Human Resource Management in Nonprofit Organizations

Routledge Studies in the Management of Voluntary and Non-Profit Organizations

Series Editor: STEPHEN P. OSBORNE (University of Edinburgh, UK)

This series presents innovative work grounded in new realities, addressing issues crucial to an understanding of the contemporary world. This is the world of organised societies, where boundaries between formal and informal, public and private, local and global organizations have been displaced or have vanished, along with other nineteenth century dichotomies and oppositions. Management, apart from becoming a specialized profession for a growing number of people, is an everyday activity for most members of modern societies.

Similarly, at the level of enquiry, culture and technology, and literature and economics, can no longer be conceived as isolated intellectual fields; conventional canons and established mainstreams are contested. Management, Organization and Society addresses these contemporary dynamics of transformation in a manner that transcends disciplinary boundaries, with books that will appeal to researchers, student and practitioners alike.

Human Resource Management in Nonprofit Organizations

Alina McCandless Baluch

Routledge
Taylor & Francis Group
NEW YORK   LONDON

First published 2012
by Routledge
711 Third Avenue, New York, NY 10017

Simultaneously published in the UK
by Routledge
2 Park Square, Milton Park, Abingdon, Oxon OX14 4RN

*Routledge is an imprint of the Taylor & Francis Group,
an informa business*

Typeset in Sabon by IBT Global.
Printed and bound in the United States of America on acid-free paper by
IBT Global.

Library of Congress Cataloging-in-Publication Data
Baluch, Alina McCandless, 1979–
    Human resource management in nonprofit organizations / by Alina McCandless
Baluch.
        p. cm. — (Routledge studies in the management of voluntary and non-profit
        organizations ; 15)
    Includes bibliographical references and index.
    1. Nonprofit organizations—Personnel management.   2. Nonprofit
        organizations—Management.   I. Title.
    HD62.6.B35 2011
    658.3—dc23
    2011025387

ISBN13: 978-0-415-89617-7 (hbk)
ISBN13: 978-0-203-14709-2 (ebk)

To Mom and Dad who always believed in perseverance and the power of a good liberal arts education—and did everything to make mine possible

Contents

Figures

Tables

Abbreviations

bill.	billion
ca.	circa
CEO	chief executive officer
cf.	confer
Doc.	document
DRG	diagnosis related groups
ed.	edition
Ed./Eds.	editor/editors
e.g.	for example
et al.	and others
etc.	and so forth
EU	European Union
EUR	euro
GmbH	*Gesellschaft mit beschränkter Haftung* (limited liability company)
gGmbH	*gemeinnützige Gesellschaft mit beschränkter Haftung* (public limited liability company)
HR	human resource/s
HRD	human resource development
HRM	human resource management
I	interview
ICNPO	International Classification of Nonprofit Organizations
i.e.	that is
IEM	internal employment market
IT	information technology
mill.	million
no.	number
NPOs	nonprofit organizations
OB	non-participant observation
OD	organizational development
org.	organization
p./pp.	page/pages

RBV	resource-based view
TQM	total quality management
U.K.	United Kingdom
U.S.	United States
vol.	volume
vs.	versus
WWII	World War II

Acknowledgments

Numerous people have played a role in completing this book, and although I will invariably neglect to acknowledge each and every one of them, I would like to express my gratitude to a few specific people who accompanied me along this journey: Professor Dr. Ridder for his academic guidance over the last years and tireless, constructive discussions about theory, contributions, and the stages in between; Professor Dr. Schmid for his constant commitment to the studies of nonprofit management; to my colleagues at the Institute of HRM for their support, friendship, and wit, without which I never could have made it to the other side; to the many student assistants who helped with the technical aspects; to the participants of several nonprofit and management conferences (AOM, ARNOVA, ISTR) for their invaluable comments; to the case study nonprofit organizations that provided me with excellent access to the field, not to mention their time and dedication; to the staff at Routledge for their assistance through this entire process; to my dear family and friends for their unwavering encouragement and support, as well as their tolerance of my resemblance to a basket case in the various stages of writing this book; and to my husband who patiently understood that leaving the office in 10 minutes could often turn into hours and never complained.

1 Introduction

More than 20 years ago, Kramer (1990, p. 13) aptly pointed out the challenges that many voluntary or nonprofit organizations (NPOs) still face today when stating they "will have to adapt to some major changes in their environment. There is considerable variation among voluntary agencies in their ability to recognize and to deal effectively with such changes." These external and internal challenges include, e.g., resource constraints and funding pressures, increasing competition, the growing demand for services, and difficulties in recruiting and retaining qualified employees (Anheier & Seibel, 2001; Bode, 2003; Salamon, 2002a; Simsa, 2002). As a result, calls for a new style of management of efficiency have emerged as NPOs need to improve their performance while spending fewer resources. Demands for the efficient and transparent use of resources as well as improved accountability have led to varied responses of increasing commercialization and professionalization within the sector. Furthermore, recent cuts in state subsidies are causing a shift toward more performance-related management in NPOs (Zimmer et al., 2001). In light of this tendency toward a more market-centered orientation, human resource management (HRM) has increased in relevance in NPOs. HRM has especially been noted for its role in aiding organizations in responding to their external and internal challenges. As mentioned above, however, NPOs vary in their ability to adapt to change.

CONTEXT OF CHANGE IN THE NONPROFIT SECTOR

Although there is a lack of consensus on which organizations make up the sector and how to term them, ranging from organizations that are nonprofit, charitable, independent, voluntary, tax-exempt, quangos, and voluntary to non- and para-governmental organizations (Lewis, 2007; Osborne, 1996; Parry et al., 2005), in the following study, the term nonprofit organization will be used to signify voluntary, charitable, independent, tax-exempt organizations because it best captures the wide array of organizations in the sector that are non-profit-distributing. The Johns Hopkins Comparative Nonprofit Sector Project considers NPOs to be formally structured, private, non-profit-distributing, self-governing, and voluntary (Salamon & Anheier, 1992). For the purpose of this book, the term nonprofit sector is understood to encompass organizations that meet the characteristics of the structural-operational definition because this definition fits the various types of organizations accorded with the nonprofit status and is best suited for comparing a broad range of NPOs.

Exploring the myriad of external and internal challenges that NPOs face, the resource constraints and funding pressures to which NPOs are subject feature most prominently in the literature. In particular, NPOs that are predominantly publicly financed are facing financial cuts (Simsa, 2002). In the fields of health care and social services, the crisis of public financing is jeopardizing the development of the nonprofit sector (Zimmer et al., 2004). Human service organizations find themselves especially dependent on public funding and vulnerable to cutbacks. In addition, the environment for social service provision has undergone major changes as fiscal crises have spread to the social insurance systems (Anheier & Seibel, 2001). Contract-based payment schemes with the state are replacing the previous system of full coverage (Ridder et al., 2004). Legal changes regarding health care and long-term care have aimed at containing costs and increasing efficiency (Anheier & Seibel, 2001). With regard to the social services field, Bode (2003) notes how nonprofit providers are increasingly forced to prove their efficiency in order to gain public money. As a result, funding is occurring more through contracts for projects rather than block grants, and these contracts are accompanied by terms or conditions and demands for professionalization (Akingbola, 2004; Brandl et al., 2006).

Not only the aforementioned financial constraints but increasing competition is also pressuring NPOs to make efficient use of their resources (von Eckardstein & Simsa, 2004). The nonprofit environment is highly competitive given the increasing demand for services and competition for contracts with the public and for-profit sectors and a tighter government funding source (Kong, 2007). This competitive and professional environment is marked by higher regulation and a strong performance-driven emphasis (Frumkin & Andre-Clark, 2000; Tonkiss & Passey, 1999). NPOs are even confronted by greater competition with other nonprofits for scarce resources (Jurkiewicz & Massey, 1998). In addition to the expanding number of nonprofit providers, commercial firms are competing as well in traditionally nonprofit areas of activity. For-profit agencies vie for contracts and clients given the devolution of previously state-funded programs (Alexander, 2000; Alexander et al., 1999). In particular, due to the deregulation of Europe's social services and social security systems, nonprofit providers face growing competition with for-profit organizations. For example, EU legislation has weakened the position of the free welfare associations in Germany by opening up their fields of services to other competitors (Anheier & Seibel, 2001; Ridder et al., 2004). The nonprofit providers are forced to compete at the local level in order to gain contracts with the public authorities (Bode,

2003). Furthermore, NPOs are also in competition for board members, clients, contracts, individual donor support, employees, volunteers, and so on (Alexander, 2000; Kong, 2007; Salamon, 2002a). This competition for skilled staff, dedicated board members, clients, and even the attention of the community is fierce. Several studies confirm that NPOs are experiencing difficulties in recruiting and retaining qualified employees (Ban et al., 2003; Fenwick, 2005; Parry et al., 2005).

Furthermore, given the turbulent and competitive external environment, NPOs are subject to the push toward performance management as they face demands from clients, funders, staff, and the public for better-managed change. Whereas funders are interested in contracts with performance requirements, the public seeks accountability (Hudson, 1999). There is greater emphasis on demonstrating efficiency, economy, and effectiveness in order to sustain funding as NPOs are under pressure to legitimize themselves economically. Yet in this respect, NPOs are criticized for acting like special interest groups seeking to expand public funding as well as for becoming too professional and thus losing touch with their client base (Salamon, 2002a). In this tight funding environment, the rules for organizational survival are being reconfigured. NPOs are forced to professionalize their management practices, display accountability, have measurable outcomes, and reduce their costs (Alexander, 2000; Alexander et al., 1999).

Finally, coupled with the decrease in state funding is an increase in the demand for programs and services delivered through NPOs (Jurkiewicz & Massey, 1998; Pynes, 1997). As public services are being transferred to NPOs, they are forced to juggle the provision of more services while receiving less state funding (Cunningham, 2010b; Simsa, 2002). Additionally, NPOs face current challenges such as demographic changes, shifts in policy and public attitudes, as well as technological and lifestyle changes. These sociodemographic changes have resulted in increased demand for nonprofit services (Salamon, 2002a), in particular in the areas of health and human services (Ridder et al., 2004). Moreover, NPOs in these areas are being confronted with dynamic market developments given changing client needs. As a result of these shifts in service demands and users' needs, there have been increasing calls for privatization in which the government plays a reduced role and the private sector takes on greater responsibilities (Anheier & Seibel, 2001).

NONPROFIT ORGANIZATIONS' RESPONSES TO THEIR CHANGING ENVIRONMENTS

From this discussion of the challenges that NPOs currently face, it becomes apparent that the need for a new style of management, one marked by efficiency, competition, and the search for new resources, has emerged as NPOs seek to improve their performance while spending fewer resources. Yet, as mentioned above, NPOs differ in their capacity and strategies used to cope with these challenges. For example, research suggests that a strategic response of differentiation is being adopted by NPOs when facing competition, such as cooperating with other organizations, increasing resources for fundraising, or diversifying revenue streams (Barman, 2002). However, one of the main responses of NPOs to these challenges can be seen in terms of commercialization. As a result of the withdrawal of government support to NPOs for delivering various services, organizations rely more heavily on fees and charges (Anheier & Seibel, 2001). NPOs face the contradiction of responding to these government cutbacks by increasing their commercial activities while simultaneously being under pressure to avoid increasing their entanglements (Weisbrod, 1998). In addition, given the decrease in private donations, NPOs are also becoming more dependent on commercial activity. Raising fees and emulating private firms, NPOs use revenue-generating activities to attract more clients and donors and to cope with these budget cuts and increasing performance expectations (Kim, 2005). Even the large welfare associations are employing more market-oriented ways of service provision and resource mobilization (Bode, 2003), suggesting that the nonprofit sector may develop more in the direction of organizations that are self-financed and rely heavily on volunteers (Zimmer & Priller, 2001).

However, the changes in the sector call for a professionalization of management in NPOs (Ridder et al., 2004). Evidence reveals that NPOs are becoming more business-like. In addition to hiring professionally trained managers, they engage in strategic planning, market analysis, cost-benefit analysis, financial information systems, and fundraising (Hall, 1990). Salamon (2002a) points to the adoption of the market culture into the operations of NPOs, affecting organizational practices and structures, as well as interorganizational behavior in the form of strategic partnerships between NPOs and businesses. Nonprofit responses to financial cutbacks have included cutting programs and rationing services, increasing marketing for charitable donations, expanding networks, increasing staff workloads to raise productivity, and relying on volunteers and recruiting board members with fundraising skills (Alexander, 2000). Moreover, NPOs exhibit copy-cat behavior to help cope with increasing financial uncertainty, thereby substituting management with financial management. Several authors provide evidence that NPOs are facing demands from the government and funders to copy for-profit practices and structure (Alexander et al., 1999; Cunningham, 2010b). In facing this competitive and performance-driven environment, the nonprofit sector has experienced rapid professionalization with professional staff developing performance measurement standards as well as drawing on reengineering processes, quality management systems, and benchmarking (Frumkin & Kim, 2001). NPOs are confronted with increasing pressure to measure performance in order to demonstrate competency, achieve legitimacy, and gain funding. Yet evaluating performance is made more difficult in the nonprofit sector because there is no single, shared criterion for success, especially given the often conflicting expectations of multiple stakeholders (Kanter & Summers, 1987; Kendall & Knapp, 2000). Research shows, however, that NPOs are using performance measurement given outside pressures of meeting grant requirements and that this has resulted in program changes, changes in general management practices, and improving accountability measures (Zimmermann & Stevens, 2006). Not only are NPOs introducing performance-related best practices from the for-profit sector in financial management and strategic planning, but recent studies suggest that NPOs are undergoing increasing professionalization in HRM as well by adopting practices from the for-profit or public sectors (Cunningham, 2010b; Hurrell et al., 2011; Kellock Hay et al., 2001; Parry et al., 2005).

INCREASING RELEVANCE OF HRM

Given this shift toward a more market-centered orientation equipped with a focus on performance-related management, HRM has grown in relevance for its role in confronting the changes in the sector. In this respect, the ability to respond to these changes is linked to HRM, especially given the labor-intensive services provided by NPOs and the relevance of employees as a primary asset (Akingbola, 2006a; McMullen & Brisbois, 2003). Nonprofit scholars have noted that "the core challenge in the nonprofit sector is to improve the efficient use of financial and human resources in the accomplishment of mission" (Chetkovich & Frumkin, 2003, p. 565). Employees are viewed as a strategically important, indispensable resource to achieving the goals of the organization's mission (Letts et al., 1999). Thus, it is clear that NPOs need to invest in their employees when facing their changing environments (Ridder & McCandless, 2010). Indeed, an improved HR function is deemed crucial for the change the nonprofit sector is undergoing (Conway & Monks, 2008). Previous research on adapting to change in NPOs reveals that many organizational responses involved their HR, such as increasing employee skills and employee participation in decision making (McMullen & Brisbois, 2003). Even HR development strategy has become more important in NPOs given the faster rate of change (Beattie et al., 2005). In summary, the need to adapt to the changing environment is linked to HRM because it can ensure that NPOs are open to change and learning (Akingbola, 2006a; Cunningham, 1999; Parry et al., 2005).

HRM is understood broadly in this study in terms of the "management decisions related to policies and practices which together shape the employment relationship and are aimed at achieving individual, organizational, and societal goals" (Boselie, 2009, p. 92). Thus, it involves the design and implementation of a wide range of HR programs and practices by both HR and line managers (Guest, 1997). In the literature, HRM has been differentiated into its component parts of HR principles, policies, programs, practices, and climate (Arthur & Boyles, 2007). This holistic understanding of HRM focuses analysis on the underlying HR policies in terms of the objectives for managing human resources. Furthermore, this approach enables an emphasis not only on the sets of formal HR practices but also the guiding HR principles that determine the choices of HR policies within organizations (Lepak et al., 2004) and represent the values that are held by the managers and drive the HR practices in the organization (Arthur & Boyles, 2007).

One strand of research in the nonprofit literature on HRM focuses on whether NPOs are becoming similar to for-profit organizations by imitating their HR programs and practices. The ongoing debate in the literature centers mainly on the transfer of best practices from the for-profit sector (Brooks, 2002; Helmig et al., 2004; Speckbacher, 2003). This is reflective of a growing body of nonprofit literature from the perspective of the neo-institutionalist approach (DiMaggio & Powell, 1983) that points toward increasing institutional isomorphism between and among the sectors (Bies, 2010; Leiter, 2008; Ramanath, 2009; Verbruggen et al., 2011). Several studies provide evidence of coercive isomorphic forces in the nonprofit sector with regard to HRM, as NPOs are professionalizing due to public sector funders' pressures and hence converging in their HR practices with public and for-profit organizations (Cunningham, 2001, 2005, 2008b, 2010b; Kellock Hay et al., 2001; Palmer, 2003; Parry et al., 2005). However, contradictory evidence suggests that NPOs may not be equipped to develop and implement their HR practices because they often lack the capabilities, resources, and expertise in HRM (Ban et al., 2003; Kellock Hay et al., 2001; McMullen & Brisbois, 2003).

Yet despite the isomorphic behavior that is present in the sector, the second strand of research in the nonprofit literature reflects that NPOs exhibit unique characteristics. As a result, they may also face different challenges in their HRM than their private or public sector counterparts, necessitating research that takes these differences into account. Overall, measuring mission impact, monitoring strategic success, and achieving strategic alignment are considered to be more difficult in NPOs (Backman et al., 2000). Not only do NPOs possess ambiguous organizational goals that are linked to the mission and numerous bottom lines, but they also lack universal measures of success. In addition, NPOs have to juggle multiple stakeholders' demands, manage their associative nature with shared organizational goals, operate under a range of financial sources with irregular funding and different employment structures, and tend to participate in discursive decision-making processes. Furthermore, the importance of values, employee commitment to the cause, and accountability to different interest groups are claimed to make HRM in NPOs more challenging (Akingbola, 2006a; Armstrong, 1992; Merlot et al., 2006; Palmer, 2003; Parry et al., 2005; Ridder & McCandless, 2010). As a result, there is a need for research on the professionalization of HRM that takes these specific nonprofit characteristics into consideration. Although these characteristics do not completely distinguish NPOs from other organizations, it is argued that NPOs have less of a possibility to cope with these conflicting demands by prioritizing them (Simsa, 2002). In light of this line of research, the purpose of this study is to empirically examine the topic of the alteration of HRM in NPOs. Investigating into this subject can provide a better understanding of the specific challenges that NPOs face in developing and implementing their HR practices.

Stemming from this brief discussion of the nonprofit literature, it can be seen that NPOs are facing uncertain, changing environments, and HRM is assumed to aid NPOs in coping with their internal and external challenges (Conway & Monks, 2008; Cunningham, 1999; McMullen & Brisbois, 2003). An in-depth review of the literature in Chapter 2 will further show that although research suggests that NPOs are undergoing professionalization of their HR practices as a response to their increasingly competitive and performance-driven environment (Kellock Hay et al., 2001; Parry et al., 2005), few studies actually examine the alteration of HRM in NPOs. Instead, this is an underdeveloped research area in which the main constructs, dynamics, and relationships are poorly understood. First, there is a lack of research that explores the various influences on the introduction of HR practices. It remains to be seen whether the distinguishing characteristics of NPOs make the alteration of HRM more challenging. In addition, while the current studies provide some insight on what is causing HRM to be altered and the implications thereof, there is still scant empirical research on how and why the alteration of HRM occurs, namely, the actual processes involved in the introduction of HR practices. These processes can be understood as the set of activities through which NPOs develop and implement their HR practices during the alteration of HRM. This book aims to bridge this gap by examining the development and implementation of HR practices and the various influences on these processes in order to better understand the specific challenges NPOs face in altering HRM. In light of this research gap, the following core research questions emerge:

How and why do NPOs develop and implement their HR practices?

and

How and why do the distinguishing nonprofit characteristics influence the development and implementation of HR practices?

RESEARCH AIMS AND CONTRIBUTIONS

The purpose of this study is to examine processes involved in the alteration of HRM in NPOs; hence, a theoretical perspective is necessary to provide the underlying logic for understanding change. The theoretical background of the dynamic capabilities approach aids in examining the organizational processes through which organizations alter their resource base to adapt to internal and external change (Eisenhardt & Martin, 2000; Helfat et al., 2007; Teece, 2007; Teece et al., 1997; Zollo & Winter, 2002). Dynamic capabilities have been defined as the "capacity of an organization to purposefully create, extend or modify its resource base" (Helfat et al., 2007, p. 4). Stemming from its focus on organizational processes, this theoretical background provides guidance in analyzing the processes or set of activities through which NPOs alter their HRM to respond to internal and external changes.

Learning processes play a central role within the dynamic capabilities approach; therefore, a focus is placed on these investments in organizational learning that facilitate the development of capabilities (Zollo & Winter, 2002). Furthermore, adapting processes can be understood as the underlying processes through which organizations identify the opportunity to alter their resource base, seize on this opportunity, and reconfigure resources to implement change (Eisenhardt & Martin, 2000; Helfat et al., 2007; Teece, 2007; Teece et al., 1997). Moreover, organizational processes evolve in a cumulative way depending on former events, experiences, and decisions (Koch, 2008; Sydow et al., 2009). With regard to this evolutionary path of an organization, the concept of path dependency conveys that an organization's future development is shaped by the narrow path it has traveled (Teece et al., 1997). Path entails the organization's values, history, routines, experience, resources, and past managerial decisions. In light of these concepts, the dynamic capabilities approach is chosen as a theoretical perspective for examining the assumption that the distinguishing nonprofit characteristics enable or constrain the learning and adapting processes through which NPOs alter their HRM given the emphasis on the influence of the organization's path on the processes through which they alter their resource base (Sydow et al., 2009; Teece, 2007; Teece et al., 1997). Because path, learning, and adapting are appropriate for understanding the alteration of HRM in NPOs, the dynamic capabilities approach aids in sharpening the focus of this study to specifically investigate two main research objectives: to examine how and why NPOs develop and implement new or modified HR practices through learning and adapting processes, and to explore how and why path influences the learning and adapting processes through which NPOs develop and implement new or modified HR practices.

Given the lack of empirical research on the alteration of HRM, the first contribution of this book is to identify core patterns and highlight the relationships between path and processes based on empirical evidence from several NPOs across different fields. The state of prior research on altering HRM in NPOs can be classified as falling between a nascent to an intermediate state (Edmondson & McManus, 2007), as the underlying processes and their influences are still poorly understood from an empirical standpoint. In this respect, this study seeks to provide, for the first time, insight into the dynamics of learning and adapting processes through which NPOs develop and implement their new or modified HR practices. This also entails yielding rich case study data on the influence of the organization's path in terms of the distinguishing nonprofit characteristics on the alteration of HRM.

Second, this study seeks to fill a critical gap in the nonprofit literature on the specific challenges NPOs face in developing and implementing their HR practices. Overall, little is known about how and why HR practices come about in NPOs and the core difficulties their design and implementation entail. Because initial evidence suggests that HRM is being altered in NPOs in distinctive ways that are not adequately explained by the aforementioned convergence across the sectors, a focus on the analysis of the influence of these nonprofit characteristics is rendered necessary. This does not imply, however, a call for a wholly distinctive approach to HRM in comparison to the public–private sectors; instead, it is argued that this approach can provide a better understanding of phenomena within the alteration of HRM that have not yet been addressed. Examining the processes of developing and implementing HR practices can contribute to the nonprofit literature in that it illustrates how these factors distinctive to NPOs affect the alteration of HRM.

The third aim of this study is to make a theoretical contribution by investigating the learning and adapting processes and the influence of path in the new context of nonprofits. Adopting the dynamic capabilities approach in the nonprofit sector can create the opportunity to extend theory by shedding new light on established concepts through the use of this novel setting. This entails empirically grounding a concept in a new context other that in which the concept was first developed (Snow, 2004). Furthermore, this book addresses the extent to which the dynamic capabilities approach aids in explaining how and why the processes through which NPOs develop and implement their HR practices emerge and are influenced. The chapter now concludes with an outline of the remainder of the book.

OUTLINE OF CHAPTERS

This book is organized into several chapters, as illustrated in Figure 1.1. Having provided a brief introduction in Chapter 1 into the study's relevance and purpose in terms of the various challenges facing NPOs and the increasing importance of HRM in NPOs, a detailed overview of the extant literature in the research area of HRM in the nonprofit sector is given in the next chapter. Chapter 2 reviews the state of the art on change and HRM in NPOs, tying together the two streams in the nonprofit research on the role of the distinguishing nonprofit characteristics in change processes and a smaller area of research on altering HRM in NPOs. In Chapter 3, the theoretical background of the dynamic capabilities approach is drawn on as a means to understand change in NPOs. After exploring the main theoretical concepts in the conceptual and empirical literature, path, learning and adapting processes and their assumed relationships are illustrated in a conceptual framework. By iterating between this theoretical framework and the prior state of nonprofit literature, theory-driven, specific research questions are developed that operationalize the theoretical concepts in the framework and provide the basis for conducting empirical research on the development and implementation of HR practices in NPOs.

Chapter 4 outlines this study's methods and proceeds by examining the methodological fit between the state of prior research, the research question, and the research design in this study, including the implications this fit entails for making a contribution to the literature. Because case study research is appropriate for analyzing how and why questions and making a contribution in research areas where constructs and linkages are poorly understood (Barr, 2004; Eisenhardt & Graebner, 2007; Yin, 2009), an exploratory multiple case study is conducted in eight German NPOs across different fields. After briefly enumerating the aims and strengths of multiple case study research and design, the study's research setting within the German nonprofit sector, sampling strategy, and the threefold research design that addresses the methodological challenges of researching into alteration of HRM in NPOs are described. Thereafter, an iterative process of data collection involving the triangulation of methods (interviews, document analysis, and non-participant observation) and within-case and cross-case analysis to identify patterns is discussed. Finally, this chapter resumes by addressing the evaluative criteria and specific strategies used throughout the research design, collection, analysis, and presentation to evaluate and ensure rigor in the multiple case study.

Chapter 5 presents the empirical findings in terms of the patterns that emerge from the cross-case analysis. There are two primary objectives with regard to the empirical case study research: to provide insight into the processes through which NPOs develop and implement their HR practices, as well as to explore the influence of nonprofit characteristics on these processes. The case stories of each of the NPOs are presented to provide an adequate picture of the context of the cases, the changes facing each NPO, and the HR practices it is currently installing. Having examined all of the cases in depth through within-case analysis for the amount and kinds of activities they engaged in with regard to the learning and adapting processes, the cases are classified along learning and adapting dimensions into groups that engage in learning and adapting to varying degrees. After identifying patterns in terms of how the groups encouraged learning and adapting during the alteration of HRM according to the conceptual framework, the groups of cases are subsequently distinguished into learning and adapting styles. These learning and adapting styles reveal in-depth insight into how the NPOs develop and implement their HR practices. Thereafter, through highlighting specific case examples of the influence of the distinguishing characteristics for each learning and adapting style, I explore why differences among the learning and adapting styles emerge. By operationalizing path with the distinguishing nonprofit characteristics, the influence of specific nonprofit features on the learning and adapting styles is assessed during the alteration of HRM.

Finally, Chapter 6 addresses the key findings on the learning and adapting styles and their relationship to path and draws initial conclusions from the exploratory case study. Tentative propositions on path are developed that account for the differences in the learning and adapting styles and entail consequences for the alteration of HRM. Both the study's contribution to the nonprofit literature and the dynamic capabilities approach are discussed in relation to the extant studies reviewed in Chapters 2 and 3. The main findings are positioned within the wider debate on convergence in HRM across the sectors by contrasting the merging elements with those that remain subject to the unique features of NPOs. A central contribution of the book is outlined in terms of the patterns identified with regard to path, which entails the relevant management concepts for exploring change in NPOs. In this respect, a series of implications are drawn that guide managers in balancing the distinguishing nonprofit characteristics with investing in learning and adapting when altering HRM in NPOs. The book closes with a brief discussion of the study's limitations and future research directions.

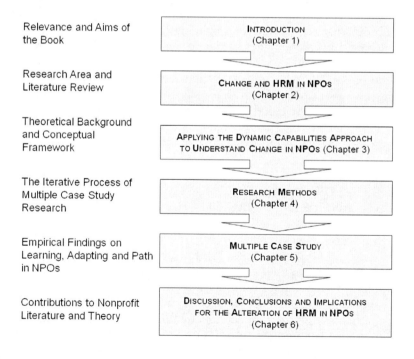

Figure 1.1 Outline of this book.

2 Change and HRM in NPOs

Although there is evidence that NPOs are imitating best practices in HRM from other sectors to be able to cope with change, rigorous empirical research is scant about the alteration of HRM. HRM may be altered in NPOs in distinctive ways that are not adequately explained by the aforementioned convergence across the sectors. Further investigation into this topic can provide a better understanding of the specific challenges that NPOs face in developing and implementing their HR practices. The purpose of this literature review is to synthesize the main themes and identify the gaps in the literature on altering HRM in NPOs (Easterby-Smith et al., 2008). In this chapter, the international findings on the central distinguishing characteristics of NPOs that are relevant for managing change will first be addressed before delving into the empirical research on HRM in NPOs. Although there are certain difficulties with comparing these studies due to their varying definitions of NPOs and the particular regulatory systems of different countries, these studies are helpful in unearthing the common themes on change and HRM that cut across these different environments. This chapter closes with identifying the research gaps about altering HRM in NPOs and developing the general research questions that guide this study.

THE ROLE OF DISTINGUISHING NONPROFIT CHARACTERISTICS IN MANAGING CHANGE PROCESSES

Although little is known about the challenges specific to nonprofit adaptation (Alexander, 2000) and studies call for a better understanding of how and why NPOs adapt to their changing internal and external environments (Galaskiewicz & Bielefeld, 1998), the literature that examines change in NPOs highlights the influence of specific nonprofit characteristics. For example, scholars propose that the unique nonprofit sectoral characteristics, such as the commitment to organizational values, lack of a market mechanism, vague goals, and diverse stakeholder objectives, can complicate change management in NPOs (Akingbola, 2006b; Kellock Hay et al., 2001; Tassie et al., 1996). Synthesizing conceptual and empirical research together suggests that change processes in NPOs are subject to the influence of the values-driven strategic orientations, multiple stakeholders' demands, unique attributes of HR, and managerial capabilities. In the following sections, the main themes in the literature will be explored for each of these distinguishing nonprofit characteristics.

Values-Driven Strategic Orientations in Change Processes in NPOs

NPOs are claimed to be prone to management challenges especially during change processes because they are values-driven. NPOs differ both from for-profit organizations and among the organizations within the nonprofit sector according to their embedded organizational values, missions, social goals, and outcomes. Not only are the shared, stable, and deeply held beliefs about organizational values and mission relevant in NPOs, but their persistence over generations has embedded them in the organization's strategies (Backman et al., 2000; Fenton & Inglis, 2007; Stone et al., 1999). Furthermore, Frumkin and Andre-Clark (2000) argue that the inimitability of NPOs lies in maintaining the special values of their distinctive missions that can yield a strategic advantage. Although research on the impact of marketization reveals the difficulties that NPOs with a strong charitable mission have in adjusting to environmental challenges (Alexander et al., 1999), organizational values are relevant for remaining competitive in effective service provision and charitable giving. Strategies sacrificing mission for margin are difficult to maintain given the alienation of stakeholders like service recipients, employees, volunteers, and the public (Alexander, 2000; Chetkovich & Frumkin, 2003; Frumkin & Kim, 2001).

Further research emphasizes the different goals and outcomes an NPO produces, such as achieving social goals and donor satisfaction of contributing to the cause (Moore, 2000, 2003). Studies suggest that the management of change may be complicated by vague, multiple social goals as well as the culture of NPOs (Kellock Hay et al., 2001; Palmer, 2003). Indeed, the specificity of mission has a crucial impact on the direction and success of organizational change (Durst & Newell, 2001). Clarity about the mission is essential to HRM in NPOs, as a strong sense of mission is claimed to seal employee loyalty to organizational norms and values (Brown & Yoshioka, 2003). Furthermore, research suggests that the concepts of traditionality and continuity can be invoked to help NPOs retain their advocacy-based missions and areas of core expertise (Salipante & Golden-Biddle, 1995). By maintaining routines and practices that are in line with the organization's core values during change, managers can assess the impact of such change on the historical mission as well as on the stakeholders' views of the organization's identity. Similarly, research demonstrates that ideological and value orientations of NPOs affect the strategies of change adopted, determining whether NPOs respond to a broad range of needs or narrow their focus to certain target groups (Schmid, 1992).

In summary, the studies emphasize that in order to remain competitive and effectively provide services in their changing environment, NPOs may benefit from translating the unique values of their mission into strategy. By maintaining routines and functions during change that are in accordance with their values-driven strategic orientations, NPOs are enabled to adapt effectively while retaining their core expertise. Yet other studies cast doubt on the incorporation of values as they point out that social goals may be vague or multiple in NPOs, thereby complicating the management of change. Thus, the findings diverge on the influence of values-driven strategic orientations on change in NPOs.

Multiple Stakeholders' Demands in Change Processes in NPOs

Diverse key stakeholders are viewed in the nonprofit literature as having a direct influence on strategic decision making and change processes in NPOs. Stakeholders are understood as any group or individual who can affect or is affected by the achievement of the organization's objective (Freeman, 1984). Research reveals the importance of sustaining trusting relationships with core stakeholders for organizational adaptation and survival (Alexander, 2000). Studies even suggest that external stakeholders may have decision-making power and influence over HR decisions in NPOs (Akingbola, 2006a; McMullen & Brisbois, 2003). NPOs are accountable to a variety of constituencies with heterogeneous needs (Speckbacher, 2003). Given the differing values and goals that external groups try to impose, these constituencies are often viewed as conflicting, which can complicate the management of change (Kellock Hay et al., 2001; Moore, 2000; Stone et al., 1999). With divergent interests trying to define organizational values, vague and difficult-to-measure goals may emerge in order for the organization to secure the support of these diverse groups (Barragato, 2002; Kendall & Knapp, 2000; Stone & Brush, 1996). Nevertheless, value-based conflict is intrinsic to NPOs given the diverse interests and interpretations of organizational missions (Simsa, 2003). As a result, change in NPOs is made more difficult given the complex web of accountability relationships toward multiple constituents and having to accommodate their diverse expectations regarding mission, conduct, and reputation (Alexander, 2000; Kim, 2005; Kong, 2007; Ospina et al., 2002).

Stakeholder groups such as funders may jar with the dominant values in the NPO (Cunningham, 2001; Stone et al., 1999). Although there is evidence of NPOs resisting funder influence (Ebrahim, 2002), NPOs often succumb solely to funders' requirements, neglecting their commitment to the beneficiaries. Studies indicate that NPOs are becoming increasingly entangled in a web of funding and contractual relations with multiple institutional actors in which a previous 'trust-based' relation is being replaced by 'confidence' based on external systems of contract and regulation (Tonkiss & Passey, 1999). Yet research also shows that nonprofit boards play the role of 'values guardians' when the organization's mission or ideology is threatened (Fenton &

Inglis, 2007; Harlan & Saidel, 1994). Provan (1991) provides evidence that the board is mainly involved in the external activities of responding to external regulatory demands, whereas studies on reorganization in NPOs indicate that the board is involved in designing reinvention, suggesting that boards try to shape major management decisions (Basinger & Peterson, 2008; Durst & Newell, 2001). Additional research emphasizes boards in terms of their complementary linkages through networks, which are important for acquiring resources (Alexander, 2000). Finally, studies on nonprofit board governance highlight the need to consider multiple stakeholders and their heterogeneous interests when formulating strategy (Brown & Iverson, 2004). Yet Hodgkin (1993) views this inclusive nature of the work of the board as partially constraining their efficiency, resulting in slower decision-making processes.

In summary, the review emphasizes, first, that multiple stakeholders' demands influence the management of NPOs, even HR decisions, and second, it overwhelmingly suggests that they can complicate addressing change in NPOs given their heterogeneous needs, values, goals, and interests. Although studies highlight broadly including external stakeholders during change processes, decision making, and resource acquisition, they also reveal some of the difficulties that arise from including these diverse interest groups, such as slower and less efficient decision-making processes. Furthermore, research on the different roles of the board presents conflicting findings on their degree of involvement in change processes. As a result, there are mixed results about the role of multiple stakeholders' demands in change processes in NPOs that render further empirical attention necessary.

Unique Attributes of HR in Change Processes in NPOs

Nonprofit employees are claimed to vary from their for-profit or public sector counterparts given their different goals, priorities, values, and needs (Fenwick, 2005; Hatten, 1982; Minkoff & Powell, 2006). They are noted for their altruistic orientations to work, are committed to certain ideals to promote the common good, and act as advocates for social change (Cunningham, 2005; Ryan, 1999). Although nonprofit employees are touted as having an advantage over for-profit employees in that they bring special values and commitment to their jobs (Ryan, 1999), the employees' personal commitment to organizational values may in fact act as a constraint on change processes (Armstrong, 1992). Yet other authors suggest that strategic change is driven by internal initiatives from staff and then relayed back to the board level; thus, there is less resistance to change from employees and volunteers (Campbell, 2008; Filipovitch, 2006; Kong, 2007). Although some research reveals that employee participation in change processes has a crucial impact on the direction and success of organizational change (Basinger & Peterson, 2008; Durst & Newell, 2001), other studies point out that greater employee participation can lead to longer decision-making processes, and employees may even serve as a barrier to change (Armstrong,

1992; Kellock Hay et al., 2001). Even the research on employee participation in decision making yields mixed results ranging from a high level of staff participation where co-determination laws are applicable (Jackson et al., 2005) to participation limited only to daily tasks as opposed to strategic issues (McMullen & Brisbois, 2003; Sheehan, 1998).

Empirical evidence suggests that nonprofit employees not only have different needs than for-profit workers due to differences in personality characteristics, values, motives, and occupational values (Rawls et al., 1975), but also stronger 'nonmonetary' orientations because they are more likely to receive intrinsic rewards from their work and exchange extrinsic rewards for commitment to the cause (Handy & Katz, 1998). Intrinsically motivated behaviors can be understood as those "that are motivated by the underlying need for competence and self-determination" (Deci & Ryan, 1980, p. 42). These unique attributes are substantiated by numerous studies that overwhelmingly confirm a stronger nonmonetary commitment amongst nonprofit workers, especially when compared to employees in the for-profit and public sectors (Almond & Kendall, 2000b; Borzaga & Depedri, 2005; Borzaga & Tortia, 2006; De Cooman et al., 2011; Light, 2002; Mirvis, 1992; Netting et al., 2005; Nickson et al., 2008; Simsa, 2004; Wittmer, 1991).

Although these studies have different definitions of and theoretical backgrounds regarding motivation, Schepers et al. (2005) cite evidence that professional efficacy, support for autonomy, preferences for working with and for people, altruism, personal growth, social contacts, skill variety, and opportunities for learning emerge as factors that motivate nonprofit employees as opposed to extrinsic rewards such as salary. A cross-sector comparison by De Cooman et al. (2011) confirms that nonprofit employees value social service more, are less concerned about career advancement, and are motivated by their appreciation of valued outcomes or personally meaningful outcomes. However, it is not possible to determine whether the organization attracts, selects, and retains employees with particular values or whether these values are influenced through socialization. Nonprofit employees are more concerned with intrinsic reasons for choosing to work and remain at their specific organization and employee satisfaction is positively related with relational and intrinsic attitudes rather than extrinsic attitudes (Borzaga & Depedri, 2005; Borzaga & Tortia, 2006).

Further literature reviews indicate that the conditions of nonprofit environments and employees' preference structures do not coincide with the motivational determinants of pay for performance systems (Theuvsen, 2004). Empirical evidence supports the overjustification and crowding-out effects (cf. Frey & Jegen, 2001) on intrinsic motivation for employees who had a high intrinsic motivation before the merit pay program (Deckop & Cirka, 2000). This research suggests that the shift toward a more performance-related HRM in NPOs may be detrimental toward employee motivation.

Finally, empirical studies also indicate the importance of the mission for attracting and retaining nonprofit employees (Ban et al., 2003; Brown &

Yoshioka, 2003; Kim & Lee, 2007; Light, 2002; Salamon, 2002b). Kim and Lee (2007) corroborate previous findings on the importance of mission attachment in retaining employees (Brown & Yoshioka, 2003), revealing that nonprofit employees' intention to stay relates positively to economic satisfaction in terms of wage and career advancement as well as to involving workers in their activity in terms of autonomy and professional growth. Furthermore, research has suggested that employees are attracted when organizational goals align with their own values. A study by Vigoda and Cohen (2003) reveals that person-organization fit and met expectations are positively related to job satisfaction and organizational commitment of nonprofit employees.

In summary, the review of the literature demonstrates that employees have different goals, priorities, needs, and values that demand special attention when managing NPOs. The employees' personal commitment to organizational values can serve as a constraint on the process of change. Empirical evidence indicates that nonprofit employees are intrinsically motivated and thus possess different reward preferences than for-profit workers. Numerous studies overwhelmingly conclude that nonprofit employees are motivated by the work itself or doing socially worthwhile, rewarding work, whereas pay and economic motivations play only a secondary role. Furthermore, the current trend toward performance-related management in HRM may have a detrimental effect on employee motivation. As different assumptions prevail regarding employees as barriers to change and there are mixed findings on the effects of involving employees in change and decision making, it still remains to be seen how their needs and values influence change.

Managerial Capabilities in Change Processes in NPOs

Finally, studies on the role of managers in change in NPOs reveal that managerial capabilities are crucial for dealing with change strategically. Research on reorganization suggests that, along with the board, executive directors are the main catalysts for undertaking change efforts (Durst & Newell, 2001). Strong executive leadership is necessary for change to occur and is essential for its success given the importance of managers in initiating and adapting to change. Findings show that the capacity for learning, development, and change is enabled when managers take their specific competencies and accumulated knowledge into account as well as the organization's internal operations, structure, and diverse internal stakeholders (Parsons & Broadbridge, 2004; van der Pijl & Sminia, 2004). When managers face a dynamic environment that renders rational decision making impractical and the balance of multiple stakeholders' interests necessary, they rely on their intuitive tacitly held knowledge bases (Ritchie et al., 2007). Managers function as facilitators of organizational and individual learning (Beattie, 2006; Beattie et al., 2005). Additional studies indicate the importance of managers emphasizing nonprofit values and their participative nature for the acceptance of change (Lindenberg, 2001). Managers in NPOs can create a self-organizing process and context for successful change to unfold by establishing a shared sense of the core vision and values informing change, yet leaving different paths to employees who pursue diverse initiatives within the entire change context domain (Tassie et al., 1996). Similarly, lacking a shared vision of change given different understandings of the organization's structure and the reasons for change can prevent the implementation of change (Dibella, 1992).

A second research stream focuses on the skills of managers, revealing the importance of board-related leadership and the need for constant efforts to maintain an effective fit among the organization, CEO, and board in order to meet the organization's needs and challenges (Bailey & Grochau, 1993; Herman & Heimovics, 1990a, 1990b, 1994). Furthermore, Heimovics et al. (1993) show how effective CEOs use their boards as strategic tools to mediate the changing environment by mobilizing constituencies, forming coalitions, creating obligations, negotiating, and bargaining. Moreover, managerial governance fosters an adaptive, learning, and resilient system in NPOs (Bradshaw, 2002). Besides board leadership skills being crucial for effective top management, accommodating divergent perspectives and demands of multiple stakeholders is also a skill utilized by effective nonprofit executives to cope with their changing resource environments (Denis et al., 2001; Herman & Heimovics, 1990a). More effective executives engage in more complex ethical reasoning and work to gather a consensus among organizational members (Jurkiewicz & Massey, 1998; Nygren et al., 1994). Managerial participation in internal and external networks helps to develop relationships and keep a high level of trust with stakeholders (King, 2004). Additionally, executives are viewed as crucial for gaining resources for the organization that are necessary for its survival (Jurkiewicz & Massey, 1998).

In summary, the nonprofit literature underscores the central role of managers when learning and dealing with change strategically, especially in terms of decision making and gaining resources. Studies highlight the inclusion of nonprofit values, managers' intuitive accumulated knowledge, and specific competencies for the acceptance of change and facilitation of learning within NPOs. Furthermore, research examining the leadership skills utilized by effective managers emphasizes certain skills that are paramount for coping with the changing resource environment. Yet these studies mainly provide descriptive accounts of the crucial role of managers; thus, it still remains unclear how and why their specific capabilities enable change and enhance the acceptance of change.

HRM IN NPOS

Having explored the literature on the influence of the unique nonprofit sectoral characteristics on managing change in NPOs, it remains to be seen whether the empirical studies on HRM take these characteristics into consideration and corroborate these assumptions. The following sections will review the literature on the HR practices in NPOs and on altering HRM in NPOs. It is important to investigate these current findings in order to come to a better understanding of the specific challenges NPOs face in developing and implementing their HR practices.

HR Practices in NPOs

HRM is claimed to be made more difficult by the specific characteristics of NPOs, such as the employee commitment to the cause, unique structure and heterogeneity of employment arrangements, and accountability to different interest groups (Parry et al., 2005; Ridder & McCandless, 2010; Zimmer et al., 2001). Furthermore, nonprofit employees may be dissatisfied if the organization is not fulfilling its mission or the espoused values conflict with the values in use (Akingbola, 2006a; Jeavons, 1992). These specific challenges are addressed to varying degrees in the HRM research on recruiting, training and retaining employees, compensation, and pay for performance.

Recruiting, Training, and Retaining Employees

The review of the research highlights recruiting and retaining employees as important HR functions (Watson & Abzug, 2005). Yet NPOs must cope with increasing costs in management, training, and recruitment while professionalizing these practices (Cunningham, 2005; Hurrell et al., 2011). Research on employee recruitment underscores the challenges of recruiting qualified staff stemming from funding pressures, a lack of qualified candidates, misconceptions about the sector and job opportunities, uncompetitive pay, and poor working conditions (Ban et al., 2003; Beck, 2002; Hurrell et al., 2011; Nickson et al., 2008; Palmer, 2003; Parry et al., 2005). For example, NPOs face difficulties in recruitment due to the shift to more project-based funding, with temporary contracts increasing, resulting in staff turnover, lowered effectiveness of services, recruiting less qualified staff, and low employee morale (Akingbola, 2004, 2006a).

Furthermore, training is viewed as important for establishing a learning culture in NPOs and the skills needed to adapt to change (McMullen & Schellenberg, 2003b), yet research indicates that resources are not being devoted to training, thereby forming a key barrier to the process of change management in NPOs (Dolan, 2002; Kellock Hay et al., 2001; Light 2002). The study by Parry et al. (2005) reveals that more financial resources were designated to training in the public sector than in NPOs. Further studies show that care organizations often fail to enquire about systematic training needs among their employees, maintain training files for their staff, and provide staff replacements when employees are in training courses (De Prins & Henderickx, 2007).

In terms of retaining employees, studies support the importance of values for employee retention (Salamon, 2002a), with employees and managers being attracted to an organization with values commensurate to their own, to their commitment to the organization's purposes and values, and to the type of work (Nickson et al., 2008). Research indicates that employees with a high ideological loyalty are more likely to leave the organization over workplace problems if these difficulties are viewed as resulting from the organization's failure to fulfill its ideological commitment (Hoffmann, 2006). Moreover, retention is aided by having rewarding work, high levels of autonomy and responsibility, a positive organizational culture with supportive colleagues, management support, and good intraorganizational communication (Ban et al., 2003; Nickson et al., 2008). Further findings suggest that nonprofit employees feel committed because they identify with the organization's values and their role in achieving the mission, which can enhance retention and reduce recruitment challenges (Cunningham, 2005; Watson & Abzug, 2005). This supports the assumption of an altruism payoff, i.e., that employees are willing to exchange their low pay for working in organizations with values similar to their own (Parry et al., 2005). However, dissatisfaction with pay is often cited as being one of the main causes of staff turnover in NPOs (Beck, 2002; Kim & Lee, 2007).

Compensating Employees

Both the nonmonetary motivation of employees and the need to reflect these nonmonetary goals to external stakeholders are claimed to influence the design of compensation systems in NPOs (Brandl & Güttel, 2007). Yet there is an ongoing debate in the literature surrounding the topic of the nonprofit wage differential. On the one hand, research indicates that wages in NPOs are equal to or even exceed those in for-profit organizations when comparing the data for industries in which both organizations operate actively (Ben-Ner et al., 2011; Leete, 2001; Salamon & Dewees, 2002). NPOs may pay higher wages given their philanthropic tendencies toward employees, attenuated property rights, and the selection of better applicants or as a means to enhance quality (for an overview, see Ben-Ner et al., 2011). On the other hand, the bulk of the studies confirms the prevalence of higher for-profit wages in specific industries (Handy & Katz, 1998; McMullen & Schellenberg, 2003a; Pitt-Catsouphes et al., 2004; Preston, 1989; Preyra & Pink, 2001; Roomkin & Weisbrod, 1999; Ruhm & Borkoski, 2003).

One possible explanation for the source of this wage differential lies in the donative labor hypothesis, i.e., that low pay in the nonprofit sector results from employees accepting a reduced wage given the different nature of the good or service being produced (Preston, 1989). Related to this explanation is the assumption that lower wages function as a screening device to attract intrinsically motivated managers and signal the effective use of donations in markets with asymmetric information (Handy & Katz,

1998; Hansmann, 1980). Another explanation for the wage differential is due to the differing characteristics of nonprofit organizations, workers, or jobs (Leete, 2001, 2006; Ruhm & Borkoski, 2003). Furthermore, proceeding from the assumption that NPOs require more intrinsically motivated employees and that wage equity is central to maintaining this intrinsic motivation, results reveal that nonprofit wages are indeed less dispersed than in the for-profit sector (Leete, 2000, 2001), although there are not substantial differences in the ratios of the highest paid staff groups to the lowest paid staff groups within the organizations across these sectors (Ben-Ner et al., 2011).

Alternatively, the wage differential may stem from accepting lower wages in exchange for compensating differentials (Cunningham, 2005). However, research provides diverse findings on the quality of working conditions and benefits in the nonprofit sector. Whereas some studies indicate that NPOs provide fewer educational and fringe benefits for their staff in certain industries (Ben-Ner et al., 2011; Emanuele & Higgins, 2000; Lynn, 2003; Parry et al., 2005), others suggest that NPOs provide benefits such as flexible working arrangements, career mobility, health insurance, life insurance, dental insurance, training, work-family policies, and child care in order to attract and retain employees (Benz, 2005; Haley-Lock & Kruzich, 2008; McMullen & Schellenberg, 2003a; Pitt-Catsouphes et al., 2004; Pynes, 1997). These results suggest that nonprofit administrators are in positions that allow them the freedom and resources to implement higher-commitment approaches toward HRM (Haley-Lock & Kruzich, 2008). Given this divided picture on the prevalence of compensating differentials, it remains unclear whether nonmonetary incentives are sufficient in attracting employees and maintaining employee commitment.

Regarding pay for performance, scholars argue that evidence that pay for performance systems fit the needs of nonprofit employees is lacking (Theuvsen, 2004). If employees self-select into NPOs because they identify with the organization's goals, pay for performance systems may result in crowding-out effects (Brandl & Güttel, 2007). Managers with the greatest risk aversion may be sorted into this sector due to the differing objectives, constraints, subsidies, or labor supply of NPOs, implying that NPOs attract different kinds of managers and provide different incentives for managers (Roomkin & Weisbrod, 1999). Studies confirm there is less dissemination of pay for performance systems in NPOs (McMullen & Schellenberg, 2003a; Preyra & Pink, 2001; Roomkin & Weisbrod, 1999). Where there is a high sensitivity to core organizational values and goals are viewed as difficult to measure, nonprofit managers are reluctant to implement pay for performance, especially given the lack of financial scope and intrinsic motivations of their employees (Brandl & Güttel, 2007; Brandl et al., 2006).

In summary, the literature on HR practices in NPOs suggests that the specific characteristics of NPOs matter for individual HR practices. Research supports the importance of organizational values for retaining employees and indicates a high level of commitment for those nonprofit employees despite dissatisfaction with pay. The lack of training in NPOs, however, relates to resource constraints and stems from the socially focused missions of NPOs, posing a barrier to change. Finally, the assumption that nonprofit employees give greater weighting to intrinsic nonmonetary rewards is predominantly substantiated by research on employee retention, compensation, and pay for performance systems, highlighting differences in nonprofit employees' motivational foundations.

Altering HRM in NPOs

Although evidence suggests NPOs are professionalizing their HR practices, little research has examined the alteration of HRM. The few studies suggest that NPOs lack the capabilities, resources, and expertise in HRM to adapt to the changing environment (Ban et al., 2003; Kellock Hay et al., 2001; McMullen & Brisbois, 2003). Research focuses predominantly on what causes HRM to be altered, the various barriers in the processes of the adoption of new HR practices, and the effects of these HRM changes on employee behavior.

Antecedents to Altering HRM

Research on the external antecedents to altering HRM emphasizes the impact of funding priorities and changing service demands, confirming an increasing professionalization of HRM toward performance-related management (Cunningham, 2001, 2008a, 2008b, 2010b; Kellock Hay et al., 2001; Palmer, 2003; Parry et al., 2005; Zimmer et al., 2001). Given the contracting of public services to NPOs, the sector faces a greater reliance on public funding and the accompanying pressure to be efficient, be effective, and show 'value for money' (Cunningham, 2005; Palmer, 2003).

Studies highlight that HR practices such as formal recruitment and selection policies and training procedures are being introduced into the sector in order to maintain funding and deal with budgetary constraints, reflecting that HRM is converging toward the approach in the public sector (Palmer, 2003; Parry et al., 2005). Findings confirm that these funding priorities and the move toward a culture that rewards performance and mimics for-profit practices led NPOs to introduce best practices and tighter performance management. On the one hand, standards are improved by introducing various employment policies in recruitment and selection and training and development, as well as disseminating best practice in discipline and grievance (Cunningham, 2008b). Yet these changes often included intensification of work, external interference in disciplinary and recruitment decisions, cuts in pay and conditions, and reliance on atypical employment forms like temporary contracts (Cunningham, 2001, 2008a, 2010b; Hurrell et al., 2011; Palmer, 2003). Cunningham (2008a) also provides evidence of

NPOs that are extremely vulnerable to state funders being unable to maintain pay and conditions that are commensurate with the public sector. The decline in nonprofit wages may result from having to provide more services, leading to reduced funding for staff (Irons & Bass, 2004). Recent research on power relations and resource dependency with regard to public fund-givers reveals business-like policies being introduced, yet the HR function remains constrained and under-resourced. Rather than wielding autonomy and strategic choice in the relations with funders, the HR function in NPOs is viewed as having a more bureaucratic, regulatory role in meeting the requirements of multiple external stakeholders or even a more administrative HR orientation as it is perceived as a cost to the organizational mission instead (Cunningham, 2010b).

Furthermore, studies cite problems in hiring and retaining professional staff members, which lead to changes in HRM (Akingbola, 2006b; Ban et al., 2003; Fenwick, 2005; Parry et al., 2005). Innovative HR practices such as flex-time, job sharing, and part-time jobs are being introduced to compensate for lower wages and benefits, professionalize the HR function, promote employee satisfaction, and enable effective hiring and retention (Parry et al., 2005). Furthermore, differentiated pay scales function as a means to attract recruits with specialist skills (Palmer, 2003). Finally, examining the relationship between change in strategy and HRM, Akingbola (2006a) concludes that changes in strategic types were not found to be related to changes in HR practices in terms of recruitment, use of temporary staff, or training. As a result, a disconnect exists between strategy and HRM in NPOs, with NPOs failing to match change in strategy with change in their internal climate. External parties being involved in HR decisions such as staffing may contribute to this disconnect between HRM and strategy and affect the organizations' abilities to align HRM with strategy (Akingbola, 2006a).

Barriers in the Processes of Introducing HR Practices

Second, the review of the research on altering HRM indicates only a limited amount of studies that focus on the barriers in the processes of introducing new HR practices, reflecting the importance of nonprofit values, organizational structure, and local autonomy. For example, a study by Alatrista and Arrowsmith (2004) reveals that high-commitment management practices are poorly implemented due to employees' competing organizational and local commitments, limited autonomy, and the organization's emphasis on business growth, rather than allowing the workers to put their own values into practice. Furthermore, Cunningham's (2001) empirical research highlights that the consistent introduction of HR policies is made difficult by the federal structure of NPOs, in which the operating units defend their tradition of defining their own HR policies. Cunningham (1999) proposes that obstacles to the introduction of HRM encompass the special characteristics of NPOs, such as professional autonomy, varying stakeholder expectations, participatory structures, existing values, loyalties of staff, and autonomy among organizational units. In addition, the internal resistance to change, lack of resources, and funding pressures are purported barriers. Further obstacles are expected to include the approach to managing volunteers, rejection of the concepts of competitiveness, a participative culture, and the increasing costs of implementation, which make even the introduction of adequate HR practices difficult, especially in terms of pay structures, training, and development. Similarly, Palmer (2003) surmises that attempts to introduce new HR practices can flounder given problems of gaining acceptance across the diverse constituencies or due to the organizational structures that lack a common perspective on goals and priorities. Yet empirical research into these expected constraints stemming from the nonprofit characteristics is still needed.

Effects of Changes in HRM

Finally, a third area of research examines the effects of professionalizing HR practices on employee behavior, suggesting that the changes in HRM predominantly have a negative impact on employee morale, satisfaction, and commitment while leading to staff turnover (Akingbola, 2004; Cunningham, 2001, 2005, 2008b, 2010a). For example, Akingbola's (2004) research on the impact of government-contract funding on recruiting, retention, and service provision reveals that motivating employees on short-term contracts results in low employee morale. Furthermore, against the backdrop of introducing more cost-effective working practices in the leisure industry, HR practices are often to the employees' detriment with less variable overtime arrangements (MacVicar et al., 2000). Additional research examining the impact of greater financial insecurity and control by funding bodies on employee commitment points toward increasing dissatisfaction, resistance, and discontent among staff (Cunningham, 2001). Work intensification and cuts in staff pay and conditions have resulted in a decline in employee commitment (Cunningham, 2005). Evidence of values displacement and eventual breaches in the psychological contracts of nonprofit workers given external pressures leads to discontent, burnout, undermined employee morale, and continuance commitment, as well as intentions to quit among nonprofit staff (Cunningham, 2010a, 2010b). However, there is also evidence of employee loyalty and commitment to the job and service users despite the challenges the NPO staff faced in their employment terms and conditions (Cunningham, 2010b).

Additional studies suggest there may be a disconnect between high performance HR practices and those valued by nonprofit employees, with 'basic' HR practices such as communication and rewards being significantly associated with higher work satisfaction and crucial for commitment to change and the success of change initiatives (Conway & Monks, 2008). Similarly, De Prins and Henderickx's (2007) findings in elderly and nursing homes reveal that instead of innovative HR principles in training, good management, and healthy mutual work, relationships contribute to outstanding quality of labor. However, conflicting results emerge, with high performance HR practices being significantly related to higher levels of employee morale and lower employee absenteeism. Yet these results are qualified by the finding that a workplace climate that stresses the value of HR in terms of employee participation, empowerment, and accountability is more important than the number of high performance HR practices for higher employee morale (Rondeau & Wagar, 2001).

In summary, HRM appears to be shifting toward more performance-related management given external funding pressures. Yet studies also convey that there still is a lack of professionalism in HR practices due in part to their resource constraints. Against this background of introducing performance-driven HR practices, the evidence points to the negative effects of these changes on employee behavior. Instead, research suggests that employees value basic HR practices that enhance their commitment to change, although conflicting findings emerge here. On the whole, empirical research is still lacking on the influence of the specific characteristics on the introduction of HR practices, although research shows that failing to consider nonprofit organizational values, the unique structure, and autonomy of organizational units of NPOs hinders the introduction of HRM. Thus, although the literature provides a few initial insights into the antecedents, barriers, and effects of altering HRM, it still remains unclear on the specific challenges NPOs face during the actual processes of altering HRM.

SUMMARY: GAPS IN THE NONPROFIT LITERATURE ON CHANGE AND HRM

This literature review has sought to synthesize the main themes and identify the gaps in the nonprofit literature on change and HRM in NPOs (Easterby-Smith et al., 2008). This synthesis of existing work highlights the role of distinguishing nonprofit characteristics, thereby providing a novel avenue for examining the alteration of HRM in NPOs. Stemming from the central implications of these literature segments, the research gaps that still remain will be discussed, leading to the development of the study's general research questions.

The review suggests that incorporating the values-driven strategic orientations of NPOs can aid NPOs to adapt effectively by retaining their mission during change. Although the inclusion of organizational values is important for the acceptance of change, research also points to the risks stemming from vague, multiple goals that can complicate the management of change. Furthermore, NPOs are accountable to multiple stakeholders' demands, yet these interests groups make addressing change problematic given their heterogeneous and often conflicting needs, values, goals, interests, and demands. Although evidence is provided that NPOs succumb to funders' requirements toward performance-related management, the influence of the board in change processes still remains unclear. Moreover, the review of the literature reveals that employees appear to have different needs and motivations that culminate in a stronger nonmonetary orientation, as corroborated by empirical studies emphasizing their preference for intrinsic rewards and the importance of the mission for nonprofit employees. However, there are conflicting findings regarding employee satisfaction, the involvement of employees in change processes, and their acceptance of change initiatives given their commitment to organizational values. Finally, research points to the importance of managerial capabilities in change processes, highlighting the consideration of nonprofit values, managers' intuitive knowledge and specific competencies, as well as the unique organizational structure for the acceptance of change and facilitating learning within NPOs.

Furthermore, studies on HR practices convey that specific nonprofit characteristics play a role in acquiring, motivating, and retaining employees in NPOs, highlighting the importance of organizational values, resource constraints, as well as the stronger nonmonetary motivational foundation and high level of commitment of nonprofit employees. Whereas research on altering HRM in NPOs confirms the assumption that an improved HR function is crucial for dealing with the increasingly competitive and performance-driven environment, there is scarce empirical research on the processes of altering HRM in NPOs. A few studies suggest that NPOs lack the resources and expertise in HRM, thereby functioning as an obstacle to change. The limited research corroborates that NPOs are professionalizing their HR practices, with the trend toward tighter performance-related management given funding pressures and further changes within the sector. Yet this shift appears to be detrimental toward employee motivation, satisfaction, and commitment. Moreover, the studies on the barriers in the processes of adopting HR practices highlight that considering the nonprofit organizational values, the unique structure, and the autonomy of organizational units of NPOs is crucial for introducing new HR practices.

From the literature review, it is evident that although the current studies provide insight on what is causing HRM to be altered in NPOs and the implications thereof, there is scant research on how and why the alteration of HRM occurs. Instead, this is an underdeveloped research area in which the main constructs, dynamics, and linkages are poorly understood. Although research on processes is important for gaining an in-depth understanding of the underlying mechanisms of the alteration of HRM, there is little insight into these processes through which managers and other organizational members accomplish the task of altering HR practices. Processes are thus understood as the set of activities through which NPOs develop and implement their HR practices during the alteration of HRM. Although a few studies have researched into the barriers in adopting HR practices, empirical research is still lacking on how HR practices come about and the challenges their design and implementation entail. Thus, a broad gap exists in the research on the processes through which NPOs develop and implement their HR practices.

Furthermore, additional research is needed to examine the assumptions about the distinguishing nonprofit characteristics that are prevalent in the literature regarding the alteration of HRM. The literature remains unclear on how and why the distinguishing characteristics of NPOs beyond values and structure may influence the alteration of HRM, especially given the complex nonprofit environment that is wrought with diverging employees' needs and multiple stakeholder interests. As the alteration of HRM is an example of organizational change in which the organization shifts its resources to introduce HR practices, further research is necessary to explore the assumptions about these influences regarding the alteration of HRM. It remains to be seen whether the distinguishing characteristics of NPOs enable or constrain the alteration of HRM. Emphasizing these distinctive features of NPOs can provide insight into the dominant beliefs, norms, and values that drive HR practices in the organization (Arthur & Boyles, 2007). Thus, this study seeks to bridge this research gap by exploring the influence of the distinguishing nonprofit characteristics on the development and implementation of HR practices. Examining both the processes and the influences on the processes in the alteration of HRM is worthy of investigation to gain a better understanding of the particular challenges that are specific to NPOs in developing and implementing their HR practices.

As research on altering HRM remains in a nascent to intermediate stage of development with the main constructs and their linkages still being explored (Edmondson & McManus, 2007), open-ended research questions can help to advance this research area. Stemming from the gaps in the research, the study will examine the following general research questions:

How and why do NPOs develop and implement their HR practices?

and

How and why do the distinguishing nonprofit characteristics influence the development and implementation of HR practices?

Thus, this study aims to bridge the aforementioned research gaps through an in-depth analysis of the sets of activities through which NPOs develop and implement their HR practices and the influence of the distinguishing nonprofit characteristics on these processes. As processes and the influences on these processes emerge as the concepts that warrant further investigation, the following chapter will address the theoretical background that will be drawn on to explore these concepts and discuss its relevance for understanding the alteration of HRM in NPOs.

3 Applying the Dynamic Capabilities Approach to Understand Change in NPOs

The previous chapter outlined that the aim of this book is to examine the processes involved in the development and implementation of HR practices in NPOs and the influence of the distinguishing nonprofit characteristics on these processes. In order to achieve this objective, it is necessary to draw on a theoretical perspective that provides the underlying logic that can explain the phenomena in question in terms of how and why these processes unfold as they do and how and why observed relationships exist (Helfat, 2007; Sutton & Staw, 1995). Certainly, there are a number of theoretical approaches that enable the analysis of change in NPOs, such as institutional theory, contingency theory, or resource dependency theory; however, a theoretical perspective is needed that makes sense of the processes through which NPOs alter their HRM. In light of this internal processual focus, the dynamic capabilities approach is drawn on because it examines the processes through which an organization alters its resource base (Maritan & Peteraf, 2007).

The dynamic capabilities approach (Eisenhardt & Martin, 2000; Helfat et al., 2007; Teece et al., 1997; Zollo & Winter, 2002) emphasizes the capacity of organizations to adapt proactively to address change. Not only is this specific theoretical perspective relevant for the present analysis of the alteration of HRM because it aids in identifying and analyzing the organizational processes that are related to the alteration of the resource base when NPOs create and modify resources to install HR practices, but also because it provides a dynamic point of view (Eisenhardt & Martin, 2000). Again, this yields the opportunity to analyze the sets of activities through which NPOs develop and implement their HR practices and gain insight into the processual aspect of the alteration of HRM from a dynamic rather than a static perspective. In addition to responding to change in the external environment, dynamic capabilities can also account for the nature of internal change (Zahra et al., 2006), which is especially relevant for a study of NPOs where external and/or internal demands may lead to pressures to alter HRM. Finally, the dynamic capabilities approach recognizes that organizational processes evolve cumulatively depending on the organization's previous path, thereby providing the opportunity to analyze the influences on the processes through which NPOs develop and implement their HR practices.

In this chapter, the theoretical underpinnings of dynamic capabilities will first be discussed to narrow the focus onto the concepts within the dynamic capabilities approach that can be applied to better understand the alteration of HRM in NPOs. Stemming from this discussion, learning and adapting processes are explored in the conceptual and empirical literature with regard to their path dependency. After establishing that path, learning, and adapting can aid in understanding the alteration of HRM in NPOs, a conceptual framework is developed by drawing on these relevant theoretical concepts. The chapter concludes with deriving theory-driven, specific research questions that operationalize the concepts represented in the framework and provide the basis for conducting the study's subsequent empirical research.

CONCEPTUALIZING DYNAMIC CAPABILITIES

The dynamic capabilities approach is a theoretical perspective that stems from the evolutionary theory of the firm (Nelson & Winter, 1982) and is an outgrowth of the resource-based view (RBV) of the firm (Barney, 1991, 2001a, 2001b; Penrose, 1959; Wernerfelt, 1984). Whereas the RBV focuses attention on the role of valuable, rare, and inimitable resources and capabilities that possess an organizational orientation, the dynamic capabilities approach investigates how organizations build, integrate, renew, and reconfigure these resources and capabilities successfully (Eisenhardt & Martin, 2000; Helfat, 2000; Teece et al., 1997).

Building on previous conceptual work on organizational routines, competences, and capabilities (Amit & Schoemaker, 1993; Barney, 1992; Collis, 1994; Grant, 1991; Nelson & Winter, 1982), the dynamic capabilities approach provides a valuable perspective for identifying and understanding the firm-specific processes through which organizations alter their resource base (Ambrosini & Bowman, 2009; Eisenhardt & Martin, 2000; Helfat et al., 2007). It has often been noted, however, that the literature on dynamic capabilities is full of inconsistencies, overlapping definitions, and contradictions (Salvato, 2003). One step in bringing clarity to the confusion is to distinguish among dynamic capabilities, operational capabilities, and organizational routines.

Capabilities have been viewed as specific types of resources, processes, or routines (Amit & Schoemaker, 1993; Collis, 1994; Grant, 1991, 1996; Helfat et al., 2007; Teece & Pisano, 1994; Winter, 2003). Within the literature, the hierarchy of capabilities ranges from lower-order operating-level capabilities to higher-order dynamic capabilities (Collis, 1994; Grant, 1996). The lower-order operational capabilities refer to the 'bread and butter' capabilities that enable the organization to earn a living presently and perform the basic activities of the organization (Helfat et al., 2007; Winter, 2003). They can be understood as a collection of organizational routines that enable the effective deployment of resources (Collis, 1994; Grant, 1991; Winter, 2003). Once the knowledge on which these capabilities is based no longer meets the current demands of the environment, these capabilities run the danger of turning into rigidities (Leonard-Barton, 1992). Therefore, an organization must not only maintain but also renew its lower-order capabilities when facing environmental change (Pavlou & El Sawy, 2006a, 2006b; Teece & Pisano, 1994). It becomes evident from this discussion that higher-order dynamic capabilities are necessary that enable the organization to respond to change (Helfat et al., 2007; Newey & Zahra, 2009).

These higher-order dynamic capabilities are the meta-routines and meta-competences that shape, revamp, and govern the rate of change of lower-order operational capabilities (Eisenhardt & Martin, 2000; Teece, 2007; Zollo & Winter, 2002). Dynamic capabilities are understood as "the capacity of an organization to purposefully create, extend, or modify its resource base" (Helfat et al., 2007, p. 4). A resource base encompasses tangible and intangible resources and assets, as well as the firm's operational capabilities. Teece (2007) contends that a scholarly consensus groups resources and competences as the firm's operational capabilities, whereas dynamic capabilities relate to high-level activities regarding the firm's ability to sense and seize opportunities, manage threats, and reconfigure assets to meet change. Dynamic capabilities revamp the lower-order capabilities, which are made up of a collection of organizational routines aimed at making better use of the organization's resources and deploying them. Thus, organizational routines form the building blocks of capabilities. Capabilities, however, are not to be equated with routines because routines are smaller in scale, typically unknown, and entail automatic behaviors (Winter, 2000, 2003). Organizational routines can be understood as tacit, learned, and recurring patterns of organized activity that are context-dependent and difficult to imitate (Cohen et al., 1996; Grant, 1991, 1996; Nelson & Winter, 1982). Figure 3.1 illustrates the relationship among dynamic capabilities, the resource base, and organizational routines.

Dynamic capabilities were originally understood as a subset of the firm's competences and capabilities used to create new products and processes and respond to the changing market conditions (Teece & Pisano, 1994). Eisenhardt and Martin (2000) focus strongly on dynamic capabilities as processes and emphasize their connection to market dynamism and the alteration of resources, rather than achieving competitive advantage. In contrast, highlighting internal change and the influence of path, processes, and market position, Teece et al. (1997) emphasize the presence of rapidly changing environments and connect dynamic capabilities to forms of competitive advantage. The numerous definitions of dynamic capabilities share the commonality that they involve changing capabilities over time, but they differ in terms of the role of market dynamism and whether dynamic capabilities provide a source of competitive advantage (Easterby-Smith et al.,

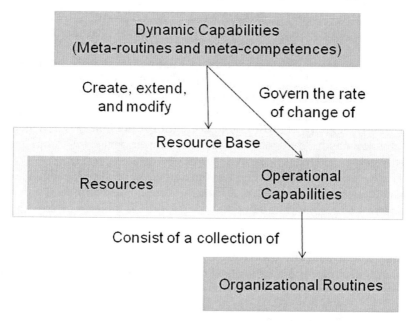

Figure 3.1   Main concepts within the dynamic capabilities approach.

2009; Zahra et al., 2006). The original definition by Teece et al. (1997) seems to require the presence of rapidly changing environments for the existence of dynamic capabilities, but firms integrate, build, and reconfigure their competences in environments subject to lower rates of change. Empirical results provide evidence that dynamic capabilities can be valuable in lower levels of environmental turbulence, thus removing the misconception that dynamic capabilities are worthless in stable environments (Pavlou & El Sawy, 2006b).

Zahra et al. (2006) note that dynamic capabilities develop in response to a variety of conditions, such as perceived external change, learning about external conditions for the first time, and internal pressures toward change. Thus, dynamic capabilities account for the nature of internal change because the need to alter capabilities "may emanate from changes in organizational conditions rather than in the external environment" (Zahra et al., 2006, p. 924). More recent work notes that dynamic capabilities operate in stable environments; therefore, 'dynamic' refers to change in the resource base (Ambrosini & Bowman, 2009).

According to the definition of dynamic capabilities by Helfat et al. (2007), altering the resource base entails creating resources by bringing in new resources, extending the existing resource base by promoting growth in the current direction, and modifying resources as a way of responding to change in the environment. This definition has been noted as being specifically applicable to NPOs given their resource base and because they are confronted by change (Helfat et al., 2007). Furthermore, this definition avoids any tautology regarding superior performance (Eisenhardt & Martin, 2000) by referring to the capacity to alter the resource base in a minimally acceptable manner that is different—but not necessarily qualitatively better than before. In addition, a capacity connotes a repeatable function that is patterned and practiced, and dynamic capabilities are purposeful, thus differing from rote organizational routines, which lack intent (Helfat et al., 2007). Finally, the definition allows for the possibility that dynamic capabilities may "address or bring about organizational changes unrelated to environmental change" (Easterby-Smith et al., 2009, p. S3).

Thus far, organizational routines, operational capabilities, and dynamic capabilities play a central role within the dynamic capabilities approach in terms of better understanding how organizations adapt. The concept of dynamic capabilities provides the missing link in explaining how organizations are able to create, extend, and modify their resource base to address change. From this discussion, it becomes clear that certain common emphases are helpful for understanding the alteration of HRM in NPOs. First, whereas earlier work on dynamic capabilities emphasized the role of a rapidly changing environment, later conceptualizations acknowledge that dynamic capabilities are necessary in environments other than those of rapid change, such as the nonprofit setting. Thus, the dynamic capabilities approach is useful for understanding organizations' responses to lower rates of change as in moderately dynamic environments or where there is perceived external change or even internal pressures toward change. Evidence from the literature suggests that NPOs are facing both internal and external changes, such as difficulties in recruiting and retaining qualified employees and increasing competition for funds and clients, with shifts in their funding and regulatory environments stemming from cutbacks and greater demands for professionalization. Thus, the dynamic capabilities approach serves as a fitting analytical tool to better understand these internal and external pressures toward altering their HRM. Finally, rather than confounding dynamic capabilities with their outcomes, dynamic capabilities can be viewed independently of their impact on organizational performance. The definition of dynamic capabilities as altering the resource base in a different manner is especially relevant for the present study because processes, rather than outcomes, are at the forefront of the analysis. The following section will explore the main concepts within the theoretical perspective of dynamic capabilities that bear further potential for exploring the alteration of HRM in NPOs.

THE ROLE OF PATH, POSITION, AND PROCESSES

Stemming from the understanding of dynamic capabilities outlined above, a myriad of influences can shape an organization's dynamic capabilities.

Teece et al. (1997, p. 518) state that "organizational processes, shaped by the firm's asset positions and molded by its evolutionary and co-evolutionary paths, explain the essence of the firm's dynamic capabilities and its competitive advantage." Path refers to the strategic options available, with path dependency conveying that an organization's future development is constrained by the narrow evolutionary path it has traveled. Position entails the firm's specific assets such as difficult to trade knowledge assets, as well as reputational and relational assets. Finally, managerial and organizational processes are referred to as the "way things are done in the firm" and its "routines, or patterns of current practice and learning" (Teece et al., 1997, p. 518). These processes have three roles of coordination/integration, learning, and reconfiguration, which are static, dynamic, and transformational concepts, respectively.

Path

Path can be understood as a constituted, recursively stabilized pattern governed by self-reinforcing mechanisms that set the pattern into motion and potentially lead to a lock-in, thereby implying a certain degree of path dependency (Sydow et al., 2009). A firm's genetics include past managerial decisions, activities, routines, decision rules, and tacit understandings that can constrain its current position or open up a range of potential strategic paths (Mahoney, 1995; Rosenbloom, 2000). For example, firms differ in their bundles of resources given their differing histories of strategic choice and performance (Rumelt, 1984). Thus, success is partially a product of the process and structures in place and previous organizational experience (Teece & Pisano, 1994).

The concept of path dependency acknowledges that history matters. It refers to a process in which the scope of variety and range of managerial discretion diminish, thus restricting the range of future decision-making options for an organization (Kay, 2005; Koch, 2008; Sydow et al., 2009). Rather than inheriting a blank slate, actors are limited in their room to maneuver by the "dead weight of previous institutional choices" that may be sticky and path-dependent (Pierson, 2000b, p. 493). Firms induce self-reinforcing processes that render reversals of course very costly given the entrenchment of certain institutional arrangements and the cumulative commitments on the existing path (Pierson, 2000a, 2000c). It not only becomes costly to create new policies, but also learning and coordination effects, and legitimation, power, and adaptive expectations are generated that provide managers with strong incentives to continue down a specific path, eventually locking in one solution (Arthur, 1994; Mahoney, 2000). These powerful mechanisms of feedback that are created can explain why organizations become self-reinforcing and resistant to change.

Therefore, the theoretical assumptions of path dependency entail that organizational processes evolve in a cumulative way depending on former events and decisions (Koch, 2008; Sydow et al., 2009). Because these processes are not easy to transform, change is assumed to be incremental (Teece & Pisano, 1994). Organizations are subject to a reality of constrained change given managerial failures and existing resource bases. Yet Teece (2007) argues that although organizations are shaped by the past, they are not necessarily trapped by it: Management has influence through investment choice and other decisions. Thus, despite the limitations, there is still a capacity for change, although the path available is narrowed by the existing capabilities (Helfat et al., 2007).

Stemming from these discussions, change can be differentiated into path-dependent or path-breaking change (Karim & Mitchell, 2000). Path-dependent change captures the notion that although change occurs, it does so within a particular set of change options. In path-breaking change, in contrast, the dissolution of paths that rely on previous routines can create new alternatives for the organization by freeing it from self-reinforcing mechanisms (Karim & Mitchell, 2000; Sydow et al., 2009). Whereas path-dependent change entails relying on past managerial decisions, activities, routines, previously gained experience, skills, and resources that foreclose the future path the organization can take (Mahoney, 1995), path-breaking change encompasses deviating from these existing skills and gaining distinct resources, thus opening up an entirely novel path (Karim & Mitchell, 2000). This new path, however, is still a product of the earlier structure of existing activities, resources, and actors (Hakansson & Lundgren, 1997). Thus, whereas in path-dependent change a critical juncture triggered by an event is followed by a self-reinforcing dynamic, in path-breaking change new events and external interventions can dislodge the equilibrium the organization has reached (Pierson, 2000a, 2000c; Sydow et al., 2009).

Position

In addition to being shaped by the firm's path, its position or its specific assets determine its competitive advantage. Assets may be technological, complementary, financial, reputational, structural, institutional, and market-based. Thus, they include knowledge assets that are not readily tradable, as well as reputational and relational assets. Teece et al. (1997, p. 529) highlight the importance of this role of assets when they argue that "competitive advantage is not just a function of how one plays the game; it is also a function of the 'assets' one has to play with and how these assets can be deployed and redeployed in a changing market." In essence, a firm's existing resources determine its position. According to Rumelt (1994), the task of management entails adapting and renewing this bundle while its value erodes. Dynamic capabilities can lead to a change in the initial resource position of the organization (Maritan & Peteraf, 2007).

Processes

Finally, recent discussions have emphasized that organizational processes are a central feature of capabilities, involving the structuring and combination of resources (Ambrosini & Bowman, 2009; Easterby-Smith et al., 2009; Wang & Ahmed, 2007). Processes are "the sets of actions that repeat over time and allow managers to accomplish some business task" (Bingham et al., 2007, p. 27). Yet the dynamic capabilities literature is marred by a lack of conceptual clarity regarding the role of processes and their link to dynamic capabilities (Maritan & Peteraf, 2007; Wang & Ahmed, 2007).

On the one hand, processes have been perceived as forming the foundation of dynamic capabilities (Dosi & Teece, 1998), with dynamic capabilities "being resident in the firm's organizational processes [. . .]" (Teece et al., 1997, p. 524). Accordingly, processes provide the elements of dynamic capabilities, rather than being dynamic capabilities themselves. Teece (2007, p. 1321) builds on his original work, making distinctions between "the organizational and managerial processes, procedures, systems and structures that underlie each class of capability and the capability itself." Processes of coordination/integration, learning, and reconfiguration form the subset of processes that support the classes of dynamic capabilities, namely, the capacity to sense and shape opportunities and threats, to seize opportunities, and to reconfigure the firm's assets and manage threats (Teece, 2007).

In contrast, other conceptual work views processes as dynamic capabilities (Ambrosini & Bowman, 2009; Eisenhardt & Martin, 2000). Eisenhardt and Martin (2000), for example, conceive of dynamic capabilities as a set of specific, identifiable strategic and organizational processes that have extensive empirical bases. They define dynamic capabilities as "the firm's processes that use resources—specifically the processes to integrate, reconfigure, gain and release resources—to match and even create market change" (Eisenhardt & Martin, 2000, p. 1107). Examples of dynamic capabilities include routines and processes such as strategic decision making for the integration of resources, transfer processes for the reconfiguration of resources, and knowledge creation routines for gaining and releasing resources.

Finally, processes have also been viewed at the micro-level as the mechanisms by which firms can develop dynamic capabilities and put dynamic capabilities into use (Maritan & Peteraf, 2007). These managerial and organizational processes are a part of the functioning of dynamic capabilities and are relevant to dynamic capabilities if they directly deal with a change in resource position and operational capabilities of the organization. Dynamic capabilities are thus related to the underlying processes that help to bring about a change in the resource base rather than those that merely maintain the status quo (Maritan & Peteraf, 2007). Research, however, is still needed on these underlying mechanisms (Easterby-Smith et al., 2009).

Following Teece (2007; Teece et al., 1997) and Maritan and Peteraf (2007), processes are viewed in this study as those underlying processes that provide the foundation of dynamic capabilities and help to bring about change in the resources and operational capabilities of an organization. These authors' complementary viewpoints of processes are both necessary for understanding change. As dynamic capabilities encompass the capacities for identifying the need or opportunity for change, formulating a response to this need or opportunity and implementing a course of action (Maritan & Peteraf, 2007), the processes that these dynamic capabilities are embedded in provide a means for analyzing the alteration of the resource base. Stemming from this understanding, processes encompass a set of activities that enable organizations to identify, respond to, and enact the alteration of the resource base by sensing and shaping opportunities, making decisions to execute on those opportunities, and reconfiguring resources when the market changes (Teece, 2007).

Summary: Path and Processes as a Foundation for Understanding the Alteration of HRM in NPOs

In conclusion, this review of the conceptual work reveals that the dynamic capabilities approach is suitable for analyzing the alteration of HRM in NPOs in several ways. First, it draws attention to the processes that provide the foundation for dynamic capabilities and are relevant to analyzing how organizations alter their resource base. Because the aim of this study is to better understand the underlying mechanisms through which NPOs develop and implement HR practices, processes lie undeniably at the heart of the present analysis. In this study, processes can be understood as the set of activities through which NPOs alter their HRM to respond to internal and external changes. Thus far, the nonprofit literature reveals little about these processes through which NPOs alter their HRM to cope with their challenges.

Furthermore, the dynamic capabilities approach takes the evolutionary path of the organization into account, as the processes enable an organization to move from its initial resource position to a new or modified path. Although the concept of resource position is important for studying how organizations achieve competitive advantage and thus not central to this study's aims, path is relevant to the present study of processes involved in the alteration of HRM in NPOs as these processes evolve cumulatively given that organizations are subject to a reality of constrained change. Although this discussion has underscored the path dependency of organizational processes, the differentiation between path-dependent and path-breaking change suggests that there is still a capacity for change. Therefore, the concept of path can direct the analysis toward the distinguishing nonprofit characteristics with regard to an organization's values, routines, past managerial decisions, and experience, which may constrain or enable the processes through which NPOs alter their HRM.

In summary, having demonstrated that the dynamic capabilities approach can provide insight into this study's research questions, path and processes emerge from the literature as the main theoretical concepts to understand the alteration of HRM in NPOs. As a result, applying the dynamic capabilities approach helps to refine the aims of this study toward analyzing the processes through which NPOs alter their HRM and the influence of path on these processes. In the following section, processes and their path dependency will be examined in the conceptual and empirical literature within the dynamic capabilities approach to enable the operationalization of these concepts.

PROCESSES AND THEIR PATH DEPENDENCY

Only recently has empirical research begun to focus on the underlying managerial and organizational processes of dynamic capabilities (Maritan & Peteraf, 2007). Conceptual and empirical work has emphasized specifying and explicating these underlying processes by which organizations can alter their resource base, highlighting learning as an important process in the development of these capabilities (Zollo & Winter, 2002). Empirical studies highlight the path dependency of learning and capability building. Furthermore, conceptual and empirical studies examining how dynamic capabilities bring about change in their resource base also reveal the importance of underlying adapting processes. A myriad of adapting processes involved in the development and deployment of capabilities has been empirically analyzed, whereas only a limited number of studies confirm the theoretical assumption that these processes are constrained by path. The following sections review the empirical research on these underlying learning and adapting processes and the extent of their path dependency.

Learning

Learning plays an important role in the alteration of the resource base and can be facilitated when directed toward areas of what is already known; thus, future learning is shaped by the current knowledge base (Cohen & Levinthal, 1990; Kogut & Zander, 1992). Learning processes of experience accumulation, knowledge articulation, and knowledge codification (Zollo & Winter, 2002) are central to creating, extending, and modifying the organization's resources and capabilities. In the following, these three underlying learning mechanisms will be briefly explored in the conceptual and empirical literature.

Experience Accumulation

In experience accumulation, internal and external knowledge can be gained either through experiential or acquisitive learning mechanisms

(Keil, 2004; Levitt & March, 1988; Luo, 2000; Mahoney, 1995; March et al., 1991; Zahra et al., 1999). The former refers to the organization's direct self-learning or learning-by-doing that occurs inside the organization and creates firm-specific knowledge, whereas the latter entails acquiring and internalizing knowledge from outside of the organization (Zahra et al., 1999). Acquisitive learning entails acquiring and internalizing knowledge from outside of the firm, through vicarious learning from other organizations, grafting or hiring new employees, and through searching and noticing, i.e., scanning the environment. Zahra and George (2002) propose that past experience, more diverse sources of knowledge, and complementarity between the knowledge base of the firm and the external sources can enhance the firm's absorptive capacity to acquire and assimilate external knowledge. Studies provide empirical support that firms are able to build new capabilities through acquisitive or experiential learning as well as by combining these learning mechanisms (George, 2005; Keil, 2004).

Knowledge Articulation

Knowledge articulation involves making the mainly tacit knowledge explicit through analysis, dialogue, debriefing, and review, and it is crucial to making sense of previous experiences and acknowledging the need for change (Kale & Singh, 1999; Keil, 2004; Zollo & Winter, 2002). It is related to knowledge sharing, which encompasses the processes of exchanging and disseminating knowledge throughout the organization and integrating this acquired knowledge with the pre-existing skills and knowledge (Kale & Singh, 1999; Luo, 2000). Informal and formal social integration mechanisms, such as social networks or the systematic use of coordinators, can enhance knowledge sharing, thereby facilitating knowledge assimilation and allowing the firm to transform and exploit the new knowledge (Zahra & George, 2002). This knowledge can be internalized within the firm or transferred via networks of individuals or organizations (Keil, 2004; Luo, 2000; Zollo & Winter, 2002). Nevertheless, barriers that are structural, cognitive, behavioral, and political can hinder knowledge internalization, sharing, and integration (Szulanski, 1996; Zahra & George, 2002).

Knowledge Codification

Knowledge codification involves documenting knowledge explicitly in written tools and activities that clearly state the rules and procedures (Singh & Zollo, 1998). In order to achieve codification, a deep understanding of processes is often necessary. Yet given the tacitness of knowledge, it can be limited because the underlying structures are not well understood (Teece & Pisano, 1994). Codification differs from articulation in that it analyzes the articulated knowledge about past experience to aid in future decision-making processes and sensemaking (Zollo & Winter, 2002). By codifying accumulated knowledge into usable guidelines or manuals, the content (know-what), methodology (know-how), and often the rationale (know-why) for tasks can be documented to guide similar future situations (Eisenhardt & Martin 2000; Kale & Singh, 1999; Zollo & Winter, 2002). Empirical research demonstrates that codification efforts encourage knowledge articulation by making knowledge easier to transfer over time and apply in future projects (Marsh & Stock, 2006). Studies show that codification supports learning from experience in which there are only a few number of cases, helping firms to develop routines for future activities and change their existing routines (Eisenhardt & Martin 2000; Kale & Singh, 1999; Keil, 2004; Singh & Zollo, 1998). Although codification processes are associated with increasing organizational inertia, research suggests somewhat counterintuitively that infrequent and heterogeneous tasks such as restructuring necessitate knowledge articulation and codification (Zollo & Winter, 2002).

The Path Dependency of Learning Processes

Learning is argued to be highly path-dependent. The way firms gain knowledge shapes how they process, store, and retrieve this knowledge (Mahoney, 1995). Thus, a firm's history of building capabilities is relevant for its current ability to absorb new knowledge (Kor & Mahoney, 2005). Teece et al. (1997) argue that learning activities must be similar to past processes in order to maintain the ability to determine cause-effect relationships. The local search for new knowledge occurs near current knowledge (Nelson & Winter, 1982) given bounded rationality and the existing accumulated knowledge base (Cohen & Levinthal, 1990; Simon, 1997). By protecting the knowledge base instead of responding to environmental changes, however, path-dependent assets may become liabilities (Helfat, 1994).

Empirical research demonstrates that organizations amass resources and develop capabilities through path-dependent learning that depends on pre-existing know-how and the development of related know-how (Camuffo & Volpato, 1996; Helfat, 1997). Knowledge retention practices are proven to enhance the organization's ability to integrate previous knowledge from past new product development projects given the path-dependent nature of these dynamic problem-solving processes (Marsh & Stock, 2006). Further studies highlight the role of path dependency in speeding up capability development by using knowledge from previous projects (Pisano, 2000). The path dependency of learning in capability development has also been explored with regard to the impact on firm performance (Helfat, 1994; Kor & Mahoney, 2005), revealing that costs remain low when firms have pre-existing knowledge that is complementary to their new knowledge base.

To sum up thus far, these learning processes entail several implications for understanding how organizations alter their resource base. Regarding experience accumulation, knowledge can be gained for identifying the need to alter the resource base either through experiential or acquisitive learning, with learning being dependent on the firm's ability to absorb new knowledge. Articulating, sharing, and assimilating this knowledge enhance the collective understanding and sensemaking of change within the organization. The codification of the content (know-what), methodology (know-how), and often the rationale (know-why) aids in sensemaking and future decision making. Finally, the path dependency of learning demonstrates that pre-existing knowledge may be crucial in enabling the alteration of the resource base.

Adapting

The literature reveals that underlying adapting processes are also necessary to bring about change in the resource base (Maritan & Peteraf, 2007). Thus, the dynamic capabilities approach is a framework for explaining how organizations spot opportunities, make decisions to act on those opportunities, and reconfigure when the market changes (Teece, 2007). Dynamic capabilities have the function of identifying the need for change, formulating a response to this need, and implementing a course of action (Helfat et al., 2007). The underlying organizational processes involved in these functions of dynamic capabilities include search, decision-making, and restructuring processes.

Search Processes

Organizations engage in search processes by which they identify and shape new opportunities for altering the resource base, scan for new ways of doing things, and acquire resources externally. Information must be gathered through internally and externally focused search, sense must be made of this information, and the implications for action must be drawn (Teece, 2007). Search includes building new thinking and creating knowledge within the organization through external linkages and bringing in new, often complementary resources from external sources (Eisenhardt & Martin, 2000; Henderson & Cockburn, 1994; Maritan & Peteraf, 2007). A firm's locus of search depends on its experience, often being local or close to the existing accumulated knowledge base and current capabilities (Cohen & Levinthal, 1990; Nelson & Winter, 1982; Zahra & George, 2002), as opposed to distant search that entails going beyond the firm's neighborhood of expertise (Cillo & Verona, 2008). Empirical studies reveal that search processes are the activities through which firms recognize opportunities, identify latent capabilities, and react to discontinuities in the environment (Maritan, 2001; Pablo et al., 2007), yet can be constrained by managerial cognitive representations (Tripsas & Gavetti, 2000).

Decision-Making Processes

Altering the resource base also includes decision-making processes about the search and selection of resources (Maritan & Peteraf, 2007). Through a series of managerial decisions preceding implementation, managers gather their expertise and integrate numerous resources to make choices (Eisenhardt & Martin, 2000; Iansiti & Clark, 1994). Thus, decision making involves the internal and external integration of activities and resources (Teece et al., 1997), entailing coordination, leadership, and routines that ensure communication as well as using the external sources of new information. However, existing capabilities and path-dependent routines may be barriers that prevent organizations from making decisions by exacerbating biases. Failure to adapt to change may stem from a lack of motivation to change and responding to threats by reverting quickly to past actions, in all of which managerial decisions play a significant role (Adner & Helfat, 2003; Helfat et al., 2007; Maritan, 2001). Indeed, further empirical research reveals that decision processes entail information flows and the important role of senior management especially in terms of firm-specific managerial experience (Kor & Mahoney, 2005). Managerial skills are required to identify, enable, and manage the use of dynamic capabilities as empirical research corroborates that they are difficult to implement (Pablo et al., 2007). Within decision-making processes, top management leadership skills play an important role in sustaining dynamic capabilities, and decision-making biases can be mitigated through lower-level decision making and reducing the number of management layers (Teece, 2007).

Restructuring Processes

Finally, restructuring processes involve the processes in change management in which the organization's resource base is changed both internally and externally (Helfat et al., 2007). It entails adding, transferring, deleting, and recombining resources, especially the allocation of scarce resources and generating new resource combinations to better match the environment (Bowman & Ambrosini, 2003; Burgelman, 1994; Galunic & Eisenhardt, 1996; Karim & Mitchell, 2000; Pavlou & El Sawy, 2006a, 2006b). Restructuring can aid in escaping unfavorable path dependencies due to narrowly focusing search activities that prohibit the organization from recognizing new opportunities. It entails revamping dysfunctional routines that no longer match the environment. A continuous strategic 'fit' among strategy, structure, and processes is required to combine resources (Teece, 2007). According to Teece et al. (1997), firms need to reconfigure through adopting best practices, scanning the environment to track external changes, and surveying the markets, which enable the firm to transform ahead of its competitors. Empirical studies indicate that decentralization, local autonomy, and strategic vision aid managers in restructuring their resources and revamping their routines in order to adapt to change (Forrant & Flynn, 1999; Rindova & Kotha, 2001; Teece, 2007; Teece et al., 1997).

The Path Dependency of Adapting Processes

Similar to learning processes, adapting processes are also path-dependent, although there are far fewer empirical studies that reveal this phenomenon. Organizations accumulate resources in search operations through path-dependent activities. This local search for new knowledge occurs near the existing accumulated knowledge base in order to maintain the ability to determine cause-effect relationships (Cohen & Levinthal, 1990; Nelson & Winter, 1982; Teece et al., 1997; Zahra & George, 2002). Empirical evidence points to the path dependency of search processes in which top managers find it difficult to adapt their mental models in rapidly changing environments (Tripsas & Gavetti, 2000). These findings confirm the danger of getting trapped when the organization protects its current knowledge base instead of responding to change (Leonard-Barton, 1992).

Furthermore, in developing, managing, and deploying capabilities, strategy formation and implementation is shown to be a gradual, cumulative, and expansive process that is path-dependent (Montealegre, 2002). Finally, empirical research on reconfiguring business resources reveals evidence of path-dependent resource-deepening that builds on an existing set of capabilities and path-breaking resource-extension with different resources and new sets of skills (Karim & Mitchell, 2000). Although these studies confirm the assumption that adapting processes are constrained by path, initial evidence is also provided regarding path-breaking change.

In summary, the aforementioned adapting processes provide valuable insight into the underlying search, decision-making, and restructuring processes through which organizations sense, seize on, and manage the alteration of the organization's resources and capabilities. These adapting processes have several implications for analyzing and understanding the alteration of the resource base. First, the search processes through which the organization scans its environment and acquires external resources are necessary for identifying the opportunity for change and often depend on past experience. Second, decision-making processes are the means through which organizations formulate a response to change, encompassing the internal and external integration of activities in which the integration of new knowledge is achieved. Furthermore, restructuring processes involve transferring, recombining, and allocating scarce resources as well as generating new resource combinations to implement change in the organization. Finally, a few studies pointing to path dependency imply that prior knowledge and organization-specific resources may inhibit the managers from adapting their beliefs to the changing environment.

Summary: Path, Learning, and Adapting Processes as a Means to Understand the Alteration of HRM in NPOs

It can be gleaned from this brief review of the conceptual and empirical literature that a focus on learning and adapting processes is necessary to better understand how NPOs alter their HRM. Path, learning, and adapting emerge as the main theoretical concepts for researching into this phenomenon. Several implications arise for this study: First, learning, with its processes of experience accumulation, knowledge articulation, and knowledge codification, can enable research into the acquisition, sharing, and codification of new and existing knowledge that is necessary for the development and implementation of HR practices. Second, adapting provides insight into the processes of search, decision making, and restructuring for analyzing how NPOs search for opportunities for altering HRM, make decisions about their HRM, and restructure their resources when altering their HRM. Moreover, the review of empirical studies has shown that both learning and adapting processes are predominantly path-dependent. Yet these studies come to different conclusions, suggesting that path can have a constraining and an enabling influence. The remainder of this chapter will illustrate the concepts of learning and adapting and their relationship to path by developing a conceptual framework.

DEVELOPING A CONCEPTUAL FRAMEWORK AND SPECIFIC RESEARCH QUESTIONS

In Chapter 2, the general research questions *"How and why do NPOs develop and implement their HR practices?"* and *"How and why do the distinguishing nonprofit characteristics influence the development and implementation of HR practices?"* were deductively developed by analyzing the research on change and HRM in NPOs. This study seeks to bridge this research gap by employing the theoretical background of dynamic capabilities to understand change in NPOs. The main theoretical concepts and the assumed relationships between these concepts will be identified and visualized with the aid of a conceptual framework. By iterating among the conceptual framework, the nonprofit literature, and the dynamic capabilities approach, specific research questions will be developed that help to operationalize path, learning, and adapting.

A framework is a representation of the main concepts and clarifies their presumed relationships that are logical or stem from previous findings (Miles & Huberman, 1994). To map a framework, the bins or main concepts need to be specified. They can stem from theory, experience, and the general objectives of the study. With its focusing and bounding function for the research, a framework ensures that not all avenues of empirical inquiry are pursued. Prior theorizing such as specifying constructs a priori from the literature (Eisenhardt, 1989) and empirical research are important inputs that give an orienting frame to the relationships that stem from the literature. The arrows clarify the relationships between the boxes, bringing order into the conceptualization by delineating patterns (Miles & Huberman, 1994; Whetten, 1989).

A theory-driven conceptual framework and specific research questions are developed in this study by iterating the theoretical concepts derived from the dynamic capabilities approach with nonprofit research. Reviewing the literature can aid in developing sharper and more insightful questions (Yin, 2009). This iterative approach reflects that the research process is not a linear progression from the literature review to research questions, design, data collection, and analysis. Instead it cycles back and forth between the prior state of research, theoretical background, conceptual framework, and research questions until an operationalized conceptual framework emerges that guides the empirical research.

Specific research questions function as a bridge between theory and data by showing how to operationalize the relationships stemming from theory, helping to narrow the relevant data and guide the subsequent analysis (Sutton & Staw, 1995; Yin, 2009). Given the poorly developed state of prior research in the nonprofit literature, conceptual work from the dynamic capabilities approach will also be drawn on to develop the specific research questions and operationalize the framework (Eisenhardt, 1989). Thus far, the iterative research process followed in this study can be displayed in the form of a funnel that narrows the focus of the research with each step, as seen in Figure 3.2.

Although the dynamic capabilities approach was developed for analyzing the sources and methods of wealth creation by private firms, it is applicable to NPOs given its focus on internal resources rather than competitive market behavior (Helfat et al., 2007; Pablo et al., 2007). Whereas learning and adapting processes are precipitated by changes in the external environment, the theory provides a perspective for understanding both external and internal changes as these processes may also have their origin in the internal organizational environment (Ambrosini & Bowman, 2009; Zahra et al., 2006). This study considers both of these environments when examining the alteration of HRM in NPOs and the dominating influences on how these organizations learn and adapt to change. In this respect, path, which entails the past managerial decisions, activities, knowledge, and routines (Mahoney, 1995; Rosenbloom, 2000), is an adequate theoretical category to examine how and why the distinguishing nonprofit characteristics influence the development and implementation of HR practices. In particular, it is assumed that path will allow insight into how these internal and external influences constrain or enable the processes through which NPOs alter their HRM.

Furthermore, processes are viewed as essential for creating, extending, and modifying the resource base of an organization to address change (Maritan

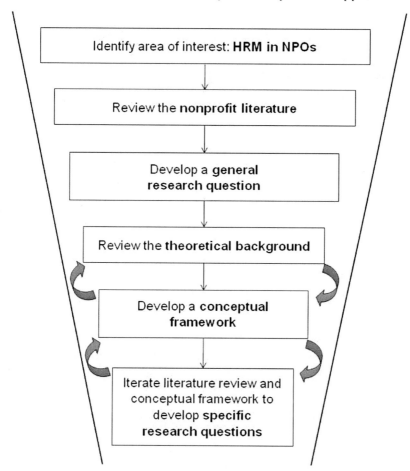

Figure 3.2 The iterative process of developing a conceptual framework and specific research questions.

& Peteraf, 2007; Teece, 2007; Teece et al., 1997). Stemming from this understanding, processes are defined in this study as a set of activities through which NPOs develop and implement their new or modified HR practices to respond to internal or external change. Because learning and adapting processes of experience accumulation, knowledge articulation, knowledge codification, search, decision making, and restructuring are central to this approach, research is needed on these sets of activities to better understand how and why NPOs develop and implement their HR practices.

Finally, altering HRM through these learning and adapting processes is assumed to result in a new or modified HR practice. New HR practices differ from modified HR practices in that the latter refer to revamping already existing HR practices, e.g., a modification of the current compensation

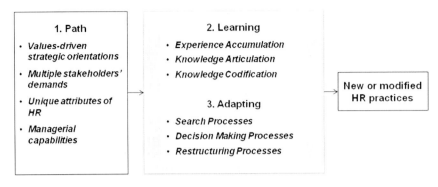

Figure 3.3   Operationalized conceptual framework.

model, whereas the former refer to installing practices that did not exist in the organization in any form before. In light of these theoretical underpinnings, this study aims to analyze the influence of path and the learning and adapting processes through which NPOs develop and implement new or modified HR practices. The following conceptual framework emerges (see Figure 3.3), which illustrates the assumed relationships between the concepts raised in the review of the theoretical literature that are subsequently operationalized in order to apply and connect the framework to empirical reality. The assumptions that lead to this operationalization will be discussed in the next section, which focuses on the mechanics of applying the theory to understand change in NPOs in terms of the alteration of HRM.

In the following, iterating among the theoretical concepts of path, learning, and adapting and the nonprofit literature leads to the development of sharper, more insightful specific research questions that operationalize the conceptual framework and guide the subsequent empirical analysis of the theoretical assumptions (Eisenhardt, 1989; Yin, 2009). Theory-driven research questions are developed that correspond to the numbered theoretical concepts in the framework.

> 1) *How and why does path influence the learning and adapting processes through which NPOs develop and implement new or modified HR practices?*

Path entails the unique histories of organizations that are reflected in their distinctive routines, with the concept of path dependency conveying that the values, experience, skills, resources, routines, and past managerial decisions shape the options available to the organization (Koch, 2008; Sydow et al., 2009). Cycling back and forth between the nonprofit and the theoretical literature reveals insight into how the theoretical concept of path can be operationalized. Processes evolve in a cumulative way (Koch, 2008), and it is assumed that the concept of path can aid in exploring how these processes emerge over time and whether they are enabled or constrained by the organization's past. Within the nonprofit literature, certain lines of inquiry have developed with regard to the various factors that influence processes in NPOs. As seen from the nonprofit literature review in Chapter 2, processes are subject to the influence of a variety of special characteristics that can be divided into values-driven strategic orientations, multiple stakeholders' demands, unique attributes of HR, and managerial capabilities. These four characteristics have been identified in the nonprofit literature as influencing organizational change and learning in different ways. They are argued to capture the path of the NPO in that they constitute its history, values, experience, skills, resources, routines, and past managerial decisions.

For example, nonprofit scholars emphasize incorporating the organization's values-driven strategic orientation, i.e., its historically embedded values and goals that are expressed in the organization's mission (Frumkin & Andre-Clark, 2000; Jeavons, 1992; Moore, 2000). Oftentimes these goals may be vague or multiple, thereby complicating the management of change in NPOs (Kellock Hay et al., 2001). Furthermore, maintaining practices that are in accordance with the organization's core values and basic mission is shown to help NPOs adapt (Salipante & Golden-Biddle, 1995). Thus, as the concept of path is constituted by the organization's history and values, it can be operationalized with the dimension of the values-driven strategic orientation. The organizational values, multiple goals, and nonprofit mission are expected to influence the processes through which they develop and implement new or modified HR practices.

The theoretical concept of path, however, is not limited to history and values but also includes the experience, skills, and resources of an organization. External stakeholders are emphasized within the nonprofit literature for bringing in their knowledge and resources through their demands in change processes (Durst & Newell, 2001; McMullen & Brisbois, 2003). However, authors also highlight how the heterogeneous needs, values, goals, interests, and demands of multiple stakeholders can complicate addressing change in NPOs (Kellock Hay et al., 2001). Varied external groups try to impose their differing values and compete for the dominance of those values in the organization (Cunningham, 2001; Tonkiss & Passey, 1999). Although the research highlights including these different interest groups, it also reveals the difficulties that arise from the external stakeholders' demands. In summary, as multiple stakeholders' demands capture the experience, skills, and resources of these stakeholders, they build the second dimension of the concept of path, which is assumed to influence the processes through which NPOs develop and implement their HR practices.

In addition to the aforementioned stakeholders, the unique attributes of HR require special attention when managing change in NPOs. Empirical research shows that employees have different goals, priorities, and values that may diverge from those of the organization (Fenwick, 2005; Minkoff & Powell, 2006). While employee participation in change management has a crucial impact upon the success of organizational change (Basinger & Peterson, 2008), studies reveal that greater employee participation can result in longer decision-making processes and even serve as a barrier to change. In light of their non-monetary motivations, the employees' personal commitment to organizational values may act as a constraint on the change process (Armstrong, 1992; Kellock Hay et al., 2001). Thus, the third dimension for operationalizing path in terms of the organization's experience, skills, and resources includes the unique attributes of HR in NPOs. Nonprofit employees are characterized by different needs, goals, and motivations, which are expected to influence the processes through which NPOs develop and implement HR practices.

Finally, in addition to experience, skills, and resources, path is constituted by managers' past decisions as managers play an important role in responding to change. The review of the nonprofit literature underscores the influence of managerial capabilities, highlighting the role of managerial knowledge and experience when learning and dealing with change, especially in terms of decision making and gaining resources (Jurkiewicz & Massey, 1998; Ritchie et al., 2007). Studies show that when managers take internal resources, knowledge about past decisions, nonprofit values, structure, operations, and internal stakeholders into account, NPOs are enabled in their capacity for learning and change (Lindenberg, 2001; Parsons & Broadbridge, 2004; Tassie et al., 1996; van der Pijl & Sminia, 2004). These studies reveal that the managerial capabilities to consider the existing internal resources, organizational structure, knowledge, and routines affect the acceptance of change and aid in learning and adapting.

Table 3.1   Operationalization of Path Dimensions Using the Nonprofit Characteristics

THEORETICAL CONCEPT OF PATH	DIMENSIONS OF PATH: NONPROFIT CHARACTERISTICS	OPERATIONALIZATION OF NONPROFIT CHARACTERISTICS
Organizational values and history	*Values-driven strategic orientation*	Organizational values, multiple goals, and nonprofit mission
Experience, skills, and resources	*Multiple stakeholders' demands*	Interests, needs, values, goals, and demands of external stakeholders
Experience, skills, and resources	*Unique attributes of HR*	Different needs, goals, and motivations of nonprofit employees
Experience, skills, resources, routines, and past managerial decisions	*Managerial capabilities*	Managerial capability to consider existing internal resources, organizational structure, organizational knowledge, and routines

Table 3.2   Specific Questions Regarding Path

---

1. How and why does **path** influence the learning and adapting processes through which NPOs develop and implement new or modified HR practices?

Values-driven strategic orientations:

1.1. How and why does the values-driven strategic orientation influence learning and adapting processes in NPOs?

- How and why do the **organizational values, multiple goals, and nonprofit mission** influence the learning and adapting processes through which NPOs develop and implement new or modified HR practices?

Multiple stakeholders' demands:

1.2. How and why do the multiple stakeholders' demands influence learning and adapting processes in NPOs?

- How and why do the **interests, needs, values, goals, and demands of external stakeholders** influence the learning and adapting processes through which NPOs develop and implement new or modified HR practices?

Unique attributes of HR:

1.3. How and why do the unique attributes of HR influence learning and adapting processes in NPOs?

- How and why do the **different needs, goals, and motivations of nonprofit employees** influence the learning and adapting processes through which NPOs develop and implement new or modified HR practices?

Managerial capabilities:

1.4. How and why do managerial capabilities influence learning and adapting processes in NPOs?

- How and why do the **managerial capabilities to consider the existing internal resources, organizational structure, knowledge, and routines** influence the learning and adapting processes through which NPOs develop and implement new or modified HR practices?

Given this influence of managers' experience, skills, resources, routines, and past decisions in orchestrating learning and change, managerial capabilities constitute the last path dimension, which is assumed to influence the alteration of HRM.

Iterating back to the previous studies on the alteration of HRM confirms that several of these factors play a role in the introduction of HR practices as well. As in the studies on organizational change, organizational values, as well as the loyalties, values, goals, and willingness to change of employees, stakeholder expectations, resources, and organizational structure and autonomy emerge from the studies on introducing HRM as potential barriers too (Alatrista & Arrowsmith, 2004; Cunningham, 1999, 2001; Palmer, 2003). Given that similar factors have been identified in both strands of research and because the alteration of HRM is an example of an organizational change, it can be assumed that these four identified specific nonprofit characteristics in change processes are expected to influence the processes in the alteration of HRM as well. As depicted in Table 3.1, these distinguishing nonprofit characteristics are understood as constituting the history, values, experience, skills, resources, routines, and past managerial decisions of the NPO and are assumed to influence the processes through which the NPO develops and implements its HR practices.

In summary, the theoretical concept of path is operationalized with the specific characteristics of NPOs. This study examines how and why these distinguishing characteristics influence the learning and adapting processes through which NPOs develop and implement HR practices, as seen in the specific questions in Table 3.2.

*2) How and why do NPOs develop and implement new or modified
   HR practices through learning processes?*

As outlined in the previous section, learning processes of experience accumulation, knowledge articulation, and knowledge codification are central to creating, extending, and modifying the organization's resources and capabilities (Zollo & Winter, 2002). Within the nonprofit literature, learning is perceived as crucial to nonprofit management, and enhancing learning is argued to improve the capacity of the NPO to achieve its mission (Buckmaster, 1999; Ebrahim, 2005). Cycling back and forth between the theoretical and nonprofit literature reveals, however, that there are empirical deficits with regard to the actual learning processes in NPOs (Beattie, 2006). Research is laden with prescriptive studies that focus on learning NPOs (Meyer & Mühlbacher, 2001; Roper & Pettit, 2002) and the design and implementation of knowledge management and information systems (Burt & Taylor, 2000; Ebrahim, 2002; Lettieri et al., 2004).

Regarding empirical research on enhancing organizational learning within NPOs, the conditions that facilitate learning include having access to information from a range of diverse external and internal sources (Fyles, 2003). Furthermore, the ability to learn is dependent on organizational culture, specifically the development of an internal culture of learning (Hailey & James, 2002). Barriers to integrating information stem from weak communication mechanisms, poor documenting and disseminating habits, and information overload, to name just a few (Fyles, 2003). Long-term processes of learning are neglected in NPOs due to the push toward short-term efficiency with regard to demands for accountability (Ebrahim, 2005). Additional empirical research shows that knowledge is maintained at an implicit and individual level and shared through informal contacts, rather than being codified and shared within a network (Lettieri et al., 2004). Specific nonprofit factors exacerbate this challenge, such as the tendency to personalize, as well as the informal structures of NPOs (Bruckner, 2001).

Iterating between the theoretical and nonprofit literature on learning processes, the three organizational learning mechanisms can be operationalized as follows: Regarding experience accumulation, it remains to

Table 3.3 Specific Questions Regarding Learning Processes

2. How and why do NPOs develop and implement new and modified HR practices through **learning processes**?

Experience accumulation:
2.1. How and why do NPOs develop and implement new or modified HR practices through experience accumulation processes?
• How do NPOs **acquire internal and external knowledge** regarding the development and implementation of new or modified HR practices through **experiential and/or acquisitive mechanisms**?
• How do **prior experience and knowledge** play a role in the acquisition of knowledge?
• How does experience accumulation influence the development and implementation of new or modified HR practices in NPOs?

Knowledge articulation:
2.2. How and why do NPOs develop and implement new or modified HR practices through knowledge articulation processes?
• How do NPOs **share knowledge** regarding the development and implementation of new or modified HR practices both **within and beyond the organization**?
• How do NPOs **utilize and integrate newly acquired and prior knowledge and experience**?
• How does knowledge articulation influence the development and implementation of new or modified HR practices?

Knowledge codification:
2.3. How and why do NPOs develop and implement new or modified HR practices through knowledge codification processes?
• How are **codification activities based on written or electronic tools** used during the development and implementation of new or modified HR practices?
• How do NPOs codify **know-what, know-how, and know-why** of developing and implementing the new or modified HR practice?
• How does knowledge codification influence the development and implementation of new or modified HR practices?

be seen how NPOs acquire internal and external knowledge for the development and implementation of the new or modified HR practice, e.g., through experiential or acquisitive learning mechanisms or a combination thereof. The nonprofit research indicates that diverse knowledge sources such as internal and external stakeholders can play a role in knowledge acquisition. In addition, it is assumed that prior experience and knowledge will enable the acquisition of knowledge regarding the development and implementation of new or modified HR practices. Furthermore, in terms of knowledge articulation, research is needed on knowledge sharing, i.e., the ways through which NPOs exchange, disseminate, and utilize prior knowledge and integrate newly acquired information. It is assumed that there are formal or informal mechanisms that support this exchange of knowledge within or beyond NPOs. Finally, with regard to knowledge codification, further investigation is needed on the codification activities based on written or electronic tools that are used to codify the content (know-what), methodology (know-how), and the rationale (know-why) behind developing and implementing the HR practice. Given the existing nonprofit research, it is expected that barriers to knowledge codification result from the organization's informal structures. In summary, experience accumulation, knowledge articulation, and knowledge codification processes enable research into the learning processes through which NPOs gain knowledge and experience as well as share and document this knowledge for the development and implementation of HR practices. The specific research questions emerge, as depicted in Table 3.3.

3) How and why do NPOs develop and implement new or modified HR practices through adapting processes?

Adapting processes can be understood as the underlying processes through which organizations identify opportunities and the need for altering their resource base, seize on these opportunities, and reconfigure resources to implement change. Iterating with the nonprofit literature, studies on change management indicate that strong executive leadership and the board are the main catalysts for undertaking change efforts. Empirical research shows that boards are involved in designing change and shape major management decisions as well (Durst & Newell, 2001). Yet other studies portray a different picture of change, with changes being initiated on the front lines and only relayed back to the board level after undertaking action (Filipovitch, 2006). Although little is known about the decision-making processes used in NPOs, managers influence change through their intuitive, strategic decision-making styles supported by accumulated tacit organizational knowledge bases (Ritchie et al., 2007). Whereas empirical studies reveal a contradictory picture about employees' participation levels in decision making, studies also show that greater employee participation results in longer decision-making processes and serves as a barrier to change (Armstrong, 1992; Jackson et al., 2005; Kellock Hay et al., 2001). Regarding resource acquisition, not only are executives viewed as crucial for gaining resources for the organization that are necessary for its survival (Jurkiewicz & Massey, 1998), but the acquisition of resources occurs via complementary linkages with clients, staff, and board members through interorganizational ties and being active in internal and external networks (Alexander, 2000; King, 2004).

Cycling back and forth between the theoretical and nonprofit literature, the adapting processes can be operationalized as follows. In terms of search processes, NPOs are assumed to initiate the alteration of HRM by exploring internally and externally for opportunities. In light of previous nonprofit research, it is expected that executive directors as well as organizational and interorganizational ties influence the search for external resources. Research is needed on whether search operations are local, i.e., conducted in a manner that is highly dependent on previous knowledge. Finally, it remains to be seen how diverse internal and external factors, such as funding priorities, HRM challenges, or the involvement of executive directors and board members, play a role in exploring for opportunities to alter HRM. Regarding decision-making processes, NPOs are assumed to make decisions through the internal and external integration of resources and activities. Both theoretical and nonprofit research on the level of decision making confirms the importance of managerial decision making. Yet it remains to be seen how the organizational hierarchy and specific values impact decision-making processes, e.g., whether employees are also involved in decision making and may function as a barrier to the alteration of HRM. Finally, with regard to restructuring processes, research is needed on how NPOs develop and implement HR practices through adding, transferring, deleting, and recombining resources. Given previous nonprofit research, the generation of new resource combinations is assumed to be aided by nonprofit goals, values, decentralization, and local autonomy. The barriers

Table 3.4 Specific Questions Regarding Adapting Processes

3. How and why do NPOs develop and implement new or modified HR practices through **adapting** processes?

Search processes:
3.1. How and why do NPOs develop and implement new or modified HR practices through search processes?
• How do NPOs **explore internally and externally for opportunities** regarding the development and implementation of new or modified HR practices?
• How does the **locus of search** influence the development and implementation of new or modified HR practices in NPOs?

Decision-making processes:
3.2. How and why do NPOs develop and implement new or modified HR practices through decision- making processes?
• How do NPOs **internally and externally integrate resources and activities** to make decisions regarding the development and implementation of new or modified HR practices?
• How does the **level of decision making** influence the development and implementation of new or modified HR practices in NPOs?

Restructuring processes:
3.3. How and why do NPOs develop and implement new or modified HR practices through restructuring processes?
• How do NPOs **add, transfer, delete, and recombine their resources** for the development and implementation of new or modified HR practices?
• How does the **generation of new resource combinations** influence the development and implementation of new or modified HR practices in NPOs?

are expected to include the lack of existing financial resources, training, and expertise in HRM. In summary, adapting processes serve as a lens for analyzing how and why NPOs engage in a search for opportunities for altering HRM, make decisions about their HR practices, and restructure their resources for the development and implementation of new or modified HR practices. Thus, the specific research questions in Table 3.4 arise.

Stemming from these specific research questions, learning and adapting dimensions are derived. These dimensions emerged from the main concepts in the dynamic capabilities literature on learning and adapting and reflect the theoretical assumptions guiding this study's conceptual framework. They are a means to operationalize the learning and adapting processes, thereby providing criteria for measuring their empirical existence (Berg, 2007, p. 36). The tables in Appendices A.1 and A.2 display these dimensions. As will be discussed in detail in Chapter 4, the dimensions will be used to assess the cases according to the degree to which they participate in the individual learning and adapting processes.

Finally, the research aim of analyzing the influence of the distinguishing nonprofit characteristics (path) and the processes (learning and adapting) through which NPOs develop and implement new or modified HR practices is also appropriate in light of the opportunity for making a theoretical contribution. The state of prior research and the choice of the nonprofit setting have implications for creating the opportunity to make a contribution to theory. The decision to conduct research in a novel research setting can reveal new aspects about the phenomenon of interest and aid in stretching the boundary conditions of a theory, thus extending the existing theory to other contexts or domains (Barley, 2006; Snow, 2004). By merging insights gained inductively from the nonprofit sector with the extant dynamic capabilities approach, this study also seeks to shed new light on the established concepts of path and processes. This entails qualifying previously established relationships and processes in a new setting, which can lead to unearthing anomalies that result in the revision of theory (Gilbert & Christensen, 2005).

SUMMARY: THE INFLUENCE OF PATH AND THE LEARNING AND ADAPTING PROCESSES THROUGH WHICH NPOS DEVELOP AND IMPLEMENT THEIR HR PRACTICES

This chapter has demonstrated that the dynamic capabilities approach is appropriate for bridging the research gap on the influence of the distinguishing nonprofit characteristics and the processes through which NPOs develop and implement their new or modified HR practices. The dynamic capabilities approach is suitable for understanding change in that it acknowledges the salient role of processes, thereby functioning as a vehicle to examine the dynamics of the alteration of the resource base. In this manner, the focus on processes in the dynamic capabilities approach provides the missing link for analyzing how organizations create, extend, and modify their resources and capabilities. Furthermore, this theoretical perspective is useful for analyzing organizations' abilities to respond to external change or internal pressures toward change. Finally, it enables investigating into the influence of the organization's history, values, past managerial decisions, routines, skills, resources, and experience on processes. Thus, it is a strategically oriented, relevant framework for thinking about change as NPOs have to adapt to changes in their environment given the increasing competition across the sectors and the need to respond to often conflicting demands of their internal and external stakeholders.

Path is relevant to the present study as processes are argued to evolve in a cumulative way. Although empirical studies confirm the path dependency of organizational processes, the differentiation between path-dependent and path-breaking change suggests that organizations may not be entirely trapped by their past and that there is still a capacity to escape path dependency. Therefore, the concept of path is assumed to enable insight into how and why the distinguishing nonprofit characteristics influence the processes and whether they enable or constrain the alteration of HRM. Furthermore, learning and adapting, as underlying processes that bring about change in the resource base, are assumed to be the main theoretical concepts for understanding the processes through which NPOs alter their HRM. Path-dependent learning enhances the learning processes of experience accumulation, knowledge articulation, and knowledge codification. The adapting processes of search, decision making, and restructuring reveal the constraining role of path dependency on these processes through which firms sense and make decisions about opportunities and reconfigure resources to implement change. The empirically robust learning and adapting processes allow a rigorous in-depth investigation of the sets of activities through which NPOs develop and implement their new or modified HR practices to respond to internal and external change. Finally, exploring this approach in the nonprofit context can create the opportunity to extend theory by shedding new light on established concepts through the use of this novel setting.

In light of these theoretical underpinnings, the aim of this study is to analyze

> *how and why NPOs develop and implement new or modified HR practices through learning and adapting processes*

and

> *how and why path influences the learning and adapting processes through which NPOs develop and implement new or modified HR practices.*

The next chapter explores the methods most appropriate for investigating these how and why questions.

4 Research Methods

Congruence among the state of prior research, the study's research questions, and the research design can ensure quality field research and promote the development of rigorous research that yields a new contribution to the literature. Edmondson and McManus (2007, p. 1155) define this concept of methodological fit "as internal consistency among elements of a research project," in which the state of prior research and theory shapes the other elements of a field research project. In the literature on theory and methods, these elements are also considered to be highly interrelated, with methods also generating and shaping theory and vice versa (van Maanen et al., 2007). Other scholars emphasize that the choice of methods stems from the research question (Barr, 2004; Punch, 2005; Yin, 2009). Furthermore, the type of research design is viewed as being related to the type of research question posed and ultimately related to the purpose of the study. Accordingly, how and why questions are associated with research that explores a process, explains the patterns related to the phenomenon in question, and identifies plausible relationships shaping the phenomenon, thus leading to a case study approach (Creswell, 2009; Yin, 2009). Not only do methods function as the tools to answer research questions, but they are also a means to limit and focus the boundaries of the study in terms of the data to be gathered and analyzed.

This chapter discusses the most appropriate method in light of the state of prior research, the study's research questions, and the aim of making a contribution to the literature. Thus, the basic idea of methodological fit guides the research process in this study. Stemming from this discussion, the aims and strengths of multiple case study research and design are briefly enumerated. With regard to the study's multiple case study research design, this chapter describes the research setting within the German nonprofit sector, sampling strategy, and the threefold design that addresses the challenges of researching into the alteration of HRM in NPOs. After recounting the data collection techniques of interviews, document analysis, and non-participant observation drawn on in the case study, the iterative process of data analysis is discussed in detail. Finally, this chapter resumes with a discussion of methodological rigor in terms of the strategies used throughout the research process to evaluate and ensure rigor.

METHODOLOGICAL FIT AMONG THE STATE OF PRIOR RESEARCH, RESEARCH QUESTION, AND RESEARCH DESIGN

The state of prior research is of central importance for methodological fit and has implications for the type of research to be conducted. Applying Edmondson and McManus's (2007) continuum of the state of prior research and theory, the state of research on altering HRM in NPOs can be classified as falling between a nascent and an intermediate state, as the main constructs and their linkages as well as the underlying processes are still poorly understood from an empirical standpoint. Constructs are tentative in nascent and intermediate research, leading to exploratory research that develops insights and new connections among phenomena, investigates unfolding processes, identifies new constructs and relationships with previously established constructs, and generates propositions (Edmondson & McManus, 2007).

The following implications regarding methodological fit arise in this study: First, as mentioned above, in terms of the state of prior research, the nonprofit literature on altering HRM is still poorly understood from an empirical standpoint because it is lacking well-researched variables and mechanisms regarding the influences on and underlying processes of developing and implementing HR practices. Second, research questions in a less developed level of prior work are more open-ended, such as novel how and why questions that focus on understanding the unfolding of processes. Having refined this study's general research questions through iterating between the nonprofit literature and theory, specific research questions emerged in Chapter 3 that operationalize the study's conceptual framework. Seeking to extend theory, these open-ended, theory-driven research questions fit with the study's aims of contributing to the nonprofit literature and dynamic capabilities approach.

Third, in this state of prior research, where little is known about the processes, qualitative methods can help to investigate constructs without having to indicate the variables or the relationships between variables a priori (Barr, 2004). As a plural domain, qualitative methods refer to a myriad of techniques that "seek to describe, decode, translate and otherwise come to terms with the meaning, not the frequency, of certain more or less naturally occurring phenomena in the social world" (van Maanen, 1979, p. 520). Rich qualitative data can aid in explaining findings that diverge from extant theory in ways that quantitative data cannot easily reveal, entailing detailed, grounded understandings and thick descriptions that allow for contextualizing the findings (Denzin, 2001; Pratt, 2008; Sutton, 1997). Thus, qualitative research can take advantage of naturally occurring data and apprehend dimensions of organizational behavior that are difficult to measure (Helfat, 2007).

Furthermore, qualitative, field-based studies can capture the dynamics and evolution of complex in-depth processes by directly examining events in order to understand how they evolve over time and why they play out in this way (Eisenhardt, 1989; Elsbach, 2005; Golden-Biddle & Rao, 1997; Langley, 1999; Langley et al., 2003; van Maanen et al., 2007). Moreover, processual and open fieldwork allows for the exploration of the break-downs that lead to producing a theoretical understanding that illuminates the underlying phenomenon (Alvesson & Kärreman, 2007). By remaining open to the raw field data and supplying the rich description that theory building requires, a qualitative approach can yield unexpected insights and serendipitous findings as well as allow for unforeseen theoretical leaps (Miles, 1979). Thus, the empirical regularities emerging from qualitative research can aid in creating and developing theories through concept for-mation, elaboration, and refinement, as well as making modifications to existing theory and extending theory to new issues or topics (Helfat, 2007; Ragin, 2004; Ridder & Hoon, 2009).

In areas in which construct definition is lacking, case studies can play a valuable part in identifying key constructs and uncovering interesting or unexpected phenomena through fine-grained insights (Barr, 2004). Case studies are detailed, holistic, empirical investigations into a complex entity that emphasize the uniqueness and situationality of the case and typically draw on a variety of data sources (Yin, 2009). In this respect, a case study design is appropriate for providing rich data when research about a phe-nomenon has little empirical substantiation, especially by revealing insight into the dynamics of processes (Eisenhardt, 1989). As congruence among the state of prior research, the research questions, and the research design is crucial for making a contribution (Edmondson & McManus, 2007), the following sections will discuss the case study as an appropriate research strategy and design for analyzing this study's research questions.

RESEARCH STRATEGY AND DESIGN: A MULTIPLE CASE STUDY

Involving concentrated inquiry into the complexity of a case, a case study is defined as "an empirical inquiry that investigates a contemporary phe-nomenon within its real-life context, especially when the boundaries between phenomenon and context are not clearly evident" (Yin, 2009, p. 18). Cases are specific, unique, bounded systems that may be defined by individuals, a group, organization, community, nation, episode or encoun-ter, event, period of time, a sustained process or spatially and temporally (Miles & Huberman, 1994; Stake, 2005). Without divorcing the phenom-enon of interest from the social context in which it is embedded, the case study approach is a way of organizing raw data that preserves the unitary character and integrity of the social object being studied. Fine-grained, process-oriented data can be gathered on the nature of the case, its his-torical background, setting and other contexts, additional cases, and their informants (Barr, 2004; Stake, 2005). Case study research aids in deeply understanding complex social phenomena, providing the necessary rich data through "thick description" of contextualized findings (Geertz, 1973) that unearth the dynamics of phenomena in their natural setting, rendering it more a research strategy than a method (Eisenhardt, 1989).

Moreover, case studies are characterized by a great deal of flexibility in employing various data collection methods and their ability to be combined with other research approaches (Dooley, 2002; Marshall & Rossman, 2006). In addition, this flexibility is ensured through the opportunity to modify methods, shift units of analysis, and add cases for comparison while the data analysis progresses (Leonard-Barton, 1990; Patton, 2002; VanWynsberghe & Khan, 2007). By allowing for both replication among individual cases to corroborate theoretical propositions and extension among multiple cases to elaborate theory, the multiple-case comparative logic is apt for generating theoretical insights (Eisenhardt, 1991). Through cross-case analysis, multiple cases can strengthen constructs and their relationships, thus offering a situationally grounded understanding of complex phenomena in their natural setting. As a result, a more accurate, robust, and generalizable theory emerges when based on multiple cases, as the theory is deeply grounded in varied evidence and constructs and relationships are able to be more precisely defined (Eisenhardt & Graebner, 2007; Yin, 2009).

A multitude of terms refers to the potential of case study research to make a theoretical contribution, such as theory generation, building, development, extension, modification, and refinement (for an overview, see Piekkari et al., 2009; Ridder et al., 2009). The emphasis is on establishing how and why the variables of a theory are related by specifying the relationships among constructs and providing theoretical explanations for these relationships (Snow & Thomas, 1994). There is widespread agreement among scholars that case study research is appropriate for staking out broader causal processes, showing violations of a theory, and understanding why results turned out differently than expected, thereby yielding rich opportunities for creating new theory or modifying established theory (Berg, 2007; Siggelkow, 2007; Walton, 1992; Yin, 2009). This approach has the potential to reveal unusual phenomena, replicate or counter the replication of findings in other cases, eliminate alternative explanations, elaborate the emergent theory, and develop hypotheses and propositions for further inquiry (Eisenhardt & Graebner, 2007; Yin, 2009).

For example, in situations where constructs and linkages are poorly understood and the existing theory is not well formulated enough to allow for explicit hypotheses, case studies can help to develop the scientific field further (Barr, 2004; Eisenhardt, 1989; Gibbert et al., 2008). In addition to substantiating understandings, case studies can also defy previous theories by revealing unseen inadequacies in the theoretical notions guiding the research, leading to a reassessment or rejection of the theory (Vaughan, 1992; Walton, 1992). Focusing attention on the deviant cases can stimulate revisions of theories, suggesting complexities for further investigation as well as helping to establish the limits of generalizability (Ragin, 2004; Stake, 2005). Furthermore, case studies can extend theory by expanding pre-existing conceptual formulations to other groups, contexts, or domains (Ridder et al., 2009; Snow, 2004). This approach entails broadening the relevance of a particular concept to a range of empirical contexts other than those in which they were first developed or intended to be used. By searching for patterns across different situations, case study research can help to qualify and specify theory by establishing the conditions under which the theory holds, i.e., when it does or does not offer potential for explanation (Snow, 2004; Vaughan, 1992). In summary, the case study approach creates or advances the conceptualization and operationalization of new theories to address new phenomena, extends extant theories to new settings, or continually refines a developed theory when the case renders another explanation more relevant (Dooley, 2002; Walton, 1992).

This study aims to make a theoretical contribution through theory extension and to gain a deeper and richer sense of how NPOs develop and implement their HR practices. In order to achieve these aims, a multiple case study is conducted because it can enable a focus on the learning and adapting processes through which NPOs alter their HRM without stripping the data of their context. Choosing a case study as the research design is the final missing piece in the puzzle of ensuring a methodological fit. Regarding the fit with the state of prior research, given that the processes and their influences within the literature on altering HRM are still poorly understood from an empirical standpoint, the case study makes an ideal choice for this study's design. Due to its in-depth view of complex phenomena in their unique locally grounded context, the case study method is suitable for examining how nonprofit characteristics may foster or hinder the alteration of HRM, as well as for unearthing the patterns across the cases that reveal and explain these differences and similarities in the processes of learning and adapting. Furthermore, because the dynamic capabilities approach suggests that processes are path-dependent in their development, detailed case-specific evidence about the processes associated with the alteration of the resource base is necessary.

Extending theory to a novel setting can aid in examining the qualitative changes in the boundaries of the theory and unearthing anomalies by exploring the theory under different conditions (Feldman, 2004). These anomalies or breakdowns in the data are understood as exceptions that the existing theory cannot account for (Gilbert & Christensen, 2005). A theoretical contribution can be constructed by showing how these anomalies affect the current understanding of the phenomena and the existing relationships (Whetten, 1989). Thus, this study seeks to qualify and extend the theoretical concepts of learning and adapting processes and path to the novel setting of the nonprofit sector. Taken together, a case study design is appropriate for ensuring methodological fit in light of the

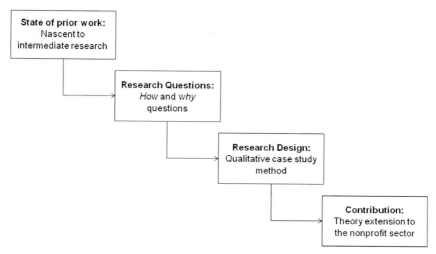

Figure 4.1 Methodological fit among the key elements of the research project.

state of prior research on altering HRM, the open-ended how and why research questions that guide the empirical research, and the potential to contribute to the nonprofit literature through theory extension. The consistency among these four key elements of the research project is depicted in Figure 4.1.

Multiple Case Study Research Design

The research design is the logical sequence that connects the empirical data to a study's research questions and its conclusions, narrows the limits of the study, and is influenced by the research perspective, theory, research questions, and methods (Flick, 2007b; Yin, 2009). According to Yin (2009), a case study design entails making specific propositions that stem from a set of how and why research questions, reviews of the literature, and new insights in order to guide further analysis. These propositions, if correct after data analysis, can contribute to theory building and refinement (Eisenhardt, 1989; Yin, 2009). The data must be reflected against and linked to the case study's theoretical propositions. In this manner, a chain of evidence of each analytical step is preserved to justify how the conclusions were reached.

In multiple case studies, each case is a single whole entity that is purposefully defined (Ragin, 2004). Multiple case study designs are considered more robust than single case designs in that they provide more compelling evidence. A multiple case study enables cross-case analysis that can verify relationships among constructs, thus offering an in-depth understanding of the processes and outcomes of cases (Yin, 2009). By including several research sites, a comparative design can enhance the understanding of relationships within processes of change (Langley et al., 2003). Regarding the number of cases in multiple case studies, Eisenhardt (1989) recommends having between four and ten cases because the complexity becomes difficult to manage upward of 10 cases. The number of cases depends instead on the state of prior knowledge and the amount of new information to be gained from incremental cases (Eisenhardt, 1991). Exploratory case studies are more unstructured and seek to generate questions and hypotheses for future research (Yin, 2009). Given the lack of knowledge of the phenomenon of developing and implementing HR practices in NPOs, this approach is based on an exploratory multiple case study of eight German NPOs in the social services, health, environmental, recreational, religious, foundation, and cultural fields. These fields were defined in accordance with the ICNPO classification scheme (Salamon & Anheier, 1996). The following sections will delineate the specific research design used in this study with regard to the research setting, sampling strategy, and the case dimensions that aid in overcoming the methodological challenges of researching into the alteration of HRM in NPOs.

Research Setting

Like the physical context of the case study, the research setting entails both the outer and inner contexts of the organization in which ideas for change are embedded. The need to explore context in studies on change has been emphasized, especially because processes are both constrained by contexts and shape contexts by preserving or altering them (Pettigrew, 1990). Through intimate knowledge of the research setting, contextual understandings are enabled in qualitative research (van Maanen, 1979). Furthermore, the choice of setting in case study research has implications for developing theory because novel research settings can shed new light on a phenomenon and extend theory to other groups, contexts or places, or socio-cultural domains (Barley, 2006; Snow, 2004).

The nonprofit sector is ideal for exploring the alteration of HRM as NPOs are professionalizing their HR practices and engaging in processes that are aimed at fulfilling their mission (Parry et al., 2005). German NPOs are appropriate research sites for examining the learning and adapting processes through which they alter their HRM because these NPOs are responding to changes in their uncertain environment. NPOs in Germany, as in their Anglo-Saxon and continental European counterparts, are facing a variety of challenges, such as an increasing demand for services, scarce resources, changing funding patterns, and increasing competition with commercial firms, all of which render the professionalization of management necessary. After briefly examining the types of organizations that make up the nonprofit sector in Germany and its constituting principles, the sector's scope and changing context in terms of employment and financing will be discussed.

The Nonprofit Sector in Germany

Analyzing the nonprofit sector in Germany reveals a multitude of terms such as *Vereine* and *Verbände* (associations) and *gemeinnützige Organisationen* (public benefit organizations), including *freie Wohlfahrtsverbände* (free welfare associations), *gemeinwirtschaftliche Organisationen* (communal economic corporations), and *Organisationen ohne Erwerbszweck* (organizations with no commercial character) (Anheier & Seibel, 1993, 2001). In addition to associations that account for more than 80% of the NPOs in Germany (Zimmer & Priller, 2001), legal forms such as the limited liability company (*Gesellschaft mit beschränkter Haftung (GmbH)*), which is common in the hospital industry, and the foundation (*Stiftung*) also make up the nonprofit sector. These organizations are tax-exempt if they meet the criteria of public benefit (*Gemeinnützigkeit*), in which the services are selfless, exclusive, direct, and timely and the organizations pursue charitable, religious, or public good-related goals (Anheier, 2005).

Applying the structural-operational definition to the German nonprofit sector (Salamon & Anheier, 1992), the organizations in the sector are formally organized and voluntary, yet the private–public distinction is blurred through the principle of subsidiarity by which the state is obligated to provide social services through nonprofit welfare associations and to support these institutions with public funds. Furthermore, the public law associations violate the private criterion so that this definition is not fully applicable to the nonprofit sector in Germany, also making the issue of self-governance a difficult criterion. Regarding the non-profit-distributing criterion, German tax law divides NPOs into their activity related to the charitable purpose that is tax-exempt and any commercial activity that is taxable. Nevertheless, the structural-operational definition enables grouping separate types of organizations together and knowing which organizations to exclude, such as private associations and corporations controlled by the government, cooperatives, mutual insurance companies, housing associations, and public law associations that are compulsory for their members (Anheier & Seibel, 1993, 2001). Accordingly, the following organizations constitute the German nonprofit sector: registered and unregistered associations, foundations, institutions run by the free welfare associations, public benefit limited liability companies, public benefit cooperatives, citizen groups and initiatives, advocacy organizations, consumer associations, self-help groups, organizations with no commercial motive, and church-related organizations.

One of the defining characteristics of the German nonprofit sector is the close cooperation between the state and NPOs. In this respect, Germany is different from other European countries in that the nonprofit sector has developed in a mutually reinforcing way with the state rather than in antithesis to it (Anheier & Seibel, 2001). The German nonprofit sector can be classified as a corporatist model in which the strong state plays a predominant role, resulting in the coexistence of extensive welfare spending and an expansive nonprofit sector (Anheier, 2005; Kramer, 1990; Salamon & Anheier, 1998; Zimmer & Priller, 2001). Under the corporatist arrangement, labor is divided between the government and welfare associations through a consensus-oriented cooperative style of interaction among the state, the parties, and the welfare associations (Seibel, 1990). However, the sector is currently in a state of major transition toward a more pluralistic model as the traditional field of welfare associations faces a surge of competition from private providers coupled with more restrictive funding (Bode, 2003).

Historically, the nonprofit sector in Germany has been shaped by the three principles of self-administration, subsidiarity, and *Gemeinwirtschaft* (communal economics) over the last two centuries. The principle of self-administration or self-governance emerged out of the 19th-century conflict between state and citizens and is reflected in the state-free organizations and professional associations, yet it led to a peculiar pattern of state-controlled autonomy. In contrast, the principle of *Gemeinwirtschaft*, which refers to the cooperative movement, implies the non-market, non-competitive production of goods and delivery of services and encompasses the primacy of maximizing public and social welfare over profit making in these organizations (Anheier & Seibel, 1993).

Most important, the principle of subsidiarity governs and divides the labor in public–private relationships and relegates the public provision of social services to the lowest level. Originally a Catholic principle, it dictates that the larger social unit, i.e., the state, should assist the smaller social unit only when it cannot rely on its own resources and has come to stand for an institutional alternative to the state as provider of welfare (Anheier & Seibel, 1993). As a result, welfare is administered through large administrative social insurance bodies, whereas social services are provided by free welfare associations that are subsidized by the state. Subsidiarity has been legally inscribed in social welfare legislation, in which the public sector is required to provide support to these welfare associations, which are in turn to be given preferential treatment, e.g., by limiting the number of additional service providers at the local level. As such, the legal foundation of subsidiarity protects NPOs from competition with for-profits and the public sector (Anheier, 1992; Anheier & Seibel, 1993). Thus, the outsourcing of public services in the health and social services sectors represents a specific historical and legally codified tradition in Germany. In contrast to the U.K., where the outsourcing of social care is a more recent development (Cunningham & James, 2011), the contracting out of health and social services in the German nonprofit landscape is a bulwark of welfare provision. Yet in the context of EU liberalization of the markets, some of the privileges stemming from subsidiarity have recently been legally removed, e.g., in the field of youth and child welfare or long-term home care, where welfare association providers are on an equal playing field with commercial providers (Zimmer & Priller, 2001).

In summary, the nonprofit sector in Germany is characterized by a highly developed associational life with an especially pronounced role for the welfare associations and close cooperation between the state and nonprofit institutions, creating a quasi-public sector stemming from the state subsidies in service provisions. Although the historical prominence of the state still echoes in the principle of subsidiarity, this model is changing with the health and social services fields facing increasing competition from private providers as EU legislation deregulates the quasi-monopolistic structures. In addition to increasing competition within and across the sectors, NPOs in Germany, much like in other European countries, are facing greater demands given shifts in demographics, financial cutbacks, and changing needs for services.

Scope and Changing Context of the Nonprofit Sector in Germany

Unfortunately, other than a few smaller scale surveys (see, e.g., Dathe & Kistler, 2005; Zimmer et al., 2001), more recent data on the German nonprofit sector are not yet available in a comprehensive form other than the Johns Hopkins Comparative Nonprofit Sector Project, which examined NPOs on an international scale from 1990 to 1995 (Salamon et al., 1999). The search for more recent data is made difficult because Germany does not have a collective register classifying the organizations in the nonprofit sector (Schneider, 2008).

According to Salamon et al. (2004), the German nonprofit sector is similar to that of France in terms of its scale and revenue structure. As a major economic force, its economic relevance is related to the functional incorporation of NPOs into executing administrative initiatives of the state (Anheier & Seibel, 2001). Rapid expansion has occurred in services with the number of health and social service institutions operated by the German free welfare associations increasing by 3.6% between 2004 and 2008 (*Bundesarbeitsgemeinschaft der Freien Wohlfahrtspflege*, 2009). Further data reveal that the expansion of the sector is not limited to services because sports, arts, culture, and leisure are the primary fields of the registered voluntary associations in Germany (Zimmer et al., 2004). The sector is expected to continue to grow given the reallocation of responsibilities of the state, transition to a service society, demographic developments, diversification of service needs, and more citizen initiatives (Zimmer et al., 2001). For example, given increased longevity, the demand for inpatient services for elderly care is rising in Germany, leading to an overall 5% increase in services and institutions and an 11% increase in inpatient services from 2004 to 2008. Not only in the area of elderly care, but institutions and services have also expanded for childcare by 5% and for the mentally disabled by 8% (*Bundesarbeitsgemeinschaft der Freien Wohlfahrtspflege*, 2009). However, the economic impact of the third sector may be diminishing as German NPOs attempt to free themselves from dependency on the state, with some larger organizations like hospitals leaving the sector (Zimmer & Priller, 2001). Similar to the development in the U.K., where the private sector is growing increasingly involved in social services and health care (Almond & Kendall, 2000a), commercial organizations in Germany are becoming more prominent in health care, social services, and higher education. As a result, the structure of the German nonprofit sector is expected to change over the next decades with the development of new organizational forms and the transition of existing ones (Anheier & Seibel, 2001).

Regarding the scope and scale of paid employment, statistics point to the relevance of the nonprofit sector in terms of employment, with more than 1.5 million persons employed in the institutions of the free welfare associations alone (*Bundesarbeitsgemeinschaft der Freien Wohlfahrtspflege*, 2009). In 2008, this amounted to employing 4% of all the working population (43.3 million) in Germany and more than 5% of the working population in the services sector (28.8 million) (*Statistisches Jahrbuch*, 2008). These figures may not even fully capture the importance of the health and social services fields for the entire nonprofit sector, with estimates from the Institute for Employment Market and Job Research of 2.5 million employees in non-profit social services when including additional paid employees such as free-lance, marginally employed jobholders, interns, and one Euro jobholders (Dathe et al., 2009). Moreover, the sector is marked by the dominance of the health and social services fields as more than the majority of all the services in the field of social services is provided by NPOs in residential care, homes for children, youth, elderly and the handicapped, kindergartens, and youth correctional schools (Anheier & Seibel, 2001). The dominance of these areas is tied in with the aforementioned legally embedded principle of subsidiarity. Recent data from the Institute for Employment Market and Job Research reveals high rates of employment in health and social services organizations (Dathe & Kistler, 2005; Schneider, 2008).

Finally, the nonprofit sector is heavily dependent on public funds, especially in the social services and health fields (Anheier & Seibel, 2001). The nonprofit sector in Germany is marked by a great deal of state subsidization in comparison with countries where NPOs are predominantly financed through fees and donations. Yet contracting and project support have become more common in the health and social services fields in Germany as state funding has declined. These healthcare and social services organizations are hard hit by the financial cutbacks because they are heavily financed through the shrinking reimbursements from the social insurance systems. As a result, NPOs are gaining their main revenue sources through the market by relying more heavily on fees and charges, thereby mimicking the revenue-seeking behavior of for-profits (Zimmer & Priller, 2001).

As a result of the changing funding relationship between the state and the nonprofit sector in Germany, funding pressures have led to more precarious and atypical employment relationships that may have a negative effect on the quality of the social services being provided. For example, the short-term project-based public funding has led to an increase in part-time and temporary workers. Part-time employment increased to 49% by 2008 in the nonprofit social services sector and is thus greater than in the private or public sectors (Dathe et al., 2009). Given cost pressures and resource constraints, the number of part-time employees in the free welfare associations has increased by 26% and exceeded the number of full-time employees (*Bundesarbeitsgemeinschaft der Freien Wohlfahrtspflege*, 2009). Moreover, the public funding of job creation programs also results in temporary contracts and has even shifted toward so-called one Euro jobs given the decline in funding (Dathe et al., 2009). In light of the emphasis on efficiency and performance-related management, NPOs face demands from clients, government, funders, staff, and the public for improved management and professionalization, with a greater focus on accountability mechanisms, monitoring systems, and contract specifications (Bode, 2003). In this respect, HRM has gained in importance as a cost-efficient instrument that can aid NPOs in dealing with the changes the German nonprofit sector is undergoing (Zimmer & Priller, 2001).

The review thus far has shown the significance of the German nonprofit sector as an expanding, changing sector and a critical source of employment, although there is a trend toward increasingly atypical and precarious forms of employment. The sector is characterized by being predominantly publicly funded, yet recent cuts in state subsidies have led to a stronger emphasis on performance-related management. Indeed, calls for the efficient and transparent use of resources have resulted in improving management within the sector. In line with these changes, the emphasis on HRM and its professionalization in NPOs has grown in relevance. Thus, the German nonprofit sector was chosen as the research setting because it is an appropriate context for observing the ongoing phenomenon of the alteration of HRM. Because nonprofit goals do not include profit maximization, this context differs from the for-profit setting in which the dynamic capabilities approach was initially applied. Not only does this novel setting construct the opportunity for making a theoretical contribution by exploring path, learning, and adapting under different conditions, it is also ripe for analyzing the topic of how organizations alter their HRM when facing uncertainty in their changing environments.

Sampling Strategy

In case study research, the focus is mainly on small samples that are selected purposefully to explore an issue in greater depth. Because cases are chosen that are linked with the purpose of the study, cases were purposefully selected in which the alteration of HRM was transparently observable (Pettigrew, 1990). In this study of an underdeveloped research field, theoretical sampling is an appropriate strategy for selecting cases that reveal manifestations of a theoretical construct of interest so as to

Table 4.1 Case Descriptions

	Case A: Social Services Association	Case B: Museum	Case C: Social Services Local Chapter	Case D: Environmental Organization
Size	90–100 employees	70–80 employees	120 employees	217 employees
HR practice	Goal setting/perfor-mance appraisal	Pay for performance system	Goal setting/perfor-mance appraisal	Compensation model
Phase at start of data collection	Planning: new HR practice	Implemented: new HR practice	Implemented: new HR practice	Implementing: modified HR practice
Reasons for introduc-ing the HR practice	"Modern HRM tool," an "absolute must" for the organization; Employees dissatisfied with current feedback from managers	Financially reward highly involved employees who work more than is stipulated in their contracts; Have regular goal assessment feedback	"Simply identified it as an HR instru-ment"; Imitated and adopted directly from the state association	Internal dissatisfaction among employees, managers, and the board with the old, static, outdated model
Goal of intro-ducing the HR practice	To clearly link depart-mental strategic goals with organizational strategic goals; To improve employee and organizational performance	To coordinate work better and increase employees' motivation through intensive dia-logue; Give employees a chance to improve their performance	To develop criteria to make well-justified HR decisions; To increase employees' motivation, commit-ment, and adaptability	To increase transpar-ency and acceptance of the compensation model; To develop a less complex model that is better suited to their current work
Mission	Help people in elderly care, emergency services, childcare, youth groups, and disaster areas	Be a service provider, advisor, initiator, and partner in cultural, scientific, social, and economic projects; To collect, preserve, research, and commu-nicate cultural history for future generations	Skills, competitiveness, improvement, and perspectives	Save the environment through peaceful mea-sures; Politically and commercially finan-cially independent
Unique attri-butes of HR	Religious ties and social work experience	Highly motivated and committed employees full of conviction regarding their work; Strongly identify with the work of the museum	Motivated to work in social services; Familiar with aid organizations; Identify with the association	Active, strong willed; High intrinsic motivation to save the environment
External stake-holders	Board, local member associations, clients	Board, development association, funders, local county, local	Board, local authority	Board, donors, advisory board, local group network
Organizational structure	Traditional hierarchy, large departments with "departmental egoism"	Flat hierarchy, greater autonomy and flex-ibility through the organizational form of a foundation	Traditional hierarchy, tight administrative structure	Flat hierarchy, interde-partmental working groups, interdisciplin-ary teams
Financial resources	Decreasing funds from the EU, government, insurance companies, donations, and mem-bership fees; Provided with the necessary resources for introduc-ing the HR practice	More autonomy and economical manage-ment within multi-year budget; Financed via fees, county subsidies, development associa-tion, and foundation grants	Flexibility and finan-cial freedom within a multi-year budget contracted with the local authority	Shrinking financial reserves, expenditures increasing, need to cut HR costs

Case E: Sports Organization	Case F: Teaching Hospital	Case G: Foundation	Case H: Religious Organization
121 employees	7,000 employees	320 employees	250 employees
Organizational development	Internal employment market	Skills analysis system	Organizational development
Decision making: new HR practice	Decision making: modified HR practice	Planning: modified HR practice	Planning: new HR practice
Internal reduction in funding, societal, and demographic changes and their impact on sports, and internal discussions about roles in the organization	Need to create and find jobs and support employees who have health restrictions, whose position is not being refinanced, or who want to switch positions voluntarily	Need to identify skills necessary for employees in foundations; "foundation work demands a more balanced skills profile" than for-profits	25% financial cuts by 2011 make organizational restructuring and tightening up the structure necessary
To avoid the duplication of work, clarify roles and responsibilities; To develop adequate structures to deal with future demands and stabilize member organizations	To place employees in permanent, limited, or service-oriented positions; To increase the quality and skills of the employees in the internal employment market	To develop employees' skills; To recruit, develop, and maintain top project managers	To work more effectively with fewer staff; To ensure and improve the quality of its work; To improve cooperation between the divisions
Contribute to the welfare of citizens through sports; Common good, sustainability, gender mainstreaming, success and performance, subsidiarity, volunteerism, humane work climate	Teaching, research, and medical services; Humane and responsible actions; Continual improvement of performance; Acting economically; Effective processes; Managers leading by example; Cooperation to achieve goals	Contribute to social progress in education, the economy, health care, civic society, and international understanding; Independent, nonpartisan	Proclamation of Protestant religious values, missionary, provision of services for congregations and institutions; Being open, experienced, full of ideas for the church and society, exploring and testing new things
Large portion of employees are highly motivated and willing to change; High degree of identification with sports	Medical staff highly motivated to help people, engaged in psychologically and physically stressful work; Teaching and research staff highly motivated	Highly intrinsically motivated experts; Strong identification with the founder, the foundation, and its goals	Highly motivated and educated experts with a theological and educational background
Board, member organizations of state sport associations and city clubs, commission, main committee political bodies	Board, senate, clinic commission, university council	Board, EU, national, state, and regional governments, and special interest groups and associations that vary by subject	Congregations and church districts, board, special interests groups, and associations that vary by subject
Rigid traditional hierarchy, informal horizontal teams, and integration	Traditional hierarchy, rigid structure with employees in departments for more than 25–30 years	Traditional hierarchy, yet also project-based working groups that vary by subject	Traditional hierarchy with large departments divided into smaller divisions according to subject
20% reduction in state funds due to massive state deficit; Financed via fees from the membership organizations; State lottery funds used to finance youth and competitive sports	Increasingly scarce financial resources and rising costs; Budget reductions across entire departments; New division of financial resources with performance-related component	Financed through the income from its holdings in the founder's company, cooperative partnerships, and the financial management of its assets	Decreasing financial support from church taxes, stable financing through public grants and subsidies, EU funds, donations; Need to cut costs by 25%

elaborate and examine the construct (Gobo, 2004; Patton, 2002). In multiple case studies aimed at extending theory, cases are chosen on the basis of relevance to the research questions and theoretical position in terms of their contribution to theory, e.g., leading to clearly contrasting patterns of central constructs and their relationships (Eisenhardt & Graebner, 2007; Silverman, 2006).

Thus, the eight NPOs in this exploratory multiple case study were selected according to a theoretical sampling strategy for their representation of theoretical concepts in order to reveal unusual phenomena and illuminate relationships between the concepts (Eisenhardt & Graebner, 2007). These cases were purposely selected across a heterogeneous set of field sites according to the ICNPO classification scheme in order to extend theory to a broad range of NPOs (Eisenhardt, 1989; Glick et al., 1990). By looking for the conditions that are common across a variety of cases (Ragin, 2004), one aim of this study is to extract the similarities of the dynamics underlying the development and implementation of HR practices. In light of the aim of extending theory, the theoretical sampling strategy also allows for contrasting patterns to be easily observed in the data to articulate the idiosyncrasies of the underlying processes (Eisenhardt & Graebner, 2007). In this manner, cases are chosen to confirm and disconfirm patterns from other cases (Pettigrew, 1990). Furthermore, the range of cases increases the external validity of the findings as common insights are drawn from NPOs stemming from different fields (Maxwell & Delaney, 2004). The types of NPOs varied across the nonprofit fields of activity (social services, health, environmental, recreational, religious, foundation, and cultural fields), and the sizes ranged from having less than 100 employees, to 100–320 employees, to the largest size of 7,000 employees. The range of HR practices can be seen in Table 4.1.

This study draws on a multiple-case holistic design (Yin, 2009), in which each NPO represents a case with the process of developing and implementing the HR practice as a single unit of analysis. In order to be able to compare the findings in one case across the multiple cases, the phenomenon being studied exhibited characteristics common to all the cases (Lee et al., 1996; Leonard-Barton, 1990). In each case, it was identified whether an entirely new HR practice or a modified version of a current practice was being introduced. The sample was designed to control for variance by ensuring the following two criteria were met: (1) limiting the sample to organizations that were currently or had only recently (within the last two years at the start of data collection) begun introducing their new or modified HR practices, and (2) ensuring a comparable context of undergoing the alteration of HRM by standardizing and consistently defining the phases (planning, decision making, and implementing) the NPOs were in for each case so that the contrasting cases could be compared. Table 4.1 provides a more detailed case description of each organization.

Threefold Research Design as a Means of Addressing the Challenges of Researching into the Alteration of HRM

In order to address the challenges associated with researching into the alteration of HRM, the exploratory multiple-case holistic design in this study is threefold, incorporating longitudinal, retrospective, and processual dimensions. A single-site, in-depth longitudinal case study was conducted (Case A) because longitudinal case studies are helpful for tracing the development of processes over extended periods of time and within a specific context (Leonard-Barton, 1990; Pettigrew, 1990). Simultaneously, two retrospective case studies (Cases B and C) were conducted to identify initial patterns involved in the processes of developing and implementing HR practices as these organizations had already implemented their respective HR practices within the last two years. In addition, the five processual case studies (Cases D–H) provided a real-time picture of the evolving patterns in their context. The diagram in Figure 4.2 visualizes the three dimensions of the case study research design.

This threefold research design aids in overcoming some of the methodological challenges associated with researching into change and HRM in NPOs. First, it is important to undertake a real-time study of processes unfolding in their natural field settings before the outcomes are known (van de Ven, 1992, 2007). The longitudinal and processual research designs can thus mitigate the problem of implicit performance theories associated with retrospective research designs in HRM research by which the respondents can be influenced by the already known outcomes of altering HRM when reporting about HR practices (Wright et al., 2005). The real-time data are richer and finer grained, allowing for a contextualization and deeper understanding of retrospective data (Jarzabkowski, 2008; Langley, 1999).

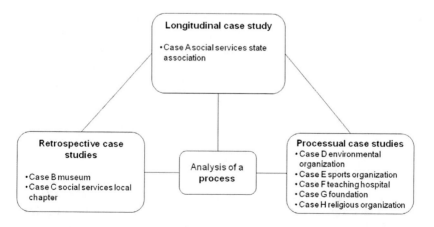

Figure 4.2 Longitudinal, retrospective, and processual case dimensions (adapted from Flick, 2007b, p. 45).

Furthermore, while the retrospective cases enable insight mainly into the content of altering HRM, the longitudinal and processual cases preserve the richness of data and interpretation regarding how and why the alteration of HRM occurred as well. Therefore, this threefold research design compensates for weaknesses by collecting comparative, processual, and historical data (Pettigrew, 1990).

Not only does this design allow for investigating the alteration of HRM over time as well as identifying patterns and underlying processes both in detail and from a broader view, combining different types of case studies of the same phenomena can also enhance construct and internal and external validity (Leonard-Barton, 1990). In terms of construct validity, the three-fold design yields the opportunity to examine phenomena over time and across different situations. The longitudinal and retrospective data also reduce the methodological risks associated with time lags between implementing HR practices and their taking effect that are well known in HRM research (Rodwell & Teo, 2004; Rogers & Wright, 1998). Furthermore, dividing the process phases into planning, decision making, and implementing helps to mitigate problems associated with the differences between intended HR policies and actual HR practices (Truss & Gratton, 1994; Wright & Boswell, 2002). Accordingly, this aids in enhancing construct validity by ensuring that researching into the phenomenon of the alteration of HRM entails the actual implementation of these HR practices rather than their mere espoused existence in HR policies (Arthur & Boyles, 2007; Boselie et al., 2005).

In addition, longitudinal and processual cases can reduce accepting respondent bias through access to confirming or disconfirming details and enhance internal validity as they enable relationships to be tracked as they evolve. These cases alert the researcher to look to confirm or disconfirm these patterns in the retrospective studies by providing in-depth understanding of the processes (Eisenhardt & Graebner, 2007). In this manner, this study seeks to shed light on an area of the HR literature that is widely neglected, namely, the underlying mechanisms in HRM, i.e., the black box of processes involved in HRM (Becker & Gerhart, 1996; Guest, 1997; Paauwe, 2009). Finally, multiple retrospective studies can increase the external validity of the research design and diminish observer biases associated with a longitudinal study of change (Leonard-Barton, 1990).

DATA COLLECTION METHODS

Qualitative case studies can rely on a gamut of data collection methods that enable the researcher to gain a close-up, detailed picture of the phenomenon of interest and in-depth insight into processes from the participants' perspectives (Barr, 2004). Case studies allow for the use of flexible multiple data collection methods that can evoke unexpected data and allow for the data collection to be modified depending on the information gained in the field (Marshall & Rossman, 2006). Because each of the data collection methods is associated with certain strengths and weaknesses, Yin (2009) maintains that data collection should be guided by the principle of multiple sources of evidence from complementary methods. This allows for the triangulation of data, i.e., the use of different perspectives on a research phenomenon to increase knowledge on different levels (Flick, 2007a). By allowing the different data sources to converge on a single fact, it strengthens the accuracy of the case study findings or conclusions, thus enhancing construct validity (Yin, 2009). If dissimilar results emerge from the different measures, the researcher may generate more complex, alternative explanations by having to account for these divergent results (Jick, 1979).

In this exploratory multiple case study, 'between (or across) methods' triangulation was employed in all of the cases, which involves using multiple qualitative data collection methods to corroborate the same phenomenon (Flick, 2007a). The aim of triangulating the different methods of interviews, non-participant observation, and document analysis was both to gain new perspectives on the data and cross-check the findings. Using a range of field methods can counter problems associated with retrospective research and reduce the researcher's bias (Eisenhardt, 1989; Golden, 1992). This added range and depth to the analysis and helped to address construct validity because it provides multiple measures of the same dimension of the research problem (Flick, 2007a).

Interviews

Interviews are a significant source of information in case studies in which key informants can provide insight into the phenomenon under study and open up access to corroboratory or disconfirming sources of evidence (Fontana & Frey, 2005; Marshall & Rossman, 2006; Seale, 1998; Yin, 2009). As the primary data source in this study, the multiple case study design draws on data collected from a combination of 22 open-ended unstructured and semi-structured in-depth interviews with five executive directors, five HR managers, and one OD manager in the NPOs. These key informants were contacted and selected according to their lead role in, knowledge of, and influence on the development and implementation of the HR practice, as well as their ability to articulate the recent HRM changes in their organization (cf. Glick et al., 1990; Huber & Power, 1985; Pettigrew, 1990). The key informants were able to provide valuable information due to their position and familiarity with the organization and its structure, history, and practices (Marshall & Rossman, 2006). Access was gained to these key informants via email or telephone. Table 4.2 yields an overview of the number and position of these key informants in each organization, as well as the method for citing the interview data from these key informants.

Table 4.2   Key Informants Interviewed

Case	No. of Key Informants	Position of Key Informants	
Case A: Social Services State Association	2	HR Manager (Case A: 1)	Head HR Manager (Case A: 2)
Case B: Museum	2	Executive Director (Case B: 1)	Director (Case B: 2)
Case C: Social Services Local Chapter	1	Executive Director (Case C: 1)	
Case D: Environmental Organization	1	Head HR Manager (Case D: 1)	
Case E: Sports Organiza- tion	2	Executive Director (Case E: 1)	OD Manager (Case E: 2)
Case F: Teaching Hospital	1	Head HR Manager (Case F: 1)	
Case G: Foundation	1	Head HR Manager (Case G: 1)	
Case H: Religious Organization	1	Executive Director (Case H: 1)	

The interviewees granted informed consent after being briefed on the purpose of the investigation and were ensured of the confidentiality of the data (Kvale, 2007). All interviewees agreed to have the interviews digitally recorded. The face-to-face interviews lasted between 50 and 142 minutes, with an average interview duration of 83 minutes, and were conducted between August 2006 and January 2009. Where additional access was granted, errors of recall were minimized by interviewing more than one person involved in the introduction of the new HR practice. When recalling past events, interviewees were always asked for detailed information about the key persons involved and when events occurred in order to diminish memory bias (Golden, 1992).

The interview questions were partially structured by categories from theory and the related literature. The sets of questions were kept as open-ended as possible, however, in order to capture the nuances of the pro-cesses, unearth insights that can then be used for further inquiry, and allow the interviewees to act as informants in the case study, reflecting on how their organization learned and adapted over time (Rapley, 2004; Yin, 2009). The aim was to let the interview flow more like a conversation with a purpose, with the interviewee's perspective unfolding while respecting how the informant framed the responses, rather than having predetermined response categories dominate (Marshall & Rossman, 2006). This enables understanding (*Verstehen*) the meaning of actions and interactions from the interviewees' point of view (King et al., 1994). Throughout the interviews, various explanatory and focused probes were used to elicit further response from the interviewees (Easterby-Smith et al., 2000). The interview questions were validated for their coherence and clarity with a team of researchers before entering the research field. The interview question guideline is provided in Appendix A.3.

Adhering to an iterative process of data collection and analysis, follow-up interviews were conducted and structured around the key events and issues that were identified in the first interview to capture the processual aspect of developing and implementing HR practices. The follow-up interviews reduced methodological error and secured the validity that the initial interpretations captured the interviewees' meanings, being conducted until a complete picture of the implementation of the HR practice was given. The interviews were typed up verbatim by research assistants, yielding 465 typed pages of transcriptions. As interviews can be marred by problems of bias and socially desirable responses (Fontana & Frey, 2005), the interview data were triangulated with other sources of data from non-participant observation and document analysis (Marshall & Rossman, 2006).

Non-Participant Observation

Non-participant or direct observation entails recording events, behaviors, and objects with the researcher usually being an unobtrusive observer (Yin, 2009); thus, data collection can be conducted without disturbing the setting. It involves a lengthy period of personal observation in which the researcher is immersed in the situation, gaining an up-front view of events as they occur in their natural setting. Combining the retrospective case history with real-time observations in the longitudinal case study (Case A) helped to understand the context, previous events, and how changes occur rather than merely identifying if and what changes occur through the interviews (van de Ven, 1992). Thus, interview data were supplemented by non-participant observation of more than 25 hours of attending internal key project group meetings, in addition to taking field notes. During non-participant observation, field notes emerge as detailed, concrete descriptions of events and behavior during a site visit. These detailed field notes incorporated participants' quotes and were written up directly during the observation of the meetings (Miles & Huberman, 1994).

The role of a non-participant observer was assumed in order to understand the setting and the members' perspectives more fully as well as obtain valid descriptions through methodological triangulation (Easterby-Smith et al., 2008). Data gathering in the longitudinal case (A) was most intense, involving prolonged engagement and persistent observation. This close-up encounter provided a proximity to the events as they occurred and allowed for the observation of alterations in attitudes and behavior that provides insight into how the organization learns and adapts over time (Elsbach, 2005). This observational evidence aided in capturing the subjective, often contradictory interpretations of actors involved in the change process (Marshall & Rossman, 2006; Pettigrew, 1990). For example, the statements made in the project group meetings often differed greatly from the interview data, and the individual participants varied in their perceptions of the consequences of implementing the HR practice. Recording the first-hand observations helped to validate data from previous interviews and develop further interview questions. In addition, informal conversations with key informants in all of the cases and taking field notes enabled gathering further real-time data (Gibbs, 2007). These conversations were held with key informants before, during, and after meetings or as part of informal encounters during lunches or hallway discussions. The field notes were typed up immediately after the data collection, totaling 163 typed pages.

Document Analysis

Documents supplemented the other data collection methods by checking and augmenting contradictory evidence as well as aiding in understanding the context surrounding the research setting. In this case study, initial analysis began with the available public documents, such as organizational brochures, charts, and annual reports that are official documentary records (Berg, 2007). It was followed by using internal organizational documents provided by key informants to examine the processes and crosscheck against the interview data to reduce over-simplification, inaccurate data, and hindsight or attributional biases, especially in the retrospective cases (Golden, 1992; Huber & Power, 1985). Inferences made from the documents also provided the basis for developing questions for further, more detailed, and extensive interviews. Finally, the documents were reviewed again after the interviews for any missing facts.

An advantage of gathering and analyzing documents is that it is unobtrusive. However, because documents are usually written for other purposes, they can be biased or inaccurate as well. Therefore, the objectives under which the documents were produced were identified and evaluated (Marshall & Rossman, 2006; Yin, 2009). The table in Appendix A.4 depicts the types of documents used in each case. Whereas the interview data were collected over a two and a half year period (summer 2006–winter 2009), the document analysis gathers data beginning in the late 1990s. The documents totaled 2,538 typed pages.

Case Study Research Design	Organization	Date	Interviews	Additional data collection methods
Single-site in-depth **longitudinal**, field case study	Case A social services state association	Summer 2006- Spring 2007	N=1 (Unstructured) N=2 (Semi-structured) Planning, decision making	• 25 hours of **non-participant observation** of 8 project group meetings • 484 pages of **document analysis** and 61 pages of field notes • Informal conversations
		Summer 2007- Winter 2009	N=3 (Semi-structured) Decision making, Implementing	
Retrospective cases	Case B museum	Fall 2006	N=1 (Semi-structured) Implemented	• 516 pages of **document analysis** and 12 pages of field notes • Informal conversations
	Case C social services local chapter		N=1 (Semi-structured) Implemented	
Multiple cases, **processual** approach	Case D environmental organization	Summer 2006- Spring 2008	N=2 (Semi-structured) Implementing	• 1,538 pages of **document analysis** and 90 pages of field notes • Informal conversations
	Case E sports organization		N=5 (Semi-structured) Decision making, implementing	
	Case F teaching hospital		N=3 (Semi-structured) Decision making, implementing	
	Case G foundation		N=2 (Semi-structured) Planning, decision making, implementing	
	Case H religious organization		N=2 (Semi-structured) Planning, decision making, implementing	

Figure 4.3   Data collection timeline and methods.

In summary, case studies are suitable for gathering fine-grained data about how processes unfold over time. Thus, the interviews were conducted in waves during each subsequent phase to capture the processual nature of developing and implementing HR practices. Figure 4.3 shows the cases were in various phases of developing and implementing HR practices at the start of data collection. Once it became apparent that no new information could be gleaned, it was determined that it was no longer necessary to continue collecting data in the cases. Figure 4.3 depicts the timeline and qualitative data collection methods in this study.

THE ITERATIVE PROCESS OF DATA ANALYSIS

At this stage in the research process, the challenge lies in "moving from a shapeless data spaghetti toward some kind of theoretical understanding that does not betray the richness, dynamism and complexity of the data [. . .]" (Langley, 1999, p. 694). Various qualitative techniques of data reduction and display were drawn on to structure the data in this study (Miles & Huberman, 1994). The iterative process of data analysis entailed moving back and forth among extant theory, the conceptual framework, and the emerging body of data. The raw data were analyzed in several

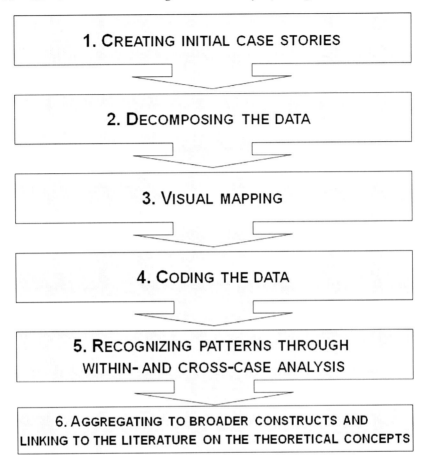

1. CREATING INITIAL CASE STORIES

2. DECOMPOSING THE DATA

3. VISUAL MAPPING

4. CODING THE DATA

5. RECOGNIZING PATTERNS THROUGH WITHIN- AND CROSS-CASE ANALYSIS

6. AGGREGATING TO BROADER CONSTRUCTS AND LINKING TO THE LITERATURE ON THE THEORETICAL CONCEPTS

Figure 4.4   Stages of iterative data analysis.

iterative analytic stages to progress up the ladder of abstraction to a higher aggregation without stripping the data of its complexity. Figure 4.4 illustrates the stages of data analysis employed in this study.

First, initial case stories were created from the analysis of public documents regarding the organization's mission, employees, stakeholders, organizational structure, financial resources, current HR practices, and history of change. This document analysis is important for establishing the chronology or the what of change first before conducting additional data collection that aids in gaining insight into the how and why of change (Pettigrew, 1990). Gaining baseline information and developing a retrospective case history of the context and related events leading up to the phenomenon of interest is crucial for the study of change (van de Ven, 1992). These case stories were validated and revised using interview and non-participant observation data. Therefore, rather than presenting a theoretical account at this preliminary stage, constructing these narratives served as a validation tool for subsequent analysis (Langley, 1999). The case stories are presented in the beginning of Chapter 5.

Second, the data from interviews, non-participant observation, and documents were broken down into the phases of planning, decision making, and implementing the HR practice. These distinct phases and the key informants' interpretations of these phases formed units of analysis that were compared within and across the cases in-depth (Langley, 1999). This entailed focusing on "the sequences of incidents, activities and stages that unfold over the duration of a central subject's existence" (van de Ven, 1992, p. 170). In order to decompose the data into the three phases, critical incidents of events were identified and specified (Poole et al., 2000). Critical incidents included, e.g., hiring HR personnel and external consultants, executive and board decisions about introducing the HR practice, rejection of alternative HR practices, and starting pilot projects. Because learning and adapting processes are not directly observable, patterns were sought among the observable activities, events, and behaviors over time. Patterns are recurring themes that group together separate chunks of data and aid in reducing a mass of data (Miles & Huberman, 1994). Breaking up and pulling out the different pieces of data allows for comparison. For example, the order and sequence of the critical incidents was compared with those of other cases to elicit patterns (van de Ven & Huber, 1990).

Third, a visual mapping strategy was used to accurately organize these main events along the phases (van de Ven et al., 1999). The goals of this strategy are to map organizational reality as accurately as possible, explain outcomes as a result of the order in which events unfold and their conjunctions with other events, and identify emerging patterns across the phases. The visual maps functioned as an intermediate step between the raw data and more abstract conceptualization. They enabled a graphical representation of parallel processes and events over time (Langley, 1999). Mapping helped to visualize and identify whether certain activities were singular or recurring across the phases, how lengthy their duration was, and whether these events were sequential (van de Ven & Huber, 1990). The visual maps were validated for their accuracy with key informants in the follow-up interviews and are presented along with the case stories in the next chapter.

Fourth, aided by the tool of the qualitative data analysis software program MAXQDA, interview transcripts and field notes were coded using pre-specified descriptive codes and more complex interpretive codes according to the conceptual framework (Gibbs, 2007; Miles & Huberman, 1994). This computer-aided method of coding can enhance the validity of findings by applying a stable coding scheme that retrieves all relevant information about a specific topic. Codes are tags or labels for assigning units of meaning to the descriptive or inferential information compiled during a study and retrieve and organize the chunks of data at different levels and times of the analysis. They represent the link between raw data and theoretical concepts (Seidel & Kelle, 1995). Using the clustering tactic that relies on aggregation and comparison (what things are like or unlike each other), these master codes were applied to the data (Miles & Huberman, 1994). In vivo codes used by the informants in the first round of interviews or categories stemming from the data that were not yet reflected in the coding scheme were adopted and guided the questions in the subsequent interviews (Gibbs, 2007). In vivo codes represent behaviors or processes that explain how problems are resolved or processed by the participants (Glaser, 1978). The master codes were divided into additional sub-codes when fieldwork indicated that the code must be further split up. The retroductive approach of coding combines a literature-driven category scheme with categories emerging from the data and led to higher inference, more explanatory pattern codes during the data analysis (Miles & Huberman, 1994; Poole et al., 2000). A structured list of codes was generated in which the codes are keyed to the study's specific research questions and framework.

The fifth stage entailed within-case and cross-case analysis to recognize initial patterns in the data. Patterns were discerned with regard to similarities and differences among concepts and processes and included particular themes that were present in more than one case (Dooley, 2002). Recurring empirical regularities provided added evidence of an identified pattern, although disconfirming evidence and counterexamples were key to forming patterns as well (Miles & Huberman, 1994). Through cross-case analysis, within-case puzzles and between-case differences emerged, with the counterintuitive or puzzling patterns being stimulating and rich for developing theory (Richards, 2005). These moments of "surprise, interruption and breakdown" in the data are opportunities for theorizing (Weick, 2005, p. 408). Using the tactic of following up surprises (Miles & Huberman, 1994), initial patterns were tested against the next wave of data collection, which entailed member checking or respondent validation to secure construct validity.

The cases were inspected to see whether they fall into groups that share certain patterns. In order to recognize patterns, the data were first coded and analyzed according to the extent to which each of the cases engaged in the learning and adapting processes. This entailed searching for similarities and differences across the different cases along the learning and adapting dimensions regarding the kinds and amount of learning and adapting activities in the cases. These learning and adapting dimensions that emerged from theory and reflect the theoretical assumptions of this study's conceptual framework were iterated with the case evidence. The dimensions functioned as a means to operationalize the processes, thereby providing criteria for measuring their empirical existence (Berg, 2007). A 5-point scale ranging from no (−−) to high (++) participation was used to score the cases according to the degree to which they engage in these learning and adapting processes. The tables in Appendices A.1 and A.2 display the theoretically derived dimensions. This led to identifying three groups of cases that engage in learning and adapting to differing degrees. Having grouped these cases into this classification scheme along the learning and adapting dimensions, further similarities and differences were looked for within the groups according to the conceptual framework. These groups were then structured and clustered according to the differences in their main patterns. By iterating with the theoretical literature for conceptual analogues that account for these differences, the groups were transferred into learning and adapting styles.

Stemming from these learning and adapting styles, relationships between path and the learning and adapting styles were explored (Carlile & Christensen, 2004). The case data were analyzed for the similarities and differences in the influence of the path dimensions on the learning and adapting styles. The direction of influence was analyzed by searching for terms in the data that indicate a fostering influence (e.g., "aided," "supported," "enabled") or a hindering influence (e.g., "blocked," "stopped," "delayed"). Using the technique of cross-case synthesis, word tables and diagrams were used to facilitate cross-case comparisons (Gibbs, 2007; Miles & Huberman, 1994). In order to maintain internal validity, divergent findings were included to allow

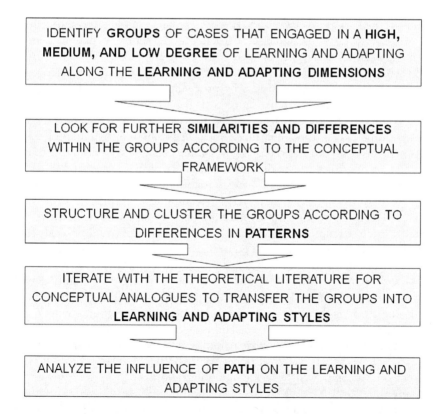

Figure 4.5 Steps within the stage of cross-case analysis.

for rival explanations (Eisenhardt, 1989). In this manner, within-case and cross-case analysis enabled the emergence of patterns that refine and expand on the original theoretical assumptions. These patterns and corresponding quotes from the data were translated by the author into English, focusing on generating accurate data by leaving phrases as close to the German meaning as possible (Marshall & Rossman, 2006).

Furthermore, patterns that cut across the cases were discerned in this stage through the use of metaphors as data-reducing, pattern-making, and decentering devices. Attaching metaphorical gerunds to the data helped to shift from facts to processes that account for the alteration of HRM (Miles & Huberman, 1994). For example, metaphorical gerunds such as disseminating knowledge throughout the organization or transferring knowledge beyond the organization were attached to the common themes surfacing from the data to make better sense of the activities that encourage learning (cf. Corley & Gioia, 2004). Figure 4.5 depicts the stage of cross-case analysis that entails grouping the cases, transferring them into learning and adapting styles, and examining the influence of path on these styles.

Sixth, the patterns and conceptual ideas derived inductively from the within-case and cross-case analysis were linked to the literature of the study's framework (Pettigrew, 1990). In a first step, this entails aggregating from patterns in the data to broader constructs in the dynamic capabilities literature on path, learning, and adapting. Iterating the empirical findings with the theoretical literature aided in transferring the patterns of the processes into learning and adapting styles. By proceeding up the abstraction ladder to broader constructs that tie the empirical findings together, the findings were connected to and discussed in light of the conceptual framework and the dynamic capabilities literature. A pattern-matching technique iterated between the data and the theoretical assumptions of the conceptual framework by comparing patterns derived from theory with the observed empirical patterns in the data (Campbell, 1975; Trochim, 2001). In addition, a special type of pattern matching, namely, the technique of explanation building (Yin, 2009), was drawn on to explain the underlying phenomena within the data. In order to maintain a chain of evidence when moving up the abstraction ladder, these techniques helped to provide a clear link from the findings and conclusions to the research questions and framework, as well as to the empirical referents (Miles & Huberman, 1994; Yin, 2009). Iterating with the literature can entail linking the findings to "overarching, across-more-than-one-study propositions that can account for the 'how' and 'why' of the phenomena under study" (Miles & Huberman, 1994, p. 261). Discussing the findings with the published empirical findings sharpens insights and the limits of external validity, as well as enriches the theoretical level to achieve analytical generalization in which the local boundaries of the cases are transcended (Eisenhardt, 1989; Yin, 2009). Thus, the findings were evaluated throughout the data collection and analysis for their correspondence to theory in order to build internal and external validity.

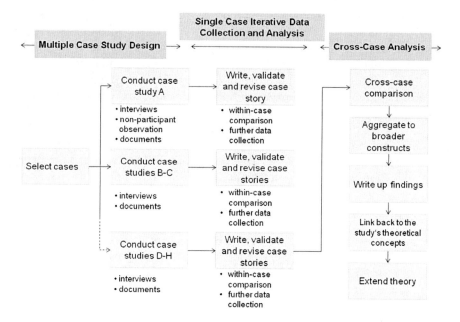

Figure 4.6   Data collection and analysis within the multiple case study design *(adapted from Yin, 2009, p. 57).*

Figure 4.6 sums up the case study method used in this study from the selection of cases to the qualitative data collection methods and the analytic stages, which culminate in the extension of extant theory. Depicting the rationale for multiple case designs, this diagram displays that the multiple case study entails both within-case and cross-case analysis to determine where the commonalities and differences in the processes of developing and implementing HR practices lie. Because the cases revealed contradictory empirical findings, each case was used to confirm or disconfirm the findings drawn from the others. The final step of extending theory encompasses a revision of the case study's initial theoretical assumptions by iterating between the empirical findings and the study's theoretical concepts. This comparison can provide the opportunity to broaden these concepts and help to move beyond the boundaries of the cases to generalize back to theory via analytical generalization (Yin, 2009).

METHODOLOGICAL RIGOR

Ensuring methodological rigor is important because case study research can generate valuable theoretical insights (Bartunek et al., 2006; Gephart, 2004; Shah & Corley, 2006). Failing to ensure rigorous research can cause problems in the later stages of research that elaborate on the relationships that have been unearthed through the case data (Eisenhardt & Graebner, 2007; Gibbert et al., 2008). Rigor in case study research encompasses, first, the standards for judging and evaluating the rigor and ultimately the quality of the conclusions drawn by the researcher (Miles & Huberman, 1994). The concern for validity and reliability is pertinent in evaluating the rigor of field research because the goal of finding plausible and credible outcome explanations is central to research (LeCompte & Goetz, 1982; Lee, 1999). Furthermore, the strategies to ensure rigor are mainly applied during the research process (Frankel, 1999; Guba & Lincoln, 1989; Seale, 1999). These guidelines enable case study research to be evaluated according to the rigor with which it has been conducted and the quality of the new insights.

Evaluating Rigor: A Discussion of Evaluative Criteria

Evaluative criteria involve the post-hoc assessment of research, representing the standards to be upheld as ideals in qualitative research (Creswell, 2009; Whittemore et al., 2001). They signify the minimum accepted level of following established norms and providing evidence that rigor has been attended to during the study. The quality of case study research can be judged against the four tests of construct validity, internal validity, external validity, and reliability, which have been modified for use in case studies. First, construct validity is the extent to which a study measures the phenomenon of interest that it intends to measure rather than some other phenomenon (Yin, 2009). It refers to whether the procedure leads to an accurate observation of reality and a correct interpretation of the constructs (Maxwell & Delaney, 2004). Therefore, the researcher must choose the appropriate method for studying the phenomenon using a well-considered set of measures and gaining full access to the informants' meanings (Dooley, 2002; Easterby-Smith et al., 2000). Furthermore, internal validity concerns the extent to which causal propositions are supported in a study (Seale, 1999). Yin (2009) defines this as establishing a causal relationship that rules out spurious relationships.

Third, external validity establishes the domain to which a study's findings can be generalized beyond the cases being studied (Dooley, 2002; Yin, 2009) and thus concerns the extent to which causal propositions are likely to hold true in larger but similar settings or in other settings or across time (Maxwell & Delaney, 2004; Seale, 1999). Showing similarities between the case's context and other contexts implies that the findings can be applied in similar contexts (Pratt, 2008). It is important to note that these aforementioned types of validity are not mutually exclusive. The absence of internal and construct validity in case study research means that no external validity exists. Thus, external validity is viewed as being dependent on the logical prerequisite of internal and construct validity given the hierarchical relationship among the three validity types. Finally, reliability refers to whether a particular research technique will yield the same insight if applied repeatedly to the same object, thereby entailing the absence of random error (Gibbert et al., 2008). In case study research, the concept does not refer to the exact replicability of findings; rather, it is understood more as the concept of internal reliability in which different researchers make similar observations and come to the same conclusions (Easterby-Smith et al., 2000; LeCompte & Goetz, 1982). Therefore, the study needs to be reported in detail so that researchers can trace the logic and evaluate the methods used (King et al., 1994).

Ensuring Rigor: Techniques to Attain Evaluative Criteria

In order to attain the evaluative criteria, techniques are used that ensure rigor and ultimately quality in the research process. These techniques include the methods employed to diminish threats to validity or reliability (Silverman, 2006; Whittemore et al., 2001). Because this study is an iterative process in which the fit between data and the analysis is monitored and confirmed constantly, techniques were used as self-correcting mechanisms to ensure the quality of the research. By being drawn on in each phase of the research process, errors can be corrected before they are built in to the design and subvert the analysis (Creswell, 2009). A variety of techniques was used in various stages in the research process to improve the quality of the case study research, as summarized in Table 4.3.

As an example of a strategy to ensure methodological rigor, maintaining a case study database allows for independent inspection of the raw data that led to the study's conclusions, thereby improving the reliability of the case study. The data set for this study encompasses the interview transcripts, documents, revised case stories, field notes, and the recording of observations. The case study database ensured a chain of evidence from the research questions and conceptual framework to the conclusions, allowing others to follow the argumentation and derivation of evidence from the empirical referents, thus enhancing reliability and construct validity (Miles & Huberman, 1994; Yin, 2009). In addition, several steps have been taken in order to ensure reliability, e.g., by citing specific data sources in the database and linking the raw data to the study's research questions. Moreover, clear cross-referencing to methodological procedures and the resulting evidence helped to enhance construct validity (Yin, 2009).

SUMMARY: THE ITERATIVE PROCESS OF MULTIPLE CASE STUDY RESEARCH

In light of the concept of methodological fit, the use of a qualitative multiple case study design was justified both with regard to the study's research questions as well as the state of prior research on altering HRM. Furthermore, it has been shown that case studies can provide fine-grained qualitative data

Table 4.3   Techniques to Ensure Methodological Rigor

Research Stage	Techniques	Evaluative Criteria
Research Design	• Threefold design (longitudinal, retrospective, processual) to examine phenomena over time and across different situations • Longitudinal cases and processual cases to enable relationships to be tracked as they evolve • Multiple retrospective studies to increase the range of the research design	Construct validity Internal validity External validity
Research Design	• Sampling decisions: theoretical sampling strategy • Maintain clear accounts of criteria used for the selection of subjects for study	External validity
Research Design	• Pre-test interview questions in discussions with colleagues	Construct validity
Data Collection	• Unobtrusive data collection methods: document analysis, non-participant observation • Prolonged engagement, persistent observation	Reliability Construct validity
Data Collection	• Between-method triangulation of multiple data sources	Internal validity Construct validity Reliability
Data Collection	• Discuss initial explanations with key informants via member checking or respondent validation during follow-up interviews	Construct validity Internal validity
Data Analysis	• Maintain a database • Field notes • Verbatim transcription	Reliability Construct validity
Data Collection Data Analysis	• Iterative interaction between data collection and analysis, e.g., following up surprises	Construct validity Internal validity External validity
Data Analysis	• Replicate findings through within- and cross-case analysis	Internal validity External validity
Data Analysis	• Include and account for negative, diverging instances • Address rival explanations by going back to the data and comparing these alternative arguments with the data set • Pattern-matching between the empirically observed pattern and predicted ones • Explanation building for the underlying phenomena within the data	Internal validity
Presentation	• Careful documentation and clarification of the research procedures	Reliability

Continued

Continued

Presenta-tion	•Thick, detailed, rich description of the setting to give a detailed picture of the context •Contextualize research setting clearly so the reader can understand the sampling choices and transfer the explanations from this setting	External validity
Presenta-tion	•Establish a logical chain of evidence and ground analysis in the data to satisfy the reader of the relationship between evidence and the conclusions •Cross-reference findings to specific data sources in the database and methodological procedures and link the raw data to the research questions •Use evidence that supports interpretations yet with a clear distinction between data and their interpretation	Reliability Construct validity

that extend theory about processes and path from the dynamic capabilities approach to the novel setting of the nonprofit sector. Through cross-case analysis, multiple case studies are ideal for offering an in-depth under-standing of the processes through which NPOs alter their HRM and the influences on these processes. Ensuring methodological fit in the selection of the cases, the exploratory multiple case study research design follows a theoretical sampling strategy in which eight German NPOs were chosen. Seeking commonalities and differences in the processes of and influences on developing and implementing HR practices, the study aims to extend theory to a broad range of NPOs. An iterative process that cycles back and forth between data collection involving the triangulation of methods and various stages of data analysis has been employed to draw out the patterns through within-case and cross-case analysis. Rather than being linear, an open-ended, iterative process emerges that involves interaction between the different stages of the research process. Finally, various techniques were drawn on to enhance the study's construct, internal and external validity, as well as reliability. In summary, this chapter has provided the logic and research design for linking the theory-driven research questions derived in Chapter 3 to the empirical findings. The next chapter discusses the case stories and empirical findings emerging from the cross-case analysis of the eight cases.

5 Multiple Case Study

This chapter presents the empirical findings of the exploratory multiple case study that emerge from the analysis of the learning and adapting processes and the influence of path on these processes in NPOs. As noted in Chapter 4, a multiple case study enables fine-grained analysis, which explains the patterns related to the phenomenon in question and identifies plausible relationships shaping the phenomenon. First, the individual case stories are presented in the next section to provide an in-depth understanding of the unique setting in each case as the NPO alters its HRM. Thereafter, this chapter displays the patterns identified in the cross-case analysis, through which the cases were grouped according to a high, medium, and low degree of learning and adapting and subsequently transferred into learning and adapting styles. Finally, using exemplary case studies for each of the learning and adapting styles, the empirical findings about the influence of path are presented. Individual case studies reveal the relationship between the unique nonprofit features and the learning and adapting processes through which the NPOs develop and implement their HR practices. Overall, this analytical procedure reflects the stages of observing phenomena of learning and adapting processes, categorizing the phenomena into a classification scheme along the theoretical dimensions, and defining relationships by exploring the association between path and the learning and adapting styles (Carlile & Christensen, 2004).

CASE STORIES

The first analytical stage entailed creating initial case stories from the analysis of public documents to provide information about the organization's mission, employees, internal and external stakeholders, organizational structure, financial resources, current HR practices, and history of change. These case stories were validated and revised with the interview data and the internal documents, thereby serving as a validation tool for subsequent analysis (Langley, 1999). The multiple data sources are designated in the case stories as interviews (I), document analysis (Doc.), and non-participant observation (OB), and the quotes were made anonymous. Thereafter, the raw data were broken down into the planning, decision-making, and implementing phases of introducing HR practices to identify and specify critical incidents along each phase. As a graphical representation of processes and events over time, visual maps organize these main events by displaying critical incidents as individual points and the parallel, recurring processes across the phases as horizontal lines (Langley, 1999; van de Ven & Huber, 1990; van de Ven et al., 1999). The following section provides these descriptive case stories and visual mapping of each of the cases (Yin, 2009).

Case A Social Services State Association: "A Modern HRM Tool"

As a member of one of the six largest free welfare associations in Germany, Case A is a social services state association founded after WWII in 1947. It is responsible for representing and consulting the 53 local chapters and 1,234 town chapters in the state of Lower Saxony. In addition, the state association runs six different social services institutions and two subsidiaries. There are 90 to 100 employees within the head organization of the social services state association whose mission is to help people in the areas of elderly care, emergency services, childcare, youth groups, and disaster zones abroad. Their employees often have religious ties and previous experience in social work. The state association is committed to following the international committee's seven principles of humanity, impartiality, neutrality, independence, voluntary service, unity, and universality (Case A: Doc. 10). The NPO is divided into eight departments, including publicity, HR, accounting, auditing, administration, national aid, social services, and the youth organization (Case A: Doc. 1). Within the traditional hierarchy, the organization encounters problems of coordination and communication among the large departments, which often suffer from "departmental egoism" (Case A: I1, 2). The HR department consists of a head HR manager as well as an HR manager and seven employees in payroll (Case A: I2, 2). The HR manager views the role of the HR department as service providers for their employees and the local and town chapters (Case A: I1, 1). The main tasks of the HR department include, e.g., HR planning, managing the HR budget, recruiting, personnel development, consulting local and town chapters, administration, compensation, retirement planning, advising on employment law, conducting wage and workers' council negotiations, and introducing HR practices such as HRM systems, time management systems, feedback talks, and goal setting and performance appraisal systems (Case A: I1, 1; Doc. 15).

At the time of data collection, the NPO was in the planning phase of developing its goal setting and performance appraisal system. The HR department had received the mandate to introduce this HR practice in November 2005 after a previous HR manager failed to develop it in 2002

(Case A: I1, 1, 2; Doc. 14). Regarding the events leading up to the search for a new or modified HR practice in Case A, hiring a new executive director from the for-profit sector served as the catalyst for introducing a series of HR practices that emphasized performance management and a more service-oriented direction within the organization. The executive director initiated this process to help the organization become more progressive and competitive (Case A: I1, 1; I2, 1). As such, the organization is being proactive in choosing to introduce new HR practices. The NPO is under financial pressure given decreasing funds from the EU, national, state, and local governments, insurance companies, donations, and membership fees, as well as increasing wage and pension costs (Case A: Doc. 10). The HR practice is seen by the HR managers as an absolute must, "a modern HRM tool," without which the organization cannot survive (Case A: I1, 1, 2). The goals of introducing goal setting and performance appraisal include more efficient HR planning and training, as well as increasing transparency and communication among the departments in order to clearly link departmental goals with the strategic organizational goals. In addition, the NPO aims to improve employee and organizational performance, employee motivation and skills, and managers' leadership of the employees, especially because the employees expressed dissatisfaction with the feedback they receive from their managers (Case A: I1, 1, 2, 3; I2, 1, 2; Doc. 12). Although the NPO

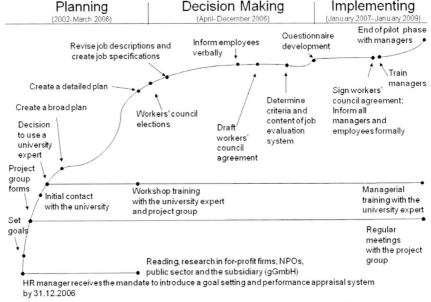

Figure 5.1   Case A social services state association.

had been given the mandate to introduce a performance appraisal system by 31.12.2006, a pilot phase of implementing the HR practice with the managers only began in November 2008 and ended in January 2009 (Case A: I1, 4). Figure 5.1 maps the main events over the planning, decision-making, and implementing phases in Case A.

Case B Museum: "Rewarding Our Employees"

Case B is an open-air, regional cultural history museum that was founded in 1953 in a county outside of a major city in Northern Germany. The museum aims to collect, preserve, research, and communicate cultural history for future generations. Furthermore, it seeks to be a service provider, advisor, initiator, and partner in cultural, scientific, social, and economic projects. As a central cultural institution, the museum is responsible for running and managing various museums, institutions, and cultural monuments at additional branch sites. The NPO views itself as being regional and decentralized, family-friendly, economical, professional, integrative, ecological, well networked, and participative (Case B: Doc. 3, 5). Their 70 to 80 employees fluctuate in number depending on the season and are perceived as being highly motivated, committed, and full of conviction regarding their work, identifying strongly with the museum's work (Case B: I2, 1). In addition to being financed through admission fees, county subsidies, and foundation grants, the museum's development association raises funds for the organization (Case B: Doc. 4). The organization has a relatively flat hierarchy and is divided into 10 departments, including controlling, public relations and marketing, folklore, general service, visitors' service, farming and groundskeeping, artisanry, cultural sites, archival work, and projects. The museum does not have its own HR department (Case B: Doc. 5). Instead, the executive director is responsible for all HR matters at the museum. The NPO has a variety of HR practices, including recruiting, HR development trainings and seminars, annual work planning, flexible working hours, employee feedback talks, and a pay for performance compensation system (Case B: I1, 1; I2, 1).

At the time of data collection, the organization had implemented its pay for performance system in the museum two years ago. The museum had hired an executive director experienced in working in the nonprofit consulting area who proactively initiated the process of introducing the HR practice into the museum's development association in 2002. At the time, the museum was still a part of the public sector, and pay for performance systems were not contractually permissible. In 2003, the museum changed its legal form to a foundation to deal with the decreasing funding. This afforded the organization with greater autonomy and more cost-effective management with a multi-year budget. The pay for performance system was then allowed to be adopted into the museum. The executive director and director wanted to use this HR practice to financially reward highly

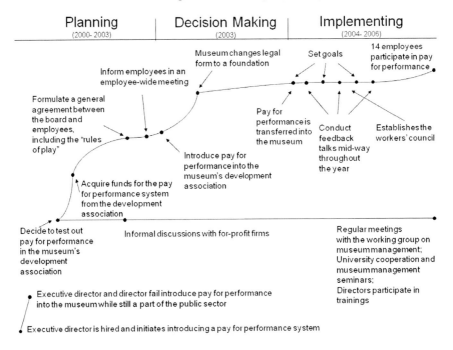

Figure 5.2   Case B museum.

involved employees who work more than is stipulated in their contracts and have regular goal setting and performance appraisal feedback talks. By introducing this HR practice, the directors aimed to better coordinate work and increase employee motivation through intense dialogue. In addition, they sought to give employees a chance to improve their performance, with feedback talks occurring mid-way through the evaluation period (Case B: I1, 1; I2, 1). At the time of developing the HR practice and introducing it into the museum's development association, there was no workers' council. A workers' council was established later in the museum once the HR practice was already accepted by the employees (Case B: I1, 1). Furthermore, the directors chose not to apply the pay for performance system to all of the employees, opting merely for those with management responsibility (Case B: I2, 1). In 2006, 14 employees had participated in pay for performance in the museum (Case B: Doc. 1). Figure 5.2 depicts these main events over the planning, decision-making, and implementing phases in Case B.

Case C Social Services Local Association: "Simply Identified It as an HR Instrument"

Case C is a social services local association, more specifically a public benefit limited liability organization (*gGmbH*), in Lower Saxony that focuses solely on providing emergency services. It is 1 of 17 local and town chapters in Lower Saxony and a member of the state association, a politically and religiously independent organization with roots in the German labor movement. The organization is affiliated with one of the six main social welfare organizations as a member of the Association of Social Movements. The organization has 120 employees who are motivated to work in social services, are familiar with aid organizations, and identify with the association (Case C: I1, 1). In the process of becoming certified in total quality management (TQM), the local association developed a mission statement that focuses on the four aspects of skills, competitiveness, improvement, and perspectives (Case C: Doc. 1). In this respect, the organization is devoted to helping others regardless of ethnicity, nationality, or creed while providing quality services and working transparently and efficiently (Case C: Doc. 5). The executive director views and runs the NPO first and foremost as a business. The local association is in the fortunate situation of having financial freedom and flexibility within a multi-year budget contracted with the local authority. Given additional contracts in emergency services, the executive director has the opportunity to hire new employees. The executive director is responsible for HRM within the local association because there is no separate HR department and the board is not involved in HR decisions. The organization relies on its state association for new developments in HRM (Case C: I1, 1).

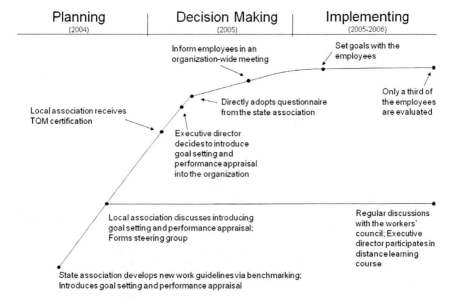

Figure 5.3   Case C social services local association.

At the time of data collection, the organization had already implemented goal setting and performance appraisal in the fall of 2005. This HR practice was imitated and directly adopted from the state association where it was already institutionalized (Case C: Doc. 2). Introducing this HR practice was reactive rather than indicative of a change-driven culture within the organization. After gaining certification in TQM, the executive director introduced the HR practice into the organization. Goal setting and performance appraisal was "simply identified [. . .] as an HR instrument" that would help to develop criteria to be able to make well-justified HR decisions, such as laying off employees in order to avoid arbitrariness (Case C: I1, 1). In addition, the NPO aims to increase its employees' motivation, commitment, and ability to change and improve throughout the year. Although the organization has a flat, democratic hierarchy and a tight administrative structure, the executive director encountered problems during implementation. As can be seen in Figure 5.3, the social services local association failed to implement the HR practice with all of the employees, evaluating only a third of the employees instead (Case C: I1, 1).

Case D Environmental Organization: "Internal Dissatisfaction among Our Employees, Managers, and the Board"

Case D, an environmental organization, is a politically, commercially, and financially independent NPO that relies on peaceful, non-violent measures to bear witness to threats to the environment. Established in 1971 as the national office of the international environmental organization in Germany, it is "autonomous in carrying out the agreed global campaign strategies within the local context [it] operate[s] within, and in seeking the necessary financial support from donors to fund this work" (Case D: Doc. 11). Its 217 employees are perceived as being active, strong willed, and intrinsically motivated to save the environment (Case D: I1, 1). At the first point of data collection in 2006, the NPO was under financial pressure to cut its HR costs because its financial reserves shrunk as expenditures increased; the HR budget decreased by 1.6 million EUR, leading to cutting 13 positions (Case D: Doc. 13). By the second point of data collection, the donations had become more financially stable as the budget reached 42 million EUR in 2007 (Case D: Doc. 12). The organization has a flat hierarchy that is marked by interdepartmental working teams and interdisciplinary teamwork (Case D: I1, 1, 2; Doc. 3). It is divided into three main departments (marketing/advertising/fundraising, campaigns, and administration) that are then broken down further into divisions. Along with divisions in the areas of finance, accounting, law, and IT, HR is a division of the administrative department (Case D: Doc. 12). The HR manager oversees the work of six employees who work in the areas of HR administration and HR development. The HR policies emphasize transparency, internationality and diversity, flexibility, a fair culture of disagreement, teamwork, a cooperative leadership style, and immaterial values (Case D: Doc. 3). There is a vast array of HR practices in the environmental organization, including recruiting, mentoring, coaching, employee talks, upward feedback talks, HR development, team development, compensation, sabbaticals, international workshops and seminars, as well as weekly or bi-monthly organization-wide plenums (Case D: I1, 1; Doc. 3).

At the time of data collection, the NPO was in the process of implementing a new compensation model. Conflicts had arisen with the workers' council and the employees regarding the pay scale groupings that led to labor court proceedings, drawing out the implementation of the HR practice over a two-year period (Case D: I1, 1, 2). In 2000, the organization hired a new HR director who was given the task of introducing a new compensation system. The employees, managers, and even the board were dissatisfied with the static, outdated compensation model (Case D: I1, 1; Doc. 5). The previous compensation model no longer reflected the current line of work of the organization and its employees. In this sense, introducing the new HR practice was a reaction to the new situation. The NPO wanted to increase the transparency and acceptance of the compensation system and develop a less complex model that is better suited to its work (Case D: I1, 1). During the planning phase of developing the HR practice, the board asked the organization to reconsider its decision not to introduce a pay for

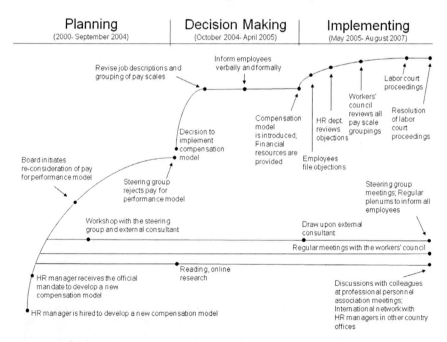

Figure 5.4 Case D environmental organization.

performance component to the compensation model, but the steering group on compensation decided against a pay for performance system because it is difficult to develop criteria and measure performance and success in their line of work. In addition, the HR manager believed it would conflict with their organizational culture, the intrinsic motivation of their employees, and the nature of their tasks, as well as be unfair to their volunteers and donors (Case D: I1, 1; Doc. 9). The decision to implement the new compensation model was not made until 2004 because other issues had priority in the organization, and the steering group engaged in broad, lengthy processes of developing the HR practice with the employees in the plenums (Case D: I1, 1, 2). These events occurring over the planning, decision-making, and implementing phases can be seen in Figure 5.4.

Case E Sports Organization: "Clarifying Our Roles and Responsibilities"

Case E, the sports organization, is an umbrella organization that represents its members in 600 sports clubs, 48 sports associations, and 58 state sport associations in Lower Saxony. The organization's mission is to contribute to the welfare of citizens in Lower Saxony through advocating for and supporting sports (Case E: I1, 1; Doc. 11). Its key activity areas encompass sports policy, sports development, education, youth sports, and OD while being guided by the principles of the common good, sustainability, gender mainstreaming, success and performance, subsidiarity, volunteerism, and maintaining a humane work climate (Case E: I1, 1; Doc. 3, 4, 11). Its 121 employees are viewed as highly motivated and willing to change, and they identify with sports to a high degree. The organization has a traditional, rigid hierarchy with cross-departmental teamwork (Case E: I1, 1, 2, 3; I2, 1, 2). After undergoing an OD process, the organization's structure was divided into three main business areas, which are each then separated into the following two main departments: sports development and organizational development, youth sports and education, and finances and administration (Case E: I2, 2). Each main business area has an executive director and a head director who presides over the entire organization as well as the individual departments of principles, legal issues, public relations, Olympics, and auditing (Case E: Doc. 1). Although there is no separate HR department, HRM falls under the responsibility of the head director. HR development is housed in its own department within the business area of finances and administration, and the OD department also addresses HR matters (Case E: I1, 3; I2, 2). HR practices within the organization include recruiting, HR development, leadership circles, goal setting, employee surveys, and volunteer management (Case E: I1, 1).

At the time of data collection, the sports organization was in the decision-making phase of its OD process. After having developed a mission statement together with representatives from the member organizations in

2000, the directors and departmental employees initiated a discussion about a change process. The NPO was facing a 20% reduction in state funds due to the massive state budget (Case E: I1, 1). The change process was introduced into the organization in 2005 given this decrease in funding but also due to societal and demographic changes and their impact on sports, as well as internal discussions about clarifying roles within and outside of the organization (Case E: I1, 1; I2, 1; Doc. 3). The managers were proactive in introducing the OD process in that they anticipated the changes facing the organization in the future. By engaging in a change process with the member organizations and employees, the sports organization sought to avoid the duplication of work, to clarify roles and responsibilities, and to develop adequate structures to deal with future demands and stabilize the member organizations (Case E: I1, 1; I2, 1). Aided by external consultants, the NPO used working groups made up of representatives from the member organizations and the steering group to determine the organization's future goals, with the board setting the goal prioritizations (Case E: I1, 1, 2; I2, 1, 2; Doc. 7). Although the organization intended to have implemented and evaluated its OD process by the end of 2007 (Case E: Doc. 3), they officially restructured with the new business area and new OD department in January 2008. Furthermore, the catalogue of planned measures and tasks

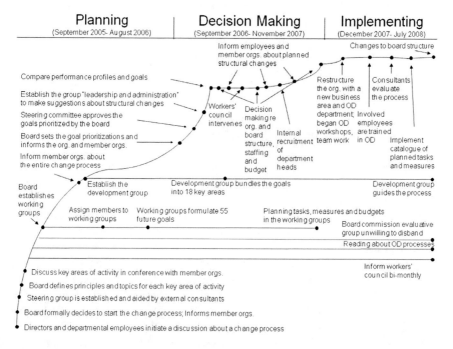

Figure 5.5 Case E sports organization.

as well as changes to the board structure were still being implemented in the summer of 2008 (Case E: I1, 3; I2, 2). The main events along the planning, decision-making, and implementing phases of the change process are displayed in Figure 5.5.

Case F Teaching Hospital: "Create and Find Jobs and Support Employees"

As a teaching hospital established in Lower Saxony in 1963 with the aim of combining teaching, research, and the provision of medical services, its mission entails being "united in principles, free in cases of doubt and charitable towards all" (Case F: Doc. 2). The hospital emphasizes humane and responsible actions, continually improving its performance, acting economically, maintaining effective processes, having managers who lead by example, cooperating to achieve goals, and HR development as a part of the organizational strategy. Its 7,000 employees can be differentiated into medical staff or teaching and research staff. The medical staff is perceived as highly motivated to help others while being engaged in psychologically and physically stressful work, whereas the teaching and research staff is considered to be highly motivated to achieve its scientific goals (Case F: I1, 1). The organizational structure follows this division between providing medical services and teaching and research. The hospital has a traditional hierarchy that is organized into three main departments (research and teaching, medical services, management and administration), which are further divided into approximately 70 departments. The HR and legal departments are situated within the management and administration department, alongside finance, technology, and logistics (Case F: Doc. 1, 10). The HR manager oversees 10 employees in the HR department as well as the area of HR development, which forms its own separate unit with 13 additional employees. The HR department focuses on job management, consulting, health management, skills management, and HR strategy development and consulting. Within the NPO, HR practices include recruiting, HR development, employee health systems, employee surveys, goal setting, and career planning (Case F: I1, 1).

Given that the hospital was facing increasingly scarce financial resources coupled with the rising costs of health care, they reacted to these changes by implementing an internal employment market (IEM) for employees whose positions were not being refinanced. Budget reductions were occurring across departments, and financial resources were being distributed according to performance-related criteria given the hospital's deficit of about 40 million EUR (Case F: Doc. 10). At the time of data collection, the organization was making decisions about extending its existing IEM to employees with health restrictions. The hospital wanted to introduce an IEM that would create and find jobs and support employees with health restrictions or even those who want to switch positions voluntarily. By introducing an IEM, the hospital sought to place these employees in permanent, limited, or service-oriented positions, thereby allowing them to maintain employment at the hospital. In addition, they aimed to increase the quality and skills of the employees being transferred through the IEM (Case F: I1, 1, 2; Doc. 6, 7). For example, employees who could no longer physically work in their previous positions were retrained into service positions. As an incentive to encourage managers to use the IEM, the HR department covered half of the HR costs of employing a person from the IEM for six months (Case F: I1, 2, 3). Although the HR manager intended to introduce the IEM for employees with health restrictions by October 2006, the workers' council agreement was not signed until June 2007 because additional negotiations were necessary with the workers' council due to their different approaches to getting employees with health restrictions to use the IEM. In November 2007, the IEM began as a pilot project in a few departments for employees with health restrictions (Case F: I1, 2, 3). As can been seen in Figure 5.6, 56 employees had been successfully transferred into new positions through the IEM by April 2008 (Case F: Doc. 12).

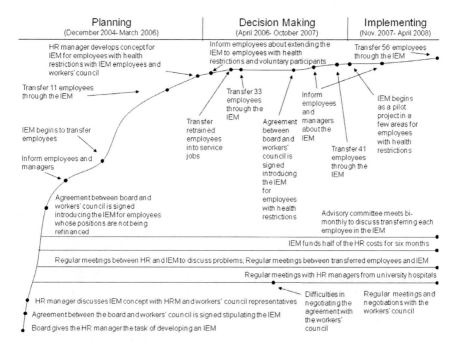

Figure 5.6 Case F teaching hospital.

Case G Foundation: "A More Balanced Skills Profile"

Established in 1977 on the values of competition, freedom, goodwill, and solidarity, Case G is an independent, nonpartisan organization with the mission to promote continual social progress in education, the economy, health care, civic society, and international understanding (Case G: Doc. 5). As an operating foundation, it solely funds its own programs, which focus on encouraging and being a catalyst for social change, thereby having a large and sustainable impact on society (Case G: Doc. 15). The foundation has 320 employees who are perceived as being intrinsically motivated experts who strongly identify with the founder, the foundation, and its goals (Case G: I1, 1; Doc. 15). The foundation is in a comfortable financial situation because it is financed through the income from its holdings in the founder's company, cooperative partnerships, and the financial management of its assets. In 2007, the foundation had a budget of 84 million EUR (Case G: Doc. 17). The NPO is a traditional line organization, yet at the same time it is divided into several competency centers according to topics and into project-based groups that are often interdisciplinary depending on the topic. The foundation was restructured in 2004 to separate the work of the board from that of the board of trustees and clearly define the areas of competencies. 'HR and Organization' make up one department alongside finance and services within the foundation. The NPO views itself as a learning organization (Case G: Doc. 2, 4). It emphasizes open and constructive dialogue, personal responsibility, a willingness to learn, a balance between work and family, cooperative leadership styles, and the idea that it is a good argument that counts rather than one's job title (Case G: Doc. 4, 18). In this respect, its HR practices encompass upward feedback talks, employee surveys, work-life balance programs, HR development, goal setting and performance appraisal, pay for performance, recruiting and online recruiting, an IEM, and a project management workbook (Case G: Doc. 9).

At the time of data collection, the foundation was in the process of planning the development of a skills analysis system. Because the NPO had developed further strategically, it wanted to determine whether the old skills analysis model appropriately captured the current and future challenges facing the organization (Case G: Doc. 1). Thus, by proactively altering the organization's HR practices, the HR manager initiated developing a new skills analysis system that entailed buying this HR practice from an external consultant from the university (Case G: I1, 1). Having finished testing the skills analysis system on the managers, the foundation wanted to determine which skills are necessary for their employees. In this respect, the HR manager strongly believes that employees in a foundation need "a more balanced skills profile" in contrast to for-profit organizations, with personal skills and social skills being stronger in foundations (Case G: I1, 1, 2). The goals of introducing the skills analysis system include developing the employees' skills, as well as recruiting, developing, and retaining

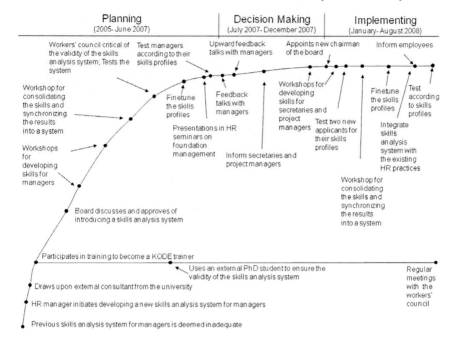

Planning	Decision Making	Implementing
(2005- June 2007)	(July 2007- December 2007)	(January- August 2008)

Workers' council critical of the validity of the skills analysis system; Tests the system

Test managers according to their skills profiles

Upward feedback talks with managers

Appoints new chairman of the board

Inform employees

Workshop for consolidating the skills and synchronizing the results into a system

Finetune the skills profiles

Feedback talks with managers

Workshops for developing skills for secretaries and project managers

Finetune the skills profiles

Test according to skills profiles

Presentations in HR seminars on foundation management

Test two new applicants for their skills profiles

Integrate skills analysis system with the existing HR practices

Workshops for developing skills for managers

Inform secretaries and project managers

Board discusses and approves of introducing a skills analysis system

Workshop for consolidating the skills and synchronizing the results into a system

Participates in training to become a KODE trainer

Uses an external PhD student to ensure the validity of the skills analysis system

Regular meetings with the workers' council

Draws upon external consultant from the university

HR manager initiates developing a new skills analysis system for managers

Previous skills analysis system for managers is deemed inadequate

Figure 5.7   Case G foundation.

top project managers because there is no market from which to 'buy' these resources (Case G: I1, 1; Doc. 9). Although the foundation had planned to be finished with developing and implementing the skills analysis system for the secretaries and project managers by May 2008, they were delayed by four months given difficulties in gathering the participants for the workshops together and in including the workers' council. The workers' council was especially critical of the validity of such a skills analysis system. The main events in planning, decision making, and implementing the skills analysis system are depicted in Figure 5.7.

Case H Religious Organization: "Restructuring and Tightening up the Structure"

Case H, the religious organization, is a dependent institution of the regional Protestant Church in Lower Saxony. Its predecessor, the office for congregational services, was founded in 1937 and oversaw various independent institutions for congregational services. With a reform process that began in 1998, the synod, i.e., the parliament, mandated that the various institutions be joined together under one organization. After developing a mission statement in March 2001, the organization was renamed in 2002 and restructured into three main departments in 2004 (Case H: Doc. 2, 3). Its mission entails the proclamation of Protestant religious values, missionary work, the provision of services for congregations and institutions, as well as the promotion of the principles of being "open and experienced, full of ideas for the Church and society, and exploring and testing new things together" (Case H: Doc. 5). Its 250 employees are considered to be highly motivated and educated experts with a theological and an educational background (Case H: I1, 1). The organization is structured into three main departmental areas (congregation support services, additional congregation services, dialogue with the church) and an administrative department that serves both the organization and the various institutions of the regional church. The three main departmental areas are further divided into departments according to topics. These divisions differ in size, location, and age, ranging from being established merely 20 to as many as 100 years ago. The administrative department is further divided into HR, finance, and general administration departments. The HR employees are responsible for employment law and compensation. The HR practices within the NPO include recruiting, HR development, quality circles, departmental goal setting, employee feedback talks, employee suggestion systems, and employee surveys (Case H: I1, 1; Doc. 3, 8, 9, 10).

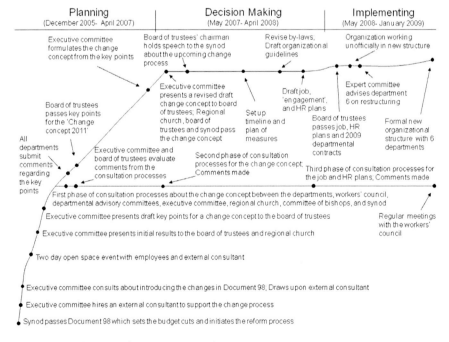

Figure 5.8   Case H religious organization.

At the time of data collection, the organization was in the planning phase of its OD process. Although the organization has received its own budget for HR and material costs since 1999 (Case H: Doc. 8), it still faces financial pressure due to decreasing income from church taxes, which has led to budget cuts. The synod passed Document 98 in 2005, which stipulated budget cuts between 10% and 50% for all the regional church institutions. Given its financial cuts of 25% by 2011, the organization was forced to restructure its areas of work and tighten its organizational structure (Case H: Doc. 3). By engaging proactively in an OD process, the NPO sought to work more effectively with fewer staff, ensure and improve the quality of its work, as well as improve cooperation between its divisions (Case H: Doc. 3, 10). The NPO was asked to present a change concept of how to implement these budget cuts by 2011. In a series of consultation processes among the departments, workers' council, regional church, committee of bishops, and the synod, the organization developed a draft change concept that was passed by the regional church. The change concept entails the new structure of the organization and which positions and fields of work are to be cut or discontinued in the future (Case H: I1, 1, 2; Doc. 2, 3). Formally, the new organizational structure was to be in place by January 2009, but the organization was already working in the new six departments that cover 45 fields of work in the summer of 2008 (Case H: I1, 2; Doc. 3, 10). Figure 5.8 captures the main events over the planning, decision-making, and implementing phases in Case H.

LEARNING AND ADAPTING STYLES IN NPOS

As developed in Chapter 3, both learning and adapting are assumed to serve as appropriate lenses for investigating how and why NPOs develop and implement their new or modified HR practices. According to cross-case analysis within the case study method, the empirical findings are displayed with explanatory information dispersed from the individual cases (Yin, 2009) and discussed across the cases regarding the learning and adapting processes. Having inspected the cases to see whether they fall into groups that share certain patterns (Miles & Huberman, 1994), they are grouped along the learning and adapting dimensions derived from theory according to a classification scheme of a high, medium, and low degree of engaging in learning and adapting. Through an iterative process that cycles back to the theoretical literature for conceptual analogues that account for the similarities and differences in the main patterns, the groups are subsequently distinguished into styles of learning and adapting. Finally, these learning and adapting styles are discussed in light of the dynamic capabilities literature.

LEARNING PROCESSES

The dynamic capabilities literature reveals the importance of learning processes as organizations alter their resource base. Therefore, learning is assumed to be an appropriate concept for researching into the way NPOs obtain, share, and document knowledge during the alteration of HRM. Stemming from Zollo and Winter (2002), experience accumulation, knowledge articulation, and codification processes are three key learning mechanisms. As delineated in Chapter 4, the cases were organized into groups by coding and analyzing the data according to the extent to which the cases engaged in these three learning processes. Within-case and cross-case analyses identified patterns that capture the similarities and differences among these cases with regard to the kinds and amount of learning activities the NPO engaged in, and the cases were grouped according to the learning dimensions for each individual learning process (Miles & Huberman, 1994). These learning dimensions emerged from theory and reflect the theoretical assumptions guiding this study's conceptual framework. A 5-point scale ranging from no (--) to high (++) participation was used to score each case. The table in Appendix A.1 lists these dimensions and the 5-point range of participation. Having grouped these cases into the classification scheme of a high, medium, and low degree of engaging in learning along the learning dimensions, patterns were sought in each of the three identified groups of cases in iteration with the conceptual framework. Within the three groups, internal homogeneity is ensured regarding the kinds and amount of learning activities. Furthermore, the validity of these groups is enhanced by ensuring external heterogeneity among the groups. In the following, the similarities and differences among the groups of cases that are characterized by a high, medium, and low degree of learning will be discussed. The final aim is to identify styles of learning among the cases that originate from aggregating the emergent patterns from the data.

High Degree of Learning

By coding and analyzing the data along the learning dimensions for the extent to which the NPOs engaged in experience accumulation, knowledge articulation, and knowledge codification, commonalities were revealed among four of the cases, cases A, D, E, and H. This group can be classified as engaging in learning to a high degree.

Experience Accumulation

In terms of experience accumulation processes, this study examines how NPOs acquire internal and external knowledge regarding the development and implementation of HR practices through experiential and/or acquisitive mechanisms as well as the role of prior experience in the acquisition of knowledge. The cross-case analysis unearths that Cases A, D, E, and H are classified as engaging in experience accumulation to a high degree along the learning dimensions of (1) external acquisitive learning, and (2) the role of internal knowledge.

External Acquisitive Learning

Iterating the data with the theoretical literature, the findings indicate that knowledge is gathered from outside the organization in these four cases. From the cross-case analysis, four external acquisitive learning patterns emerged inductively from the data: learning from written material, vicarious learning, participating in training programs, and hiring external support. Learning from written material involved mainly gathering information from books in Cases A, D, and E to gain external knowledge (Case A: Doc. 10; Case D: I1, 1; Case E: I2, 1). Vicarious learning occurred in Cases A, D, E, and H and entailed learning informally from for-profit, nonprofit, and public organizations' experiences with the respective HR practice. For example, Case D (I1, 1) learned vicariously through informally discussing with for-profit organizations about their experiences with compensation systems at HR professional association conferences. In Cases A, D, E, and H, vicarious learning also occurred through learning from NPOs, public sector organizations, or consultants who specialized in these NPOs. Vicarious learning took place in Case H through learning from other NPOs and their experiences in a quality management seminar. Despite the differences in the nonprofit subsectors, the executive director still deemed a transfer to the religious organization possible:

> "And we were able to all sit down at the table and learn from each other. And in this respect you can say that religious organizations can certainly adopt things and learn from each other if similar training opportunities are there." (Case H: I1, 2).

In Cases A, E, and H, the managers all participated in various training programs, which aided in acquiring external, explicit knowledge about the development and implementation of the respective HR practice (Case A: Doc. 10; Case E: I2, 1, 2; Case H: I1, 2). For example, employees in Case E formally gained information through their participation in OD training courses to be able to guide the change process within the organization (Case E: I2, 2). Finally, in Cases A, D, E, and H, hiring external support assisted in the development of the HR practice. In three of the cases, external support was hired that had specific nonprofit experience with regard to the HR practice or other HR practices in the NPOs (Case A: I1, 1, 2; I2, 1, 2; Case E: I1, 1; Doc. 2, 3, 5, 8; Case H: I1, 2). In Case A, non-participant observation of project group meetings indicated that they repeatedly considered the input of a university expert in NPOs and HRM (Case A: OB, 1, 6). They decided against hiring an external consultant because they often fail to tailor their advice to the needs and goals of NPOs:

> "We have certain rules of thumb from our experiences. You can see how important it is, perhaps from today's discussion, that people working in the project group know the organization, its employees, [. . .] where an external consultant is used, an instrument is developed, introduced and goes into effect and the problems of the organization are not really acknowledged. And we try to address and consider these problems." (Case A: I1, 2).

This finding regarding the importance of considering the organization, its problems, and its employees is triangulated by the data gained through non-participant observation of project group meetings, which revealed that the HR managers and workers' council representatives discuss sensitive issues regarding their employees' situations (Case A: OB, 1, 6, 7). In this sense, they maintained current practices of experience accumulation that are in line with their organization's needs, thus customizing the alteration of HRM to fit with their employees' needs and organizational goals. Similarly, in Case H, an external consultant with previous experience in the organization was hired because he understands the organization and the 'language' they speak:

> "Basically we brought in people who we know from some other processes or events. Where we knew that they know a little bit about the church and know how we tick and which language we speak as well." (Case H: I1, 2).

Thus, there is the commonality that external consultants have previous experience with NPOs, which signals that they will consider nonprofit goals. Furthermore, regarding hiring external support, each of the cases emphasizes the necessity of organizational autonomy in accumulating knowledge and not receiving too much input. Data drawn from interviews and non-participant observation corroborates that it did not fit their culture to yield consultants too much scope in this information gathering stage (Case A: OB 1, 6, 7; Case E: I2, 1; Case H: I1, 1). As seen in Case D,

> "We didn't use this consultant for the compensation model that much. It was more like I would always call him and tell him where we stand, what should we do and is it okay, just to get only a little bit of an adjustment because in all processes we don't like to let go of the reins." (Case D: I1, 1).

One idiosyncratic result among these four cases was that Cases A and H acquired their knowledge about the HR practice by copying HR practices, i.e., learning through imitation. In Case A, this entailed copying materials from for-profit organizations, as seen in the documents in which there was a "[d]raft of a job evaluation questionnaire in the state association, adopted from an anonymous organization" (Case A: Doc. 5). Triangulating this finding with non-participant observation of the project group meetings showed that they copied the wording and structure of for-profit organizations' question-naires, for example, by directly copying the dimensions from questionnaires from an industry and a transportation firm (Case A: OB, 1, 2, 7). Field notes taken reveal that the workers' council representatives felt that "[w]e don't need to reinvent everything. We can steal the information on questionnaires here" (Case A: OB, 2). Furthermore, another representative admitted later that, "I think we let ourselves be too led by the sample questionnaires. [. . .] We have to see if we really need [those performance dimensions]" (Case A: OB, 7). Observation of the project group meetings, however, also unearthed the HR manager, emphasizing, "we have to tailor it to the needs of our organization" (Case A: OB, 4). This can be corroborated by interview data:

> "And we developed a lot on our own where we thought that the organi-zational requirements must be taken into consideration and I wrote the workers' council agreement alone, okay there were examples but I knew what our main organization needs and it's 100% us." (Case A: I2, 1).

Likewise, Case H imitated adult education centers in terms of success measurements yet also adapted them to their needs (Case H: I1, 2; Doc. 10). These idiosyncratic findings about learning through imitation are rel-evant because they also highlight the importance of adapting the externally acquired knowledge to the organizations' needs and goals.

Role of Internal Knowledge

The cases possess direct previous knowledge about the HR practice, with the exception of Case D, where there was only limited previous knowledge about the compensation model. The HR manager and the steering group members had limited, indirect previous job experience with compensation models, and this previous knowledge was not deemed transferrable in terms of content (Case D: I1, 1). The rest of the cases had direct knowledge about the HR practice. In Case E, the OD department head and the executive director had initiated change processes in the organization in the past. This direct internal knowledge entails implicit organization-specific knowledge about change processes:

> "We have initiated change processes here, started further developments and so we were familiar with change relatively early." (Case E: I1, 1).

Document and interview analysis provides further evidence of direct previous knowledge in Case A, in which the HR manager wrote a report on goal setting in NPOs as part of a further education program (Case A: I2, 2). In this report, it is evident that the organization possesses explicit first-hand previous knowledge of how to combat problems when introducing the HR practice, such as the importance of the workers' council as "[i]n the past it has proven successful to include the workers' council early on in the change process" (Case A: Doc. 10).

In summary, triangulating the findings from interviews, document analysis, and non-participant observation indicates that these cases engaged in various external acquisitive learning activities that are crucial for building up new knowledge. Although the cases learned both informally and formally from the experiences of for-profits and public sector organizations, the necessity of maintaining practices that are in line with the organization's needs and goals emerged as playing a crucial role in gaining knowledge. This was seen especially with regard to vicarious learning from nonprofits' experiences, hiring external support versed in the specifics of NPOs, and adapting the imitated materials to the organization's values. Furthermore, the data reveal that most of the cases drew on the internal resource of direct, organization-specific knowledge, i.e., knowledge stemming from previous experience. The cases can be classified as engaging in experience accumulation to a high degree along the two learning dimensions. As a result, the cases first display the pattern of participating in a mixture of several external acquisitive learning activities, and, second, most of the cases possess direct previous knowledge about introducing the HR practice. Case D participates in experience accumulation to a fair degree because it had limited previous knowledge.

Knowledge Articulation

Concerning knowledge articulation processes, this study researches how NPOs share knowledge regarding the development and implementation of HR practices as well as utilize and integrate newly acquired and prior knowledge. Triangulating the data stemming from the interviews, documents, and non-participant observation unearths that Cases A, D, E, and H are classified as partaking in knowledge articulation to a high degree along the learning dimensions of (1) knowledge sharing within and beyond, and (2) applying and integrating knowledge.

Knowledge Sharing Within and Beyond

Cases A, D, E, and H all share the commonality of engaging in the first knowledge articulation dimension of knowledge sharing within and beyond the organization. These cases can be grouped according to the similarity that they display the pattern of participating in the knowledge articulation activities of discussing in small, diverse groups in the organization, disseminating knowledge throughout the organization, and transferring knowledge beyond the organization. In terms of discussing in small, diverse groups in the organization, the cases all tended to articulate diverse opinions, viewpoints, and concerns and make sense of the effects of the HR practice in discussions that took place in small, diverse groups. Some of these groups were informal and were used to coordinate and inform about the progress of the process as in Case E (I2, 1). Multiple sources of data also confirm that each case established a formal working group and/or steering group made up of diverse employees and positions so as to include the staff as broadly in the process as possible (Case A: OB 1, 2, 3, 4, 5, 6, 7; Case D: I1, 1; Doc. 5, 6; Case E: I1, 3; I2, 1; Doc. 2, 3, 7; Case H: I1, 1; Doc. 2). This enabled the employees to put their own values into practice when developing the HR instrument and enhanced their acceptance of the instrument. In Case D, document analysis depicts the broad composition of the steering group on compensation as "six equal members from different areas and functions" (Case D: Doc. 6). The HR manager discussed the broad participation in terms of enhancing acceptance:

> "[It] slowed down the process fundamentally. Quite clearly. But it also makes it, if you really use it to steer the process and listen attentively to all the participants' concerns, it makes it more acceptable." (Case D: I1, 2).

In Case A, non-participant observation of project group meetings unearths how debates between the employer's and workers' council representatives helped them to understand the performance implications of the HR practice better (Case A: OB, 5, 6; Case A: I1, 3). Attempting to make sense of the potential effects on the employees, the head HR manager commented that "[t]he employees will block it. The atmosphere is bad and then this is being added on to it" (Case A: OB, 5). However, the HR manager argued that "[i]t will increase motivation!" (Case A: OB, 6). In short, these discussions in small, diverse groups enable the organization to make sense of the HR practices. In Case E, sensemaking about the change process was enabled at a meta-level through these discussions with colleagues:

> "I have been able to open my perspective that has possibly been influenced or constricted by the consultants. [. . .] The whole thing enabled me to remove myself and look at it from a meta-level." (Case E: I2, 1).

Moreover, the data reveal the distinction between knowledge articulation and knowledge sharing as disseminating knowledge throughout the organization. Each of the four cases used various platforms to inform the employees. For example, organization-wide meetings were used to inform employees about the status of the HR practice (Case A: I1, 3, 4; I2, 1; Case

E: I1, 1, 2, 3), and open-space workshops with the employees were a means to discuss with the entire organization (Case H: I1, 1; Doc. 2). Yet the four cases varied in terms of intensity of information, ranging from Case A (I1, 1, 2, 3), which briefly informed the employees that the HR practice was being developed, to Case D (Doc. 5, 6, 7, 8), in which the employees were involved in weekly plenums to discuss the HR practice. Whereas non-participant observation of project group meetings in Case A reveals disagreements about when and how much to inform the employees (Case A: OB, 7), in Case D, the "compensation model was presented regularly during the planning phase to gain feedback" (Case D: I1, 1). Furthermore, because knowledge articulation also includes written form, the cases inform the employees by letter, email, and the Intranet (Case D: Doc. 10; Case E: Doc. 4, 8; Case H: Doc. 3).

The cross-case analysis also demonstrates that these cases participate in several activities of transferring knowledge beyond the organization using, e.g., the Internet to inform about their HR practice. Moreover, knowledge exchange beyond the organization is supported through discussions in interorganizational (Case D: I1, 1) or intraorganizational networks within the same local (Case E: I2, 2) or international association (Case D: I1, 1):

> "There are different offices of our organization in other countries that have changed their compensation models and I had an international exchange with them." (Case D: I1, 1).

In contrast, Cases A and H did not have such networks at their disposal. Case H is a unique exception to the aforementioned activities as the knowledge flow beyond the organization functions in a cascading process. Both interview and document data support that the flow of knowledge within and beyond the organization moves in a process of consultation from the executive committee, departments, and workers' council to the regional church, the committee of bishops, synod, and board of trustees (Case H: Doc. 2). The interview data indicate how knowledge sharing beyond the organization was not only necessary for the exchange of information but also for making decisions about the HR practice:

> "And then there was a consultation, that means that the workers' council was involved, the committee of bishops [. . .]. Then it went back to the executive committee and next week it'll go to the board of trustees and hopefully they will pass the decision so that we can implement it starting in June 2008." (Case H: I1, 2).

Finally, the dissemination of written materials was a means of sharing knowledge beyond the organization in the cases. For example, Case E informed its member organizations and the general public about the ongoing change process through its weekly newsletter in addition to the Internet

(Case E: I1, 3; Doc. 2). Triangulating the multiple data sources validates the evidence of these informal and formal mechanisms through which the cases transferred knowledge beyond the organization to inform their stakeholders and aid in making decisions.

Applying and Integrating Knowledge

Cases A, E, and H participate both in utilizing pre-existing knowledge and integrating the externally acquired knowledge. These activities were facilitated by the compatibility of previous job experience or the knowledge gained from various external sources. For example, in Case E, the head of the OD department applied his compatible pre-existing knowledge gained from prior experiences with change processes:

> "It all developed quite organically and because I had already been involved in these questions with regard to our city clubs so I could say: Yes, the development of our organization is a really important point. And I participated, brought in ideas, made suggestions, prepared decisions for the board in my department." (Case E: I2, 1).

Case D proves to be an exception to the aforementioned pattern because it was constrained in utilizing the limited pre-existing knowledge from the HR manager's previous job experience. The integration of externally acquired knowledge from intra- and interorganizational networks was also limited given cultural and sectoral differences. As the HR manager commented on these differences,

> "It was the case that here in Germany we were a bit ahead of the others [. . .]. But it wasn't far enough that I could really make a comparison." (Case D: I1, 1).

In summary, triangulating the data reveals that Cases A, D, E, and H included a broad range of participants to gain transparency and acceptance for the HR practice as well as enact the employees' own values. By exploring the cause and effect relationships of the HR instrument through intense dialogue, the cases were better able to engage in sensemaking about the need for the alteration of HRM (Weick, 1995; Zollo & Winter, 2002). They use various platforms to disseminate information, albeit the intensity of information and involvement of employees varied in each case. The cases rely on informal and formal mechanisms that support knowledge exchange beyond the organization to exchange ideas, inform stakeholders, and foster decision making. In addition, both utilizing and integrating knowledge was facilitated by compatible pre-existing experience or externally acquired knowledge. These cases can be classified as engaging in knowledge articulation processes along the two learning dimensions to a high degree. As a result, the cases first display the patterns of engaging in several activities of knowledge sharing within and beyond the organization and second, they both utilize pre-existing knowledge and integrate externally acquired knowledge. Case D participates in knowledge articulation to a medium degree because it was limited in utilizing pre-existing knowledge and integrating externally acquired knowledge.

Knowledge Codification

Regarding the codification of accumulated knowledge, this study investigates the codification activities and how NPOs codify know-what, know-how, and know-why behind developing and implementing the HR practice. Analyzing the data reveals that Cases A, D, E, and H can be classified as participating in knowledge codification to a high degree along the learning dimensions of (1) codification activities using written or electronic tools, and (2) codifying the content, method, and rationale.

Codification Activities

The knowledge codification activities in Cases A, D, E, and H include both written and electronic tools and activities. Triangulating multiple sources of data indicated that these four organizations began the development of their HR practices with a written working paper (Case A: I2, 2; Doc. 10; Case D: I1, 1; Doc. 9; Case E: I2, 1; Case H: I1, 1; Doc. 3). This commonality shows the importance of codifying the reasons for altering HRM in the organization at the initial stages of the process for sensemaking purposes. For example, in Case E, a paper written by the former club services department head outlined the necessity for change and was circulated among the board and the directors of the organization:

> "I wrote a draft paper and presented that in different contexts. That was the starting point for what developed out of it. Because it was important for me to write down what our fundamentals, our basic values are that stemmed from my work in the department club services, from the necessity that arose out of that." (Case E: I2, 1).

In all of these cases, a common effect of codification in written form was that it served as a means to reduce the complexity of the process (Case A: I1, 1, 2; Case D: I1, 1; Case E: I1, 1; Doc. 4, 6, 7; Case H: I1, 1). In Case D (I1, 1), the HR manager noted that the process of developing the compensation model had become so complex that careful documentation of steering group discussions and changes became necessary due to the complexity and amount of examples. Codification activities in electronic form also occurred (Case A: Doc. 2, 3, 7, 8, 9, 11, 12; Case D: 10; Case E: Doc. 7; Case H: I1, 2). In Case A, non-participant observation of project group meetings revealed the use of real-time electronic documentation (Case A: OB 5, 6). Interview data confirm that the electronic documentation of changes during negotiations aided making decisions with the workers' council:

> "[Real-time electronic documentation] allows for huge progress in the negotiations because we used to have a hard copy and sit together [. . .] and we had to make the changes in the original document and now where we work with the LCD projector that gives us a huge advantage." (Case A: I2, 1).

Cases D, E, and H all pursued a high level of detail in their codification activities, especially to ensure the acceptance of decisions and clarify decision-making competences (Case D: Doc. 5, 6, 7, 8; Case E: I1, 1; Doc. 4, 6, 7; Case H: I1, 1; Doc. 1, 2, 3). For example, Case D became more detailed in its codification activities once the organization began to implement the HR practice. As a result of an intervention by the workers' council, the HR manager became more formal in the negotiations with the workers' council, precisely documenting all decisions in addition to the formal applications to avoid similar future legal disputes. Detailed documentation functions as a guideline for future negotiations with the workers' council:

> "I document their participation a lot more carefully. Because I found this extra loop which they built in really unpleasant [. . .] So I've become a bit more careful there." (Case D: I1, 1).

Case A differed from the rest of the group, however, in terms of how detailed the codification activities were. Combining interview data with non-participant observation and document analysis indicates that this case advocated documenting only simple guidelines rather than detailed minutes to enable following the progress of the process, completing the tasks ahead (Case A: Doc. 4; OB 1, 4, 5), and avoiding "document[ing] yourself to death" (Case A: I1, 1). Thus, triangulating interview data and document analysis reveals the mixed result that both detailed and simple codification are perceived as necessary for providing guidelines.

Codification of Content, Method, and Rationale

By iterating the analysis of the documents, non-participant observation, and interview data with the theoretical background, the codification of accumulated knowledge documents the content (know-what) in HR practice guidelines, organizational and departmental goals, a written catalogue of criteria, and letters to employees that highlight the easily transmittable content of the HR practice (Case A: Doc. 5, 13; Case D: Doc. 7, 10; Case E: Doc. 4, 6). Case H formulated its by-laws and organizational guidelines as part of their change process, thereby codifying the changes that came

about in the scope of reorganization (Case H: I1, 2; Doc. 3). More important, however, is that these cases document the meeting minutes, project
outlines, PowerPoint presentations, and working papers to also codify the
method of developing and implementing the HR practice (know-how) or
the rationale behind it (know-why). Some cases indicated that they were
codifying the content and method to provide guidelines for future employees carrying out tasks in the organization (Case A: I1, 3; Doc. 4, 14; Case
D: Doc. 5, 6, 7, 8; Case H: Doc. 2), as in Case A:

> "For all of our projects we have a plan [. . .] and try to document all
> of it for the people who come after us. Who knows who'll sit here in
> 30–40 years? [. . .] How did it come about, who was involved and you
> need it for that and the documentation is always the part with a lot of
> work." (Case A, I2:2).

The cases also codified the content and rationale behind the practice (Case
A: Doc. 10; Case D: Doc. 9; Case E: I2, 1). In Case E, after numerous discussions with the employees, the external consultants wrote a report that dealt
with the employees' wishes and suggestions for the organization in the future
(Case E: Doc. 8). This report served to clarify the core problems within the
organization that provided the rationale for engaging in a change process. It
served as an exercise in sensemaking about the change process:

> "[. . .] they formulated the core problems. [. . .] From their point
> of view it became evident that the main problems for us [. . .] has
> to do with the leadership in our organization, that's what's wrong."
> (Case E: I2, 1).

Moreover, a further similarity is that the cases codify content, method, and
rationale at once. All the cases engaged in specific codification activities, such
as the documentation of workers' council agreements and final reports that
codified the content, method, and rationale behind the HR practice (Case A:
I2, 2; Doc. 6, 12; Case D: 5, 6, 7, 8, 9; Case E: Doc. 3, 7; Case H: 1, 2, 3). In
Case E (Doc. 5), the consultants codified these three types in a final evaluative
report by reviewing and comparing the phases with the goals of the process:

> "The final report basically referred to the individual phases that are
> described in the rocket diagram, to review them so to speak and to look
> what happened in the individual phases, which results were achieved,
> and to what degree we remained true to the concept as it was described
> in the conceptual paper." (Case E: I2, 2).

In summary, triangulating multiple sources of data demonstrates that not
only did these cases engage in codification activities of the content of the

HR practice in both written and electronic form, but these activities were also a means to codify the method and rationale to reduce complexity and provide guidelines for executing future negotiations. The cases corroborate that knowledge codification aids especially when engaging in infrequent tasks, e.g., initiating the alteration of HRM. Similarly, they provide empirical support that codification analyzes the articulated knowledge about past experience to aid decision making and sensemaking (Zollo & Winter, 2002), while it also ensures openness and transparency and reduces complexity. Codification was enabled by varying the level of detail to fit the needs of the organization, with most of the cases engaging in detailed codification. Thus, Cases A, D, E, and H share the commonality of engaging in knowledge codification to a high degree. As a result, each case first illustrates the pattern of several written and electronic codification activities, and, second, each engages in various combinations of codifying content, method, and rationale.

Group of a High Degree of Learning

The analysis of the data along the learning dimensions unearths that these cases are classified as engaging in experience accumulation, knowledge articulation, and knowledge codification processes to a high degree. The first result is that these cases are characterized by the common patterns of participating in a mixture of several activities of external acquisitive learning, knowledge sharing within and beyond the organization, and written and electronic codification. Furthermore, most of these cases exhibit the commonalities of possessing direct previous knowledge about the HR practice, utilizing pre-existing knowledge, integrating externally acquired knowledge about the HR practice, and engaging in different combinations of codifying the content, method, and/or rationale behind the HR practice. Thus, there is internal homogeneity with regard to the kinds and amount of learning activities. A first group of NPOs with a high degree of learning can be identified that is characterized by strongly encouraging experience accumulation, knowledge articulation, and knowledge codification during the development and implementation of HR practices. Table 5.1 illustrates the similarities and differences in the learning patterns in this group and scores each case according to its level of participation along the learning dimensions.

Medium Degree of Learning

Coding and analyzing the data along the learning dimensions that stem from the study's theoretical assumptions also reveals a second group of cases that engaged in the individual learning processes to a medium degree.

Table 5.1   Emergent Patterns in the High Degree of Learning

CASE	Experience Accumulation	HIGH DEGREE OF LEARNING	
		Knowledge Articulation	Knowledge Codification
	Extent of engaging in external acquisitive learning activities; has internal knowledge	Extent of knowledge sharing within and beyond the organization; utilizes pre-existing knowledge and integrates externally acquired knowledge	Extent of engaging in codification activities; codifies the content, method, and rationale
Case A	(++) High • **Engages in several external acquisitive learning activities** (Learning from written material, vicarious learning, participating in training programs, hiring external support, learning through imitation) • **Direct previous knowledge**	(++) High • **Engages in several activities of knowledge sharing within and beyond the organization** (Discussing in small, diverse groups in the organization, disseminating knowledge throughout the organization, transferring knowledge beyond the organization) • **Utilization of pre-existing knowledge and integration of externally acquired knowledge**	(++) High • **Engages in several codification activities** (Written and electronic form, simple) • **Codifies content and method; Codifies content and rationale; Codifies content, method, and rationale**
Case D	(+) Fair • **Engages in several external acquisitive learning activities** (Learning from written material, vicarious learning, participating in training programs, hiring external support) • *Limited* **previous knowledge**	(0) Medium • **Engages in several activities of knowledge sharing within and beyond the organization** (Discussing in small, diverse groups in the organization, disseminating knowledge throughout the organization, transferring knowledge beyond the organization) • *Limited* **utilization of pre-existing knowledge and limited integration of externally acquired knowledge**	(++) High • **Engages in several codification activities** (Written and electronic form, detailed) • **Codifies content; Codifies content and method; Codifies content and rationale; Codifies content, method, and rationale**
Case E	(++) High • **Engages in several external acquisitive learning activities** (Learning from written material, vicarious learning, participating in training programs, hiring external support) • **Direct previous knowledge**	(++) High • **Engages in several activities of knowledge sharing within and beyond the organization** (Discussing in small, diverse groups in the organization, disseminating knowledge throughout the organization, transferring knowledge beyond the organization) • **Utilization of pre-existing knowledge and integration of externally acquired knowledge**	(++) High • **Engages in several codification activities** (Written and electronic form, detailed) • **Codifies content; Codifies content and rationale; Codifies content, method, and rationale**
Case H	(++) High • **Engages in several external acquisitive learning activities** (Learning from written material, vicarious learning, participating in training programs, hiring external support, learning through imitation) • **Direct previous knowledge**	(++) High • **Engages in several activities of knowledge sharing within and beyond the organization** (Discussing in small, diverse groups in the organization, disseminating knowledge throughout the organization, transferring knowledge beyond the organization) • **Utilization of pre-existing knowledge and integration of externally acquired knowledge**	(++) High • **Engages in several codification activities** (Written and electronic form, detailed) • **Codifies content; Codifies content and method; Codifies content, method, and rationale**

Experience Accumulation

The cross-case analysis along the learning dimensions of (1) external acquisitive learning, and (2) the role of internal knowledge unearths that two of the cases, Cases F and G, engage in experience accumulation processes to a fair to medium degree.

External Acquisitive Learning

When examining the patterns of the external acquisitive learning activities, the cross-case analysis demonstrates that Cases F and G engaged to a varying degree in learning from written material, vicarious learning, participating in training programs, and hiring external support. Whereas Case F participates in few acquisitive learning activities, Case G participated in several. For example, both interview and document analysis indicate that Case G engaged in learning from written material by using a book that contained explicit examples about skills training and coaching manuals on the KODE system, a pre-developed skills management system, which they were adopting (Case G: I1, 1; Doc. 14). Case F did not acquire any external knowledge in this way, claiming instead that it fully developed the concept of the IEM on its own. This case provides evidence of experiential learning with knowledge development occurring inside the organization and relying on the tacit knowledge of its HR:

> "No there was basically nothing we could have copied. Instead we simply developed it, looked at what we want to achieve and how we will get there and how we will get structures so that it'll also function." (Case F: I1, 1).

Yet Case F did engage in vicarious learning from the experiences of other nonprofit hospitals that had or were implementing IEMs (Case F: I1, 1; Doc. 6). In Case G, both the HR manager and HRD employee participated in a training program to become an official KODE trainer (Case G: I1, 1; Doc. 12). Case G also hired external support from a university expert who was a consultant in skills analysis systems and from a PhD student who was hired to ensure that the validity of the KODE instrument would not be compromised. The combination of data from the interviews and documents shows that not only did the HR manager emphasize hiring a consultant but also 'buying' the KODE instrument developed by this university consultant (Case G: Doc. 12, 13):

> "Yes, that's the one we bought. That is this KODE, it's a trademarked brand. A professor or a couple of professors developed it at universities and provide it as an instrument." (Case G: I1, 1).

In addition, the external acquisitive learning pattern of learning through imitation emerges from the interview data and document analysis as being a way of learning in Case G (Case G: I1, 1, 2; Doc. 8, 9, 10, 11, 13). They openly admitted to directly copying the KODE system with the HR manager conjuring up the metaphor of reinventing the wheel when candidly stating that "[w]hat we did was we looked at where the right wheel is. And we found that in KODE" (Case G: I1, 1). However, Case G did not emphasize adapting the externally acquired knowledge to the nonprofit's goals. Instead, the HR manager views the analysis tool as universally applicable to all sectors:

> "I think that this instrument is so universal that it wasn't necessary [to adapt it to the needs of the foundation]. But what was interesting was that one could see from the first results that we had from some of the tests that there were differences to the for-profit sector." (Case G: I1, 2).

Thus far, combining these multiple data sources reveals the focus on experiential learning and vicarious learning in Case F versus several external learning activities in Case G.

Role of Internal Knowledge

Regarding the role of prior knowledge in the accumulation of knowledge, the analysis of the documents and interview data shows that the previous internal knowledge is limited in both Cases F and G. In contrast to most of the cases with a high degree of learning, which had previous, direct organization-specific knowledge, these cases possess only limited previous knowledge. In both cases, this knowledge is indirect. In Case F, neither the HR manager nor the board member who suggested introducing IEM had previous experience with the HR practice (Case F: I1, 3). As the HR manager recalled about the lack of direct, previous experience of the board member,

> "That wasn't experience [of the board member]. That was just the decision that we will do something too and I actually designed it." (Case F: I1, 3).

Similarly, Case G is also marked by having only limited prior knowledge with its previous skills analysis system (Case G: I1, 2). The HR manager's experience with this prior skills analysis system for managers was indirect because he was not employed in the organization at the time. The HR manager claimed that the previous system was complicated and difficult to use:

> "[. . .] before we had a skills analysis system for managers but [. . .] it was supposed to be able to do everything. That was developed before and no one was really satisfied with the system." (Case G: I1, 1).

In summary, combining the data from multiple sources indicates that Case F is idiosyncratic, in that it provides support for experiential rather than acquisitive learning, and Case G yields further confirming evidence for learning through imitation, although it was not deemed necessary to adapt the HR practice being copied to the organization's needs. Engaging in external acquisitive learning activities to a differing extent in these cases appears to stem from Case F not perceiving any external knowledge to acquire other than from vicarious learning from nonprofit hospitals, relying instead on developing the HR practice themselves. Thus, these cases can be classified as engaging in experience accumulation processes to a fair to medium degree along the two learning dimensions. On the one hand, divergent findings show that Cases F and G participate in few or several external acquisitive learning activities; on the other hand, both display the pattern of limited previous knowledge about the HR practice. Given these differences along the learning dimensions, Case F engages in experience accumulation to a medium degree and Case G to a fair degree.

Knowledge Articulation

The examination of the data along the learning dimensions of (1) knowledge sharing within and beyond, and (2) applying and integrating knowledge reveals that Cases F and G participate in knowledge articulation processes to a medium degree.

Knowledge Sharing Within and Beyond

Unlike the first group with a high degree of learning, Cases F and G share the commonality of engaging in several knowledge articulation activities of knowledge sharing within the organization, yet only Case F participates in numerous activities for knowledge sharing beyond the organization. Both cases frequently engaged in discussing in small, diverse groups in the organization, with knowledge articulation taking place in informal and formal discussions. For example, triangulating interview data with document analysis in Case F reveals holding bi-monthly meetings of the diversely composed advisory council when implementing the HR practice for employees with health restrictions (Case F: Doc. 5, 6, 7). These formal discussions enabled decision making about the IEM and consequences for individual employees with health restrictions:

> "[. . .] and every 14 days we meet with the advisory council- with the workers' council, the organization's medical services, and then we go through all of the cases and talk about what has happened, what is planned, how it should continue and that is where the decisions are made." (Case F: I1, 2).

In terms of disseminating knowledge throughout the organization, similar to the first group, they used employees' meetings as a platform to inform all of the employees about the HR practice throughout the organization (Case F: I1, 2; Case G: I1, 2). Yet unlike the first group, Cases F and G also relied on word of mouth propaganda to share positive information about the HR practice in the organization. For example, Case G exhibited evidence of using employees who participated in the workshops to develop the skills analysis system as 'informal informants' who spread the good word about this HR practice (Case G: I1, 2). Similarly, Case F used this method to pass on information about the benefits of the IEM from the department heads to the organizational areas, thereby enhancing the acceptance of the IEM:

> "That has gotten around more and the word of mouth propaganda amongst the department heads has led to the acceptance of the internal employment market being larger. [. . .] I believe we have reached a really good base and most of them will turn to us if they have a problem." (Case F: I1, 3).

Whereas Case G limited the amount of information given to its employees so as not to re-open the process of developing the skills analysis system (Case G: I1, 1, 2; Doc. 8, 11), Case F (I1, 2, 3) used additional platforms such as board meetings with department heads and project leaders and the Intranet to inform about the workers' council agreement and the IEM (Case F: Doc. 4, 5). It engaged in these additional informational efforts because its organization-wide meetings were poorly visited by the department heads, physicians, and researchers (Case F: I1, 1). Moreover, because knowledge articulation also includes knowledge in written form, both of these cases informed employees about the HR practice using written materials such as letters, information packets and brochures, and skills profiles' evaluations (Case F: I1, 3; Doc. 8, 9; Case G: I1, 2; Doc. 12, 13, 14).

In addition, Case G only participated in one activity of transferring knowledge beyond the organization by giving external presentations about the skills analysis system in a course on foundation management (Case G: Doc. 9, 10). In contrast, Case F not only participated regularly in interorganizational networks with university hospitals to discuss its experiences with the IEM, but it also gave presentations to other organizations (Case F: I1, 3; Doc. 6, 7). It even partook in a university study about European IEMs to exchange information and gain input (Case F: I1, 3; Doc. 10). In summary, Cases F and G share the commonality that they were both involved in knowledge sharing within and beyond the organization, although they were idiosyncratic with regard to their extent of participation in the knowledge sharing activities outside of the organization.

Applying and Integrating Knowledge

Cases F and G both engage in utilizing pre-existing knowledge and integrating the externally acquired knowledge, but they differ from the group of a high degree of learning in that they were both constrained in utilizing pre-existing knowledge. Regarding the utilization of pre-existing knowledge, Case F employed the knowledge of the employees involved in the first run of the IEM. However, this knowledge was limited in its applicability because it referred to a different group of employees. The HR manager was thus limited in applying the internal resources of the employees within the IEM during the development of this HR practice for employees with health restrictions (Case F: I1, 2, 3). Furthermore, Case F integrated the knowledge gained from its interorganizational network with other university hospitals. The HR manager specifically mentioned that it was able to gain and integrate information on how other hospitals financed their employees' trainings:

> "Cologne, for example, got in contact with the employment administration relatively early and they got funding for re-training their employees [...] and these are things that we have major problems with getting information about and we discuss with them about how they did it, who did they talk to [...]." (Case F: I1, 3).

However, the data reveal that Case F was also limited in integrating the externally acquired knowledge from other university hospitals, citing fundamental differences in the implementation of the IEM systems (Case F: Doc. 6):

> "Instead we will have incentives and we got the departments by saying that we will pay their HR costs for the first half a year if they take someone from the internal employment market. And that is one of the fundamental differences to Hamburg. They implement it directly." (Case F: I1, 1).

Case G faced constraints in utilizing the limited pre-existing knowledge about the previous skills analysis system for managers because this was purported to be an unsuccessful, all-in-one instrument for managers rather than all employees (Case G: I1, 1, 2):

> "The biggest problem was that we already had a firm here that developed a skills analysis system but it was discussed to death by the managers that it became such an all-in-one instrument, which means that it should have fit everything [...]. And that's why it was a bit difficult." (Case G: I1, 2).

Yet Case G was not limited in integrating the knowledge gained from the external university consultant. The KODE system was brought into the organization because it was deemed to fit the needs of the organization best and viewed as a universally applicable instrument (Case G: I1, 1).

Overall, triangulating the findings from interviews and document analysis indicates that, as in the first group, knowledge sharing within and beyond enabled decision making and enhanced acceptance, especially through word of mouth propaganda. Cases F and G additionally display the common pattern of facing constraints in utilizing pre-existing knowledge and integrating externally acquired knowledge. This lack of complementary knowledge limited their knowledge articulation processes, providing insight into why these cases engage in knowledge articulation to a lesser degree than the first group. Applying the learning dimensions highlights fine-grained differences that do not fit the patterns of the first group. Cases F and G differ in their extent of transferring knowledge beyond the organization, with Case G engaging in only a few activities of knowledge sharing beyond the organization. Both are limited in utilizing pre-existing knowledge and/or in integrating externally acquired knowledge by lacking complementary knowledge. Given these limitations along the two dimensions, Cases F and G are classified as engaging in knowledge articulation to a medium degree.

Knowledge Codification

Assessing the data along the learning dimensions with regard to knowledge codification, the analysis of the interview data and documents unearths that Cases F and G engage in knowledge codification to a fair to medium degree.

Codification Activities

The cross-case analysis reveals that Cases F and G varied in their level of participation in knowledge codification activities. Combining the multiple sources of data shows that Case G engaged in few codification activities using only written tools to document the workshop results and information about the skills analysis system in PowerPoint presentations (Case G: I1, 2; Doc. 1, 9, 10, 11). In contrast, Case F participated in several codification activities in both written and electronic forms. The variety of written tools encompassed key points papers, information packets, brochures, statistics, and presentations as well as electronic tools such as the Intranet and an online databank with job ads and applicants' profiles (Case F: I1, 1, 2, 3; Doc. 3, 6, 7, 9, 11, 12, 13). As demonstrated above, Case F engaged more in experiential learning than in external acquisitive learning. Combining the interview data with document analysis unearths that frequent codification occurs with experiential learning in this case. Furthermore, Cases F and G both pursued simple codification activities. Case G kept the codification of the process of developing the ideal skills profile in the workshops simple, focusing on the basics and milestones reached thus far (Case G: Doc. 1, 11). This simple codification of the progress of each workshop was not only necessary for steering the process but also for providing guidelines for future workshops in the process:

> "[Documenting the results of the workshops] helped especially in steering the process and simply to document the milestones and where we are now. And these are documents of course that we need to be able to work further on the process. It flows, this information flows into the next workshop." (Case G: I1, 2).

Similarly, Case F engaged in simple codification about the IEM because the employees were overwhelmed by an influx of daily information in the hospital (Case F: Doc. 8, 9). The HR manager lamented the problem of getting the managers to read the materials about the IEM and emphasized the importance of keeping documentation short so as to ensure the transfer of knowledge:

> "It might be that with the amount and influx of information goes to the desk of the managers each day, that they simply do not have the time to look at it in detail. And that is why we have noted that everything that is longer than a page won't be read anymore." (Case F: I1, 2).

Yet Case F also pursued a high level of detail in its codification activities. The HR manager maintained the importance of detailed documentation in the presentations for enhancing transparency about the processes and those responsible for the IEM (Case F: I1, 3; Doc. 6, 7). The detailed documentation of statistics about the number of employees to be placed in the IEM served as a justification for the internal market to the executive committee (Case F: I1, 3; Doc. 11, 12).

Codification of Content, Method, and Rationale

Applying the second learning dimension with regard to knowledge codification reveals the patterns that Cases F and G either solely codify content (know-what) or codify all three of these aspects, i.e., content, method, and rationale. In Case F, documenting statistics, advisory council discussions, and sample forms were all means to codify the content of the HR practices. They provided sample forms with criteria for sending an employee into the IEM, which were solely used to document the content of the HR practice (Case F: I1, 2; Doc. 13). The second commonality that emerged from the document and interview analysis in Cases F and G was that they participate in specific codification activities, such as documenting presentations, key points papers, workers' council agreements, and information packets that codified the content, method, and rationale behind introducing the HR practice (Case F: Doc. 3, 4, 5, 6, 7; Case G: Doc. 1, 11). Not only did Case G codify the results of workshops in PowerPoint presentations, which contain content about skills analysis, but these presentations also documented the method of how they proceeded in developing the skills profile according to a four-phase model and delineated the rationale for introducing this new system (Case G: Doc. 1, 11):

> "Since 2003 the foundation has developed further both in terms of content and strategically and that is why it needs to be examined if the skills analysis system captures the current and future demands." (Case G: Doc.1).

Thus, even when NPOs engage in few codification activities, such as Case G, they still codify the content, method, and rationale while partaking in infrequent tasks. In contrast to the first group of cases, triangulating the data suggests that these cases tend toward simple codification. This group yields evidence that codification steers the process, enhances transparency, provides guidelines for future work, ensures knowledge transfer, and serves as a justification for the HR practice. An idiosyncratic result suggests that frequent codification supports experiential learning. Applying the learning dimensions with regard to knowledge codification reveals that Cases F and G engage in knowledge codification processes to a fair to medium degree. First, there are idiosyncrasies within this second group of cases because they range from participating in few to several written and electronic codification activities. Second, Cases F and G share the pattern of engaging in codifying content and codifying all three aspects. Given the varying extent of participation along these two learning dimensions, Case F is classified as participating in knowledge codification to a fair degree and Case G to a medium degree.

Group of a Medium Degree of Learning

Assessing the cases along the learning dimensions unearths that Cases F and G can be grouped as engaging in experience accumulation, knowledge articulation, and knowledge codification processes to a medium degree. Granted, there are idiosyncratic patterns regarding the kinds and amount of participation in knowledge sharing beyond the organization, the integration of externally acquired knowledge, the extent of codification activities, and the external acquisitive learning activities given the prominence of experiential learning in Case F. Despite these idiosyncrasies, these cases are bound together through exhibiting common patterns of being constrained in learning by possessing limited previous knowledge and facing limitations in utilizing the pre-existing knowledge about the HR practice. Furthermore,

Table 5.2   Emergent Patterns in the Medium Degree of Learning

CASE	Experience Accumulation	MEDIUM DEGREE OF LEARNING	Knowledge Codification
		Knowledge Articulation	
	Extent of engaging in external acquisitive learning activities; has internal knowledge	Extent of knowledge sharing within and beyond the organization; utilizes pre-existing knowledge and integrates externally acquired knowledge	Extent of engaging in codification activities; codifies the content, method, and rationale
Case F	**(0) Medium** • **Engages in *few* external acquisitive learning activities** (Vicarious learning, yet evidence of experiential learning) • **Limited previous knowledge**	**(0) Medium** • **Engages in several activities of knowledge sharing within and beyond the organization** (Discussing in small, diverse groups in the organization, disseminating knowledge throughout the organization, transferring knowledge beyond the organization) • **Limited utilization of pre-existing knowledge and limited integration of externally acquired knowledge**	**(+) Fair** • **Engages in *several* codification activities** (Written and electronic form, simple and detailed) • **Codifies content; Codifies content, method, and rationale**
Case G	**(+) Fair** • **Engages in *several* external acquisitive learning activities** (Learning from written material, participating in training programs, hiring external support, learning through imitation) • **Limited previous knowledge**	**(0) Medium** • **Engages in several activities of knowledge sharing within the organization, but *few* activities of knowledge sharing beyond the organization** (Discussing in small, diverse groups in the organization, disseminating knowledge throughout the organization, transferring knowledge beyond the organization) • **Limited utilization of pre-existing knowledge, integration of externally acquired knowledge**	**(0) Medium** • **Engages in *few* codification activities** (Written form, simple) • **Codifies content; Codifies content, method, and rationale**

both cases participate in several activities of knowledge sharing within the organization and codify solely the content and all three aspects of the content, method, and rationale behind the HR practice. Given this external heterogeneity to the first group of cases, a second group can be identified with a medium degree of learning. This group is characterized by moderately encouraging experience accumulation, knowledge articulation, and knowledge codification during the development and implementation of HR practices. Table 5.2 depicts the learning patterns in this second group of cases and scores them according to their degree of participation in the learning processes.

Low Degree of Learning

A third group of cases can be identified from the rich data that participated in the learning processes to a lesser degree than the previous groups. Assessing the data along the learning dimensions reveals that a third group of cases (Cases B and C) engages in learning to a low degree.

Experience Accumulation

The cross-case analysis unearths that Cases B and C engage in experience accumulation to a low degree along the learning dimensions of (1) external acquisitive learning, and (2) the role of internal knowledge.

External Acquisitive Learning

Unlike the former groups of cases, Cases B and C engaged in few external acquisitive learning activities. Neither of the cases hired external support. Case B only engaged in learning from written material and vicarious learning when introducing their pay for performance system (Case B: I1, 1; Doc. 1). Case C participated in training programs and in learning through imitation. The rich case data revealed that both of these cases engaged in these activities to a very low extent in comparison with the other cases. In contrast to the groups with a high or medium degree of learning, vicarious learning in Case B consisted solely of learning informally from for-profit organizations' experiences with the HR practice given the perceived lack of information in the nonprofit sector. As the executive director stated,

> "When introducing it, of course, reading, discussing with institutions who had implemented something similar. Those weren't museums, rather they were classic for-profit organizations. Because if I think about it, we've been doing this for almost six years and hardly anyone in the cultural sector has thought about this." (Case B: I1, 1).

There is no evidence of maintaining practices that are in line with nonprofit needs and goals in gaining knowledge. Instead, the interview data from Case B indicates that acquisitive learning was constrained due to the lack in organizations, which introduce pay for performance systems into the cultural sector (Case B: I1, 1; I2, 1). This evidence suggests that barriers to experience accumulation may stem from a lack of knowledge and experience in the nonprofit sector. Case C also only engaged in a few acquisitive learning activities. Regarding participating in training programs, the executive director took part in a distance learning course in social and health services that covers the issue of goal setting among other topics (Case C: I1, 1). In addition, interview and document data demonstrate that learning through imitation occurred as they acquired their knowledge about the HR practice by directly copying the materials from their state association (Case C: Doc. 2, 3):

> "Then we looked at the appraisal questionnaire which our state association had developed. Then we said 'we'll take it like it is.' It fits to us too and we then started with having the talks." (Case C: I1, 1).

As with the second group of cases of a medium degree of learning, Case C did not deem it necessary to adapt the HR practice to its own organizational needs. When asked about how the state association developed the HR practice, the executive director answered,

> "No, the state association didn't hire any external people for it. They developed it themselves and in the context of benchmarking they looked at how it's done elsewhere. You don't always have to reinvent the wheel." (Case C, I1:1).

Again, the metaphor of reinventing the wheel surfaces as justification for copying HR practices.

The Role of Internal Knowledge

The interview data reveal that these cases share the commonality of having limited pre-existing knowledge about implementing the HR practice. In Case B, the executive director commented that, although previous contact with pay for performance elements did exist in a previous job, this explicit knowledge was limited in that it did not encompass direct implementation:

> "I didn't implement it anywhere else but there was contact before with having worked with a flexible element in contracts." (Case B: I1, 1).

Furthermore, the data from Case C specifically demonstrate that it possessed limited previous knowledge about HR practices in that the executive director lacked experience in implementing goal setting and performance appraisal:

> "I have been dealing with this for a long time even if I have never implemented it." (Case C: I1, 1).

Additionally, the members of the steering group in charge of coordinating the implementation of the HR practice also did not have prior knowledge (Case C: I1, 1). Although having dealt with other HR practices before, the executive director's knowledge was constrained with regard to the current situation. In particular, in Cases B and C, direct previous knowledge about the implementation of the HR practice was not available as an internal resource.

Thus, the patterns that emerge from these two cases differ from the previous two groups of cases in several respects. First, unlike the first group, Cases B and C engaged in few external acquisitive learning activities, and experience accumulation did not require acquiring knowledge that is in line with nonprofit values, needs, and goals. Yet these cases yield new evidence that a lack of nonprofit-specific knowledge may be related to engaging in less experience accumulation. Second, although additional empirical support is provided for learning through imitation, in contrast to the first group, imitation does not require adapting the HR practice to organizational needs because these practices are viewed as universally applicable. Despite the similar metaphor of reinventing the wheel as in the second group, there is less experience accumulation given the lack of experiential learning and external support in these cases. Finally, the analysis reveals that the previous knowledge in both Cases B and C is limited, given the limited explicit knowledge about the implementation of the HR practice. As a result, in contrast to the previous groups of cases, assessing the cases along the learning dimensions reveals that they can be characterized as engaging in experience accumulation processes to a low degree. This low degree of learning holds along both of the learning dimensions of experience accumulation in terms of displaying the patterns of participating in few external acquisitive learning activities and possessing limited previous knowledge.

Knowledge Articulation

When assessing the data with regard to knowledge articulation along the learning dimensions of (1) knowledge sharing within and beyond, and (2) applying and integrating knowledge, Cases B and C are classified as engaging in knowledge articulation to a low degree.

Knowledge Sharing Within and Beyond

In contrast to the previous groups, Cases B and C do not share the commonality of engaging in knowledge sharing within and beyond the organization. Only Case B engages in knowledge sharing within and beyond the organization, with Case C engaging solely in knowledge sharing within the organization. These cases are similar, however, in that they display the pattern of participating in few knowledge articulation activities. For example, Case B only engages in disseminating knowledge throughout the organization and transferring knowledge beyond the organization. Case C, in contrast, only participates in discussing in small, diverse groups in the organization and disseminating knowledge throughout the organization. For example, Case C formed a steering group that was broadly composed of different levels of employees and representatives of the workers' council. In regular meetings, the steering group coordinated the introduction of the HR practice:

> "That's our steering group. We have the total quality management specialist, departmental heads, executive director and of course the workers' council is always at the table for these types of things." (Case C: I1, 1).

Yet, unlike the first and second groups, these diverse employees were not involved in developing the HR practice because it was copied directly from the state association (Case C: Doc. 2, 3). Instead, these meetings were solely used to coordinate and steer the implementation of the HR practice (Case C: I1, 1). Both Cases B and C disseminated knowledge about the HR practice throughout the organization via the platform of employees' meetings. Case B used these meetings to inform the employees and allay their fears about pay for performance:

> "Uncertainty arises when people are not informed correctly and we got that under control really well. And of course the employee breakfasts also play a certain role. That is definitely the case." (Case B: I2, 1).

Correspondingly, Case C informed the employees about the introduction of the HR practice during an employees' meeting (Case C: I1, 1). Both of these cases, however, emphasize that the employees were merely informed about the HR practice rather than being involved in its development. Only Case B transferred knowledge beyond the organization. In addition to engaging in informal discussions about the pay for performance system with for-profit organizations, knowledge exchange beyond the organization in Case B was supported through discussions in interorganizational networks (Case B: Doc. 6). For example, triangulating document analysis with interview data reveals that they were able to share their experiences with the implemented HR practice and provide support for other museums through the workshops of the working group museum management (Case B: Doc. 1):

> "[. . .] and what will interest my colleagues from other museums and cultural organizations the most is how we implemented it. [. . .] using our example here at the museum to show how we did it, how time-consuming the whole thing is and to provide support if another museum is planning on implementing it as well." (Case B: I1, 1).

The analysis of the multiple data sources in Cases B and C depicts these patterns of knowledge articulation with an emphasis on informing employees rather than involving them as well as on the formal mechanisms for transferring knowledge beyond the organization.

Applying and Integrating Knowledge

Furthermore, Cases B and C do not share the commonality of applying and integrating knowledge. These cases did not participate in utilizing pre-existing knowledge because previous knowledge about the implementation of the HR practice was unavailable within the organizations, as discussed in previous section on experience accumulation (Case B: I1, 1; I2, 1; Case C: I1, 1). Nevertheless, both cases engaged in integrating externally acquired knowledge. With regard to the compatibility of external knowledge, Cases B and C display similarities to the previous groups. Similar to the group of a high degree of learning, the integration of externally acquired knowledge in Case B was facilitated by complementary knowledge. They were able to integrate the knowledge from the interorganizational working group with members from the cultural sector directly into their work (Case B: Doc.1):

> "The working group on museum management [. . .] is a permanent body for sharing and discussing ideas [. . .] It's always the case that we incorporate the results directly into our work here in the museum." (Case B: I2, 1).

Likewise, the knowledge gained from the state association in Case C was fully integrated when altering HRM (Case C: Doc. 2, 3). The state association's specific experience was deemed compatible with the local chapter so that it would be introduced in entirely the same way:

> "It was a good experience and I wanted to adopt it here in the exact same way." (Case C: I1, 1).

These case examples highlight the importance of sector-specific or organization-specific knowledge for the assimilation of externally acquired knowledge. Similar to the group with a medium degree of learning, Cases B and C also faced constraints in integrating externally acquired knowledge. The knowledge gained from the distance learning course in Case C (I1, 1) was inapplicable to the situation because it was too theoretical. Furthermore, in Case B, the differences between the employees in the for-profit sector and in the museum also rendered integrating the externally acquired knowledge from discussions with for-profit firms difficult. It is characteristic of the museum that their employees vary from academics to gardeners and handymen (Case B: I2, 1; Doc. 5):

> "What was probably different [from for-profits]—and still is—is this situation that we have here in the museum that people are employed here with really different backgrounds." (Case B: I1, 1).

Thus, in contrast to first and second groups of cases, triangulating the findings drawn from interview and document analysis reveals that these cases engaged in few activities of knowledge sharing within and beyond the organization. Case C did not engage in transferring knowledge beyond the organization at all. Unlike the previous groups of cases, the evidence demonstrates that whether discussing in small, diverse groups or disseminating knowledge throughout the organization, there is little employee involvement in these knowledge articulation activities. On the one hand, Cases B and C differ from the previous groups of cases in that they do not engage in the activity of utilizing pre-existing knowledge due to the limited state of previous knowledge in these organizations. On the other hand, they exhibit similarities to both the previous groups by being enabled to integrate externally acquired knowledge that is sector-specific or organization-specific, yet are limited in integrating externally acquired knowledge given sectoral differences and the type of knowledge. Nevertheless, the analysis of the data highlights that when assessing the cases along the two learning dimensions with regard to knowledge articulation, the cases exhibit patterns that do not match the previous groups of cases. Instead, Cases B and C are classified as engaging in knowledge articulation processes to a low degree. First, Cases B and C exhibit the pattern of only engaging in a few activities of knowledge sharing within and beyond the organization. In this respect, Case C participates even less by not sharing knowledge beyond the organization at all; thus, it renders this learning dimension only partially applicable. Second, the pattern emerges that neither of the cases utilizes pre-existing knowledge, and both of the cases are limited in integrating externally acquired knowledge. Yet the cases provide new evidence that sector-specific or organization-specific external knowledge plays a crucial role in facilitating the integration of acquired knowledge. Taking these two learning dimensions together, Cases B and C participate in knowledge articulation processes to a low degree.

Knowledge Codification

Finally, by analyzing the data along the learning dimensions with regard to knowledge codification, Cases B and C engage in these processes to a low degree.

Codification Activities

Both Cases B and C engaged in few codification activities, using only written tools that ranged from a binding general agreement to conference proceedings to a handbook (Case B: Doc. 1; Case C: Doc. 1). Electronic tools were not used in either of these cases. The least amount of codification activities occurred in Case C because it imitated the HR practice directly from the state association. It directly took over its questionnaires rather than developing the HR practice (Case C: Doc. 2, 3). This is corroborated by the interview data as follows:

"That was all from our state association." (Case C: I1, 1).

"The state association developed it themselves. [. . .] they had the guidelines from somewhere." (Case C: I1, 1).

Thus, it is not surprising that the codification activities in Case C are limited to documenting the advent of goal setting and performance appraisal within the TQM handbook. The employees had all read and signed this handbook, which indicated that goal setting and performance appraisal would be introduced into the organization (Case C: I1, 1; Doc. 1). Case B also displayed a low level of participation in codification activities. These activities were limited to a written binding general agreement about the pay for performance system and publishing their experiences with the HR practice in the conference proceedings of the interorganizational museum management workshop (Case B: Doc. 1). Coinciding with this low degree of knowledge codification, Cases B and C both pursued simple codification activities. Document analysis shows that the binding general agreement in Case B merely covers the basic principles of the HR practice rather than going into detail:

"This general agreement entitled 'Using Goal Setting in the Museum' has the 'rules of the game' for formulating individual goals and was developed and accepted by all the participants as a basis." (Case B: Doc. 1).

Thus, similar to the second group of cases, Cases B and C participated in simple codification activities while they engaged in the infrequent task of introducing an HR practice.

Codification of Content, Method, and Rationale

With regard to the codification of content, method, and rationale behind the HR practice, these cases do not fit the patterns in the first or second group. Instead, the interview data and document analysis reveals that Cases B and C codify only the content and rationale behind the HR practice. Unlike the previous groups of cases, they did not engage in codifying the method of developing and implementing the HR practice. For example, in Case C, the TQM handbook mentions both the know-what of the HR practice and the reasons for introducing it into the organization in terms of defining goals (Case C: Doc.1):

> "You have to define goals. Without goals you go through things aimlessly. Working together towards goals, involving the employees, making it clear to them how important they are as employees for the organization. And to also give the employee a chance to change if necessary if there are critical issues." (Case C: I1, 1).

In Case B, both the conference proceedings of the interorganizational museum management workshop and the binding general agreement codify the content and the rationale. The proceedings titled "Goal Setting as a Sensible HR Instrument: A Case Study of the Museum" describe the concept, basic principles, stages, and activities of the HR practice (Case B: Doc.1). Document analysis shows that this contribution not only encompasses the content of the HR practice but also the reasoning behind introducing the HR practice:

> "[. . .] the employees are informed about the goals of the organization and are simultaneously urged to make a personal contribution to the organization's success through dialogue. In this manner the organization aligns its employees with the success of the organization." (Case B: Doc. 1).

These examples indicate that although the content and rationale were codified in these cases, the method was not. Case C copied rather than developed the HR practice, thereby rendering a method of developing the HR practice obsolete (Case C: Doc. 2, 3). Case B followed its own method of developing the HR practice, as illustrated by the following quote:

> "A lot of different people have thought about this, developed performance appraisal systems, be it for social behavior or with weighted answers—we don't do that at all." (Case B: I2, 1).

Thus, the case data suggest that these NPOs do not codify the method while partaking in the infrequent task of altering HRM. Unlike the previous groups of cases, neither of these cases developed the HR practice together with their employees. Both when copying an HR practice or having only the directors design the HR practice, the method of developing and implementing the HR practice is not documented. In contrast to the second group of cases, these cases provide new evidence that suggests NPOs may engage in low codification and fail to codify the method depending on their method of developing the HR practice (or lack thereof). Furthermore, unlike the first group, mostly simple codification of the development and implementation of the HR practice occurs. Given the low extent of participation along the two learning dimensions, both cases are classified as participating in knowledge codification to a low degree. As a result, they first engage in few codification activities only in written form. Second, Cases B and C differ from the first and second groups of cases in that they do not codify the method of developing and implementing the HR practice.

Group of a Low Degree of Learning

Having applied the learning dimensions to the data in cross-case analysis, Cases B and C are characterized as engaging in experience accumulation, knowledge articulation, and knowledge codification processes to a lesser degree than the previous groups. These cases are marked by common patterns in the amount of participation in learning activities, with both engaging in only few external acquisitive learning, knowledge articulation, and codification activities. Furthermore, the utilization of pre-existing knowledge does not hold as a pattern in these cases given the limited previous knowledge about the implementation of the HR practice. Finally, both cases are limited in integrating the externally acquired knowledge and only codified the content and rationale behind introducing the HR practice. In addition to internal homogeneity along the learning dimensions among the two cases, there is also external heterogeneity to the first and second groups of learning. Engaging in learning to a low degree, this group is characterized by rarely or not encouraging experience accumulation, knowledge articulation, and knowledge codification during the development and implementation of HR practices. Table 5.3 illustrates the learning patterns for this third group and the scores for each case along the learning dimensions.

Learning Encouragement and Styles of Learning

Through cross-case analysis of the eight NPOs, patterns were identified within each of these three groups that provide in-depth insight into the theory-driven research question of how NPOs develop and implement new or modified HR practices through learning processes. By empirically grounding the learning dimensions derived from theory, these patterns were sought, which help to understand how NPOs engage in the individual learning processes and allow for a precise differentiation among the degrees

Table 5.3   Emergent Patterns in the Low Degree of Learning

CASE	LOW DEGREE OF LEARNING		
	Experience Accumulation Extent of engaging in external acquisitive learning activities; has internal knowledge	**Knowledge Articulation** Extent of knowledge sharing within and beyond the organization; utilizes pre-existing knowledge and integrates externally acquired knowledge	**Knowledge Codification** Extent of engaging in codification activities; codifies the content, method, and rationale
Case B	(–) Low • **Engages in few external acquisitive learning activities** (Learning from written material, vicarious learning) • **Limited previous knowledge**	(–) Low • **Engages in few activities of knowledge sharing within and beyond the organization** (Disseminating knowledge throughout the organization, transferring knowledge beyond the organization) • **No utilization of pre-existing knowledge and limited integration of externally acquired knowledge**	(–) Low • **Engages in few codification activities** (Written form, simple) • **Codifies content and rationale**
Case C	(–) Low • **Engages in few external acquisitive learning activities** (Participating in a training course, learning through imitation) • **Limited previous knowledge**	(–) Low • **Engages in few activities of knowledge sharing within the organization,** *no* **knowledge sharing beyond the organization** (Discussing in small, diverse groups in the organization, disseminating knowledge throughout the organization) • **No utilization of pre-existing knowledge and limited integration of externally acquired knowledge**	(–) Low • **Engages in few codification activities** (Written form, simple) • **Codifies content and rationale**

of learning. The groups of learning that have been identified differ in the kinds and amount of learning activities they engage in during the development and implementation of HR practices: The group of a high degree of learning strongly engages in and thereby encourages the individual learning processes, the group of a medium degree of learning is characterized by moderately engaging in and encouraging learning, and the group of a low degree of learning rarely engages in and encourages learning when developing and implementing the HR practices.

In order to capture the extent of encouraging learning processes during the development and implementation of the HR practice, each case is scored along the learning dimensions for its level of 'learning encouragement.' This construct emerges from the characterization of the groups and is a measure of the patterns of specific actions taken by the NPOs to encourage the learning processes. Each action that encouraged learning, such as engaging in several codification activities, was coded as plus one point. No points (0) were given for actions that encouraged learning to a lesser degree, such as a limited utilization of pre-existing knowledge. Furthermore, each action that failed to encourage learning, such as not possessing previous knowledge, was coded as minus one point (–1). These points were added up in each of the cases into a score, and the differences in scores represent the variations in the patterns regarding learning in each case. Scoring these patterns serves as a preliminary tool to structure and cluster these patterns and reveals that there are differences that cannot be explained by the three degrees of learning.

Following Miles and Huberman (1994), these learning patterns were aggregated by looking for broader constructs that group the cases together according to their common patterns. This entails naming the patterns and identifying corresponding constructs by finding conceptual analogues in iteration with the theoretical literature that help to explain why these patterns occur. By aggregating the patterns according to these broader constructs, the cases are transferred into four main styles of learning, namely, integrative learning (Cases A, E, H), experiential learning (Cases D, F), exploratory learning (Case G), and administrative learning (Cases B, C) that can be seen along a continuum of encouraging learning. This continuum of encouraging learning reveals the gradual differences in encouraging learning across the four learning styles. As a result, these styles emerged in an iterative process of initially scoring and placing the cases along a continuum of encouraging learning to structure the emerging patterns and seeking broader constructs to cluster the cases according to their common patterns by cycling back to the theoretical literature. Table 5.4 displays the patterns of actions encouraging learning, levels of learning encouragement, and the four main styles of learning that emerged across the eight cases.

These varying levels of learning encouragement suggest that the NPOs differ substantially in terms of how and to what extent they encouraged the learning processes through which they developed and implemented their

Table 5.4 Level of Learning Encouragement and Styles of Learning

CASE	LEARNING PROCESS	PATTERNS OF ACTIONS ENCOURAGING LEARNING	LEVEL	STYLE
Case A	*Experience Accumulation:*	**Several** external acquisitive learning activities; **Direct** previous knowledge	10	Integrative Learning
	Knowledge Articulation:	**Several** activities of knowledge sharing within the organization; **Several** activities of knowledge sharing beyond the organization; Utilization of pre-existing knowledge; Integration of externally acquired knowledge		
	Knowledge Codification:	**Several** codification activities; Codifies content and method; Content and rationale; Content, method, and rationale		
Case E	*Experience Accumulation:*	**Several** external acquisitive learning activities; **Direct** previous knowledge	10	Integrative Learning
	Knowledge Articulation:	**Several** activities of knowledge sharing within the organization; **Several** activities of knowledge sharing beyond the organization; Utilization of pre-existing knowledge; Integration of externally acquired knowledge		
	Knowledge Codification:	**Several** codification activities; Codifies content; Content and rationale; Content, method, and rationale		
Case H	*Experience Accumulation:*	**Several** external acquisitive learning activities; **Direct** previous knowledge	10	Integrative Learning
	Knowledge Articulation:	**Several** activities of knowledge sharing within the organization; **Several** activities of knowledge sharing beyond the organization; Utilization of pre-existing knowledge; Integration of externally acquired knowledge		
	Knowledge Codification:	**Several** codification activities; Codifies content; Content and method; Content, method, and rationale		
Case D	*Experience Accumulation:*	**Several** external acquisitive learning activities; **Limited** previous knowledge	8	Experiential Learning
	Knowledge Articulation:	**Several** activities of knowledge sharing within the organization; **Several** activities of knowledge sharing beyond the organization; **Limited** utilization of pre-existing knowledge (0); **Limited** integration of externally acquired knowledge (0)		
	Knowledge Codification:	**Several** codification activities; Codifies content; Content and method; Content and rationale; Content, method, and rationale		
Case F	*Experience Accumulation:*	**Few** external acquisitive learning activities (0); **Limited** previous knowledge (0)	5	Experiential Learning
	Knowledge Articulation:	**Several** activities of knowledge sharing within the organization; **Several** activities of knowledge sharing beyond the organization; **Limited** utilization of pre-existing knowledge (0); **Limited** integration of externally acquired knowledge (0)		
	Knowledge Codification:	**Several** codification activities; Codifies content; Content, method, and rationale		
Case G	*Experience Accumulation:*	**Several** external acquisitive learning activities; **Limited** previous knowledge (0)	5	Exploratory Learning
	Knowledge Articulation:	**Several** activities of knowledge sharing within the organization; **Few** activities of knowledge sharing beyond the organization; **Limited** utilization of pre-existing knowledge (0); Integration of externally acquired knowledge		
	Knowledge Codification:	**Few** codification activities (0); Codifies content; Content, method, and rationale		
Case B	*Experience Accumulation:*	**Few** external acquisitive learning activities (0); **Limited** previous knowledge (0)	0	Administrative Learning
	Knowledge Articulation:	**Few** activities of knowledge sharing within the organization (0); **Few** activities of knowledge sharing beyond the organization (0); **No** utilization of pre-existing knowledge (0); **Limited** integration of externally acquired knowledge (0)		
	Knowledge Codification:	**Few** codification activities (0); Codifies content and rationale		
Case C	*Experience Accumulation:*	**Few** external acquisitive learning activities (0); **Limited** previous knowledge (0)	-1	Administrative Learning
	Knowledge Articulation:	**Few** activities of knowledge sharing within the organization (-1); **No** knowledge sharing beyond the organization (0); **Limited** utilization of pre-existing knowledge (-1); **Limited** integration of externally acquired knowledge (0)		
	Knowledge Codification:	**Few** codification activities (0); Codifies content and rationale		

Actions that encourage learning   Actions that fail to encourage learning (-1)

(0) learning to a lesser degree   (-1)

new or modified HR practices. At the highest level of learning encouragement, the style of *integrative learning* emerges (Cases A, E, H). This style is characterized by the pattern of integrating all three key learning mechanisms identified in the theoretical literature, namely, experience accumulation, knowledge articulation, and knowledge codification. Integrative learners share the patterns of not merely strengthening their learning activities in areas of existing knowledge but also going beyond to acquire new sources of knowledge when they develop and implement their HR practices. Aggregating these patterns from the data, integrative learning highlights the interplay between exploration through acquisitive learning, exploitation of the existing knowledge within the organization, knowledge articulation and sharing, as well as various combinations of knowledge codification (Levinthal & March, 1993; March, 1991). Zollo and Winter (2002) emphasize that organizations adopt an "opportune" mix of behavioral and cognitive processes by being able to articulate and codify knowledge while facilitating the accumulation and absorption of experience. Because there were no corresponding constructs in the literature that adequately capture the patterns of the variation, mixture, and interplay of these three learning mechanisms during the development and implementation of the HR practices, this style was subsequently termed integrative learning.

In contrast, the *experiential learning* style (Cases D, F) emerges where there are fewer actions encouraging learning as compared with the integrative learning style. Although learning is encouraged through engaging in several activities of knowledge sharing within and beyond as well as several codification activities, the patterns in this style focus mainly on the limitations in previous knowledge and the constraints in the utilization of this pre-existing knowledge and integration of externally acquired knowledge. These patterns of limitations stem from a lack of complementarity between the knowledge base of the firm and the external sources (Zahra & George, 2002). Exploitative learning did not occur because the existing knowledge was limited in this style. Aggregating these patterns of the limitations in both internally and externally acquired knowledge by iterating with the literature on experience accumulation led to identifying a style of learning that is characterized by self-learning. This style entails a strong emphasis on the pattern of introducing the HR practice through first-hand internal experiential learning that occurs inside the organizations and creates organization-specific knowledge (Zahra et al., 1999), thereby being termed experiential learning.

Although the third style of *exploratory learning* (Case G) encourages learning to a similar degree as the experiential learning style, it nevertheless forms a heterogeneous style. A different pattern emerged from the experiential learners in that the main emphasis is on acquiring knowledge about developing and implementing the HR practice from the outside rather than by engaging in self-learning. This style evolved from aggregating the prominent patterns of engaging in several acquisitive learning activities and integrating externally acquired knowledge given that the previous knowledge was limited in its applicability. The search for a corresponding construct in iteration with the literature led to the identification of a style of exploratory learning that involves innovation and discovery to develop new knowledge and expertise (Levinthal & March, 1993). Exploratory learning is critical for the organization's capacity to adapt, but too strong an emphasis on change can be detrimental for learning if the existing knowledge bases are not drawn on. This style of learning is characterized by the patterns such as the pursuit of new knowledge and new approaches when developing and implementing the HR practice. Thus, it was termed exploratory learning.

Finally, the fourth style of *administrative learning* (Cases B, C) captures the patterns in which the NPOs rarely or do not engage in actions that encourage learning other than codifying the content and rationale behind the HR practice. Aggregating these patterns of an overall low extent of engaging in acquisitive learning, knowledge sharing, and codification activities, and utilizing pre-existing knowledge, as well as being limited in the integration of externally acquired knowledge led to the identification of a fourth style of learning. This style of learning encompasses a bare minimum

Integrative Learning
(Cases A, E, H)

• characterized by **integrating all three key learning mechanisms** of experience accumulation, knowledge articulation and knowledge codification;

• do not merely strengthen their learning activities in areas of **existing knowledge**, but also go beyond to acquire **new sources of knowledge**;

• highlights the **interplay** between exploration through acquisitive learning, exploitation of the existing knowledge within the organization, knowledge articulation and sharing, as well as various combinations of knowledge codification.

Experiential Learning
(Cases D, F)

• faces limitations in previous knowledge, **constraints** in using this **pre-existing knowledge** and integrating **externally acquired knowledge**;

• **lacking complementarity** between the knowledge base of the organization and the external sources;

• characterized by **self-learning**; strong emphasis on introducing the HR practice themselves through **first-hand internal experiential learning** that occurs inside the organization and creates organization-specific knowledge.

Exploratory Learning
(Case G)

• main emphasis is on **acquiring knowledge from the outside** rather than by engaging in self-learning;

• engaging in several acquisitive learning activities and integrating externally acquired knowledge, with the **previous knowledge limited** in its applicability;

• characterized by the **pursuit of new knowledge and new approaches** when developing and implementing HR practices.

Administrative Learning
(Cases B, C)

• **rarely** or does **not engage in actions that encourage learning** other than codifying the content and rationale behind the HR practice;

• **low extent** of engaging in acquisitive learning, knowledge sharing, using pre-existing knowledge, integrating externally acquired knowledge, and codification activities;

• bare minimum of learning, e.g. merely **imitating best practices** by attempting to integrate external knowledge;

• phenomenon of rarely encouraging learning, as organizations are **not able or willing to invest in learning**.

Figure 5.9 Emergent learning styles and their main patterns.

of learning, e.g., merely imitating best practices by attempting to integrate knowledge that is gained externally. Because there was no corresponding construct in the literature that captures this pattern of the phenomenon of rarely encouraging learning, this style was termed administrative learning to depict these organizations that are not able or willing to invest in learning. Figure 5.9 displays that each of these learning styles is characterized by the main emphasis of their patterns stemming from the data.

As a result, evidence has been provided for four styles of learning and how these styles differ in encouraging the learning processes when altering their HRM. Learning has served as an appropriate lens to examine how NPOs obtain, share, and document knowledge to develop and implement HR practices. Iterating between these styles and the theoretical literature on organizational learning and dynamic capabilities entails several implications about how these NPOs learn in the alteration of HRM that confirm and add on to the literature.

First, in contrast to the literature in which the highest investment in learning occurs in knowledge codification processes given the time, effort, and resources associated with codification (Zollo & Winter, 2002), the findings from the integrative learning style reveal that high investments in learning stem from the co-presence of all three learning mechanisms. Accordingly, a high investment in learning is made through the combination of experience accumulation and knowledge articulation processes in addition to knowledge codification. Beyond codification, the integrative learners have mastered the balance between exploration through acquisitive learning and exploitation of the existing knowledge within the organization (March, 1991).

Furthermore, confirming the literature on experiential learning as purposefully engaging in acquiring knowledge through direct experience given the lack of complementary knowledge (Huber, 1991; Zahra & George, 2002), experiential learners in this case study can be understood as intentionally engaging in self-learning and generating ideas about the HR practice that lead to the creation of organization-specific knowledge. The experiential learners distinguished themselves from the other learning styles because they did not perceive that they could orient themselves to any models of HR practices, suggesting that these learners may only be convinced by experience that the frame of reference from vicarious learning is valid for learning in the organization (Huber, 1991). In line with the well-known difficulties associated with learning from experience, especially because the implications of experience are likely to be lost given the turnover of personnel (Levitt & March, 1988), the data confirm that detailed codification is crucial for learning from experience. Furthermore, the analysis of the experiential learning style also indicates that knowledge articulation and knowledge codification are related to each other. Codification aids knowledge articulation by ensuring knowledge transfer about the HR practice throughout the organization. This corroborates the initial findings in the literature on the interactions between the learning processes (Verona & Ravasi, 2003; Zollo & Winter, 2002).

Although learning through imitation (Levitt & March, 1988) emerged in several learning styles, the learning styles differed as to whether the HR practice being copied was adapted to the organization's needs. Encouraging learning to a lesser degree is associated with less concern for sector-specific barriers to imitative learning, as in the exploratory learning style. Moreover, exploratory learning is discussed in the literature as acquiring second-hand experience. This entails learning about the strategies, practices, and technologies of other organizations (Huber, 1991). The study confirms that rather than acquiring knowledge through direct experience, second-hand experience about the HR practice was acquired by the exploratory learner through learning from written material, participating in training programs, hiring external support, and learning through imitation. Exploratory learning aided the alteration of HRM by emphasizing external knowledge acquisition and buying the HR practice on the external market, especially as it was deemed unnecessary to reinvent the HR practice.

Finally, the literature on organizational learning emphasizes that organizations and individuals are more likely to learn if information is widely distributed throughout the organization (Huber, 1991). This is supported by the findings, which show that the administrative learners only engage in a few activities of knowledge sharing within the organization, failing to invest in discovering what their organizational members know. When the NPOs neglect the opportunity to distribute information, involve employees in processes of learning, and draw on their potential skills and experiences during the alteration of HRM, administrative learning results, in which the organizations are not able or willing to invest in learning. The next section will examine the adapting processes through which the NPOs alter their HRM.

ADAPTING PROCESSES

According to the dynamic capabilities approach, adapting can be understood as a variety of organizational processes through which organizations alter their resource base (Maritan & Peteraf, 2007). The theoretical literature indicates that organizations create, extend, or modify their resource base through processes involving search, decision making, and restructuring. Thus, adapting is assumed to serve as an appropriate lens to analyze how NPOs search for opportunities for altering HRM, make decisions, and restructure their resources when developing and implementing HR practices. Following the same procedure as with learning, the eight cases were assessed along the adapting dimensions as seen in Appendix A.2, leading to the identification of three groups that engage in adapting to a high, medium, and low degree. The next sections discuss the similarities and differences in the kinds and amount of participation in adapting for each group. The final aim is to identify styles of adapting that stem from aggregating the patterns from the data.

High Degree of Adapting

Assessing the data for the extent to which the NPOs engaged in the processes of search, decision making, and restructuring along the adapting dimensions unearths similarities and differences across the cases. Given their common patterns, Cases A, D, E, and H are classified as engaging in adapting to a high degree.

Search Processes

In terms of search processes, this study researches how NPOs explore internally and externally for opportunities regarding the development and implementation of HR practices and the influence of the locus of search on the alteration of HRM. The cross-case analysis of the eight cases according to the adapting dimensions of (1) exploration within and beyond the organization, and (2) engaging in local and distant search unearths that Cases A, D, E, and H are classified as engaging in search processes to a high to fair degree.

Exploration Within and Beyond the Organization

Assessing the cases along the first adapting dimension, Cases A, D, E, and H stood out in the cross-case analysis because they each participated in several activities of exploration within and beyond the organization of introspective searching within the organization using external linkages to gain new knowledge and determining the direction of search. With regard to introspective searching within the organization, each of these cases initiated the alteration of HRM through drawing on internal resources. For example, Case E initiated its change process through internal discussions among the club services department, executive directors, and external consultants, thereby spurring on the need for change in the organization:

> "The actual impetus came from the work being done in the club services department [. . .] These questions came up in the scope of this discussion in the area of club services and really led into the question-how should the entire organization set itself up? That really got its push from this discussion." (Case E: I2, 1).

In addition, all of the cases engaged in exploration beyond the organization by using external linkages to gain new knowledge. Case H drew on the external stakeholders in the advisory committees to gain advice about the change concept. Case D drew on its inter- and intraorganizational networks to gain information on compensation models. Similarly, Case A used its external linkages to the university for expertise in developing and implementing the HR practice:

> "And we thought it over [. . .] and we tried to get experts from the outside and I believe it was my colleague who had studied at the university and came up with the professor." (Case A: I2, 1).

These cases also share the commonality that a variety of different stakeholders determined the direction of search. Case E was a unique case in which the external consultants determined the direction of search. Interviews with the executive director and the head of the OD department confirm the strong role the external consultants had in steering the goals in the working groups:

> "I think they did influence the result, I think so. That their ideas and the impetus they provided- it did steer it in one direction. No question." (Case E: I2, 1).

Although the synod, i.e., the parliament, set the boundaries for search activities in the change process in Case H (I1, 1), it still gave the directors scope to develop the change concept internally.

Engaging in Local and Distant Search

The emergent patterns from the data along the second adapting dimension reveal that the locus of search in these four cases is local or a combination of local and distant searches. Local search entails being close to the organization, whether it is a different level of the same organization, the reliance on the same external consultants or stakeholders, or within the nonprofit sector. In contrast, distant search is classified as going outside of the nonprofit sector, e.g., into the for-profit or public sector. First, these cases are bound by the commonality that they all conduct local search. In Case H, local search occurred by drawing on the same external consultant used in previous organizational processes. Additionally, search was local in Case H because the organization relied on the advisory committees, committees of external stakeholders that the organization regularly uses for guidance, in developing the change concept in the departments:

> "Those are committees where external people sit who advise and guide their work. They too were allowed to participate in this process. So really everyone could provide comments." (Case H: I1, 1).

Nevertheless, case evidence suggests that the organizations also engage in distant search when local search was unsuccessful. For example, Case

A not only searched locally in its organization's subsidiary, but it also scanned locally for the experiences of NPOs. The rich case data indicate that neither of these local searches was successful in identifying opportunities for developing and implementing the HR practice. On the one hand, the subsidiary's HR practice was deemed such a catastrophe that the knowledge was inapplicable, and, on the other hand, there was a perceived lack of knowledge in the nonprofit sector. Thus, Case A was forced to engage in a distant search in for-profit and public sector organizations in order to recognize information:

> "We also looked at a performance appraisal instrument in a bank. But in the nonprofit area we didn't find anything. It doesn't exist." (Case A: I1, 3).

Moreover, Case D engaged in a local search in the intraorganizational HR managers' network of country offices and distant search in an interorganizational network of HR professionals from the for-profit sector. Yet Case D emerges as somewhat of an anomaly in the analysis because neither a local nor a distant search was entirely appropriate for developing the compensation model. For example, sectoral differences in the interorganizational network prohibited the search for information about the compensation model. The HR manager spoke of these sectoral differences as limitations:

> "[. . .] we exchange our experiences although these are mainly in the for-profit sector. [. . .] and there are always colleagues from other firms with whom I've talked to about it although that always has its limitations because the profit and nonprofit sectors tend to differ from each other very strongly." (Case D: I1, 1).

In summary, the case examples provide evidence of an internally focused search in addition to an externally focused search. Introspective searching within the organization entailed drawing on internal resources to identify and recognize opportunities, problems, and areas for altering HRM. In an externally focused search, for-profit and public sector organizations, the university, external stakeholders, as well as interorganizational and intraorganizational ties were used to search for opportunities. Furthermore, although a local search did not deviate from its past experience, two of the cases reveal the idiosyncrasy of a distant search to for-profit and public sector organizations when a local search did not prove to be successful. Assessing the data along the adapting dimensions highlights that these cases can be classified as engaging in search processes to a high to fair degree. As a first result, Cases A, D, E, and H illustrate the pattern of participating in several activities of exploration within and beyond the organization. Second, they all engage in local searches, with some cases engaging in a distant search, too. Given this distinction, Cases A and D are

classified as participating in search processes to a high degree and Cases E
and H to a fair degree.

Decision-Making Processes

This study examines how NPOs internally and externally integrate
resources and activities to make decisions and the influence of the level of
decision making on the development and implementation of HR practices.
Examining the cases according to the adapting dimensions of (1) internal and external integration of resources and activities, and (2) lower and
higher level decision making unearths that Cases A, D, E, and H engage in
decision-making processes to a high to fair degree.

Internal and External Integration of Resources and Activities

Cases A, D, E, and H emerged from the cross-case analysis of the data as
sharing the commonality of participating in several activities of internal
and external integration of resources and activities, such as negotiating
internally, pooling internal and external resources, providing decision-
making input, and addressing conflicts. In terms of negotiating internally,
each of the cases engaged in intense negotiations during the development
and implementation of the HR practice. Case H (I1, 1) had a consultative
decision-making process that flowed from the top to the bottom and back
to the top of the organization. In Case A, intense internal negotiations with
the workers' council took place in order to reach a consensus:

> "We negotiate them, every single point . . . we negotiate every single
> word and think about what do we need and why do we want to do it
> that way." (Case A: I1, 2).

In terms of pooling internal and external resources, the internal expertise of employees, managerial knowledge, and the external resources of the
board or external stakeholders were pooled. Case A was the only exception that did not engage in the external integration of resources because it
only pooled the internal expertise of the employers' and employees' representatives in making decisions. Case D gathered its employees together to
transparently discuss decisions in the weekly plenums, thereby emphasizing
the necessity of building a lobby before the plenum. Pooling together key
persons to form a lobby for the HR manager's cause was valuable for successfully communicating information (Case D: I1, 2).

In addition to drawing on internal expertise, in Case H (I1, 2), the external expertise of the various external stakeholders in the expert committee
was pooled to aid in making decisions with regard to the new work concept in one of the departments. Similarly, in Case E, external resources
were pooled in meetings with the member organizations to gather external

expertise to build a political majority and garner support for future decision making in the parliament:

> "[. . .] it is about soliciting for the structures, not within the organization because that is the realm of the board and the directors, but adapting the board structure to the key activity areas and creating a political majority so that by the time the parliament meets in 2008 this fall—these rulings will be made." (Case E: I2, 2).

In terms of providing decision-making input, steering groups, HR managers, directors, and middle managers all provide input into the decision-making process. This appeared to speed up the introduction of the HR practice by having managers prepare these decisions in advance. In Case E, the executive directors make an effort to prepare these decisions before the board meetings to ensure that these decisions get made within the strict timeframe:

> "That is the decisive point as to why we can decide so quickly and of course because currently the executive directors have the opportunity to bring about decisions in the board. [. . .] During these four weeks we try to decide things at the level of the executive directors as is practically possible." (Case E: I1, 2).

In contrast, addressing conflicts with the workers' council, supervisory committees, or external stakeholders slowed down the decision-making process in the cases. For example, non-participant observation of project group meetings with the representatives of the workers' council in Case A provided up close and real-time evidence of the critical issues that needed to be addressed. The working group members clashed over how to best name the HR practice so that the employees would not reject it. One of the members was strongly opposed to the term 'appraisal' because it sounded too harsh for the organization (Case A: OB, 1). This drew out the negotiations on the development of the HR practice, with an entire working group meeting devoted to how to name the HR practice. In Case H (I1, 2), addressing conflicts of interest with the internal supervisory committees and the external committee of bishops necessitated the organization to go through additional rounds of consultative decision-making processes.

Lower and Higher Level Decision Making

The data regarding lower and higher level decision making reveals that most of these cases engage in both lower and higher level decision making. For example, in Case A, the HR manager spoke of using the scope within decision making given to him by the executive director in order to develop the HR practice. Exercising this autonomy in decision making enhances implementing the HR practice, rendering additional coordination between him and executive director unnecessary:

> "I think that my boss gave me a lot of scope within decision making through this appointment or else he wouldn't need a head HR manager. [. . .] I can back it and I can stand behind it and then it'll most likely be implemented in that way." (Case A: I2, 2).

In Case D (I1, 1), while the executive director and board make the final decisions regarding the compensation system, the steering group members are also involved in decision making. The HR manager described this as a top to bottom and bottom to top decision-making process. Although lower level decision making served to delay the development of the HR practice, it was viewed as a necessary tradeoff to increase the acceptance of the HR practice:

> "We don't try to have a small group come up with the cure for everyone and introduce it. Instead we really try to lay it out as broadly as possible [. . .]." (Case D: I1, 2).

Similarly, in Case H, the decision-making process encompasses both lower and higher level decision making, underscoring its cooperative, consultative, and democratic nature. The final decisions are made by the board of trustees and the synod, but only after engaging in several rounds of consultations with the workers' council and employees who suggested changes that influenced decisions (Case H: I1, 2). Case E (I1, 3), in contrast, poses an idiosyncratic result because decision making occurred only at the higher levels: The division heads, employees, workers' council, and member organizations were excluded from making decisions concerning the organizational structure. Higher level decision making ensued, with the board and steering committee being solely responsible.

In summary, all of these cases engaged in internal negotiations that point to a strong emphasis on consultative and discursive decision-making processes. Second, decision making was aided and support for decisions was garnered by pooling the internal and external expertise of employees and external stakeholders, managerial knowledge, or the external resources of the board. Third, the cases share the commonality of providing input and addressing conflicts as activities that enabled the organizations to reach a consensus, gain support for, and prepare decisions in advance. Furthermore, most of these cases also participate in lower level decision making, as seen in the employees' autonomy in decision making. The lengthier decision-making processes arising out of including employees are viewed as necessary to enhance the acceptance of the HR practice. As a first result, the cases illustrate the pattern of engaging in several activities of internal and external integration of resources and activities. Second, most of the cases share the pattern of lower and higher level decision making. Based on the varying extent of participation, Cases D and H are classified with a high degree of engaging in decision making and Cases A and E as a fair degree.

Restructuring Processes

This study investigates how NPOs reconfigure their resources for the development and implementation of new or modified HR practices. Furthermore, it examines the influence of the generation of new resource combinations on the alteration of HRM. The cross-case analysis according to the adapting dimensions of (1) resource reconfiguration activities of adding, transferring, deleting, and recombining resources in the alteration of HRM and (2) generating new resource combinations to better match the environment reveals that Cases A, D, E, and H are classified as participating in restructuring processes to a high degree.

Resource Reconfiguration Activities

Cases A, D, E, and H display the common pattern that each of these organizations engages in several resource reconfiguration activities. Regarding resource addition, the four cases added financial resources, human resources, new positions, departments, and hierarchical levels during the development and implementation of their HR practices. For instance, Case D provided supplementary financial resources for the difference between the old and new salaries while restructuring the compensation model (Case D: I1, 1, Doc. 1). Moreover, adding human resources to "disburden" the HR manager in Case A was perceived as making these employees more responsive during the implementation of the HR practice (Case A: I2, 2). Similarly, Case E not only added human and financial resources but it also added new departments and hierarchical levels to the organization in the change process. This new business area represented reverting to old organizational structures. Namely, it previously had this same three-part structure but had changed it when it proved unsuccessful. Yet even these negative experiences were not sufficient to overcome this past structure:

> "We already had this in 1998. But it didn't prove to be successful back then. That's why we changed it then. But now we are of the opinion that after all of the results, the goals, the performance profiles, after all the discussions in the meantime—that we have to create this new area again." (Case E: I1, 3).

In terms of transferring resources, several of these cases transferred their financial, managerial, human, and physical resources and fields of work. For example, Case A transferred financial resources during the implementation of the HR practice by allocating these resources to the HRD measures. After implementing the HR practice, there was a heightened responsiveness to the employees' needs as funds were transferred for further development training courses (Case A: I1, 4). In Cases E and H, human resources were transferred with resource deepening occurring as positions were filled internally rather than acquiring new resources externally. In Case H (I1, 2), in addition to human resources, physical resources were also transferred to different departments to enable them to work after implementing the change process. Furthermore, because of financial cuts, they were no longer able to work on all of their topics and were thereby forced to transfer these areas of work to religious institutions that are affiliated with the organization (Case H; I1, 2). Case A (I1, 3, 4) transferred its scarce HR managerial resources from completing daily HR tasks to providing longer-term support to guide the implementation of HR practices:

> "You need someone who works on it and implements it into practice, who steers it and advises the employees and helps them and makes it understandable and deals with the problems." (Case A: I1, 3).

In addition, Cases D and H participated in resource deletion. In Case H (I1, 2), positions were reduced within the organization as a result of funding cuts. During the implementation of the compensation model in Case D, they had to lay off several employees and recombine their departments according to the changes that were being made in the content and direction of their work:

> "We are still restructuring but we have made a lot of changes regarding our work [. . .] we haven't had to cut salaries, so we have maintained the status quo there. We have had to lay people off. We have reduced our amount of jobs and changed the content of our work. We have combined departments and so on." (Case D: I1, 2).

Finally, resource recombination in terms of organizational structure occurred as well (Case H: I1, 2). In Case E, the employees were recombined into new positions and new modes of working in teams and in cross-departmental cooperation. This entailed resource deepening rather than extending resources through the acquisition of new employees. Previous division heads were reduced to less prestigious positions, which caused some problems:

> "And one group is especially affected, namely the division heads. Because they face grave changes. Either they will be promoted 'up top' to become a departmental head or they will descend 'down below' in the direction of participating in a team which will be built in the future." (Case E: I2, 1).

These examples of reconfiguration activities strongly drew on the employees, especially in the addition and transfer of human, financial, and work resources as well as through resource deepening and shifting fields of work.

Generating New Resource Combinations

These four cases also illustrated the pattern of generating new resource combinations. In Case A (I1, 4), the HR head manager and HR manager integrated the HR practice together horizontally with existing HR practices in a human capital management system to be able to better adapt the employees' skills to the demands on the organization. In Case D, the new compensation model is claimed to be flexible enough to enable the organization to adapt to the external and internal changes it encounters. The modification of the HR practice serves as a means to cope with change:

> "In our restructuring process we noticed that we needed a new level which we then introduced as team leader. [. . .]. So we had to add in a new level. And that's proof that we have this flexibility." (Case D: I1, 2).

Furthermore, in Case E, the structural changes in the board and organization were aligned to the content, and through this alignment the organization managed to have a continuous correspondence among the structure of the board, the organization and the fields of activity (Case E: I1, 2). By following this simple rule of aligning structure to content, Case E perceives it will enhance its ability to meet future challenges (Case E: I1, 3; I2, 2). This case example conveys the importance of achieving a fit between the strategic goals and the organizational structure. Furthermore, the structural changes led to creating a lean leadership structure that would aid them in providing services for their member organizations. The strategic vision of freeing the directors from operative work to follow the strategic goals was viewed as central to the success of restructuring the organization:

> "[. . .] the executive directors get released from doing operative work and instead do what they are actually supposed to be there for—strategically following goals, representing the sports interests, working in networks and representing interests in this area." (Case E: I1, 3).

Finally, in Case H, by combining the employees into new modes of working in interdisciplinary teams and project groups and consolidating the organization's resources into a new organizational structure (Doc. 3), the organization views itself as better able to meet its funding challenges and fulfill its goals (Case H: I1, 1).

In summary, not only were financial and human resources, new positions, departments, or hierarchical levels added, but the cases also all

Table 5.5 Emergent Patterns in the High Degree of Adapting

CASE	HIGH DEGREE OF ADAPTING		
	Search Extent of exploring within the organization and beyond; engages in local and distant search	**Decision Making** Extent of internally and externally integrating resources and activities; engages in lower and higher level decision making	**Restructuring** Extent of adding, transferring, deleting, or recombining resources; generates new resource combinations to better match the environment
Case A	**(++) High** • **Exploration within and beyond the organization** (Introspective searching within the organization to draw on their internal resources, using external linkages to gain new knowledge, variety of stakeholders play a role in determining the direction of search) • **Local and distant search**	**(+) Fair** • **Internal integration of resources and activities, *no external integration*** (Negotiating internally, pooling only internal resources, providing decision making input, addressing conflicts) • **Lower and higher level decision making**	**(++) High** • **Engages in several resource reconfiguration activities** (Addition and transfer of resources) • **Generates new resource combinations to better match the environment**
Case D	**(++) High** • **Exploration within and beyond the organization** (Introspective searching within the organization to draw on their internal resources, using external linkages to gain new knowledge, variety of stakeholders play a role in determining the direction of search) • **Local and distant search**	**(++) High** • **Internal and external integration of resources and activities** (Negotiating internally, pooling internal and external resources, providing decision making input, addressing conflicts) • **Lower and higher level decision making**	**(++) High** • **Engages in several resource reconfiguration activities** (Addition, transfer, deletion, and recombination of resources) • **Generates new resource combinations to better match the environment**
Case E	**(+) Fair** • **Exploration within and beyond the organization** (Introspective searching within the organization to draw on their internal resources, using external linkages to gain new knowledge, variety of stakeholders play a role in determining the direction of search) • *Local search*	**(+) Fair** • **Internal and external integration of resources and activities** (Negotiating internally, pooling internal and external resources, providing decision making input, addressing conflicts) • **Higher level decision making, *no lower level decision making***	**(++) High** • **Engages in several resource reconfiguration activities** (Addition, transfer, and recombination of resources) • **Generates new resource combinations to better match the environment**
Case H	**(+) Fair** • **Exploration within and beyond the organization** (Introspective searching within the organization to draw on their internal resources, using external linkages to gain new knowledge, variety of stakeholders play a role in determining the direction of search) • *Local search*	**(++) High** • **Internal and external integration of resources and activities** (Negotiating internally, pooling internal and external resources, providing decision making input, addressing conflicts) • **Lower and higher level decision making**	**(++) High** • **Engages in several resource reconfiguration activities** (Addition, transfer, deletion, and recombination of resources) • **Generates new resource combinations to better match the environment**

participated in transferring financial, managerial, human, and physical resources, thereby keeping the employees involved and responsive in the restructuring activities. Resource deletion took place with regard to human resources and the number of positions in some of the cases. Oftentimes resource deepening occurred as positions were filled internally, and most cases recombined their organizational structures and modes of working too. Moreover, the finding of reverting to old organizational structures suggests that reconfiguration entails managers relying on their past decisions. Assessing the cases along the adapting dimensions, Cases A, D, E, and H share the commonality of engaging in restructuring to a high degree. As a first result, each case participates in several resource reconfiguration activities. Second, they display the pattern of generating new resource combinations as a means to meet the challenges stemming from internal or external demands by integrating and modifying HR practices, achieving a fit between goals and structure, and combining employees into new working modes.

Group of a High Degree of Adapting

The cross-case analysis along the adapting dimensions unearths the commonality that Cases A, D, E, and H engage in search, decision-making, and restructuring processes to a high degree. These cases are characterized by the common patterns of participating in several activities of exploration within and beyond the organization, internal and external integration of resources and activities, and resource reconfiguration activities of adding, transferring, deleting, and recombining resources. In addition, they are all classified as conducting local search, engaging in lower and higher level decision making, and generating new resource combinations to better match the environment. The cases display internal homogeneity along the adapting dimensions so as to enable the identification of a first group of NPOs with a high degree of adapting. This group is grounded in the empirical data through the triangulation of multiple data sources. It is characterized by strongly encouraging adapting during the development and implementation of HR practices. Table 5.5 illustrates the patterns of adapting among this group and scores each case according to its level of participation along the adapting dimensions.

Medium Degree of Adapting

Examining the data according to the adapting dimensions revealed a second group of cases that engaged in search, decision-making, and restructuring processes to a medium degree. Cross-case analysis identified patterns that capture the similarities and differences among these cases with regard to the individual adapting processes.

Search Processes

Assessing the cases along the adapting dimensions of (1) exploration within and beyond the organization, and (2) engaging in local and distant searches, the cross-case analysis unearths that two of the cases, Cases F and G, can be classified as engaging in search processes to a medium degree.

Exploration Within and Beyond the Organization

Like the first group, Cases F and G share the commonality of engaging in exploration within and beyond the organization. Yet in contrast to this first group, these cases are limited in exploring through introspective searching within the organization. Cases F and G both only drew partially on their internal resources in initiating the alteration of HRM, which was viewed as aiding the development of the HR practice. For example, in Case F, the HR manager solely developed the IEM. Only after it was developed did he recognize the internal expertise of those already working in this area and the workers' council by putting his developed concept to discussion:

> "The basic concept [. . .] is actually a development that I conceived of for myself and in the context of how I imagined the procedures to be I developed this concept and then discussed it and presented it with the people who already have responsibility in the internal employment market and in the workers' council." (Case F: I1, 2).

In a similar vein, Case G only drew partially on the internal expertise of its employees in developing the skills analysis system. Instead of having them identify opportunities to develop the necessary managerial skills, the HR manager presented them with the 64 skills fields of the established KODE system. They admitted that they had made the employees "believe" they had created the skills profile themselves (Case G: I1, 2), which fostered its development:

> "And in this way we got to the managerial skills and then I, I don't want to say secretly, but in the background, I provided them with the 64 skills fields of KODE instead of making the managers think of such things themselves. And that's how we got it sorted and then the instrument was introduced here. [. . .]." (Case G: I1, 1).

Similar to the first group, Cases F and G engaged in exploration beyond the organization by using external linkages to gain new knowledge. In Case F, the HR manager used ties to other university hospitals to search for opportunities about introducing the IEM:

"And there are regular meetings of HR managers in the university hospitals [. . .]. And we exchange ideas. We look at what they are doing, what is working well, what isn't working so well." (Case F: I1, 2).

The HR manager in Case G similarly drew on external ties to the university in the search for the appropriate skills analysis system:

"Mr. H was one of the founding professors of the technical university of medium-sized businesses in Bielefeld and I knew him through my previous job. He presented that to us back then and he always developed it further and we simply believe that it is one of the best instruments on the market." (Case G: I1, 1).

In contrast to the first group of cases, only the HR managers play a role in determining the direction of search, rather than having a variety of different stakeholders dominate. In Case G, the HR manager solely conducted the search activities for developing the skills analysis system. He noted that the board was not involved in identifying opportunities for its introduction, having merely approved the HR practice "on a purely strategic level" (Case G: I1, 2). Similarly, in Case F (I1, 1), the HR manager solely directs the search activities and has scope in developing the concept for the IEM.

Engaging in Local and Distant Search

The emergent patterns from the data reveal that the organizations' locus of search is solely local. Cases F and G either search within the nonprofit sector or rely on the same external consultants. For example, in Case F, the locus of search was local in nonprofit university clinics. Furthermore, the idea to have an IEM stemmed in part from the board member who was previously employed at one of these university hospitals:

"The idea was there quite often. It simply came from the fact that the board member Mr. B used to be at the university hospital in Hamburg and back then they had an internal employment market." (Case F: I1, 2).

Likewise, in Case G, the HR manager conducted a search locally because he knew the consultant who developed the skills analysis system from working with him in a previous job (Case G: I1, 1). There is no case evidence that these cases were constrained in the search for opportunities as in the first group. For example, in Case G, sectoral differences did not pose a problem in gaining new knowledge about the HR practice. Instead, the HR manager noted that this universally applicable HR practice provided the chance to learn more about skills profiles of employees in foundations (Case G: I1, 2).

In summary, the local search activity indicates that these two cases identify opportunities for altering HRM in ways that remain close to past processes. It is noteworthy, however, that neither case provided evidence of being constrained in identifying opportunities in their search activities. Instead, the recognition of opportunities appeared to be enabled by searching close to their existing knowledge. Furthermore, they are limited in exploring within the organization with the HR managers drawing partially on their employees and dominating the search for opportunities because this was viewed as fostering the development of the HR practice. Thus, analyzing the data along the adapting dimensions shows deviating case data that do not fit the patterns in the first group. The rich case data provide evidence of the common patterns that exploration within the organization is limited and both engage only in a local search. Thus, the cross-case analysis unearths that Cases F and G differ from the first group by participating in search processes to a medium degree.

Decision-Making Processes

Assessing the cases according to the adapting dimensions of (1) internal and external integration of resources and activities, and (2) lower and higher level decision making reveals that Cases F and G engage in decision-making processes to a medium degree.

Internal and External Integration of Resources and Activities

Cases F and G engage in fewer decision-making activities that involve the internal integration of resources and activities and none externally integrate resources such as the expertise of external stakeholders. With regard to negotiating internally, both of the cases participated in intense internal negotiations with the workers' council, which delayed the processes. In Case F, intense negotiations took place among the workers' council, managers, and the employees from HR departments in order to agree on the concept for the IEM for employees with health restrictions and to optimize the processes of the IEM. The HR manager commented that it took a year longer due to the different perspectives that needed to be negotiated:

> "We needed a whole other year. [. . .] And that was because with regard to the ill employees we developed an entire concept with the workers' council and there were very different perspectives at first. That required a few discussions and we optimized the current procedures and processes [. . .]." (Case F: I1, 2).

Similarly, in Case G (I1, 1), intense negotiations took place in several rounds of discussions with the workers' council given its repeated criticism of the reliability of the skills analysis system. In terms of pooling internal and external resources, in both of the cases, only the internal resource of the expertise of the employees was drawn on in both cases. In Case F, the HR manager drew on the expertise of the employees within the IEM to determine the practicality of the concept and make changes to the concept he had developed:

> "I am more of a theorist because I don't do the basic work and those are areas that I can't really have an overview on from my desk. And it is also important to me to see what it is that I want to implement into practice. And they say because of these and these reasons it won't work and then you can adjust it." (Case F: I1, 2).

An idiosyncratic result emerged as Case F also engaged in providing decision-making input. The HR manager together with his employees from the HR and HRD departments provided input on the subject of the design of IEM. As the HR manager noted, providing feedback to the board enabled decision making:

> "And then we did it that we had relatively large scope and we always tried to determine the key points, how it can work and then we gave them feedback and presented these key points to the board. Then they gave their okay and we did the detailed implementation and that actually worked." (Case F: I1, 1).

Given the lack of evidence of addressing conflicts and externally integrating resources in decision making, Cases F and G engaged in less decision-making activities than the first group of cases.

Lower and Higher Level Decision Making

The two cases both engaged in lower and higher level decision making. For example, in Case F, the board, HR manager, and representatives of the workers' council are responsible for decision making. Although the board makes the final decisions regarding the IEM, the HR manager and the workers' council reach a consensus about the content and details of the HR practice. As the HR manager commented on this process of finding a common ground with the workers' council,

> "[. . .] and then it was about coordinating with the workers' council to reach a consensus, where are the areas of conflict and how do we find a common ground. And to get this basic agreement." (Case F: I1, 3).

Accordingly, in Case G, the HR manager makes decisions about the introduction of the skills analysis system together with the managers and employees in the workshops and the workers' council. The data indicate that integrating employees delays decision making given the difficulty of finding the time to include the managers, employees, and the workers' council, yet it enhances the acceptance of the HR practice (Case G: I1, 2).

In summary, the analysis confirms the first group of cases regarding the effects of including lower levels in decision making on the pace of developing and implementing HR practices and on enhancing the acceptance of the HR practice. In addition, these cases share the commonality of engaging in intense internal negotiations, suggesting again that decision making in NPOs is discursive and aims at finding a consensus. In contrast to the first group, however, the HR managers did not draw on external resources. Instead they negotiate internally and only pool together the internal expertise of their employees. Thus, the dimension of internal and external integration of resources and activities does not entirely capture the extent of their participation. Although these cases display the pattern of lower and higher level decision making, these cases engage in decision-making processes to a medium degree. As a first result, the cases illustrate the pattern of not participating in the external integration of resources and activities. Second, they engage in fewer decision-making activities, with only Case F providing decision-making input and neither case addressing conflicts.

Restructuring Processes

By examining the data along the adapting dimensions of (1) resource reconfiguration activities, and (2) generating new resource combinations to better match the environment, the analysis demonstrates that Cases F and G can be classified as engaging in restructuring processes to a high to medium degree.

Resource Reconfiguration Activities

The rich evidence from the cases indicates that Cases F and G engaged to a varying degree in resource reconfiguration activities. Case G only participated in a few activities by transferring and recombining its resources during the development and implementation of the skills analysis system. For example, resources were transferred by shifting resources to the managers so that they could be multipliers for the system to make the employees more willing to accept the HR practice (Case G: I1, 1). Furthermore, there was only one instance of resource recombination in Case G as the skills profile was integrated with the managers' performance appraisal and the employees' feedback on managers' performance, rendering the strategically integrated skills analysis system the center of the managerial instruments:

> "[It] influenced the tasks-goal discussions [. . .] the capability analysis- they flow into there too. And in the HRD analysis. We tried to develop it into a strategically integrated skills model. It is not just about

any applicants' tests or something but it should serve as the nucleus, as the center of the managerial instruments." (Case G: I1, 2).

In contrast, Case F participated in several resource reconfiguration activities. For example, resource addition occurred as another position was added for the IEM and the tasks of a position in HRD were transferred to the IEM so as to provide ongoing support for the employees and department heads. The addition and transfer of these human resources enable the hospital to support the employees entering the IEM for up to six months and support the department heads using the IEM. Moreover, resource addition occurred as the board added financial resources for the incentive system:

> "The tipping point was the question of the incentive system. [. . .]
> But that went relatively well and thus the board really provided support where it was necessary and then also the money for the incentive system." (Case F: I1, 1).

In addition, given the nature of the HR practice, human resources were transferred in the IEM. When these employees with health restrictions are placed successfully through the IEM, they are transferred into service and DRG documentation positions in a relatively short time period. The HR manager in Case F (I1, 3) also threatened to remove these human resources from the departments in order to exert pressure on the departments to invest financially in these employees and transfer financial resources back to the HR department. Furthermore, financial resources were transferred during the implementation of the IEM from the state employment office. After engaging in interorganizational networks with other university hospitals, Case F (I1, 2) learned that the financial resources spent on training courses for the employees within the IEM can be reimbursed by the employment office. Problems arose, however, when the department heads attempted to transfer employees through the IEM due to issues related to employment laws rather than health restrictions. In this respect, Case F was supported by the round table, which was made up of HR employees, workers' council representatives, and the organizational physician, who were charged with assessing the transfer of employees:

> "[. . .] then the HR employees have to convene this round table and assess if it is actually a health problem or an employment law issue. [. . .] and then we had this mixing of the health and employment law issues and that has to be kept separate and worked on separately." (Case F: I1, 3).

Whereas Case G engages in only two instances of the transfer of work resources and the recombination of existing HR practices, Case F participated in several resource reconfiguration activities of resource addition and transfer.

Generating New Resource Combinations

Both of the cases exhibit the common pattern of generating new resource combinations to better match the environment. For example, in Case F, interview data reveal that transferring employees with health restrictions is important in light of the current demographic developments, the longer working periods until retirement, and the need for flexibility within the organization. By deploying these human resources into new areas in the organization and retraining these employees into service positions, Case F was able to unburden the physicians in their daily work from operative tasks:

> "And because it is important for ensuring revenues we developed the concept that the documentation assistants do the coding, the physician reviews it and signs it and they are disburdened. A few of the ill employees [. . .] have switched into these positions and are working successfully there." (Case F: I1, 2).

The rich case data also yielded empirical support that the IEM is becoming institutionalized as a means to determine which competences the current employees have, which competences are needed for the types of jobs in the future, and how this fits to the overall organizational strategy (Case F: I1, 2, 3). Thus, this case provides new evidence that deploying human resources through the IEM helps to recombine and retrain the human resources to better fit the organizational strategy and meet the challenges that the departments will face in the future. Similarly, in Case G, not only was the skills management system used to derive the necessary HRD measures for the managers and employees in order to better equip them for addressing the challenges in their work, but it was also integrated for new job applicants in top managerial positions. The organization aimed to be able to better attract and identify top managers; thus by integrating the HR practice into the applicant process, the organization is better able to identify these qualified managers:

> "We had two pilot phases [with new applications for managerial positions] and are thinking about expanding it because it really was beneficial." (Case G: I1, 2).

In summary, both of these cases provide rich evidence that the combination of resources is perceived as aiding the organizations in ensuring a fit with the organizational strategy, meeting their challenges, and fulfilling their organizational goals. Overall, both Cases F and G share the pattern of engaging in the transfer of resources including human, managerial, and work resources. Managers played a crucial role in resource reconfiguration, and interorganizational ties are central to the transfer of resources. Unlike the first group, resource recombination occurred less in the development and implementation of the HR practice. Assessing the cases along the adapting dimensions, the analysis reveals that Cases F and G are characterized by a high to medium degree of participation in adapting. First, idiosyncrasies emerge because these two cases differ in the extent to which they participate in resource reconfiguration, ranging from few to several resource reconfiguration activities. Second, Cases F and G share the similar pattern of generating new resource combinations. Given their differing degrees of participation, Case F is classified as participating to a high degree, whereas Case G is classified as participating to a medium degree.

Group of a Medium Degree of Adapting

The cross-case analysis of the data along the adapting dimensions unearths that Cases F and G can be grouped as engaging in adapting processes to a lesser degree than the first group. Granted, these cases are characterized by the same patterns of engaging in exploration beyond the organization, higher and lower level decision making, and generating new resource combinations to better match the environment, yet they differ from the first group by having only limited exploration within the organization, only local search, and participating to a lesser extent in the internal integration of resources and activities, with external integration not occurring at all. Furthermore, the search for opportunities to alter HRM is enabled locally, and the cases vary in their extent of resource reconfiguration activities. The analysis has thus revealed that there is evidence of internal homogeneity along the adapting dimensions as well as external heterogeneity to the first group. This second group of adapting to a medium degree is characterized by moderately encouraging search, decision making, and restructuring during the development and implementation of HR practices. The patterns of adapting in this group and the levels of participation along the adapting dimensions are illustrated in Table 5.6.

Low Degree of Adapting

Coding and analyzing the data along the adapting dimensions reveal a third group of cases (Cases B and C) that is characterized by being engaged in the adapting processes to a low degree.

Search Processes

Applying the adapting dimensions of (1) exploration within and beyond the organization, and (2) engaging in local and distant searches, Cases B and C differ from the first and second groups by participating in search processes to a low degree.

Table 5.6 Emergent Patterns in the Medium Degree of Adapting

CASE	MEDIUM DEGREE OF ADAPTING		
	Search Extent of exploring within the organization and beyond; engages in local and distant search	**Decision Making** Extent of internally and externally integrating resources and activities; engages in lower and higher level decision making	**Restructuring** Extent of adding, transferring, deleting or recombining resources; generates new resource combinations to better match the environment
Case F	**(0) Medium** • **Limited exploration within the organization; Exploration beyond the organization** (Introspective searching within the organization to draw partially upon their internal resources, using external linkages to gain new knowledge, only the HR managers play a role in determining the direction of search) • **Local search**	**(0) Medium** • **Internal integration of resources and activities, no external integration** (Negotiating internally, pooling only internal resources, providing decision making input) • **Lower and higher level decision making**	**(++) High** • **Engages in *several* resource reconfiguration activities** (Addition and transfer of resources) • **Generates new resource combinations to better match the environment**
Case G	**(0) Medium** • **Limited exploration within the organization; Exploration beyond the organization** (Introspective searching within the organization to draw partially upon their internal resources, using external linkages to gain new knowledge, only the HR managers play a role in determining the direction of search) • **Local search**	**(0) Medium** • **Internal integration of resources and activities, no external integration** (Negotiating internally, pooling only internal resources) • **Lower and higher level decision making**	**(0) Medium** • **Engages in *few* resource reconfiguration activities** (Transfer and recombination of resources) • **Generates new resource combinations to better match the environment**

Exploration Within and Beyond the Organization

Cases B and C share the commonality of engaging in exploration within and beyond the organization to a low extent. These cases only use their external linkages to gain new knowledge. In Case B, the executive director and director draw on their interorganizational ties to for-profit firms that had implemented similar pay for performance systems when initiating the alteration of HRM (Case B: I1, 1; I2, 1). Similarly, Case C solely uses its external linkages to its state association to sense for information and developments about HR practices (Case C: Doc. 2, 3). They followed the state association, which had just introduced this HR practice:

> "That was all from our state association. We had finished the process of getting certified in TQM and our TQM had been introduced. We then talked about whether we wanted to also do such an appraisal." (Case C: I1, 1).

Neither of these organizations drew on their internal resources in initiating change. A further commonality is that in both of the cases, only the executive director determines the direction of search activities. In Case C, the executive director "simply identified it as an HR instrument" (Case C: I1, 1). The executive director in Case B determined the direction of search regarding the development of the HR practice. The idea to introduce a pay for performance system stemmed from the executive director's previous job experience as a cultural consultant:

> "The idea came from Mr. P. I was involved in the planning, and we implemented it together, but someone always has the idea. Sometimes it emerges from discussions, but Mr. P came from . . . it has to do with his resume." (Case B: I2, 1).

Thus, the case evidence emphasizes a low level of exploration for opportunities beyond the organization but none within the organization.

Engaging in Local and Distant Search

The cases display idiosyncratic patterns in terms of the locus of search. For example, Case C (Doc. 2, 3) only engaged in a local search. A local search depended on past experience of following the developments in the state association:

> "It all started with our state association. They developed new work guidelines which got rid of the automatic grouping into a higher pay scale. [. . .] That was all from our state association." (Case C: I1, 1).

Case B, however, only engaged in a distant search, a finding that is idiosyncratic from both of the previous groups of cases. The locus of search was distant because information was sought solely from for-profits; there was no perceived information in the cultural sector (Case B: I1, 1). Thus, a local search consisted of identifying opportunities from a different level of the same organization and occurred similarly to past processes. The result of a distant search, however, entailed searching for opportunities for the alteration of HRM in for-profit firms without even considering scanning within the cultural organizations in the nonprofit sector.

Combining the interview data with document analysis reveals an emphasis in these cases on external search solely because there is no recognition of the internal resources and capabilities during the development of the HR practice. Only the executive directors determine the direction of search, relying on external linkages to gain new information through inter- or intraorganizational ties. The rich case data indicate that Cases B and C engage in search activities to an even lesser degree than the other groups of cases. For instance, these two cases display the pattern that search can fully occur externally in organizations because exploration did not occur within the organization. Second, these cases highlight idiosyncratic results regarding the locus of search, with Case C solely searching locally and Case B providing empirical evidence of a distant search. Thus, the cross-case analysis unearths that these cases are distinct in that they engage in search processes to a low degree in comparison with the previous groups of cases.

Decision-Making Processes

The analysis of the case data along the adapting dimensions shows that Cases B and C are classified as having a low degree of participation in decision-making processes.

Internal and External Integration of Resources and Activities

Neither of these cases engages in external integration of their resources to make decisions about the development and implementation of the HR practice. Instead, both of the cases only pool their internal expertise. Case B (I2, 1) drew on the internal managerial knowledge of the executive director for decision making about the pay for performance system. Case C (I1, 1) gathered the expertise of different employees and the workers' council together in the steering group for making decisions about the HR practice. Only Case C engaged in negotiations with the workers' council regarding the introduction of goal setting and performance appraisal. These negotiations, however, were not described as being critical or intense as in the previous groups. Instead, it was more symbolic because the workers' council merely needed a bit of clarification before it approved of introducing the HR practice (Case C: I1, 1). Case B did not engage in any internal negotiations with its employees. At the time of introducing the pay for performance system, it did not have a workers' council (Case B: Doc. 2). The executive director and director merely decided to introduce the HR practice into the museum's development association because the previous organizational form did not allow for it. Once the museum was reorganized as a foundation with a workers' council, the already well-accepted HR practice was adopted directly without any difficulties (Case B: I1, 1).

Lower and Higher Level Decision Making

In terms of the second adapting dimension, both Cases B and C illustrate the pattern of only participating in higher level decision making. This result contradicts the previous case evidence, which suggests NPOs tend toward democratic, discursive decision-making processes. Instead, in Case B (Doc. 1), solely the executive director and director decided how the practice would be developed and implemented in the organization. This finding is corroborated by the interview data:

> "Mr. P was a member of the development association and he suggested this instrument and we tentatively started with it." (Case B: I2, 1).

In addition, in Case C, only the executive director decided to introduce goal setting and performance appraisal. As the executive director commented on quickly making the decision,

> "I sat down with the steering group and decided to introduce it here." (Case C: I1, 1).

In summary, neither of these cases provides evidence of lower level decision making. Instead, decision making ensued relatively quickly, taking place only at the level of the top managers. Thus, these cases yield deviating evidence from the pattern of consultative decision-making processes in NPOs. In Case B, this may be due in part to the lack of a workers' council, but even in Case C, there was still little evidence of involving the employees in decision making. Furthermore, there was no evidence of addressing conflicts or providing decision-making input. Instead, the cases participate in few decision-making activities that are limited to the internal integration of managers' and employees' expertise as external resources were not drawn on. Triangulating multiple sources of data reveals that not only do Cases B and C share the pattern of participating in less internal integration of resources and activities and no external integration, but they also engage only in higher level decision making. In summary, assessing the cases according to the adapting dimensions shows that these cases differ from the previous groups by engaging in decision-making processes to a low degree.

Restructuring Processes

Analyzing the interview data and document analysis according to the adapting dimensions indicates that Cases B and C engage in restructuring processes to a non-existent to low degree.

Resource Reconfiguration Activities

In terms of the resource reconfiguration activities of adding, transferring, deleting, and recombining resources, Cases B and C illustrate the pattern of not engaging or only participating in a few of these activities. In neither of the cases were resources added, deleted, or recombined during the development and implementation of the HR practice. Only in Case B did the transfer of resources occur. As part of the pay for performance system that had been introduced, financial resources were transferred to the employees in the form of a bonus (Case B: Doc. 1). The director noted the freedom of resource allocation it has in terms of the amount of financial resources being transferred:

> "And the reality is that about 70% get the maximum bonus, 20–25% get less than that, but 3–4% are above the bonus. This means that there are employees who are so involved that we say 'okay, you have done your job so well that you don't get 15 but 20'. That's the leeway that Mr. P and I have." (Case B: I2, 1).

In contrast, Case C did not participate in any resource reconfiguration activities. The executive director did not perceive the need to add or transfer any supportive resources for the implementation of goal setting and performance appraisal. The executive director noted that they ran out of time and failed to implement the HR practice for all of the employees:

> "We did it in a way that was really time-consuming. Unfortunately we weren't able to evaluate all the employees last year because there were just too many. But we'll improve it this year." (Case C: I1, 1).

Case C recognized the benefits of decentralizing the implementation of the HR practice to the respective department levels during the next implementation round:

> "I am going to do it differently now. I will only personally have the talk with my administrative employees. The departments will then do it themselves." (Case C: I1, 1).

Overall, these cases are characterized by the pattern of non-existent to low participation in the resource reconfiguration activities. The data in Case

B corroborate the role of managers in restructuring processes, pointing to the importance of managerial freedom to allocate their financial resources. Case C is idiosyncratic in that it failed to implement the HR practice for all employees by not adding or transferring supportive resources.

Generating New Resource Combinations

Neither of the cases provides evidence of generating new resource combinations during the development and implementation of the HR practice. Unlike the previous groups, the data from interviews and documents do not suggest that the HR practices were integrated with other HR practices to aid the organization in meeting its challenges. Instead, in Case B, the pay for performance system was not integrated into the HR practice of work planning but merely viewed as the next logical step for certain employees in higher positions to have their performance evaluated and rewarded (Case B: I2, 1; Doc. 5). Correspondingly, in Case C (Doc. 2, 3), the HR practice was not modified or integrated with the existing HR practices. Rather, the executive director wanted to let the process of goal setting and performance appraisal evolve over time in each implementation round (Case C: I1, 1). The HR practice was simply viewed in terms of enabling the director to make less arbitrary decisions with regard to which employees to lay off:

> "Sometimes you have to decide whether you want to lay off an employee. I can use these criteria, these results. I then have some indication for saying I would rather lay him off than him." (Case C: I1, 1).

Similarly, in Case B, the HR practice is not viewed in terms of enabling the organization to meet its external challenges. Instead, the goal setting aspect of the pay for performance system is perceived as internally structuring the employees' work (Case B: Doc. 1):

> "The monetary aspect is just one aspect. [. . .] But to talk to him about content three or four times that is much, much more important. That has something to do with content, structure, work structure and the appraisal has something to do with social aspects [. . .]." (Case B: I2, 1).

In summary, these two cases are bound by the common pattern that resources were not combined to better match the environment. The data indicate that the HR practices were not integrated with existing HR practices, and the HR practices were viewed internally in terms of aiding in operational decision making and structuring work, rather than adapting to change. Furthermore, the case evidence reveals that resources are not added, deleted, or recombined, with financial resources being transferred only in Case B given the managers' freedom to allocate their financial resources. Case C yields evidence that a failure to perceive the need to add or transfer supportive resources is associated with being unable to implement the HR practice. As a result, applying the adapting dimensions indicates that these cases diverge from the patterns in the previous groups. First, the cases are characterized by low to non-existent participation in resource reconfiguration activities. Second, unlike the previous groups, resource combinations are not generated to better match the environment. In conclusion, these cases do not participate in restructuring (Case C) or to a low degree (Case B).

Group of a Low Degree of Adapting

Having assessed the data along the adapting dimensions, these cases are characterized as engaging in search, decision-making and restructuring processes to a low degree. Cases B and C differ from the groups of a high and medium degree of adapting, with both cases exhibiting common patterns of engaging only in exploration beyond the organization, the internal integration of resources and activities, and in no or only few resource reconfiguration activities. Furthermore, the cases display idiosyncratic patterns in terms of their locus of search and the dimensions regarding decision-making activities only apply partially to these cases. Cases B and C share the pattern that they do not participate in the external integration of resources and activities and engage only in higher level decision making. In terms of restructuring, both cases do not generate resource combinations to better match the environment. Having achieved internal homogeneity between the two cases and external heterogeneity to the previous groups reveals the third group, which is classified by low encouragement of search, decision making, and restructuring during the development and implementation of HR practices. Table 5.7 displays both the extent of engaging in adapting processes according to the patterns in this group and the scores for each case along the adapting dimensions.

Adapting Encouragement and Styles of Adapting

As a result, three distinct groups of adapting have been identified that differ in terms of their extent of engaging in the adapting processes to a high, medium, or low degree. These groups provide in-depth insight into this study's theory-driven research question of how NPOs develop and implement new or modified HR practices through adapting processes. Patterns were sought within each of the groups by empirically grounding the theoretically derived dimensions of the adapting processes. Stemming from these commonalities and differences, the case study evidence has shown that the groups of adapting differ in the kinds and amounts of adapting activities they engage in during the development and implementation of HR practices. Namely, the findings range from a group of a high degree

Table 5.7   Emergent Patterns in the Low Degree of Adapting

CASE	LOW DEGREE OF ADAPTING		
	Search Extent of exploring within the organization and beyond; engages in local and distant search	**Decision Making** Extent of internally and externally integrating resources and activities; engages in lower and higher level decision making	**Restructuring** Extent of adding, transferring, deleting or recombining resources; generates new resource combinations to better match the environment
Case B	(-) Low • **Exploration beyond the organization, not within the organization** (Using external linkages to gain new knowledge, only the executive directors play a role in determining the direction of search) • *Distant* **search**	(-) Low • **Internal integration of resources and activities, no external integration** (Pooling only internal resources) • **Higher level decision making, no lower level decision making**	(-) Low • **Engages in *few* resource reconfiguration activities** (Transfer of resources) • **Does not generate new resource combinations to better match the environment**
Case C	(-) Low • **Exploration beyond the organization, not within the organization** (Using external linkages to gain new knowledge, only the executive directors play a role in determining the direction of search) • *Local* **search**	(-) Low • **Internal integration of resources and activities, no external integration** (Negotiating internally, pooling only internal resources) • **Higher level decision making, no lower level decision making**	(--) None • **Engages in *no* resource reconfiguration activities** • **Does not generate new resource combinations to better match the environment**

of adapting that is characterized by participating in several activities that strongly encourage adapting, to a group of a medium degree of adapting that is limited in its adapting activities and classified as moderately encouraging adapting, to a group of a low degree of adapting that is characterized by a rarely encouraging adapting, engaging in no to few adapting activities during the development and implementation of HR practices in NPOs.

In order to capture how extensive the encouragement of adapting processes is during the development and implementation of the HR practice, each case is scored for its level of 'adapting encouragement.' This construct emerges from the characterization of the groups and measures the specific actions the NPOs use to encourage the adapting processes. Each action that encouraged adapting, such as the internal integration of resources and activities or several resource reconfiguration activities, was coded as plus one point. No points (0) were given for actions that encouraged adapting to a lesser degree, such as limited exploration within the organization. Finally, each action that failed to encourage adapting, such as not generating new resource combinations to better match the environment, was coded as minus one point (–1). These points were added up for each case and summed into a score that reveals the differences in patterns among the cases in terms of adapting. As with learning, the scores function as a preliminary tool to structure and cluster the patterns detected in the three groups. The remaining differences among the cases require aggregating the various patterns by using corresponding constructs from the theoretical literature or naming the overarching patterns that emerge inductively from the data to capture these differences (Miles & Huberman, 1994). By aggregating the common patterns in an iterative process with the dynamic capabilities literature, the cases are transferred into three main styles of adapting, namely, decentralized adapting (Cases D, A, H), local adapting (Cases E, F, G), and managerial adapting (Cases B, C) that are placed along a continuum of encouraging adapting. This continuum displays the gradual differentiation among the cases according to their patterns to which they encourage adapting across the three adapting styles. Table 5.8 displays the patterns of actions encouraging adapting, levels of adapting encouragement, and the three main styles of adapting that emerged across the eight cases.

The range in the level of adapting encouragement indicates that the NPOs vary in terms of how and to what extent they encouraged the adapting processes through which they developed and implemented their HR practices. The style of *decentralized adapting* (Cases D, A, H) captures the highest levels of adapting encouragement in all three adapting processes. Most important, however, the decentralized adapting style is characterized by the pattern of engaging in the three adapting processes at the lower levels of the organization. For example, in addition to scanning the environment, exploration occurs within the organization at the level of the employees. Beyond mere higher level decision making, lower level decision making ensues. Finally, resource reconfiguration involves the employees as well and

Table 5.8 Level of Adapting Encouragement and Styles of Adapting

CASE	ADAPTING PROCESS	PATTERNS OF ACTIONS ENCOURAGING ADAPTING	LEVEL	STYLE
Case D	Search:	• Exploration within the organization; Exploration beyond the organization; Local search; Distant search	10	Decentralized Adapting
	Decision Making:	• Internal integration of resources and activities; External integration of resources and activities; Lower level decision making; Higher level decision making		
	Restructuring:	• Several resource reconfiguration activities—addition, transfer, deletion, and recombination of resources; Generates new resource combinations to better match the environment		
Case A	Search:	• Exploration within the organization; Exploration beyond the organization; Local search; Distant search	8	Decentralized Adapting
	Decision Making:	• Internal integration of resources and activities; No external integration of resources and activities (−1); Lower level decision making; Higher level decision making		
	Restructuring:	• Several resource reconfiguration activities—addition and transfer of resources; Generates new resource combinations to better match the environment		
Case H	Search:	• Exploration within the organization; Exploration beyond the organization; Local search; No distant search (−1)	8	Decentralized Adapting
	Decision Making:	• Internal integration of resources and activities; External integration of resources and activities; Lower level decision making; Higher level decision making		
	Restructuring:	• Several resource reconfiguration activities—addition, transfer, deletion, and recombination of resources; Generates new resource combinations to better match the environment		
Case E	Search:	• Exploration within the organization; Exploration beyond the organization; Local search; No distant search (−1)	6	Local Adapting
	Decision Making:	• Internal integration of resources and activities; External integration of resources and activities; No lower level decision making (−1); Higher level decision making		
	Restructuring:	• Several resource reconfiguration activities—addition, transfer, and recombination of resources; Generates new resource combinations to better match the environment		
Case F	Search:	• Limited exploration within the organization (0); Exploration beyond the organization; Local search; No distant search (−1)	5	Local Adapting
	Decision Making:	• Internal integration of resources and activities; No external integration of resources and activities (−1); Lower level decision making; Higher level decision making		
	Restructuring:	• Several resource reconfiguration activities—addition and transfer of resources; Generates new resource combinations to better match the environment		
Case G	Search:	• Limited exploration within the organization (0); Exploration beyond the organization; Local search; No distant search (−1)	4	Local Adapting
	Decision Making:	• Internal integration of resources and activities; No external integration of resources and activities (−1); Lower level decision making; Higher level decision making		
	Restructuring:	• Few resource reconfiguration activities—transfer and recombination of resources (0); Generates new resource combinations to better match the environment		
Case B	Search:	• No exploration within the organization (−1); Exploration beyond the organization; No local search (−1); Distant search	−1	Managerial Adapting
	Decision Making:	• Internal integration of resources and activities; No external integration of resources and activities (−1); No lower level decision making (−1); Higher level decision making		
	Restructuring:	• Few resource reconfiguration activities (0); Does not generate new resource combinations to better match the environment (−1)		
Case C	Search:	• No exploration within the organization (−1); Exploration beyond the organization; Local search; No distant search (−1)	−2	Managerial Adapting
	Decision Making:	• Internal integration of resources and activities; No external integration of resources and activities (−1); No lower level decision making (−1); Higher level decision making		
	Restructuring:	• No resource reconfiguration activities (−1); Does not generate new resource combinations to better match the environment (−1)		

(0) Actions that encourage adapting to a lesser degree   (−1) Actions that fail to encourage adapting

keeps them responsive to ongoing changes through the addition and transfer of human and work resources. Aggregating these common patterns and iterating with the literature on adapting for corresponding constructs led to identifying a style of adapting that emphasizes the role of decentralization in change processes. Decentralization can help to sustain the ability to adapt to change as it reduces the organizational layers that create structural rigidities and constrain responsiveness (Teece, 2007; Teece et al., 1997). Given this participation in all three of the adapting processes at the lowest possible level during the development and implementation of HR practices, this style was termed decentralized adapting.

Second, the *local adapting* style (Cases E, F, G) is marked by patterns of less actions encouraging adapting in contrast to the decentralized adapting style. The patterns in this style highlight an emphasis on local rather than distant search and reveal the failure to engage in the external integration of resources and activities. Further patterns illustrate adapting locally in terms of restructuring processes, with changes in organizational structure occurring close to the organizations' past change experiences when developing and implementing HR practices. Instead of searching beyond the organization's accumulated knowledge base (Cohen & Levinthal, 1990; Zahra & George, 2002) or integrating external sources of new information (Iansiti & Clark, 1994), this style is characterized by remaining close to its experience and protecting its current knowledge base when engaging in adapting activities. Iterating with the literature for a conceptual analogue to the aggregated patterns led to naming this style local adapting.

Finally, the third *managerial adapting* style (Cases B, C) emerges where there are patterns of rarely or even an absence of actions that encourage adapting. The common patterns in these cases mainly emphasize that executive directors steered the direction of search and dominated decision-making processes, with decision making about the development and implementation of the HR practice only occurring at a higher level. Furthermore, the pattern emerged that the managers rarely or failed to engage in resource reconfiguration. Iterating these patterns with the literature highlights that managers can constrain organizational change through their beliefs, and managerial decisions can play a role in the failure to adapt to change (Helfat et al., 2007; Tripsas & Gavetti, 2000). Given the dominance of managers in adapting during the development and implementation of HR practices, a third style was subsequently termed managerial adapting. Figure 5.10 captures the main patterns stemming from the data on these adapting styles.

As a result, three styles of adapting have been identified, and an analysis of how these styles differ in encouraging the adapting processes has been provided. Adapting serves as an appropriate lens for examining how the NPOs identify the opportunities for the alteration of HRM, make decisions, and restructure their resources to develop and implement new or modified HR practices. Iterating between these styles and the dynamic

Decentralized Adapting
(Cases D, A, H)

- encourages all three adapting processes of search, decision making and restructuring processes when developing and implementing HR practices;
- characterized by engaging in adapting processes at the lower levels of the organization, e.g. scanning the environment and exploration within the organization at the level of the employees, higher and lower level decision making, and resource reconfiguration involves the employees through the addition and transfer of human and work resources;
- emphasizes the role of decentralization in change processes.

Local Adapting
(Cases E, F, G)

- emphasis on local rather than distant search and failed to engage in the external integration of resources and activities or lower level decision making;
- adapting locally in terms of restructuring processes, with changes in organizational structure occurring close to the organizations' past change experiences;
- characterized by remaining close to its capabilities and experience and protecting its current knowledge base when engaging in adapting processes, rather than searching beyond the organization or integrating external sources of information.

Managerial Adapting
(Cases B, C)

- rarely or an absence of actions that encourage adapting;
- emphasizes that executive directors steered the direction of search and dominated in decision making processes, with decision making about the development and implementation of the HR practice only occurring at a higher level;
- rarely engaged in or failed to engage in resource reconfiguration.

Figure 5.10   Emergent adapting styles and their main patterns.

capabilities literature reveals several findings that confirm and expand on this literature and entail several implications about how these NPOs adapt during the alteration of HRM.

The dynamic capabilities literature suggests that decentralization is crucial for being able to recognize opportunities and sense developments (Teece, 2007; Teece et al., 1997). The analysis of the decentralized adapting style is in line with this view as particularly the internally focused search with organizational members at the lower levels of the organization was helpful in recognizing opportunities for altering HRM. In contrast to claims of decentralization enabling rapid decision making (Teece, 2007), there is mixed evidence of decision-making processes being both accelerated and delayed through the involvement of lower level employees. Going beyond the emphasis in the literature on managerial decision making, autonomy is given to the lower level managers and employees in order to minimize resistance to the HR practice and coordination difficulties during the implementation of the HR practice, as well as enable consensus making. Finally, this study confirms that decentralization aids organizations in their ability to accomplish reconfiguration and transformation (Teece et al., 1997). Restructuring is encouraged at the lower levels of the organization through the addition and transfer of human and work resources that allow for employee responsiveness. In summary, the findings reveal more specifically how the decentralized approach aids the alteration of resources by minimizing resistance to the HR practice and coordination difficulties during the implementation of the HR practice, as well as enabling consensus making and employee responsiveness.

Furthermore, the literature on search emphasizes that organizations must overcome a narrow search horizon, constantly scanning and exploring across technologies and markets that are both local and distant in order to recognize opportunities (Teece, 2007). The findings of this study reveal that the local adapting style is distinct from the other adapting styles in that they only engage in local search within the nonprofit sector or by relying on the same external consultants when altering their HRM. This local search activity suggests path-dependent behavior (Cohen & Levinthal, 1990; Teece et al., 1997; Zahra & George, 2002) because searching for opportunities to alter HRM was enabled by remaining in proximity of the organization's past experience. The local adapting style is also characterized by making the decision during the alteration of HRM to revert to an old organizational structure that did not prove successful in the past. A possible explanation for the unusual decision-making behavior in the local adapting style has been referred to in the literature as negative transfer (Finkelstein & Haleblian, 2002). Accordingly, managers draw on lessons from past processes in their next decisions even when the situation differs substantively given their deeply embedded knowledge sets (Helfat et al., 2007; Leonard-Barton, 1992). In contrast to the assumption that reconfiguration can aid in escaping unfavorable path dependencies (Teece, 2007), this study demonstrates instead that reconfiguring the organizational structure in the local adapting style maintained a path dependency by reverting to the past structure. Confirming the literature, the local adapters framed their new problems in terms of their outdated knowledge base rather than adjusting them to the changing environment (Tripsas & Gavetti, 2000). In summary, these findings imply that drawing heavily on the past experience of altering HRM can constrain the perception of new alternatives, decision making, and restructuring by relying on an outdated knowledge base, as seen in the local adapting style.

Moreover, there is an emphasis in the theoretical literature on the importance of top management leadership skills, especially as managers must interpret new events and developments. Yet given that managers can become "prisoners of the deeply ingrained assumptions," it is better to embed scanning processes inside the organization rather than leave these functions to a few individuals (Teece, 2007, p. 1322). Similarly, the managerial adapting style confirms the danger of having only managers engage in these search processes, leaving the organization vulnerable to missing important developments when relying solely on the cognitive traits of the managers. Furthermore, evidence is provided of mainly higher level decision making, thereby neglecting the importance of garnering the input and loyalty of the employees for making quality decisions and communicating values and goals (Teece, 2007). Given bounded rationality, managers often do not see what is changing or respond in a timely fashion, failing to adapt their mental models to the current demands (Helfat et al., 2007; Tripsas & Gavetti, 2000). The present study expands on this literature to show how narrow managerial beliefs hindered restructuring processes as managers did not perceive the need to add or transfer the necessary resources for the implementation of the HR practice. Thus, the managerial adapting style makes clear that when managers fail to garner input from within the organization for search and decision making, as well as fail to engage in restructuring processes, they do not act in ways that purposefully create, extend, and modify the organization's resource base (Helfat et al., 2007). The analysis especially suggests that managerial judgments and beliefs are critical to the alteration of HRM.

SUMMARY: LEARNING AND ADAPTING STYLES

Thus far in the analysis, the key learning and adapting processes that have been touted in the literature as those through which organizations alter their resource base have been examined. The cross-case analysis has highlighted significant differences among the eight cases in terms of their extent of engaging in and encouraging learning and adapting during the alteration of HRM. Thus far, four learning styles termed *integrative learning*, *experiential learning*, *exploratory learning*, and *administrative learning* and three adapting styles, *decentralized adapting*, *local adapting*, and *managerial adapting*, have been identified from the cross-case analysis of the data. Each of these styles is an aggregation of the different emphases of the patterns stemming from the data and is characterized by the way in which it encourages learning or adapting during the alteration of HRM. Finally, the theoretical claims stemming from these learning and adapting styles through which NPOs develop and implement their new or modified HR practices have been discussed in relation to the dynamic capabilities literature.

When viewing the learning and adapting styles together, the findings reveal that some of the cases encourage both learning and adapting to a similarly high extent as seen in the integrative learning styles and the decentralized adapting styles. The cross-case analysis indicates that Cases A and H, which highly encouraged learning by combining all three learning processes, also encouraged adapting to a high degree by engaging in adapting processes at the lowest levels of the organization. At the other end of the spectrum, the same cases that rarely encouraged learning had low participation in adapting, as seen in the administrative learning and managerial adapting styles (Cases B, C). This finding suggests that the learning and adapting processes are related, but it still remains unclear how they are linked to each other. Extending these arguments, the fine-grained view of the individual processes in the learning and adapting styles indicates that not only do knowledge articulation and knowledge codification support each other (Verona & Ravasi, 2003; Zollo & Winter, 2002), with evidence of codification aiding knowledge articulation by ensuring knowledge transfer throughout the organization, but they also support adapting processes such as decision making. This is in line with prior nonprofit research that has shown that improving knowledge sharing leads to high-quality decision making (Perry et al., 2006). These findings suggest that the individual learning processes need to be viewed both in relation to each other and in relation to their impact on the adapting processes.

Learning processes are viewed in the literature as enhancing an organization's ability to change as routines become established and standardized (Nelson & Winter, 1982). Yet, thus far, the focus in the literature has been on explicating the relationship between learning and dynamic capabilities (Maritan & Peteraf, 2007; Rindova & Kotha, 2001; Teece, 2007, Teece et al., 1997; Zahra et al., 2006; Zollo & Winter, 2002), rather than the linkages among the processes themselves. Only recently has research begun to conceptualize about the relationship between individual learning and adapting processes. Teece (2007) views learning and search processes as central to the capability of sensing new opportunities, arguing that this capability depends in part on the knowledge and learning capabilities of the organization. In addition, competences must be maintained and improved for making decisions that seize on opportunities. Finally, when managing threats and reconfiguration, the generation of new knowledge, knowledge transfer, and knowledge integration are perceived as critical. Learning is conceived of as an enabling process whose role it is to facilitate the process of reconfiguring resources to better match the environment (Easterby-Smith & Prieto, 2008; Pavlou & El Sawy, 2005, 2006b).

As a result, the recent literature on the dynamic capabilities approach puts forth the assumption that adapting is dependent on and facilitated by learning, but it has not provided fine-grained empirical research on the linkages between learning and adapting. The present study has yielded initial support that learning and adapting processes are associated with each other as seen in the commonalities across the learning and adapting styles. Not only does the analysis suggest that the individual learning processes support each other, but further evidence is provided that learning functions as an enabling process for individual adapting processes as well.

Furthermore, although the analysis of the rich data from the exploratory multiple case study has unearthed *how* the styles of learning and adapting differ in terms of their aggregated patterns, it still remains unclear *why* these differences among the styles emerge. The contrast among integrative, experiential, exploratory, and administrative approaches to learning and among decentralized, local, and managerial approaches to adapting implies that both the learning and adapting styles were influenced differently. Although there are several possible explanations for this variation among the cases, the theoretical foundations of the dynamic capabilities approach are followed, which point to the importance of path in shaping learning and adapting processes. In the next section, the influence of the distinguishing nonprofit characteristics as a possible source of this variation across the styles of learning and adapting will be examined.

THE INFLUENCE OF DISTINGUISHING NONPROFIT CHARACTERISTICS ON LEARNING AND ADAPTING

As delineated in Chapter 3, the dynamic capabilities approach maintains that path encompasses the organization's history, values, experience, skills, resources, and managerial decisions and is embedded in the routines of an organization. Processes evolve in a cumulative way (Koch, 2008), with the theoretical literature emphasizing the path dependency of learning and adapting processes. Path dependency conveys that these past managerial decisions, routines, and experience shape and restrict the options available to the organization (Sydow et al., 2009). Stemming from this theoretical background, this study aims to examine how path influences the learning and adapting processes through which NPOs develop and implement their HR practices. Iterating between the nonprofit and the conceptual literature has revealed that the theoretical concept of path can be investigated into using the distinguishing nonprofit characteristics. Previous studies indicate that change in NPOs is subject to the influence of a variety of distinguishing nonprofit characteristics that can be divided into values-driven strategic orientations, multiple stakeholders' demands, unique attributes of HR, and managerial capabilities. Given that similar factors have also been identified in the literature on the introduction of HR practices and because the alteration of HRM is an example of an organizational change, it is assumed that these identified specific nonprofit characteristics will influence the alteration of HRM as well. These four nonprofit characteristics represent the dimensions of path that enable investigation into this latent concept. They capture the organization's values, history, experience, skills, resources, routines, and past managerial decisions, which are claimed to influence learning and adapting processes.

Prior empirical findings from nonprofit studies have provided insight into how to operationalize these four specific nonprofit characteristics. Previous research suggests that maintaining practices that are in accordance with the nonprofit's historically embedded core values and social goals as expressed in the mission can aid NPOs in survival and adapting to change (Frumkin & Andre-Clark, 2000; Moore, 2000; Salipante & Golden-Biddle, 1995). In addition, studies suggest that the failure to consider nonprofit values can serve as a barrier to the implementation of HR practices (Alatrista & Arrowsmith, 2004; Cunningham, 1999). As path entails an organization's values and history, nonprofits' *values-driven strategic orientations* constitute a dimension of path and can be operationalized in terms of nonprofit values, multiple goals, and nonprofit mission. Furthermore, nonprofit studies indicate that *multiple stakeholders' demands* on NPOs during change processes may be conflicting given their various interests, values, needs, and goals (Moore, 2000; Ospina et al., 2002; Stone et al., 1999). The nonprofit literature suggests that multiple external stakeholders such as funders, donors, service recipients, members of the community, regulatory bodies, and board members place demands on NPOs during change processes (Basinger & Peterson, 2008; Durst & Newell, 2001). Similarly, varying stakeholder expectations and problems of gaining acceptance across diverse constituencies have been discussed in the literature as proposed obstacles to introducing new HR practices (Cunningham, 1999; Palmer, 2003). Yet studies have shown that with these demands, stakeholders bring in a wealth of knowledge and experience, as well as their external connections and resources to NPOs (Basinger & Peterson, 2008; Durst & Newell, 2001; McMullen & Brisbois, 2003). Thus, the experience, skills, and resources that can be gained from these external stakeholders and constitute path are operationalized by their interests, needs, values, goals, and demands.

In addition, because nonprofit employees have different goals, priorities, and values that may diverge from those of the organization (Fenwick, 2005; Minkoff & Powell, 2006), their personal commitment to organizational values may act as a constraint on change processes (Armstrong, 1992), whereas their stronger nonmonetary orientation may foster the willingness to learn (Borzaga & Tortia, 2006). Failing to let workers put their values into practice, professional autonomy, loyalties of staff, and internal resistance to change have been identified in the literature as possible constraints on introducing HRM (Alatrista & Arrowsmith, 2004; Cunningham, 1999). Depending on whether the nonprofit employees are involved in change and decision-making processes (Basinger & Peterson, 2008; Durst & Newell, 2001; Kellock Hay et al., 2001), NPOs can draw on their wealth of experience, skills, and resources as well. Thus, these elements that constitute path are operationalized by the *unique attributes of HR* in terms of their different needs, goals, and motivations. Finally, in addition to experience, skills, and resources, path is also embedded in organizational routines and past managerial decisions. Managerial experience has been shown to be relevant for decision-making processes and gaining resources given their accumulated knowledge bases (Jurkiewicz & Massey, 1998; Ritchie et al., 2007). Previous nonprofit research has pointed to the influence of managers in taking nonprofit values, internal resources, organizational structure, operations, and diverse internal stakeholders into account for the success of learning and change (Parsons & Broadbridge, 2004; van der Pijl & Sminia, 2004). Further studies corroborate that failing to consider the organizational structure and autonomy of organizational units in NPOs can serve as a barrier to the implementation of HR practices (Alatrista & Arrowsmith, 2004; Cunningham, 2001), especially because these structures lack a common perspective on goals and priorities (Palmer, 2003). In addition, a lack of resources features as a barrier with regard to HRM (Cunningham, 1999; Kellock Hay et al., 2001). Therefore, the final path dimension of *managerial capabilities* is operationalized by the managerial capability to consider existing internal resources, organizational structure, knowledge, and routines.

Because the theoretical literature has indicated that path shapes organizational processes, these dimensions of path are assumed to influence the processes through which NPOs develop and implement their HR practices. Coinciding with the theoretical literature on path-dependent and path-breaking processes (Sydow et al., 2009), these path dimensions are appropriate for examining the assumption that distinguishing nonprofit characteristics may constrain or enable learning and adapting during the alteration of HRM. Whereas stability and path dependence in learning and adapting are expected to be associated with sticking to the organization's traditional values and mission, managerial capabilities may be related to change and path-breaking behavior if managers can instigate a shift from the organization's previous decisions, routines, and values. Depending on the degree to which the experience, skills, and resources of multiple stakeholders and employees are included in and can exert influence on the alteration of HRM, these path dimensions may have the potential to bring about path-breaking learning and adapting in NPOs as well.

As noted in Chapter 4, by triangulating multiple sources of data, each case was analyzed for similarities and differences in the influence of these path dimensions on learning and adapting. Patterns stemming from the path dimensions were sought that could be compared within and among the learning and adapting styles. Metaphorical gerunds were attached to the activities stemming from the data to discern these patterns and make cross-case comparisons (Gibbs, 2007; Miles & Huberman, 1994). Furthermore, the influence of path was analyzed by searching for terms in the data that indicate a fostering (e.g., "aided," "supported," "enabled") or a hindering influence (e.g., "blocked," "stopped," "delayed"). Using individual case studies as examples, the theoretical concept of path will be examined in the following sections for the patterns in the influence of the distinguishing nonprofit characteristics on the learning and adapting styles. The exemplary case studies are presented for each of the learning and adapting styles by cycling back to the case data and subsequently discussing the findings with the literature on path dependency and the nonprofit characteristics.

CASE STUDIES OF THE INFLUENCE OF PATH ON LEARNING STYLES

Concerning the influence of the path dimensions on learning styles, triangulation of the multiple data sources demonstrates that there are substantial differences in the influence of path. Drawing on individual case studies representative of each of the learning styles, the empirical findings on the relationship between the unique features of NPOs and the learning processes are presented. Each of the distinguishing nonprofit characteristics that represents the dimensions of path, i.e., the values-driven strategic orientation, multiple stakeholders' demands, unique attributes of HR, and managerial capabilities, is explored with regard to how and why it influences the various learning styles. After carefully searching the data for commonalities and idiosyncrasies, several patterns emerged. The next sections discuss the differing patterns in terms of how these unique nonprofit features influence one of the case studies from the integrative, experiential, exploratory and administrative learning styles. In a final step, the influence of path as a source of variation in the four learning styles will be discussed in iteration with the theoretical and nonprofit literature, and implications about the relationship between path and learning in NPOs will be drawn.

Case H: An Integrative NPO

The integrative learners are characterized by a mixture and interplay of all three learning mechanisms, combining experience accumulation, knowledge articulation, and knowledge codification in the alteration of HRM. Case H exemplifies the integrative learning style through which NPOs strengthen their learning activities in areas of existing knowledge and go beyond to acquire new sources of knowledge when they develop and implement their HR practices. Namely, the organization introduced an OD process to restructure its areas of work and tighten its organizational structure due to drastic budget cuts reducing funds by 25% (Case H: Doc. 3). This proactive OD process was introduced in the organization to work more effectively with fewer staff, ensure and improve the quality of its work, as well as improve cooperation between its divisions (Case H: Doc. 3, 10). The departments, workers' council, regional church, committee of bishops, and the synod all engaged in a series of experience accumulation, knowledge articulation, and knowledge codification activities with the executives to develop a draft change concept of how to structure and organize work within the organization. In the following, the influence of the four path dimensions on the integrative learning style will be analyzed for Case H.

Living the Organizational Culture and Aligning the Values-Driven Strategic Orientation

As a religious organization, the organizational values in Case H center around the mission of the proclamation of Protestant religious values, missionary work, the provision of services for congregations and institutions, and a culture of being open, democratic, and experienced, full of ideas for the Church and society, and exploring and testing new things (Case H: Doc. 5, 8). With regard to the influence of the values-driven strategic orientation on the learning processes through which Case H developed and implemented its change process, the analysis showed that the pattern of *living the organizational culture* emerged from the data as fostering learning processes in the integrative learning style. In the integrative learning style, living the participatory culture influenced knowledge sharing within and beyond the organization by facilitating the cascading consultation processes (Case H: I1, 1, 2). In light of this open, democratic culture (Case H:

Doc. 8), external stakeholders and employees in their department meetings were all given the opportunity to exert influence on the change process through the system of knowledge sharing. As a result, democratic consultation processes occurred within the organization and cascaded beyond the organization through intense discussions with the synod, board of trustees, supervisory committees, advisory committees, and the committee of bishops about the change process, the concept, and the job plan.

Iterating back to the data unearths the further pattern that there was a need to *align the values-driven strategic orientation* with the development and implementation of the HR practice. Case H emphasized a fit between its religious mission and the acquisition of external knowledge. For example, this fit to organizational values played a role in influencing the choice of employing an external moderator for their change process who is "familiar with the church and the language [they] speak" (Case H: I1, 1). Furthermore, aligning the introduction of the HR practice with the mission of the organization even encouraged additional knowledge articulation processes in the integrative learning style. Considering the organization's religious message and mission enabled further knowledge exchange about the future content of their work within the change process. The executive director commented on how these discussions about substantive issues were conducted in line with their mission:

> "[. . .] we always tried to ask ourselves—the substantive part of what we—not related to the structures, you can't do much there, but related to the substantive issues that were determined in this process. That we said which topics do we also want to convey?" (Case H: I1, 2).

Thus far, the analysis reveals that living the organizational culture and the necessity to align the organization's values with introducing the HR practice influenced the way the integrative learner both acquired and exchanged knowledge about the HR practice.

Multiple External Stakeholders' Input, Level of Expertise, and Conflicting Interests

In Case H, the interests of several church organs such as the synod, advisory committees, board of trustees, supervisory committees of the head church, and the committee of bishops played a role in the change process. Concerning the influence of these multiple external stakeholders on the learning processes, the integrative learning style shows the emerging patterns that the external stakeholders' input and level of expertise both fosters and hinders the three individual learning processes. On the one hand, incorporating the *input of these numerous external stakeholders* fostered the learning processes. The synod assisted knowledge accumulation by giving the organization and its employees enough scope to develop its own change concept as they saw fit (Case H: I1, 1). Furthermore, the advisory committees who have guided the individual departments in the past supported the acquisition of knowledge about the change concept by providing suggestions on aspects that could be altered. Overall, the stakeholder input, which reflects the experience of external stakeholders who have participated in change processes in the organization in the past, aided both knowledge articulation via intense consultations about the change concept and knowledge codification through the provision of written comments:

> "And then there was a consultation, that means that the workers' council was involved, the committee of bishops, because we work in the regions [. . .]. The supervisory committees of our head church organization were involved and of course the current department heads who will be working in different structures were also included. And they could turn in comments which many of them did." (Case H: I1, 2).

Following this practice of drawing on the expertise of these external stakeholders from past change processes reflects the path-dependency of learning as their prior experience is reproduced in the current alteration of HRM. Possessing a high *level of expertise*, the external stakeholders enabled knowledge to be integrated into developing the change concept. Not only did this occur with each departments' advisory committees (Case H: I1, 1), but also by setting up an expert committee of external stakeholders who had expertise in a certain area of work with regard to the church:

> "And we added in an extra loop and said—they won't just be the employees who are formulating their concept in a new way. Instead we have a, we called it an expert committee, the name already says a lot—where people are there who have something to do with the church and the working world. [. . .] People who know about the church and the working world and we asked this small committee to advise us with the demands they have on such a department." (Case H: I1, 2).

However, including external stakeholder input also hindered the knowledge articulation processes when developing the HR practice. Not only did the board of trustees make several changes to the initial draft of the change concept due to their own interests (Case H: I1, 1; Doc. 3), but the committee of bishops also had conflicting interests with the organization. The executive director in Case H noted how these conflicts of interest blocked discussions about the change process, delaying the development of the change concept:

> "[. . .] but if it weren't for that [the conflicting interests] we would be able to reach our goal much faster alone." (Case H: I1, 2).

It is noteworthy that the highest degree of learning occurs in the integrative learning style, despite being hindered in learning by the demands of multiple stakeholders. On the surface, it would seem that the more actors that are involved in the development and implementation of the HR practice, the more the NPO engages in several learning activities. This explanation, however, does not fully capture the data. First, there are not more actors involved in the introduction of the HR practice in the integrative learning style, and, second, its learning processes are both aided and hindered by the demands of external stakeholders. Cycling back and forth between the raw data and the initial theoretical explanations (Yin, 2009) unearths the underlying phenomenon that the more the integrative learner was blocked in its learning activities by external stakeholders, the more it responded to these constraints by engaging in further learning activities with their stakeholders to counteract and compensate. Case H provides rich confirmatory evidence for this pattern of participating in further learning activities when the stakeholders' conflicting interests posed a hindrance to the consultative knowledge articulation processes. The executive director responded to these conflicts of interest with the committee of bishops by engaging in further learning activities:

> "At the same time we have this committee of bishops [. . .] and they have an interest in having as many of our positions being spread across the state. [. . .] There were simply conflicts of interest. They also blocked or inhibited the process. This required additional consultation processes and so on." (Case H: I1, 2).

Thus, the rich case evidence led to the detection of an anomalous relationship in the data because this learning style encourages learning to the highest degree, although its learning activities are also constrained by the external stakeholders. This reflects the emphasis in the literature on the hindering role of external stakeholders' conflicting interests, needs, values, goals, and demands. In an iterative process of explanation building (Yin, 2009), the underlying phenomenon was unearthed that the integrative learning style responds to path constraints on learning by engaging in even more learning activities in order to counteract this negative influence. Even the path-dependency of learning processes is demonstrated in the integrative learning style through relying on the prior experience of external stakeholders. Thus, the path dimension of multiple stakeholders' demands further reveals how the integrative learning style was influenced in its combination of learning processes in the alteration of HRM.

Breadth of HR, Acceptance of HR, and the Workers' Council as a Guardian

Concerning the influence of the unique attributes of the human resources, the employees in Case H are considered to be highly motivated and educated experts who vary in terms of having a predominantly theological or educational background (Case H: I1, 1). Yet the employees' motivational base was not found to influence the learning processes in the integrative NPO. Although the employees are perceived as highly motivated given their specialized training and expertise (Case H: I1, 1), the analysis indicates that this high degree of motivation behind their tasks was not interpreted as impacting how they learned during the development and implementation of the change concept. Instead, the integrative learning style displays evidence of the first pattern that they were influenced by the *breadth of HR* or the degree to which the different organizational levels of employees were included. Case H demonstrated how including the breadth of HR fostered a broad discussion about the change process. Incorporating all employees in the workshops aided in sharing knowledge throughout the organization:

> "Then we did a two day open space workshop with all the employees. [. . .] That really ran wild to a certain degree. Some went really structured over the two days. Some developed in all directions and everything that came out of it we sifted through it and tried to bundle it again and to get a picture of it." (Case H: I1, 1).

Participating in consultations regarding the change concept and the job plan, the employees and supervisory committees, which were made up of various employees from the departments, aided the executive directors in acquiring department-specific information (Case H: Doc. 3). The employees incorporated their specific knowledge of the work being done in the departments, thereby bringing about concrete changes regarding the restructuring of departments and the positions slated to be cut:

> "And because of a comment that came out of this area of work [. . .] both departments were asked again with the result that it went from department 1 to 6. [. . .] Or that there was a concrete suggestion for a certain job cut— [. . .] And those were the details that were then changed." (Case H: I1, 2).

Furthermore, the case data indicate that including the breadth of HR is also suggestive of relying on a past practice in the integrative learning style. In Case H, the executive director commented on the repeated practice of including various employees from the departments who not only fostered intense discussions, but also knowledge codification by providing written comments about the change concept and job plan in a cascading process:

> "What does work is a stepwise process of consultation in which certain committees such as the workers' council or supervisory councils are involved and on the other side the employees are given the chance

to exert influence through a cascade system. We pass on the plan to the department heads, they discuss it in their area and can absorb any ideas, hints, suggestions, but also criticism of course, and they pass it on again." (Case H: I1, 2).

An additional pattern emerged from the data that the overall *acceptance of HR*, i.e., the extent to which the employees accept change and are willing to change, also enabled knowledge articulation. Given this lack of resistance to change on behalf of the employees, discussions were thus able to occur objectively in the integrative NPO:

> "And they were really pragmatic about it, discussed it objectively and said 'how can we do it despite this?' And that wasn't an attitude of resistance in which they said they think it's outrageous that funds are being cut." (Case H: I1, 1).

Furthermore, an additional pattern emerged in the integrative learning style that the *workers' council acted as a guardian of the employees' interests*, thereby fostering discussions about the HR practice. For example, in Case H, the workers' council was highly involved from the beginning, yielding them the opportunity to discuss the change concept and provide comments (Case H: I1, 1). The openness of the workers' council fostered the exchange of knowledge, as the executive director noted:

> "There was simply— they [the workers' council] were involved from the beginning. They could bring in their suggestions and ideas. They did that especially with regards to the job plan." (Case H: I1, 2).

As a result, the patterns of the breadth of HR, acceptance of HR, and the role of the workers' council as a guardian provide in-depth insight into how the unique attributes of HR influenced the integrative learning style, with evidence of this path dimension having a fostering effect on a series of knowledge acquisition, exchange, and codification activities. In particular, including the breadth of HR reflects the path-dependency of learning processes as it entails relying on past practices of consultations that had benefited the organization during the previous alteration of HRM. Furthermore, the willingness to accept change and the guardian role of the workers' council fostered knowledge articulation.

Managerial Capabilities to Integrate Past Change Experience and Employ Learning Routines

Exploring the data with regard to managerial capabilities, the analysis specifically indicates the first pattern of deploying the *managerial capability to integrate past change experience* in which managers drew on their previous experiences and learned from their past mistakes in change processes. In Case H, the executive director considered his previous change experience in the church district, thereby deciding against involving the organization broadly at first. This past experience had taught that structuring knowledge management by formulating suggestions before broad discussions fosters disseminating knowledge throughout the organization:

> "That is really demanding because it has been tried in the church district and that hasn't been very successful. [. . .] you find a structure in which you can develop suggestions as alternatives and then to enter the process more broadly with these suggestions. But not to start off broadly to do it." (Case H: I1, 1).

Furthermore, considering past change experiences influenced the acquisition and exchange of knowledge within the current OD process. Through an intervention by the external consultant, the organization was forced to address its taboos about the change process concerning the organizational structure and its future structure of work. Considering the past structural change experiences aided the organization in gaining an understanding in their current change process of coming to an even closer, more consolidated structure. In this sense, deploying this managerial capability assisted the executive director in making fundamental structural changes that deviate from the previous structure. The executive director noted these differences to the mistakes associated with the past organizational structure:

> "Cooperation all of that has to happen because we have already seen that the resources are dwindling. We have to work differently, more effectively. It's different and with the new structure we are really going to consolidate it. [. . .] We have to move closer together there. That was a guiding reason for me in order to find a new structure." (Case H: I1, 1).

Another pattern that emerged from the data is the *managerial capability to employ learning routines*. Reflecting the path-dependency of learning, this managerial capability entails drawing on existing organizational learning practices during the development and implementation of the HR practice, which fostered learning. For example, the managers utilized the routine of relying on the same external consultants, which aided in the acquisition of external information. The benefits of acquiring knowledge from the same external consultant were described in Case H as follows:

> "Exactly, he knows our institution. He doesn't know each individual employee, but he knows our mandate and already knows how to assess us." (Case H: I1, 1).

Taken together, these managerial capabilities foster several of the individual learning processes by learning from past mistakes and relying on past routines in the integrative NPO, suggesting the crucial role that managers and path-dependent learning play in encouraging a high degree of learning.

Discussion of the Integrative Learning Style

Thus far, the analysis suggests that when NPOs consider their values-driven strategic orientation, multiple external stakeholders' demands, unique attributes of IIR, as well as their managerial capabilities, they are more likely to combine all three learning processes (integrative learning style). In integrating several learning mechanisms, Case H seeks to fit learning to the organizational values of the religious message and mission and draw on the breadth of employees and input of multiple stakeholders, while considering past change experiences and learning practices. Characteristic of the integrative learner are the consultation processes with employees and external stakeholders through which they strengthen their learning activities in areas of existing knowledge, but they also go beyond to acquire new sources of knowledge. Although all of the distinguishing nonprofit features foster learning, the multiple stakeholders' demands also hinder learning. These conflicts of interest with external stakeholders block learning, yet also account for the high degree of learning in the integrative NPO as managers engage in further knowledge articulation processes to counteract and compensate.

The rich data reveal that engaging in several learning activities in all three learning processes is encouraged by all the distinguishing nonprofit characteristics. First, integrative learners emphasized needing to ensure a fit among their mission, goals, and culture and the introduction of the HR practice, which fostered experience accumulation and knowledge articulation activities. In addition, the integrative learners incorporated the knowledge and experience of their external stakeholders and nonprofit employees (Fyles, 2003) in a series of knowledge acquisition, exchange, and codification activities during the alteration of HRM. External stakeholders' expertise as well as including the breadth of HR emerge from the analysis as path-dependent factors in the integrative learning style. According to the literature on path-dependent processes, self-reinforcing or positive feedback forces are the source of path dependence and can help to explain why the learning processes in the integrative learning style are sticky or persistent (Mahoney, 2000; Pierson, 2000a, 2000c). These self-reinforcing dynamics include large set-up or fixed costs, learning effects, coordination effects, adaptive expectations, direct and indirect network externalities, and complementary effects (Arthur, 1994; Koch, 2008; Pierson, 2000a; Sydow et al., 2009). Given these effects, reversals of course become increasingly unattractive. Additional scholars have expanded these conditions conducive to path dependence to rules and routines (Hakansson & Lundgren, 1997) or go beyond non-increasing returns-based explanations to address functional, power, and legitimation explanations of self-reinforcing processes (Mahoney, 2000). Iterating back to the data, the external stakeholders' expertise has a path-dependent influence on learning that reproduces their prior experience with the alteration of HRM, with the external stakeholders benefiting from the existing arrangement in which they are involved and seeking to uphold their power and influence. In addition, including the breadth of HR reflects the path-dependency of learning processes in the integrative learning style because this had become an established, legitimate practice that yielded benefits for learning as well.

The managerial capabilities aided all three learning processes in the integrative learning style through employing path-dependent learning routines and the integration of managerial experience to avoid the constraints of previous change processes. The analysis also reveals that path-dependent learning occurred in the integrative learning style with respect to pursuing the tried and true learning routine of relying on the same external consultants. As the integrative learning style gains from following these routines in terms of learning and coordination benefits, they continue to rely on their current, well-established practices rather than look for new alternatives. These findings confirm the nonprofit literature, which has identified the past experience of leaders and entrenched routines as path-dependent factors (Ramanath, 2009). In summary, including the experience from the values-driven strategic orientation, multiple external stakeholders' demands, the unique attributes of HR, and managerial capabilities influenced the combination of all three learning processes in the integrative learning style. The integrative learning style of participating in a combination of the three learning processes emerges from the analysis as encouraging this mixture through the influence of all four path dimensions and the path dependency of learning with its self-reinforcing mechanisms.

Case D: An Experiential NPO

Experiential learners are characterized by self-learning. This style entails a strong emphasis on introducing the HR practice themselves through first-hand internal experiential learning that occurs inside the organizations and creates organization-specific knowledge. Learning in the experiential NPO is encouraged through engaging in several activities of knowledge sharing within and beyond the organization, yet there are limitations in previous knowledge and constraints in the utilization of this pre-existing knowledge and integration of externally acquired knowledge. Case D is an example of the experiential learning style. Marked by the pursuit of self-learning, the organization implemented a new compensation model as employees, managers, and even the board were dissatisfied with the previous compensation model that no longer reflected the current line of work of the organization and its employees. They saw the need to react to their changing internal and external environment and develop a less complex model that is suited to their work, more transparent, and better accepted (Case D: I1, 1; Doc. 5).

Aligning the Values-Driven Strategic Orientation

This experiential NPO stresses its political, commercial, and financial independence and values peaceful, non-violent measures to bear witness to threats to the environment. Stemming from this mission, the organization's HR policies emphasize transparency, internationality and diversity, flexibility, a fair culture of disagreement, teamwork, a cooperative leadership style, and immaterial values (Case D: Doc. 3). Similar to the pattern identified in the integrative learning style, in the experiential NPO, the values-driven strategic orientation also aids in knowledge articulation. For example, the organizational culture of accountability to donors in Case D was one of the reasons for transferring knowledge about the compensation model beyond the organization. Document analysis revealed this sense of accountability: "As a nonprofit organization we receive funds primarily from our donors, we deal carefully and respectfully with these donations" (Case D: Doc. 2). This was corroborated by interview data about publishing the new pay scales on the Internet:

> "We also have a responsibility that we feel responsible to all the people who give us donations and finance us that we are open and say: 'Look here. This is what we are. We are not hiding anything'." (Case D: I1, 1).

Furthermore, the pattern emerged of emphasizing the *alignment of the values-driven strategic orientation* with the development and implementation of the HR practice. In the experiential learning style, the HR manager explained engaging in the broad knowledge articulation processes in terms of aligning the introduction of the compensation model with their organizational culture of transparency (Case D: Doc. 2):

> "It's because we have a culture here of making internal processes transparent and although only those responsible decide and as a last resort always the management. But they want to do it with as broad an acceptance as possible." (Case D: I1, 1).

In addition, the need to fit the introduction of the HR practices with the organization's values-based nonprofit orientation encouraged knowledge articulation about the possibility of introducing a pay for performance system (Case D: I1, 1, Doc. 9). This, in turn, triggered the acquisition of external resources to gain new knowledge and expertise, by drawing upon an external consultant for his expertise on pay for performance systems.

The HR manager and the steering group members debated heavily about the problems of assessing nonprofit success and influence in their area of work, the lack of fit with employees' intrinsic motivations, the organization's image and culture, as well as the difficulties of assessing performance in teamwork. The need to ensure a fit with the organization's image and culture served to dictate the types of HR practices being introduced, leading to the steering group's decision against introducing a pay for performance component within their new compensation model:

> "We decided against a pay for performance system because it would have caused problems for the way we work because we are very team oriented. . . . This whole team culture and how we use ideas here makes a pay for performance model difficult." (Case D: I1, 1).

Thus, in Case D, knowledge acquisition and articulation activities within the self-learning process through which the experiential learner developed its own compensation model were facilitated by the necessity of aligning the introduction of the HR practice with their nonprofit orientation and organizational culture and image.

Lack of External Stakeholder Involvement

External stakeholders in Case D include the board, donors, advisory board, the organization's local group network, and the state government. However, in the experiential learning NPO, there was evidence of a *lack in external stakeholder involvement* in the individual learning processes. Instead, when knowledge integration about the compensation model was not possible because the external consultant was not experienced in the nonprofit sector, the organization pursued self-learning with its organizational members (Case D: I1, 1). The board was one of the main drivers behind introducing the HR practice, having initiated the decision to introduce the compensation model (Case D: I1, 1; Doc. 5). Granted, the involvement of the board in this process was mandated by their by-laws because the compensation model was related to a certain volume of the budget. Although the board helped to initiate the process through its criticisms of the previous model, it gave the HR manager the scope to develop and implement the practice with the steering group:

> "No, the board wasn't involved in planning. Our board is a sort of supervisory body ultimately. They control the executive director and there is the internal rule that above a certain financial amount the board decides. In addition, the compensation model is really a management issue and that's why the board joined in, but the board wasn't involved directly in the discussions." (Case D: I1, 1).

Instead of external stakeholders' demands and expertise being incorporated, the experiential learner relied on its steering group and the broad base of employees. Thus, the lack in external stakeholder involvement is also associated with a learning style that emphasizes creating knowledge within the organization through developing the HR practice itself.

Breadth of HR, Lack of Acceptance of HR, and the Workers' Council as a Guardian

In Case D, the employees are perceived as being active, strong willed, and intrinsically motivated to save the environment. Surprisingly, the perceived high level of intrinsic motivation of the employees was not deemed to have an impact on how they learned (Case D: I1, 1). Instead, the key informants emphasize the *breadth of HR* supporting knowledge articulation about the HR practice. Including all employees in the organization-wide plenums in Case D enabled broad, intense discussions about the compensation model (Case D: I1, 1, 2). The employees were highly involved and provided their feedback about the HR practice in these weekly plenums, aiding the process of self-learning. This finding suggests relying on a past practice of knowledge articulation in which they always discuss topics with all levels of employees in the plenum:

> "The plenum always occurs and sometimes we present the work we are doing. But there are also internal discussions. So if we are discussing the compensation model, then that's a topic." (Case D: I1, 2).

While the HR manager noted the importance of the support of "different people who had different perspectives" in negotiations with the steering group (Case D: I1, 2; Doc. 5), the breadth of HR also hindered knowledge articulation. For example, exchanging knowledge about the compensation model was made more difficult in the steering group due to the members' different backgrounds and levels of knowledge about the HR practice.

> "[. . .] there are certain complex issues that are incredibly difficult to discuss with people who don't do this in their job. If I have a campaigner for forestry here, then he has completely different interests and topics. I found that to be difficult at times. [. . .] and it was simply difficult to discuss it with everyone on equal footing." (Case D: I1, 1).

Furthermore, in its pursuit of generating organization-specific knowledge about the compensation model in the plenums, incorporating the different employees' ideas and opinions on the compensation model rendered the process of developing the HR practice within the organization especially ineffective:

"Sometimes we have too much feedback, too many discussions are held and offered so that all ideas are taken into account, which can sometimes be ineffective." (Case D: I1, 1).

However, these ineffective discussions and negotiations with the employees were perceived as necessary for pursuing self-learning. Delays also stemmed from the HR practice not being given priority in comparison to other work. The HR manager admitted that these knowledge articulation processes take time but also expressed the wish that the process would have been given priority:

"It's because we have these discussions added on in certain points that take time and because there were more important things that we couldn't push back. As the HR manager I sometimes wished that we would have at least had the pretense of doing nothing else for three months, just the restructuring process and then we would be done." (Case D: I1, 2).

Although some of the employees did not necessarily accept the new compensation model, even this *lack of acceptance* and willingness to change fostered knowledge sharing within the plenum. Employees had existential fears connected with introducing the new compensation model, leading to these plenums "having the most people when the compensation model was on the agenda" (Case D: I1, 1).

A further pattern that emerged was the role of the *workers' council as a guardian of employees' interests* and its fostering and hindering influence on learning processes in the experiential learning style. The workers' council was well involved in the development and implementation of the HR practice by being a part of the steering group and knowledge sharing about the compensation model occurred in regular meetings with the workers' council. Despite its continual involvement, the workers' council severely guarded the interests of its employees by insisting on having formal hearings for the pay scale groupings for each employee (Case D: Doc. 8). On the one hand, having to make 190 formal applications to the council hindered the exchange of knowledge with the workers' council. The workers' council hindered knowledge articulation by delaying and drawing out discussions when it represented the interests of employees that differed from those of the executive directors and responsible HR managers. The HR manager commented on the delays stemming from the involvement of the workers' council, even leading to a labor court procedure in two of the cases:

"[. . .] so we subsequently had to add this step in and have the workers' council hearings although they had been in the steering group. Then the workers' council didn't agree in this one case regarding the pay scale grouping and the job description and that's why we are in a labor court procedure at time being. It's gotten really complicated and complex." (Case D: I1, 1).

On the other hand, the hindrances to learning stemming from the active role of the workers' council resulted in engaging the workers' council in further learning activities to counteract for this negative influence. Namely, severely guarding the employees' interests before implementing the compensation model led the organization to respond with increased knowledge sharing between the HR manager and the workers' council. The HR manager explained the implications for additional knowledge exchange as follows:

> "In general, I drew the conclusion that we needed to have a weekly meeting with the workers' council. And this refers to all of our coop- eration not just regarding compensation but all possible topics. And because it's clearer and they're informed about this or that and that's good." (Case D: I1, 1).

In this respect, further validation for the phenomenon of this pattern of response to path constraints is unearthed in the experiential NPO as well. When confronted with hindrances stemming from the unique attributes of HR, the organization engages in further knowledge articulation activities with their employees in order to cope with the workers' council. Again, the anomalous relationship between engaging in several knowledge articula- tion activities in the experiential learning style and facing hindrances to learning was detected in the data.

Overall, the unique attributes of HR in terms of the breadth and accep- tance of HR as well as the role of the workers' council as a guardian had both a fostering and hindering effect on knowledge articulation in the experiential NPO. This is in line with nonprofit research suggesting that the different needs and goals of nonprofit employees are expected to vari- ously influence the processes through which NPOs develop and implement HR practices. In particular, including the breadth of HR revealed that the experiential NPO generates organization-specific knowledge by relying on past experience and routines of including all levels of employees in broad discussions through which the organization pursues self-learning.

Managerial Capabilities to Integrate Past Change Experience and Employ Learning Routines

Finally, the *managerial capability to integrate past change experience* emerged as a pattern that helped the organization to introduce the HR practice itself through first-hand internal experiential learning. For exam- ple, in Case D, self-learning occurred through knowledge articulation processes with the entire organization within regular plenum meetings. In this respect, the HR manager incorporated the experience gained from previous change processes in the organization in which failing to build a lobby before the plenum became a hindrance. Drawing on this past experience of the necessity of building a lobby enabled the process of knowledge articulation during the plenum:

> "But generally in the plenum it's important to get a lobby for yourself in advance, to give these people information and warm them up beforehand. This is so that they won't be surprised or overwhelmed in the plenum." (Case D: I1, 1).

Given the limitations of pre-existing knowledge about the HR practice that are characteristic of the experiential learning style, Case D encourages learning to occur within the organization by *employing routines of knowledge exchange* that emphasize self-learning. This second pattern emerging from the data shows that as the steering group members were limited in their knowledge about compensation models, Case D drew on a variety of learning practices for sharing knowledge that ranged from the weekly plenums, regular meetings with the workers' council, and discussions with colleagues from other firms at professional personnel association meetings to international exchange with the organization's country offices (Case D: I1, 1, 2). The emphasis, however, in the knowledge sharing routines was placed on letting the organization develop the HR practice itself. Drawing on the learning routine of knowledge sharing in the international network, the HR manager still emphasized the need to develop their own compensation model:

> "[. . .] we discussed it according to our situation and that was totally interesting for me to gain so much criticism and different perspectives. [. . .] One could only fall back on old models and I knew them because we also had looked around beforehand. [. . .] So that's why we didn't absolutely orient ourselves towards these models." (Case D: I1, 1).

Even this learning routine exemplifies the challenges that the experiential NPO faced in integrating its externally acquired knowledge. In summary, both the managerial capability to integrate past change experience and the capability to deploy knowledge sharing routines within and beyond the organization facilitated self-learning and generating organization-specific knowledge about the HR practice in the experiential NPO.

Discussion of the Experiential Learning Style

The analysis suggests that NPOs are more likely to engage in self-learning about the HR practice when they consider the values-driven strategic orientation, breadth and acceptance of HR, concerns of the workers' council as well as managerial capabilities (experiential learning). Characteristic of experiential learners is their creation of organization-specific knowledge, which the analysis has shown is predominantly facilitated through the employees' varying perspectives in broad and intense organization-wide discussions. Thus, the experiential learners are distinct from the other learning styles in that they draw more on the knowledge and experience of their employees, showing no evidence of external stakeholder involvement. The limitations of pre-existing knowledge and constraints to integrating externally acquired knowledge of the experiential learning style are compensated for by the breadth and acceptance of IIR promoting knowledge sharing. Even the hindrances to learning stemming from the active role of the workers' council led to the experiential NPO engaging the workers' council in further learning activities to counteract for this negative influence. Furthermore, including the breadth of HR was associated with path-dependent learning, again given the legitimacy and learning benefits gained from repeatedly employing this practice (Mahoney, 2000; Pierson, 2000c). This finding fits with the literature highlighting the path dependency of experiential learning (Levitt & March, 1988). Reflecting the focus in the experiential NPO on introducing the HR practice through first-hand internal experiential learning that occurs inside the organizations, HR managers are given the scope to develop and implement the practice with the employees, remaining free from external stakeholder involvement. Finally, deploying managerial capabilities enabled the knowledge articulation that is crucial for self-learning in which understanding is improved through deliberation (Zollo & Winter, 2002).

Case G: An Exploratory NPO

Exploratory learners are characterized by acquiring knowledge about developing and implementing the HR practice from the outside rather than by engaging in self-learning. As an example of the exploratory learning style, Case G engages in several acquisitive learning activities and integrates externally acquired knowledge given that the previous knowledge was limited in its applicability. The exploratory NPO seeks the pursuit of new knowledge and new approaches when developing and implementing the HR practice. Through exploratory learning, the organization sought to introduce a skills analysis system that better captures the current and future challenges facing the necessary managerial and employee skills (Case G: Doc. 1). In this proactive approach to altering HRM, the new skills analysis system was bought from an external consultant from the university (Case G: I1, 1).

Aligning the Values-Driven Strategic Orientation

Regarding the influence of the values-driven strategic orientation, the analysis of the data demonstrated that considering nonprofit goals influenced learning in the exploratory learning style. As an independent, nonpartisan organization with the mission to promote continual social progress in education, the economy, health care, civic society, and international understanding (Case G: Doc. 5), the values of Case G entail competition, freedom, goodwill, and solidarity, as well as encouraging and being a catalyst for social change (Case G: Doc. 15). The HR manager maintained that employees in a foundation need "a more balanced skills profile" in contrast to for-profit organizations, with personal and social skills being stronger in foundations (Case G: I1, 1, 2). The HR manager repeatedly mentioned how the consideration of the foundation's goals encourages learning in the organization during the external acquisition of the skills management system (Case G: I1, 1, 2). Specifically, it fosters knowledge articulation about these differences between skills profiles in for-profit organizations and foundations:

> "We always say here that in nonprofit organizations, different employees are needed in comparison to for-profit organizations. [...] And if I were to be asked what skills profiles look like in a foundation and how they are different from the for-profit sector. What is the difference actually and what do I actually have to watch out for if I work in a foundation, if I employ people in a foundation [...]." (Case G: I1, 1).

Seeking to *fit the nonprofit culture and goals with the introduction of the HR practice* in their learning processes was also characteristic of the exploratory learning style. The HR manager stated that the foundation has tried to maintain its organizational culture of "freedom, self-realization, personal initiative and creativity" (Case G: Doc. 4) in discussions when implementing the externally acquired HR practice (Case G: I1, 2). In its pursuit of new knowledge, this is reflective of the organization seeking to emphasize open and constructive dialogue, personal responsibility, a willingness to learn, and the precedence of good ideas over hierarchy (Case G: Doc. 4, 18). The knowledge articulation processes through which the organization integrated externally acquired knowledge exhibit the alignment to the values-driven strategic orientation in the exploratory learning style.

Lack of External Stakeholder Involvement

The exploratory learner is confronted with a wide variety of external stakeholders ranging from the board, EU, national, state, and regional governments, special interest groups, and associations that vary by subject (Case G: I1, 1). Yet acquiring the HR practice externally is associated with a *lack in external stakeholder involvement* in learning. Regarding the influence of multiple external stakeholders, the board gave the HR manager scope to develop and implement the HR practice, placing no demands on the organization in its acquisition of external knowledge (Case G: I1, 1, 2). Commenting on the lack of board involvement, the HR manager notes:

> "When I say that the board was not involved, then I have to say not officially. [. . .] It was told how it came about and then it was approved of—on a purely strategic level." (Case G: I1, 2).

Thus, although the organization purchased the skills analysis system from an external consultant from the university, the analysis shows that this learning style was not subject to the demands of any external stakeholders.

Workers' Council as a Guardian

In Case G, the employees are perceived as being intrinsically motivated experts who strongly identify with the founder, the foundation, and its goals (Case G: I1, 1; Doc. 15). In terms of the unique attributes of employees, the exploratory learning style was neither influenced by their highly motivated employees nor by the breadth and acceptance of HR. Only the *workers' council acting as a guardian of the employees' interests* hindered knowledge articulation in the exploratory NPO. Instead of a broad base of employees being involved in developing the skills analysis system, a cross-section of different employees from various departments such as IT, service, HR, event management, controlling, and marketing was included in the working groups (Case G: I1, 2; Doc. 11). The breadth of HR did not emerge as a pattern as the employees had relatively little influence on developing the skills analysis system:

> "Because of the fact that we didn't place KODE at all in the forefront, the influence [of the employees] wasn't that large." (Case G: I1, 2).

Moreover, the rich case data in Case G (I1, 2) indicate that the employees were generally skeptical of the skills analysis system, yet this lack of acceptance of change did not even have an opportunity to influence the acquisition of external knowledge. Unlike the integrative or experiential learning styles, the employees were simply given the final product of the HR practice rather than including the broad base of the employees in the development of the skills analysis system (Case G: Doc. 8). This approach was chosen so as not to re-open the process of developing the HR practice:

> "They get the final result. The skills profile. And they get an overview of how the current profile was created. [. . .] We wouldn't—maybe you know this if you have finished a process and then you put all this information back into the process, then the process will repeat itself. The process would be opened up again." (Case G: I1, 2).

Furthermore, although a workers' council representative was involved in the development of the skills analysis system, Case G provides empirical evidence that knowledge sharing was made more difficult by the lower levels of knowledge regarding the HR practice in the rest of the workers' council, thereby "making it difficult to convince the others" (Case G: I1, 2). This resulted in more difficult negotiation processes with the workers' council, "hindering, rather than fostering the process" (Case G: I1, 2). Having to involve all of the members of the workers' council constrained the exchange of knowledge and slowed down the development of the HR practice:

> "It is a bit difficult. [. . .] But they ultimately take a final vote and then you have to involve all the members in the process. And that is really unbearable because you develop a certain skills profile during these workshops for the topic and of course most of the members of the workers' council don't have that." (Case G: I1, 2).

Iterating back to the data reveals that the exploratory NPO engages in further learning activities as a result of the hindering influence of the critical workers' council on knowledge articulation. Some members of the workers' council were extremely skeptical of the skills analysis system in terms of its reliability. The HR manager engaged these workers' council members in further knowledge articulation processes, even having them participate in taking the questionnaires themselves:

> "And still this little step that was necessary to go into the method was criticized again and again by managers and by the workers' council. [. . .] And then I let the workers' council fill it out and then I gave them the questionnaire again and let them fill it out again and oddly enough it was exactly the same except for a 1 or 2 point deviation. Very high reliability." (Case G: I1, 1).

Thus, the underlying phenomenon emerged that the exploratory style of learning also engages in additional learning activities with their employees when confronted with hindrances stemming from the unique attributes of HR in order to cope with this negative influence. The case evidence thereby provides further validation for the phenomenon of this pattern of response to path constraints. On the whole, however, the unique attributes of HR have little influence on the exploratory learning style, which acquires HR practices externally rather than involving a broad base of employees in developing the HR practice.

Managerial Capabilities to Integrate Past Change Experience and Employ Learning Routines

In Case G, the acquisition of external knowledge was aided by the *managerial capability to integrate past change experience*. Drawing on past mistakes in hiring external support during change processes, the HR manager noted the importance of using external consultants who are compatible with the employees and the nonprofit consensus-oriented culture:

> "We look for them [external consultants] very, very carefully and check if they are compatible with our employees in the foundation. We have already been shipwrecked because the employees felt they were being dealt with too roughly. Too much emphasis on achieving goals and maximizing profits. [. . .] It's much more about coming to a consensus and not such an authoritarian, regulative culture." (Case G: I1, 2).

Furthermore, engaging in several acquisitive learning activities and integrating externally acquired knowledge was also fostered by the *managerial capability to employ existing organizational learning routines*. The analysis reveals that the exploratory learning style is aided in knowledge acquisition by buying in many of its HR instruments (Case G: I1, 1, 2; Doc. 9). Alluding to the metaphor of re-inventing the wheel, the HR manager noted that they often employ the routine of acquiring HR tools from outside of the organization rather than rethinking such instruments anew:

> "Yeah, we've done that with goal setting talks regarding SMART goals. [. . .] Then in terms of assessing employees' potential we got that from another firm and transferred it [. . .]. We basically don't have to rethink everything anew. Instead we just have to look at what fits us and introduce these things." (Case G: I1, 2).

Possessing the capability to learn from past mistakes in change processes and to deploy previous learning routines fosters the pursuit of new knowledge beyond the organization in the exploratory NPO. In particular, a strong emphasis is placed on following the past practice of acquiring HR practices outside of the organization.

Discussion of the Exploratory Learning Style

Thus far, the analysis suggests that NPOs are more likely to acquire knowledge about the HR practice externally when they limit their focus to the values-driven strategic orientation and the concerns of the workers' council, as well as managerial capabilities (exploratory learning). Characterized by the pursuit of external approaches when developing and implementing the HR practice, the exploratory NPO maintains its nonprofit goals and organizational culture when integrating externally acquired knowledge. In its several acquisitive learning activities and exchange of this acquired knowledge, external stakeholder involvement is rare. In contrast to the experiential learner, in the exploratory learning style, employees had little influence on developing the HR practice other than the critical and less informed workers' council. Again the phenomenon is unearthed of engaging in further learning activities as a response to the hindering influence of the unique attributes of HR. Finally, in deploying managerial capabilities, the characteristic acquisition of external knowledge in the exploratory learning style was aided by integrating past change experience and employing the routine of acquiring HR tools from outside of the organization.

Case B: An Administrative NPO

Administrative learners are characterized as not being able or willing to invest in learning. The administrative learner has a low extent of engaging in acquisitive learning, knowledge sharing and codification activities, and utilizing pre-existing knowledge, while being limited in the integration of externally acquired knowledge. Case B exemplifies this bare minimum of learning in the administrative learning style, which rarely engages in actions that encourage learning. Having changed its legal form from a public sector organization to a foundation with greater autonomy to deal with decreasing funding, a pay for performance system was adopted from the museum's development association (Case B: I1, 1). Engaging in few learning activities, the organization had implemented its pay for performance system for employees with management responsibility (Case B: I2, 1). This HR practice was introduced to financially reward highly involved employees and have regular goal setting and performance appraisal feedback talks. The directors sought to better coordinate work, increase employee motivation through intense dialogue, and improve employee performance with the pay for performance system (Case B: I1, 1; I2, 1).

No Necessity of Aligning the Values-Driven Strategic Orientation

Aiming to collect, preserve, research, and communicate cultural history for future generations, the museum seeks to be a service provider, advisor, initiator, and partner in cultural, scientific, social, and economic projects. Case B stresses the values of being family-friendly, professionalism, integration, and cooperation (Case B: Doc. 3, 5). Concerning the values-driven strategic orientation, the aforementioned values and mission of the NPO were not found to impact the learning processes. In contrast to the other learning styles, administrative learners did *not perceive the need for aligning the introduction of the HR practice with the nonprofit goals, culture, or the mission.* The case evidence from this learning style reveals that the managers viewed knowledge acquisition that did not consider the organization's values-driven strategic orientation as unproblematic. As the executive director in Case B commented on acquiring knowledge about the HR practice from organizations that were not in the nonprofit cultural sector:

"I think, as far as I can remember, it wasn't a problem [that these discussions were only with for-profit organizations]." (Case B: I1, 1).

Instead, aligning the values-driven strategic orientation with the introduction of the HR practice in learning processes was not deemed necessary by the managers in Case B because sectoral differences were not perceived as posing barriers to experience accumulation and knowledge articulation. Instead, the low investment in learning in this style is characterized by adopting best practices from for-profit organizations. These findings help to further understand the imitation of for-profit HR practices that is characteristic of the administrative NPO. The analysis reveals that lacking a perceived necessity to align with the values-driven strategic orientation is associated with investing in fewer learning actions.

Lack of External Stakeholder Involvement

Case B is confronted in its external operating environment with stakeholders such as the board, development association, funders, local county, local bank, regional park association, political parties, foundations, museums, and the university. Yet in the administrative NPO where the managers solely engaged in learning activities, the *external stakeholders were not involved* in learning. Not even the demands of external stakeholders such as the board influenced learning processes when introducing the pay for performance system. Instead, the executive director and director solely initiated and made the decision to introduce the pay for performance system into the development association in Case B. The board was not involved with the introduction of the pay for performance system as it was first introduced in and funded entirely by the sponsors within the museum's development association. As the director explained how he and the executive director initiated the introduction of the HR practice,

> "We thought about it and made the suggestion that we would get certain sum of money from our sponsors, 20,000 DM, was the idea at the time and we would distribute it to the employees through bonuses to the museum that was part of the public administration at that time." (Case B: I2, 1).

Instead, the board was merely involved in appraising the performance of the managers who also set goals and were subject to the HR practice themselves:

> "By the way, the executive directors also have goal setting. We have it with the foundation board. Ultimately we have to live by example." (Case B: I2, 1).

Therefore, with the board not being involved in the managers' few learning activities in developing the HR practice, a lack in external stakeholder involvement in learning is also associated with the administrative learning style that invests little in learning.

Lack of Encouraging Employee Learning

Although employees are perceived as being highly motivated, committed, and full of conviction and identification with their work (Case B: I2, 1), the unique attributes of HR did not shape the individual learning processes because *little investment is made in encouraging learning among the employees.* Neither the breadth nor the acceptance of HR played a role in learning. First, because the employees were not involved in developing and implementing the HR practices in this learning style, the pattern of the breadth of HR did not emerge in the administrative NPO. Second, while the key informants stated that the employees were accepting of change, this was not viewed as influencing the learning processes in a positive or negative way (Case B: I1, 1; I2, 1). Similar to the other learning styles, employees' motivational foundations did not play a role in learning but were cited as the reason for rewarding the "value of the employees" with the HR practice (Case B: I2, 1). Thus, the high level of motivation is not associated with learning processes but with the goals for introducing the practice and its effects. Furthermore, the workers' council did not influence the few learning activities either. In Case B, this stems from the unique exception that there was no workers' council at the time of introducing the HR practice (Case B: Doc. 2):

> "We had introduced [the HR practice] first into our development association. The development association did not and does not have a workers' council. It transferred directly to the foundation when the foundation was established. [. . .]. This means we introduced it when we didn't have a workers' council and once we had a workers' council it was already accepted amongst the employees." (Case B: I1, 1).

Thus, rather than encouraging the employees to engage in individual learning processes in the administrative learning style, the managers dominate the low extent of acquisitive learning, knowledge sharing, and codification activities as seen in the following section.

Managerial Capabilities to Integrate Past Change Experience and Employ Learning Routines

Reflective of the common pattern across all the learning styles, the *capability to integrate experience from previous change processes* also fostered the few learning activities in the administrative NPO. The managers had introduced the pay for performance system into the museum's development association first because the museum's previous organizational form did not allow for this HR practice. Once the museum was reorganized as a foundation, the already well-accepted HR practice was adopted directly without any difficulties. Using a pilot phase in the development association as a testing ground for altering HRM in the museum, the organization was able to learn from the experiences it had gathered previously with the instrument:

> "Back then we introduced it first with our employees in the development association. The development association is an employer and has the advantage that it can determine its contracts alone. And we simply said we'll try it out. [. . .] And we gathered experience with it there [. . .]." (Case B: I2, 1).

In addition, the *managerial capability to employ learning routines* positively influenced learning in the administrative learning style as well. In Case B (I, 1), following the routine of repeatedly engaging in informal talks with for-profit organizations that had implemented similar HR practices enabled the managers to acquire knowledge about pay for performance. Furthermore, the organization repeatedly stayed abreast of developments in the field through drawing on regular collaborations with the university:

> "The university is really important for us because we get wind of the most recent developments in our field in this way and because some of our employees offer courses at the university, sometimes regularly. So it's important both for us and for the standard in the academic field." (Case B: I2, 1).

Characteristic of the dominant role of managers in the administrative learning style, both the managerial capabilities of integrating past change experiences and utilizing learning routines facilitated the few acquisitive learning and knowledge sharing activities.

Discussion of the Administrative Learning Style

The analysis suggests that when NPOs merely rely on their managerial capabilities, they are more likely to neglect investing in learning and focus instead on copying best practices (administrative learning style). Administrative learners are characterized as not being able or willing to invest in learning. The data reveal that the investment in encouraging learning among the employees remains low, and learning does not consider the organizations' values nor is it influenced by the experience of external stakeholders.

Investing little in learning, administrative learners did not view the need for aligning the introduction of the HR practice with the nonprofit goals, culture, or mission. Instead, sectoral differences were not perceived as posing barriers to experience accumulation and knowledge articulation, and for-profit practices were imitated in the integration of externally acquired knowledge. This finding adds on to the nonprofit literature confirming that NPOs copy best practices from the for-profit sector without a synergistic relationship to the existing HR practices or the organizational strategy (Akingbola, 2006a) or, as seen in this study, without a relationship to the organizational mission and values. Furthermore, there is little investment in involving the employees in learning. Instead, the managers solely engaged in the learning processes, rather than including the knowledge and experience of a broad base of employees or external stakeholders in developing the HR practices. Only incorporating managerial experience encouraged the low extent of engaging in acquisitive learning activities and utilizing pre-existing knowledge. Thus, learning in the administrative learning style was solely encouraged by the managerial capabilities to rely on their path-dependent past routines of knowledge acquisition and learn from previous change experiences.

PATH AS A SOURCE OF VARIATION IN THE LEARNING STYLES

This analysis suggests that the nonprofit characteristics that constitute an organization's path dimensions influence learning and thereby confirm the theoretical literature in terms of the importance of path for learning (Nelson & Winter, 1982; Teece et al., 1997). Idiosyncrasies in the patterns of the influence of path on learning, however, provide insight into the variation across the learning styles. Namely, the values-driven strategic orientation, multiple stakeholders' demands, and unique attributes of HR were the most germane to understanding how and why the learning styles varied considerably across the cases. Table 5.9 depicts the path dimensions and whether they fostered, hindered, or had no influence on learning, as well as their further consequences on learning. This table entails several perspectives from which implications on the relationship between path and learning can be drawn.

Managerial Capabilities

First, the managerial capabilities influenced all four styles of learning. Not only in the styles in which an interplay of the three learning processes (integrative), self-learning (experiential), or the acquisition of external knowledge (exploratory) occurred, but also in the administrative style in which the managers engaged in few learning activities,

Table 5.9   Influence of Path Dimensions on Learning Styles

	FOSTER LEARNING	HINDER LEARNING	NO INFLUENCE ON LEARNING	FURTHER CONSEQUENCES ON LEARNING
VALUES-DRIVEN STRATEGIC ORIENTATION	Exploratory learning Experiential learning Integrative learning		Administrative learning	
MULTIPLE STAKEHOLDERS' DEMANDS	Integrative learning	Integrative learning	Administrative learning Exploratory learning Experiential learning	Integrative learning: hindrances on learning *encourage* further learning knowledge activities (knowledge articulation)
UNIQUE ATTRIBUTES OF HR	Experiential learning Integrative learning	Exploratory learning Experiential learning	Administrative learning	Exploratory learning, experiential learning: hindrances on learning *encourage* further learning activities (knowledge articulation)
MANAGERIAL CAPABILITIES	Administrative learning Exploratory learning Experiential learning Integrative learning			

managerial capabilities emerge as common, central influences on learning. As the only of the four path dimensions to influence learning regardless of learning style, managerial capabilities provide little insight into the variation among the learning styles. The analysis reveals instead that both of these managerial capabilities foster all of the individual learning processes by learning from past mistakes and relying on past routines, suggesting the crucial role that managers and the organization's path play in encouraging learning. The managerial capabilities emerging from the analysis of the data fit with the conceptual literature on path as encompassing the routines and past managerial decisions within an organization (Mahoney, 1995; Rosenbloom, 2000). This study suggests the importance of managers' reliance on path-dependent learning routines for encouraging learning. The NPOs were path-dependent in the pursuit of their learning routines of relying on the same external consultants, repeatedly acquiring HR practices externally, and engaging in past practices of incorporating a broad base of stakeholders or in discussions with the same organizations. These routines confirm that learning occurs more easily in ways that are close to the past processes (Teece et al.,

1997). These findings are in line with conceiving organizational learning as routine-based and history-dependent, in which organizations learn by "encoding inferences from history into routines that guide behavior" (Levitt & March, 1988, p. 320).

These findings from the data analysis also echo the focus in the non-profit literature on the role of organizational knowledge and routines (Bruckner, 2001; Meyer & Mühlbacher, 2001). Yet, in contrast to the negative effects of routines being rationalized and professionalized without questioning organizational knowledge or its past usage (Meyer & Mühlbacher, 2001), this study contributes to the nonprofit literature to show that routines in learning are not necessarily detrimental and can aid the organization in gaining, sharing, and documenting its knowledge during the alteration of HRM. It corroborates that path dependency enables learning, in that the way an organization has gained knowledge in the past is relevant for its current ability to absorb new knowledge (Kor & Mahoney, 2005). Furthermore, in contrast to NPOs drawing on knowledge regardless of its usefulness in the past, all of the learning styles identified in this study examined their previous knowledge, as managers learned from their past mistakes and broke away from their previous behavior. Finally, the prevalence of the influence of the managerial capabilities on learning in all of the styles also has relevance for research on managerial skills and knowledge (Ritchie et al., 2007), in that it underscores the importance of managers and the deployment of their capabilities for encouraging learning in these values-driven and inclusive organizations. A clear finding from this study is that including the manager's accumulated knowledge has implications beyond the mere acceptance of change (Parsons & Broadbridge, 2004) because this managerial experience is key to facilitating learning in NPOs.

Unique Attributes of HR

Second, the unique attributes of HR reveal the variation in the learning styles across the cases because this path dimension encouraged learning in the integrative, experiential, and exploratory learning styles. Although not as prominent in their influence as the managerial capabilities, this path dimension still played a substantial role in shaping the learning processes. Employees are noted in the nonprofit literature as being the most important assets in NPOs (Letts et al., 1999), helping to ensure that organizations learn and are open to change (Conway & Monks, 2008). The breadth of HR, acceptance of HR, and the workers' council as a guardian emerged from the analysis as influencing the learning processes through which the alteration of HRM occurred. First, extending upon the literature on employee participation (Basinger & Peterson, 2008), the analysis reveals that the encouragement of learning depends on involving a broad base of employees that preserves organizational heterogeneity. Furthermore, a tension emerged given the focus on the employees' acceptance or resistance to change in the integrative and experiential learning styles, over an emphasis on how highly motivated their employees are. Indeed, it was surprising that the motivational background of the employees did not play a role in learning, especially as the nonprofit studies suggest that nonprofit employees are motivated by learning opportunities (Schepers et al., 2005). Instead, gaining the support of employees in the alteration of HRM is pivotal for learning because even employee resistance to change spurs on learning. Third, the analysis focuses on the role of employees' needs and goals as represented by the workers' council, an aspect that has not been highlighted in the nonprofit literature. The workers' council plays a dual role in that it can aid and limit learning processes in the integrative, experiential, and exploratory learning styles, thereby shedding further light on the complicated influence of employees in change processes. Representing interests of employees that differed from those of the executive directors and responsible HR managers often hindered knowledge articulation by delaying and drawing out discussions. Yet the active role of the workers' council resulted in increased knowledge sharing, and the openness of the workers' council encouraged collective learning between the representatives of the workers' council and the HR managers.

Multiple Stakeholders' Demands

Third, the multiple stakeholders' demands had an idiosyncratic influence on the learning styles, influencing learning processes only in the integrative learning style. Instead, the lack in external stakeholder involvement in learning is associated with the learning styles that emphasize self-learning (experiential learning), acquiring external knowledge (exploratory learning), or investing little in learning (administrative learning). Although the multiple stakeholders' demands have the least impact on learning in NPOs, it is still revealing that they influenced learning given that the previous nonprofit studies mainly point to their involvement in decision making and change (Basinger & Peterson, 2008; Durst & Newell, 2001). The findings confirm the negative impact of external stakeholders (Cunningham, 2001; Kellock Hay et al., 2001; Stone et al., 1999), as seen in their conflicting interests and demands, revealing that they block and slow down knowledge exchange. Regarding learning from employees' interactions with external stakeholders (Fyles, 2003), the present study specifically reveals how this occurs through incorporating their input and experience from the past alteration of HRM. Adding on to findings on accumulated tacit organizational knowledge bases (Ritchie et al., 2007), a high level of external stakeholder expertise can aid the assimilation of new knowledge in the organization. Thus, not only managers' but also external stakeholders' level of expertise is crucial for ensuring integrative learning.

Values-Driven Strategic Orientation

Fourth, the values-driven strategic orientation has a varying influence on the learning styles, encouraging learning in the exploratory, experiential, and integrative learning styles. The analysis has shown that ensuring a fit between the nonprofit mission, culture, and goals and the introduction of the HR practice fosters knowledge articulation during the development and implementation of HR practices across these learning styles. Needing to align with the organizational culture and nonprofit goals encourages NPOs to engage more in learning processes, except for the administrative style. These findings add on to the discussion in the nonprofit literature on the conditions that enhance organizational learning in NPOs, such as establishing an internal culture of learning within the NPO that derives from the leaders' attitude toward learning (Hailey & James, 2002) or a value-based organizational culture (Strichman et al., 2008). In contrast, managers in the administrative learning style invest in fewer learning activities that consider the organizational values as sectoral differences were not perceived as posing barriers to gaining and exchanging information about the HR practice. These findings provide further insight into the imitation of best practices from for-profit organizations in NPOs (Parry et al., 2005). Expanding on the current nonprofit research to show the centrality of organizational values for learning as well, the findings extend the argument of maintaining traditionality (Salipante & Golden-Biddle, 1995). Moreover, the need for a fit with the nonprofit orientation affected the organizations' decisions about what type of knowledge to gain and where to gain this knowledge from. This study reveals that knowledge that reflects nonprofit values and goals is central to exploratory, experiential, and integrative learning because differences between the sectors often limited knowledge sharing and the ability to locate new information. As such, it provides insight into the connection between the adherence to organizational values and the way the organization learns (Hailey & James, 2002).

Influence of Path on Learning Styles

In terms of gaining a deeper understanding of the consequences of the influence of path on learning, the managerial capabilities and values-driven strategic orientations had a fostering influence on the learning styles. Managerial capabilities supported learning across all learning styles in that these competences facilitated gaining, exchanging, and documenting knowledge given the path dependency of routines and the integration of past experience. These findings coincide with nonprofit studies that look to the role of managers as facilitators of learning, emphasizing the experience of leadership (Strichman et al., 2008) and highlighting that managers act as knowledge generators and encourage staff to participate in new learning experiences (Beattie et al., 2005). Furthermore, the values-driven strategic orientation enabled learning in the integrative, experiential, and exploratory learning styles, as learning activities arose out of needing to align the mission, culture, and goals of the NPO with the introduction of the HR practice. Demonstrating further support of the importance of a values-driven organizational culture for learning (Strichman et al., 2008), the act of ensuring a fit between the culture and the introduction of the HR practice leads to the encouragement of learning.

In contrast, the multiple stakeholders' demands and unique attributes of HR exerted both a fostering and hindering influence on the learning styles. Noteworthy, however, is that the analysis unearths the underlying phenomenon that the hindering influence of these path dimensions encouraged the response of engaging in further learning activities in the organizations. When the external stakeholders or employees blocked the learning processes, the managers in the integrative, exploratory, and experiential learning styles responded by drawing on subsequent learning activities. The literature suggests that managers draw selectively on and activate practices or mechanisms once the strategic direction of the organization changes, whereas less adaptable organizations are limited in the latent routines, capabilities, and knowledge that can be drawn on to respond to their changing environment (Collinson & Wilson, 2006; Kogut & Zander, 1992). Similarly, the current study suggests that further experience accumulation and knowledge articulation processes were drawn on and activated by the managers in the integrative, experiential, and exploratory learning styles once the direction of learning shifted as it was constrained. In this manner, path can lead managers to mobilize subsequent learning processes. In contrast, the administrative learning style is not influenced by the path dimensions of values-driven strategic orientations, multiple stakeholders' demands, or the unique attributes of HR, and the managers do not mobilize learning processes. Instead, the investment in learning in the administrative learning style remains low.

In summary, several findings on the relationship between path and the learning styles have arisen from the cross-case analysis. Given that there is a relationship between path and learning, these findings suggest that when organizations need to invest in integrative, experiential, or exploratory learning, they cannot merely copy HR practices from the for-profit sector, as in the administrative style, because the specific values-driven strategic orientations and unique attributes of HR play a role in learning in these styles. Because the organizational values and proclivities of employees differ across NPOs, this may prohibit the development of integrative, experiential, or exploratory learning. Furthermore, in addition to differences in experience gained from following the mission and involving the employees, incorporating the knowledge and experience of the external stakeholders also appears to account for the differences in the integrative learning style, prohibiting the direct transfer of HR practices as well. Thus, the findings convey that experience serves as a crucial factor in understanding the relationship between path and the learning styles. Specific differences have been identified among the individual path dimensions, their influence on the learning styles, and on the relationship between path and the learning styles. The analysis has shown thus far that the concept of path sheds light on both how and why the styles of learning vary considerably in the NPOs.

CASE STUDIES OF THE INFLUENCE OF PATH ON ADAPTING STYLES

With regard to the decentralized, local, and managerial adapting styles, common and idiosyncratic patterns were sought concerning how the path dimensions influenced their search, decision-making, and restructuring processes. The emergent patterns were triangulated across the adapting styles with multiple data sources from the interviews, document analysis, and non-participant observation. The rich case data reveal that substantial differences were incurred concerning the influence of path on the adapting styles, displaying idiosyncrasies in terms of how the unique nonprofit characteristics affected adapting. Employing individual case studies that exemplify each of the adapting styles in the following subchapters, an overview of the findings of the influence of the path dimensions on the adapting processes will be presented. The final section addresses the concept of path as a source of variation across the adapting styles and draws implications for the relationship between path and adapting by cycling back to the theoretical and nonprofit literature.

Case A: A Decentralized NPO

Decentralized NPOs are characterized by encouraging all three adapting processes of search, decision-making, and restructuring processes to a high degree when developing and implementing HR practices. Case A exemplifies this adapting style of engaging in the three adapting processes at the lowest level possible of the organization when introducing its goal setting and performance appraisal system, with exploration, lower level decision making, and resource reconfiguration involving the employees. After hiring a new executive director from the for-profit sector, the social services state association introduced a series of HR practices that emphasized performance management and a more service-oriented direction to help the organization become more progressive and competitive (Case A: I1, 1; I2, 1). In developing its goal setting and performance appraisal system together with the HR department and the employees' representatives in the workers' council, Case A sought more efficient HR planning and training, as well as increased transparency and communication among the departments in order to clearly link departmental goals with the strategic organizational goals. In addition, the NPO aimed to improve employee and organizational performance, employee motivation and skills, and managerial feedback to the employees (Case A: I1, 1, 2, 3; I2, 1, 2; Doc. 12). In the following, the influence of the path dimensions on the decentralized adapting style in Case A will be examined.

Lacking a Fit to the Values-Driven Strategic Orientation

In Case A, the mission is to help people regardless of creed, background, or political affiliation in the areas of elderly care, emergency services, child-care, youth groups, and disaster zones abroad. In its day-to-day work, the state association is committed to following the international committee's seven principles of humanity, impartiality, neutrality, independence, voluntary service, unity, and universality (Case A: Doc. 10). Yet, in seeking commonalities and idiosyncrasies regarding the influence of these values and the mission of the NPO on adapting, the *lack of a fit between the values-driven strategic orientation and the development and implementation of the HR practice* influenced the adapting processes in the decentralized adapting style. In Case A, the push toward performance-related management fostered the decision to introduce the HR practice. Over the past few years, Case A has been on a path of modernizing its management, coinciding with the critical juncture of hiring an executive director from the banking sector. This executive director began an organizational-wide discourse on this performance-driven mentality. In accordance with this culture of change, the introduction of goal setting and performance appraisal was perceived as an "absolute must" for organizational survival in the competitive environment (Case A: I1, 1, 2). Non-participant observation of project group meetings in which lower level decision making occurred by incorporating the employees unearths that the executive director's course of introducing performance-related HR instruments was viewed by the HR managers as crucial (Case A: OB, 1, 5, 6, 7). The introduction of the HR practice stemmed from the executive director's background and was influenced by issues of remaining competitive:

> "The impetus came from our executive director who is very innovative and thinks differently regarding our organization. He is from a completely different sector, from the for-profit sector, and in comparison to our other member organizations, we are really progressive. We want to get out of certain structures because we already feel the competition and are afraid that the competition will get worse." (Case A: I2, 1).

Thus, the lack of a fit with the values-driven strategic orientation is associated with the adapting style that emphasizes engaging in the adapting processes at the lower levels of the organization. The emergence of this pattern makes sense within the decentralized adapting style, as the push toward performance-related management aided in making decisions at the level of the HR managers and involved the lower levels of employees in an organization-wide dialogue. Namely, this tendency is associated with adapting that diverges from the organization's existing values in its strategic direction as the non-profit mission plays little role in altering HRM. The advent of the executive director and engaging the entire organization in dialogue about the organization's procedures brought performance issues to the agenda and aided in shifting the organization toward a new path of modernization.

External Stakeholders' Input and a Lack of Board Involvement

The data were also analyzed for commonalities and differences in the influence of the needs, values, goals, and demands of multiple stakeholders on the adapting processes through which the NPO developed and implemented the HR practice. In Case A, the external stakeholders include the board, local member associations, and their clients (Case A: I1, 1; I2, 1). The analysis demonstrates that external stakeholders influenced the adapting processes in the decentralized adapting style. First, the data reveal that the *external stakeholders' input* aided decision-making processes in the decentralized adapting style. On the one hand, decisions about introducing the HR practice into the local member associations were enabled through these external stakeholders' openness:

> "We view ourselves as quasi-guinea pigs. We want to introduce it here first and see what experiences we can gather and then we will introduce it into our member organizations. [. . .] They are really open. They are really open and some of them are employers with over 1,000 employees. You can't forget how big they are. But like I said, we want to have uniformity and transparency." (Case A: I1, 3).

Thus, rather than adopting a centralized approach to developing and implementing the HR practice throughout the member associations in the organization's federalist structure, Case A prefers an adapting style of gaining decentralized experience with the introduction of the HR practice. On the other hand, however, local search processes were hindered in Case A by the organization's subsidiary. Although the decentralized NPO engaged in externally focused search activities with other NPOs, the organization's subsidiary had poor direct experience with the design and implementation of its own goal setting and performance appraisal practice. Their low level of external input prohibited the organization in its search for external knowledge:

> "We haven't adopted anything from them and haven't discussed it with the developers of that system because we fundamentally think the system is really bad. It's difficult to follow and you can't understand it." (Case A: I2, 1).

Although being hindered in their search processes, the decentralized NPO still engages in adapting processes to a high degree when developing and implementing HR practices. Because this anomaly was detected with the learning processes in the previous section, it was examined whether the organization responded similarly to this path constraint by cycling back and forth between this emergent finding and the raw data. Similarly, these constraints stemming from the path dimension of multiple external stakeholders led to the response of engaging in further learning activities. For example, this response pattern is evident in Case A, where the low levels of input of the organization's subsidiary hindered external search processes about the HR practice, leading the organization to engage in further experience accumulation and knowledge articulation processes with their employees. Because the organization was not successful in local search with the subsidiary, the employees' representatives were forced to acquire knowledge from other organizations in the public and for-profit sectors (Case A: I1, 3) and exchange knowledge about their experiences with the HR practice (Case A: I1, 1). This finding provides initial evidence for the underlying phenomenon of path constraints on adapting, resulting in further learning activities.

More telling aspects about the decentralized adapting style can be seen in the areas where the external stakeholders had little influence. It is characteristic of this adapting style to engage in decision-making processes at the lowest level possible with the employees. External stakeholders provide the decision-making scope to the lower level employees. This decentralized approach to adapting is evident in the *lack of board involvement* in Case A:

> "No, that's day-to-day business here and the executive director does that. He might present it to the board someday when it's finished so that they can see what happens here in the state association [...]." (Case A: I2, 2).

Furthermore, although the decentralized adapting style is characterized by encouraging all three adapting processes, external stakeholders were not involved in the restructuring processes. This finding is typical of the decentralized adapting style because the employees rather than external stakeholders were involved in carrying out the resource reconfiguration activities (Case A: I1, 2, 3, 4; I2, 2).

In summary, this path dimension reveals how adapting is encouraged in the decentralized adapting style by enabling the decision-making processes through incorporating the demands of external stakeholders. Furthermore, the lack of the role of the board sheds light on how the external stakeholders influenced the adapting processes by providing decision-making scope to the employees. This is indicative of the decentralized adapting style in which decisions were also made at the lower levels in the organization.

In contrast, the low input of external stakeholders emerged from the data as prohibiting employees in their search for external knowledge. The case evidence led to the detection of the phenomenon that the decentralized adapting style's pattern of response to the hindering influence of the external stakeholders included engaging in further learning activities with the employees' representatives. This finding provides initial empirical support that learning reinforces adapting processes.

Lack of Acceptance of HR, Variety of HR, and Degree of Involvement of Workers' Council

The analysis of the data also sought commonalities and differences about the influence of the different needs, goals, and motivations of nonprofit employees. In Case A (I1, 1), the employees in the social services state association often have religious ties and previous experience in social work. Although the key informants in the decentralized adapting style suggested that the employees' high level of motivation was "the starting point" for introducing the HR practice and the employees are generally open to change (Case A: I1, 3; I2, 1, 2), there is a limited willingness to change among the employees that stemmed from their initial fears and skepticism regarding the HR practice. This *lack of acceptance of HR*, which captures the extent to which the employees are accepting of change and willing to change, hindered the adapting processes in the decentralized style. For example, in Case A, the employees had already been thrown into a general state of wariness of change given the professionalization efforts of the executive director. Non-participant observation of the first few project group meetings between the HR managers and the representatives of the workers' council indicated how decision making about the design of the HR practice was delayed by the employees' skepticism. The workers' council representatives complained that the HR practice was too complicated, inflexible, and confusing and would only cause stress for the managers and employees (Case A: OB, 1, 2, 4). As corroborated by interview data, the HR head manager remarked how the employees' skepticism and resistance to change hindered the introduction of the HR practice:

> "It was a bit obstructive that we are in a certain period of upheaval, in the organization as a whole and with regard to the staff. Our executive director has introduced a lot of things [...] there is a certain skepticism in both parts of the staff and there was resistance to change. And when they heard that now another one of these systems is being introduced they then ... the skepticism rose again. So and that was really hindering [...]." (Case A: I2, 2).

However, the additional pattern of the *variety of HR*, i.e., the different levels, background, and knowledge of the employees, emerged from the data as fostering search about the goal setting and performance appraisal HR practice. Namely, developing the instrument by including the variety of employees' perspectives in the working group aided the internal search processes in the organization. These employees from various backgrounds are valuable because they "bring new experiences from their areas of expertise" (Case A: I1, 1). Going beyond a mere employer's view, as is characteristic of internal search incorporating employees in the decentralized adapting style, the HR manager commented on the benefits of these employees' experiences for the exploration of internal information:

> "I have learned from discussing with the representatives of the workers' council that we have to improve the goal setting sessions which were implemented in the past. I have learned how our colleagues experienced that, especially these two managers, what went well. [. . .] You see what problems we have and how we have to improve ourselves." (Case A: I1, 2).

However, the data indicate that the variety of HR also hindered the adapting processes in the decentralized adapting style. In Case A, for example, the differing level of knowledge of the employees in the working group delayed the search process for information about the HR practice. These employees refused to be trained by the HR manager, citing the differing employees' and employers' perspectives and levels of knowledge about the HR practice as reasons to hire a neutral external expert (Case A: I2, 1). Furthermore, incorporating the different employees' emotions and sensibilities regarding the goal setting and performance appraisal practice delayed decision making about the design of the HR practice:

> "It's really detailed in terms of the performance evaluation questionnaires and you really have to make sure that they are done well. But there are a lot of subjective things that play a role for the employees, a lot of emotions play a role and these are sensibilities amongst our staff that have to be respected. Because a lot of them are afraid of it." (Case A: I2, 1).

This is corroborated by non-participant observation of the meetings between the workers' council and the HR managers. The employees' representatives delayed making decisions about the design of the HR practice by relaying the fears and questions of its members into these working group meetings (Case A: OB, 2, 4, 7).

Moreover, the data demonstrate that the *degree of involvement of the workers' council* both fostered and hindered the adapting processes in the decentralized adapting style. Granted, consultation with the workers' council is mandated by law in the NPOs, yet the styles differed significantly in the degree to which they involved the workers' council in the processes of developing and implementing the HR practice. In the decentralized NPO, for example, representatives of the workers' council were sufficiently involved from the beginning in the development and implementation of the HR practice (Case A: I1, 1, 2; I2, 1, 2). On the one hand, their early involvement was viewed pragmatically in terms of co-determination laws:

> "The workers' council has to be there. Without the workers' council you can't arrange something like this. It is because of the right to co-determination. And with goal setting it is because they impact compensation. You can't do anything without the workers' council." (Case A: I1, 2).

On the other hand, the organization can still influence the involvement of the workers' council. For example, the organization benefited from selecting which workers' council members serve as working group members. Being able to purposefully select these members aided decision making about the HR practice, as the HR department head commented:

> "The way the group is composed is really important. In the forefront we always control who is part of the working group from the workers' council because it's really important. [. . .] And it's really super important that although these are really different, relatively different people in the workers' council and with some of them it's easier and with others it's more difficult. Who sits in the working group is always really important." (Case A: I2, 2).

Nevertheless, the data show that the degree of involvement of the workers' council often hindered the adapting processes. As corroborated by non-participant observation of project group meetings, the workers' council delayed decision making by failing to share the burden of preparatory work (Case A: OB 1, 2, 3, 4, 5, 6, 7). The head HR manager criticized the lack of the workers' council participation in preparing the negotiations:

> "In the future I want the workers' council to have more responsibility. [. . .] right now 80% of the work is left to me and my colleague. Although I have to say that our relationship with the workers' council is great—there are no problems. [. . .] But it was never said that they should do the questionnaires and present them to us. And that's a procedure that I will definitely change next time." (Case A: I2, 2).

In order to validate the emerging underlying phenomenon with regard to the response to constraints on adapting, cycling back and forth to the data occurred. However, the evidence suggests that Case A did not respond at all to the hindering effects of the lack of acceptance of HR, variety of HR, and insufficient participation of the workers' council. The prevailing attitude in the decentralized adapting style was a resigned acceptance that employee resistance to change and incorporating the specific employees' needs would lead to delays in decision-making processes. Instead of responding to the employees' skepticism of the HR practice by engaging in broad knowledge articulation processes, the organization kept delaying informing the employees:

> "What has gone poorly is that we haven't stuck to certain milestones in our time schedule, like informing the employees, which I think is a really important part that the employees are always informed." (Case A: I2, 2).

Furthermore, as the aforementioned example with the unequal burden of sharing work in the workers' council reveals, the head HR manager did not respond but planned to transfer this insight into a routine for future joint projects. The lack of acceptance of HR, variety of HR, and degree of involvement of the workers' council hindered the adapting processes, yet the decentralized adapting style accepted the delays as tradeoffs for including the employees.

In summary, each of the emergent patterns provides in-depth insight into how the unique attributes of HR both fostered and hindered the adapting processes in the decentralized style. Not only the employees' limited willingness to change, their varied perspectives, and level of knowledge, but also the lack of the workers' council involvement share the commonality of delaying the search and decision-making processes about the design of the HR practice. These findings provide a better understanding of the decentralized adapting style in which the decision-making processes that occurred at the lowest level of the organization were blocked by the employees' fears, skepticism, resistance to change, and different views from those of the employers. Sufficiently involving the workers' council early on in the change process, drawing on the employees' experiences, and carefully selecting the members of the council for the working group fostered both search and decision making. Despite involving the workers' council in the beginning, they also delayed decision making by failing to participate to a sufficient degree. Rather than respond to hindrances stemming from these unique attributes of HR, however, the organization adopts a resigned approach that entails accepting delays and creating routines for developing and implementing future HR practices instead. This implies that the inclusion of diverse employees in adapting processes is viewed in the decentralized adapting style as a necessity even though the negative effects of their involvement on the development and implementation of HR practices are well understood.

Lacking the Managerial Capability to Consider Organizational Structure and Deploying the Managerial Capability of Resource Allocation

Searching for commonalities and idiosyncrasies within the data regarding the influence of the managerial capabilities to consider the existing internal resources, organizational structure, knowledge, and routines reveals several insights within the decentralized adapting style. Overall, the data in Case A points to leadership deficiencies among the managers (Case A: I1, 2; I2, 1), and these deficiencies are partially reflected in the patterns that were identified. Confirming the importance of considering organizational structure during the development and implementation of the HR practice, the analysis unearths the pattern that *lacking the managerial capability to consider organizational structure* hinders adapting. As Case A demonstrates, the traditional hierarchical organizational structure restricted restructuring processes occurring with the department heads (Case A: Doc. 1). While formulating the departmental goals, the department heads failed to consider the organizational hierarchy and different organizational levels, leading to difficulties in terms of conflicting goals and communicating changes in goals within the organization. Iterating back to the data for the pattern of response to these constraints, non-participant observation reveals that the managers did not undertake any further action. Observations drawn from the working group meetings demonstrate that the hindering effect was acknowledged by the group but not acted on because it would require changes at the managerial level of the department heads (Case A: I1, 2, 3; I2, 2; OB, 1, 2, 3). Instead of attending to the restructuring processes with the department heads, the decentralized adapting style restricts its focus to engaging in all three adapting processes at the lower levels of the organization.

In addition, the deployment of the *managerial capability of resource allocation* emerged as a pattern from the data that fostered the adapting processes. For example, in the decentralized adapting style, the managers deployed the capability of resource allocation because they were not limited to their existing resources in the process. Instead, they had a broad range of discretion in making decisions with the employees' representatives about the implementation of the HR practice that was relatively independent of resource constraints. The capability to have access to external financial and human resources enhanced the decision-making processes in the working group by providing the organizations with the necessary inputs to enact changes, as illustrated by the statement of the HR manager in Case A:

> "[. . .] we get support for whatever we need from the executive director. We can read everything. We can order everything. We can hire external consultants. We can hire specialists and retrain them. These are all the inputs we need for the whole process." (Case A: I1, 3).

In summary, the patterns of lacking the managerial capability to consider organizational structure and deploying the managerial capability of resource allocation yield insight into how the path dimension of managerial capabilities influences adapting in the decentralized style. Although this style of adapting is characterized by engaging in all adapting processes with the employees, managerial capabilities nevertheless emerge as central influences on adapting. On the one hand, the lower level decision-making processes characteristic of the decentralized adapting style were encouraged by the deployment of the capability of resource allocation because it gave the managers broad discretion for implementing the HR practice with the employees' representatives. On the other hand, the decentralized adapting style suggests that the absence of the capability to consider organizational structure is detrimental for adapting by restricting restructuring processes occurring with the department heads. Yet, the managers do not respond to this constraint because they failed to address the changes needed at the level of the middle managers, focusing instead on engaging in all three adapting processes at the lower levels of the organization. Again, these findings reflect tolerating the managerial deficiencies in the decentralized adapter and imply that the managers failed to reflect on their own role in the alteration of HRM.

Discussion of the Decentralized Adapting Style

The analysis reveals that the decentralized adapting style is influenced by all four of the path dimensions when engaging in adapting processes to a high degree. In particular, the lower level search and decision-making processes characteristic of the decentralized NPO were encouraged by the push toward performance management, external stakeholder input, lack of board involvement, employees' experiences, selection and early involvement of the workers' council, as well as the allocation of financial and human resources. These patterns shed light on the decision-making scope and broad discretion that the managers had in developing and implementing the HR practice with the involvement of the employees' representatives. Although the decentralized adapters were also hindered by the employees' limited willingness to change, varied employees' perspectives and knowledge, the level of the workers' council participation, and the failure to consider organizational structure, managers do not respond to these constraints. Instead, they accepted them as tradeoffs for including the employees or failed to address the changes needed at the level of the middle managers, focusing on engaging in all three adapting processes at the lower levels of the organization. Only in response to the low levels of external input of the organization's subsidiary did the decentralized NPO engage in further experience accumulation and knowledge articulation processes with the employees' representatives given that they were hindered in their external search processes.

Furthermore, this style provided evidence of path-breaking behavior being associated with lacking a fit to the values-driven strategic orientation. Although the literature on path dependency acknowledges that paths can be dissolved or escaped through external perspectives (Karim & Mitchell,

2000; Sydow et al., 2009), little empirical research has been conducted on this topic thus far. Path-breaking activities can arise through interventions that interrupt the logic of the self-reinforcing patterns of the process by, e.g., unearthing the hidden dynamics for critical reflection in organizational discourse, addressing emotional barriers to unlock the cognitive blinders, and irritating systems of long-standing routines and rules (Sydow et al., 2009). These interventions encourage dialogue to address hidden defenses and embrace errors (Bradshaw, 2002). In the decentralized adapting style, the push toward performance-related management is associated with path-breaking change in that it causes the organization to diverge from its past inefficient practices and strategic direction. Performance issues were brought to the organization-wide discourse after hiring the new executive director. With the advent of this new manager, the lower levels of the organization were engaged in this dialogue about performance management, which aided in irritating the system of rules and routines that had dominated the organization over the past years. This finding coincides with the literature, which maintains that organizations can be willing to switch to a new regime of rules if this is mandated by a change agent or project group (Sydow et al., 2009). In addition, it confirms the study's initial assumption that managerial capabilities are associated with change and path-breaking behavior if managers can instigate a shift from the organization's previous decisions, routines, and values. In summary, the analysis provides initial empirical evidence that a decentralized approach to altering HRM may aid in breaking up path dependency.

Case E: A Local NPO

The local adapting style is characterized by remaining close to its experience and protecting its current knowledge base when engaging in adapting activities. When developing and implementing HR practices, the emphasis is on local rather than distant search and changes in organizational structure occur in similar ways to the organization's past change experiences. In developing and implementing its OD process, Case E exemplifies this adapting style through which the umbrella organization sought to avoid the duplication of work, clarify roles and responsibilities, and develop adequate structures to deal with future demands and stabilize the member organizations (Case E: I1, 1; I2, 1). Proactively anticipating the changes facing the organization in the future, the change process was not only introduced given a decrease in funding, but also due to societal and demographic changes and their impact on sports, as well as internal discussions about clarifying roles within and outside of the organization (Case E: I1, 1; I2, 1; Doc. 3). Case E engaged in local adapting activities in its change process with external consultants, a steering group, and working groups made up of representatives from the member organizations (Case E: I1, 1, 2; I2, 1, 2; Doc. 7).

Lacking a Fit to the Values-Driven Strategic Orientation

The mission of Case E is to contribute to the welfare of citizens in Lower Saxony through advocating for and supporting sports (Case E: I1, 1; Doc. 11), guided in its work by the principles of the common good, sustainability, gender mainstreaming, success and performance, subsidiarity, volunteerism, and maintaining a humane work climate (Case E: I1, 1; Doc. 3, 4, 11). In maintaining this humane work climate, the executive director spoke of ensuring openness and transparency:

> "We've gotten a lot of feedback out of this process that says—'it's important to have this openness.' So that nothing is being kept hidden, rather that everything is being addressed. Of course, you can't go too far with this. But openness is one of the fundamental requirements for successful, positive results [. . .]." (Case E: I1, 3).

Although the executive director repeatedly emphasized the need to live the organizational mission of openness and transparency (Case E: I1, 2), the local adapting style also displayed the pattern of lacking a fit between the values-driven strategic orientation and the development and implementation of the HR practice. In Case E, the *lack of a fit with the mission* enabled restructuring processes within the organization's change process. Granted, both interview data and document analysis in Case E confirmed that the main values, fundamental principles, and mission statement were considered the starting point for the change process (Case E: I1, 1, 2, 3; I2, 1, 2; Doc. 2, 3, 4, 6, 7). These values were used to identify key activity areas that the organization would work on in the future and were intended to determine the subsequent structural changes. Yet the change process became heavily influenced by past organizational structural issues and less by the mission of the organization. This development occurred over time during the change process and was discovered in the later interviews (Case E: I1, 2, 3; I2, 2). The structures were not aligned to the values; rather, the values were aligned to the changes in structure. One of the key informants even admits that the structural changes that occurred in the organization did not actually fit the mission:

> "Other things from the mission statement can be interpreted differently, can imagine it differently with regard to what I was saying before about reducing hierarchies. That something else would have resulted out if that would have fit to the mission more in my opinion." (Case E: I2, 2).

However, neglecting a fit with their mission by prioritizing structure over content also led to difficulties in making decisions about the change process. Alluding to the disharmony in the organization and the member organizations, the OD department head commented:

"And right now this is what is making it difficult to make it more precise and intensified. On the one hand and then on the other hand to already think about structural changes. Right now we are thinking about structures and making the content more precise at the same time. This is something that should be done strictly after the other. And it should be done with the involvement of the entire organization and that is where there are some inharmonious points. I would just like to formulate that carefully." (Case E: I2, 1).

Thus far, case evidence has been provided of the local adapting style engaging in several adapting processes despite being hindered in their decision-making processes by the lack of a fit with their mission. Iterating back to the data, it was examined whether a similar pattern emerged in which the organization employed learning processes to support adapting. Yet rather than engaging in additional learning activities as a response, Case E merely lamented how further knowledge articulation processes did not occur to a sufficient degree:

"That the involvement of all colleagues did not occur sufficiently—which is catching up to us right now as a problem. And I would have liked for there to have been more open discussions with all the participants regarding the structural changes. A lot more openness than what we had here." (Case E: I2, 1).

Although the local adapters recognize the importance of responding to this constraint of path on adapting by engaging in further learning activities, they failed to engage their employees in additional knowledge articulation processes, restricting themselves instead to relying on their current knowledge base.

In summary, the lack of a fit with the values-driven strategic orientation is associated with the adapting style that emphasizes protecting the accumulated knowledge base (local). Case E demonstrates that neglecting a fit with their mission both fostered and hindered adapting processes in the local adapting style, yet it did not lead the organization to engage in further learning activities. Instead, in the local adapting style, emphasizing structural issues over values enabled restructuring processes that remained in line with past changes in the organization. This is associated with path-dependent adapting that entailed reinstating the previous organizational structure as is characteristic of the local adapting style in which restructuring processes occur close to past change experiences. Yet its hindrance to decision-making processes suggests that the lack of a fit between the values-driven strategic orientation and the development and implementation of the HR practice had an idiosyncratic influence on adapting in the local NPO. Thus, the influence of values and the mission of the NPO on adapting indicate that there are even varied effects within the individual adapting styles.

Trusting Role of the Board, External Stakeholders'
Demands, and Conflicting Interests

The external stakeholders in Case E range from its board to member organizations of state sport associations and city clubs, commission, and the main committee political bodies (Case E: I1, 1; I2, 1). Case evidence indicates that the external stakeholders fostered and hindered decision-making processes in the local adapting style. Indicative of this style in which decisions occur at higher levels, in Case E, the board played an active role in adapting in making decisions about the structural changes in the organization by making changes to its own board structure, which then influenced the further structure of the organization. Given the *trusting relationship between the board and the executive directors*, the board delegated these decisions to the executive directors, thereby enabling quick decision making within the change process:

> "It's because the leadership and executive directors here in the organization are accepted by the board. Accepted and they trust our work. That's why a lot of decisions get delegated to us. That is the decisive point as to why we can decide so quickly [. . .]." (Case E: I1, 2).

Yet at the same time, there is case evidence of external stakeholders hindering the higher level decision-making processes characteristic of the local adapting style. Case E provides evidence of external stakeholders being a barrier to the change process through their *demands and conflicting interests*. For example, reaching a consensus during decision making was blocked by power struggles with the member organizations. Both of the key informants suggested that such power struggles were a hindering factor (Case E: I1, 1, 2, 3; I2, 1, 2). The interview data indicate that these struggles stem from past grievances about negative experiences of the member organizations. The past experiences of the multiple stakeholders hindered reaching a consensus in the working groups:

> "There were individual representatives who possibly had not such good experiences in their previous cooperation with the organization or felt that they hadn't been treated adequately or fairly [. . .] it's from past situations that have fed into here so that one couldn't constructively reach a consensus." (Case E: I2, 1).

These past grievances of the external stakeholders are reflective of the local adapting style, which remains close to its past change processes. Furthermore, the representatives of the member organizations blocked decision making by seeking to achieve their own aims in the course of the process (Case E: I1, 1, 2). For example, the members of the board commission evaluative group thought they had decision-making powers in the change process and sought to exert influence in their interest:

"We have the board commission evaluative group which is unwilling to stop working because leaders from the entire organization are in this group who are not in the decision making bodies. [. . .] they have the feeling that they can make decisions as the formal decision making bodies do. This was never planned, however. [. . .] And this has to do with human psychology—everyone wants to be in a decision making position." (Case E: I1, 1).

Seeking to validate the emergent pattern of response to path constraints, closer analysis of the data reveals that, instead of engaging in further learning activities, the evidence in Case E indicates that the organization responded to this power struggle by intentionally allowing the group to continue to work. Through threatening to veto certain decisions within the organization, the group pressured the organization into letting them continue to exist:

"[. . .] some of the representatives of the board commission evaluative group said 'we will only vote for things if the group continues to work.' There was a lot of pressure for this group to keep working and that's yeah, it's ultimately a political, political sacrifice that one has to pay in the organization." (Case E: I1, 2).

Thus, these hindrances from multiple stakeholders' demands were tolerated in order to carry on with the introduction of the HR practice and because the managers felt they had no other choice but to be subject to their influence. Additional knowledge articulation processes were not viewed as an option, as the executive director commented on the futility of engaging the member organizations in further discussions:

"We hope that then at some point the complaining will get quieter in certain areas. For some strange reason that doesn't really work. And the more you inform [. . .], the more discussions there are." (Case E: I1, 1).

In summary, in the local adapting style, the patterns of the demands, the conflicting interests of external stakeholders, and the trusting role of the board reveal how the external stakeholders influenced the adapting processes. Although trust with the board sped up decision-making processes, the demands and conflicting interests of the external stakeholders emerged from the data as delaying decision-making processes. Overall, the board took on an active role in the introduction of the HR practice, thereby fitting the local adapting style, which is characterized by higher level decision making, as seen by the rich case data, which show that the external stakeholders in the higher decision-making bodies are responsible for making decisions. Furthermore, the findings on the external stakeholders shed light on the local adapting style itself. The constraining role of external stakeholders stemming from their past grievances provides further insight into local adapting, in which the organization remains close to its past change experiences. Finally, rather than engaging in further learning activities to counteract these hindrances, the local adapting style protects its current knowledge base, allowing the conflicts with the external stakeholders to continue instead of encouraging knowledge articulation.

Lack of Acceptance of HR, Variety of HR, and Degree of Involvement of Workers' Council

In Case E, the employees identify with sports to a high degree and are viewed as highly motivated and willing to change (Case E: I1, 1, 2; I2, 1, 2). Despite their given willingness to change, it was not able to take effect during the change process in the local adapting style. As a result, the employees' readiness to participate in and accept the changes emerging from the change process remained low. The results of an informal survey show that the employees were willing to embrace fundamental change, yet this willingness to change could not unfold properly in Case E (Doc. 10). This is corroborated by interviews conducted later during the change process, which indicate that the now *limited willingness to change* had manifested itself in utter dissatisfaction (Case E: I1, 3; I2, 2). Because the employees were not involved well enough, they did not identify with the change process. The OD department head commented on the perceived insufficient employee involvement as follows:

> "I believe it's because, like I said before, they weren't involved enough in the entire process and that's why a true identification with the whole thing never happened." (Case E: I2, 1).

> "The employee satisfaction regarding this process, in their involvement, also in the further substantive development and in the further structural development—in my opinion that hasn't happened enough [. . .] and that does not really boost employee motivation. On the contrary. And to break all that up and get back and bring it up to speed—that is not that easy." (Case E: I2, 2).

This had a hindering effect on the restructuring activities when implementing the change process, such as transferring employees into different departments or engaging in cross-departmental cooperative modes of working (Case E: I2, 3). By failing to include the lower levels of employees in the change process, Case E (I1, 1) was repeating its mistakes from previous change processes. This behavior fits with the local adapting style in which restructuring processes occur close to the organization's past change experiences, and, as a result, adapting is hindered by the lack of employee acceptance of the change process.

In addition, the data indicate that the *variety of HR* fostered and hindered the adapting processes in the local adapting style. On the one hand, the heterogeneity of perspectives in the working groups facilitated the entire change process. In Case E, the executive director commented on the benefits of including various employees:

> "I have drawn from personal experience that it is really worth it to involve other people and the whole organization in some form, even if that means that they are really heterogeneous because it is really fruitful for the entire process and I already noticed back when we were developing the mission [. . .]." (Case E: I1, 3).

As the organization relied on its past practice used when developing the mission, this finding reveals further how the local adapting style remains close to the organization's accumulated knowledge base and its previous change experiences. However, the variety of HR prolonged the decision-making and restructuring processes during the development and implementation of the change process. For example, the differing levels of expertise of the working group members limited reaching a consensus about the goals of the organization. Because the levels of expertise and the ways of dealing with the content varied greatly among the employees and the external stakeholders in the working groups, it was time-consuming to bring these less experienced members up to speed and help them to understand the process. The executive director commented on how the different levels of expertise slowed down the change process:

> "You could see that there was a huge discrepancy regarding the quality of formulating the goals. We had absolute experts and people who you could really say were amateurs. It was necessary there to translate the individual measures. That cost a lot of time—translating it, putting it in different words." (Case E: I1, 3).

Moreover, with regard to restructuring processes, the transfer of employees to new departments was delayed due to the employees' different career stages and preferences. This prohibited the new structures and measures from being implemented uniformly throughout the organization:

> "Yeah, it's not finished yet because especially in my area there are still personnel shifts. One colleague is leaving because of her age. [. . .] One colleague has been sick for a long time. Another staff position has to be filled due to some internal shifts. So there is still a bit of turbulence. It's basically not completed yet—can't yet say that it is running smoothly." (Case E: I2, 2).

Furthermore, the data demonstrate that the *degree of involvement of the workers' council* both fostered and hindered the adapting processes in the local adapting style. In the beginning, decision-making processes about the planned structural changes in the board and organization were fostered by keeping the workers' council's involvement to a minimum. Because the managers felt the structural issues were not the concern of the employees, the workers' council was merely informed by the director:

> "We are thinking about whether to add a member of the workers' council directly to the working group 'leadership and administration,' but I don't believe so. Rather, we have ensured that the director—he meets with the workers' council every 14 days and the workers' council is already informed about the most important steps in the change process." (Case E: I1, 1).

Yet a negative side effect emerged as this approach of failing to involve the workers' council on time and to a sufficient degree significantly stopped decision making within the change process. Although the key informants were aware of the necessity of involving the workers' council in the working group given co-determination laws, this did not occur; the interview data reveal that they chose not to do so in the beginning (Case E: I1, 1). Once the workers' council was involved later, the members had objections regarding the structural changes being proposed (Case E: I1, 2; I2, 1). Failing to include the workers' council sufficiently led to interventions and objections, stopping the change process:

> "And then it came to a point where the workers' council said 'it can't go on like this from our viewpoint. We want to be involved and participating differently than we are currently in the change process'. [. . .] Regarding the process the workers' council was obviously irritated. Obviously they were not involved sufficiently. That definitely stopped the process a bit." (Case E: I2, 1).

In light of the hindering effect of these unique attributes of HR on the adapting processes, the data were examined for the organization's response to these constraints. However, the evidence suggests that Case E did not respond to the constraints stemming from the lack of acceptance of HR, variety of HR, and degree of involvement of the workers' council. Similar to the approach in the decentralized adapting style, it was viewed as inevitable that the unique attributes of HR would lead to delays in the decision making and restructuring processes. For example, although the organization knew from the beginning to incorporate the workers' council, they failed to involve them sufficiently:

> "We said from the beginning that the workers' council has to be involved. That's also in the written version that workers' council are a participant group. But this obviously didn't happen to the extent that the workers' council had wished for." (Case E: I2, 1).

Thus, the organization's response reflected the perceived inevitability of the hindering effects, rather than engaging in further learning activities. The patterns of low willingness to change, variety of HR, and insufficient involvement of the workers' council provide in-depth insight into how the unique attributes of HR shaped the individual adapting processes in the local adapting style. First, the variety of HR both fostered and hindered adapting processes given the employees' heterogeneity, differing levels of expertise, career stages, and preferences. Again the emphasis on the inclusion of heterogeneous employees reflects the reliance on past practices of change processes that is characteristic of the local adapting style. Yet these findings are in stark contrast to the dominant findings with regard to the remaining patterns. As the limited willingness to change had a hindering effect on the adapting processes, this finding yields insight into the local adapting style in that the employees' dissatisfaction and resistance to change stemmed from repeating the failure to include lower levels of employees in the alteration of HRM as in the past. This path-dependent behavior hindered the restructuring processes, which remain close to the organization's past change experiences and current knowledge base in this adapting style. Similarly, a complex picture emerged from the data of failing to involve the workers' council on time and to a sufficient degree, which hindered decision making, although the organization was aware of the necessity of including these employees. Thus, contradictory results emerge with regard to the consideration of the unique attributes of HR in the local adapting style.

Managerial Capabilities to Consider Organizational Structure and Resource Allocation

In the local adapting style, the pattern of deploying the *managerial capability to consider organizational structure* emerged as both fostering and hindering the adapting processes. In Case E, for example, this allowed for quick decision making about the future direction of the organization within the adapting processes. Deploying this capability entailed reverting to a previous, albeit unsuccessful, organizational structure that had been used in the past, thereby fitting with the typical characteristics of the local adapting style:

> "There was a structure that did not prove to be successful that was then dismantled for a different structure. But now because of the change process it's actually come to the result that actually the structure that was back then is the right one for us. Now this structure is back again." (Case E: I2, 2).

Yet deploying this capability to consider the past structure simultaneously hindered the restructuring activities necessary for achieving the organization's goals of the change process. The key informants in Case E noted how the organization got too caught up in these structural decisions at the expense of considering the content, values, and goals of the change process (Case E: I1, 2, 3; I2, 1, 2):

> "What didn't go so well was that [. . .]. The structures and divisions had a very, very strong influence on the content and that's a point that I would be clearer about during the next change process. This principle—let us talk about goals and content first. Everything else is secondary and once we have finished with that, only then are we ready to talk about which structures we'll do that with [. . .]." (Case E: I1, 3).

Cycling back to the data regarding this constraining effect of path on adapting, no evidence was provided that the organization responded to this hindrance by engaging in further learning activities. Instead, the case data demonstrate that the managers did not show any signs of attempting to counteract this effect. The document analysis reveals that the managers were criticized by the employees for their role in the change processes, failing to exercise the necessary leadership qualities (Case E: Doc. 8). The interview data display the lack of a response on behalf of the managers and corroborate the managerial tendency to revert to structural considerations:

> "Instead they are only talking about how to change our structures and they are trying to solve the problem in this way." (Case E: I2, 1).

Furthermore, an additional pattern emerged in the data of deploying the *managerial capability of resource allocation*, which enabled the adapting processes. In Case E, for example, the managers had the foresight to anticipate the financial consequences of the change process and thereby strategically allocate available resources to support the restructuring processes. This forward-looking visionary thinking on the part of the managers allowed them to steer the change process appropriately. As the executive director commented on these leadership qualities,

> "I could go in on more detail, but it was really keeping to the time schedule, working consistently and stringently, allocating finances for it, anticipating, looking forward. In a lot of areas we made decisions, for example, we already thought two years ago about the finances we would need to progress with the organizational development process. In some areas we simply assumed that it would come like this." (Case E: I1, 3).

Thus, the data show how the adapting processes were encouraged by the deployment of this managerial capability, in that it enabled the provision and strategic allocation of the necessary resources for bringing about change. The managerial capability of resource allocation fosters adapting by anticipating change through forward-looking thinking. Furthermore, the rich case data reveal the counterintuitive finding that the managerial capability to consider organizational structure is not only beneficial for adapting by facilitating decision-making processes but can also have a hindering influence if it detracts from pursuing the organization's goals. Thus, in the adapting style, which remains close to the organization's knowledge base, these managerial capabilities emerge as central influences on adapting. The pattern of the managerial capability to consider organizational structure points to the path dependency and rigidity of adapting in the local adapting style. Deploying this capability aided the decision-making processes in a path-dependent manner that followed past managerial decisions about organizational structure, providing further insight into how the local adapting style remains close to the organization's past change experiences and managerial decisions. The local adapter did not respond to the constraint posed by the managerial capability to consider the past organizational structure as the managers succumbed to path dependencies of the prior alteration of HRM, rather than reflecting on their own role in the alteration of HRM.

Discussion of the Local Adapting Style

Influenced by all four dimensions, the findings reveal that path-dependent adapting processes predominantly occurred in the local adapting style. The higher level decision making that is characteristic of the local adapters was encouraged by the active role of the board, a trusting relationship between the board and executive directors, as well as the heterogeneity of employees' perspectives, whereas the restructuring processes benefited from being heavily influenced by past structural issues and strategic resource allocation. Moreover, the analysis of each of the four distinguishing nonprofit characteristics reveals how the local adapting style remains close to its previous change experiences, managerial decisions, and structures in its adapting processes given the lack of a fit with the mission, struggles with external stakeholders due to past grievances, reliance on the past practice of including heterogeneous employees, the repeated failure to include lower levels of employees, and the managers' consideration of past organizational structure. This coincides with the literature on path dependency as these local adapters engage in local search, decision-making, and restructuring processes that remain in line with past change processes and problem solving (Cohen & Levinthal, 1990; March et al., 1991; Zahra & George, 2002). The mechanisms of self-reinforcement that are the source of path dependency will be explored to help explain why adapting processes in the local adapting style were sticky or persistent (Pierson, 2000c; Sydow et al., 2009).

First, the lack of a fit with the mission encouraged adapting by enabling path-dependent restructuring processes that reinstated past structural changes in the organization that were unsuccessful. Those responsible for the changes benefit from the prioritization of organizational structure over values and may thus reproduce this pattern as a means to increase their power. In particular, the board and top managers pushed for following the old organizational structure rather than the organizations' fundamental principles. This became a source of conflict for the less advantaged groups within the organization, such as lower level employees (Mahoney, 2000). Furthermore, even deploying the managerial capability to consider organizational structure encouraged path-dependent adapting processes that adhered to past managerial decisions and structures. The local adapters relied on past experience and reverted to previous organizational structures despite being inefficient in the past. Path dependency is often associated with inefficiency because organizations become locked in to one path regardless of new alternatives (Sydow et al., 2009). Learning effects can be associated with reinstating the previous organizational structure. Namely, the knowledge gained and skills accumulated from the use of the structure in the past aids in reproducing the path of relying on the prior structure. Again, organizations tend to use their well-established organizational practices rather than look for alternative solutions and examine their routines (Arthur, 1994; Pierson, 2000a).

In addition, even the employees' resistance to change reflects the ways in which the restructuring processes in the local adapting style occur close to the organization's past change experiences. In particular, repeating the failure to include lower levels of employees in the alteration of HRM as in the past led to employee dissatisfaction, confirming the importance of including employees in change processes (Armstrong, 1992; Kellock Hay et al., 2001). Because the managers felt the structural issues were not the employees' concern, they chose not to involve them. Reproducing this practice of not sufficiently involving the employees is a means for the managers to maintain their power within the organization. These managers benefit from the existing arrangement in which they are determining the issues within the process. Thus, they promote its reproduction and attempt to increase their power and influence over the process, which can result in conflict (Mahoney, 2000). The lack of legitimacy of this practice, however, contributed to the employees' dissatisfaction with the alteration of HRM overall. Finally, concerning the multiple stakeholders' demands, the failure to respond to hindrances from the conflicting interests of external stakeholders and the struggles stemming from their past grievances yields further insight into how the local adapting style protects its current knowledge base at the expense of responding to change (Gavetti & Levinthal, 2000; Helfat, 1994; Leonard-Barton, 1992). These findings emphasize the dangers of focusing on past experience. Studies have shown that in path-dependent adapting processes, prior knowledge may inhibit the managers from adapting their beliefs to the changing environment (Tripsas & Gavetti, 2000). Again, these findings reflect that path dependency stems from being dependent on previous experience. Local adapters engaged in highly path-dependent adapting processes because they rely heavily on the previous experience gained from their prior alteration of HRM.

Case C: A Managerial NPO

The managerial adapting style entails rarely encouraging adapting or even an absence of actions that encourage adapting. Marked by the dominance of managers during the development and implementation of HR practices, executive directors in the managerial NPO steered the direction of search, partook in only higher level decision making, while rarely engaging in or failing to engage in resource reconfiguration. Representative of this managerial adapting style, Case C is a social services local association in which the executive director is responsible for HRM. After gaining certification in TQM, the executive director introduced goal setting and performance appraisal into the organization as a means to develop criteria to be able to make well-justified HR decisions such as laying off employees (Case C: I1, 1). Through implementing this HR practice, the NPO also aimed to increase its employees' motivation, commitment, and ability to change and improve throughout the year. The executive director imitated the goal setting and performance appraisal system, directly adopting it from their state association (Case C: Doc. 2).

Aligning the Values-Driven Strategic Orientation

As a politically and religiously independent organization with roots in the German labor movement, the mission of Case C is devoted to helping others regardless of ethnicity, nationality, or creed, while providing quality services and working transparently and efficiently (Case C: Doc. 5). The analysis of the data unearths the first pattern that *aligning the values-driven strategic orientation* with the introduction of the HR practice fostered the adapting processes in the managerial adapting style. Valuing skills, competitiveness, improvement, and perspectives in its work (Case C: Doc. 1), the manager emphasized a fit with the espoused mission through living by example by also undergoing the HR practice himself:

> "I have been dealing with this for a long time even if I have never implemented it. Job evaluation, performance reviews, HRM in and of itself, goal setting. [. . .] I myself have been evaluated by my board as executive director. I was also evaluated which ultimately led to a different salary classification. So I have personally experienced it as well." (Case C: I1, 1).

The case data show that the managerial NPO seeks to live out its mission of constant improvement when engaging in adapting processes. This finding reflects the dominance of managers in this adapting style who perceive the fit between their espoused mission and the implementation of the HR practice in terms of their managerial experience of the HR practice. In summary, the findings reveal that only in the managerial adapting style in which the managers directed and dominated the few adapting activities, the need to ensure a fit with the values-driven strategic orientation fostered adapting.

Lack of External Stakeholder Involvement

Case C (I1, 1) considers its board and the local authority to be its main external stakeholders. In the managerial adapting style in Case C, there is evidence of a *lack of external stakeholder involvement*. This organization developed and implemented its HR practice without any involvement from the board, funders, or any external regulators, relying instead on its managers' past decisions, experience, and skills with the HR practice or similar practices, as is characteristic of the managerial adapting style:

> "I have been dealing with this for a long time even if I have never implemented it. Job evaluation, performance reviews, HRM in and of itself, goal setting." (Case C: I1, 1).

Although the organization adopted the HR practice directly from its state association, the executive director solely initiated and made the decision to introduce the goal setting and appraisal practice. The executive director imitated the HR practice directly from the state association, which, "in the context of benchmarking [. . .] looked at how it's done elsewhere" (Case C: I1, 1). As the executive director commented on the minimal role of the board in HRM:

> "With regards to HRM the board doesn't have any influence. No. They can regulate things according to the by-laws. For example they approve of hiring decisions. But they don't do that." (Case C: I1, 1).

In summary, external stakeholders did not influence the adapting processes in the managerial adapting style because they were not involved in the development and implementation of the HR practice, with this style relying instead on the managers' past decisions and experience with the HR practice. This pattern fits with the characteristics of the managerial adapting style in which managers dominate the few adapting activities, as executive directors steer the direction of search, dominate decision-making processes, and rarely or fail to engage in resource reconfiguration.

Acceptance of HR

The employees in Case C are motivated to work in social services, are familiar with aid organizations, and are individuals who identify strongly with the association (Case C: I1, 1). Although employees do vary in terms of their different backgrounds and skills in various areas of health and social services, this variety of HR did not emerge from the analysis as exerting any influence on adapting processes (Case C: I1, 1). Instead, the managers dominated and directed the few adapting activities, and the employees were not highly involved in the adapting processes. In the managerial adapting style, the case data only revealed the influence of the pattern of the *acceptance of HR* or the extent to which the employees are accepting of change and willing to change. The employees' acceptance of change in Case C was seen as preserving the work climate:

> "I realized one thing—that the work climate has not gotten worse. [. . .] Everyone who went out of here had the feeling that it was okay and they knew where I was going with this." (Case C: I1, 1).

Granted, the employees were not heavily incorporated in developing and implementing the HR practices in the managerial adapting style as the managers dominated search, decision-making, and restructuring processes. Yet the willingness to change on behalf of the employees emerged from the data in terms of the commitment of the middle managers. The commitment of the department heads was cited as fostering decision making about the next round of implementation. As the executive director commented on their commitment,

> "My guy is already getting on me for when we'll start setting the goals for next year. The department heads are absolutely committed to it." (Case C: I1, 1).

Furthermore, the data in the managerial adapting style reveal that the workers' council did not have an influence on the adapting processes. Wheras there is evidence in Case C that the workers' council had some concerns regarding the HR practice, the workers' council was only symbolically involved in developing and implementing the HR practice because it was directly imitated from the state association. Although interview data show that failing to sufficiently involve the workers' council had led to "drama" in past change processes, the executive director symbolically included the workers' council for its mutual consent in the steering group when introducing the HR practice (Case C: I1, 1). The case data suggest that the workers' council neither fostered nor hindered the processes but merely gave its rubber stamp of approval of goal setting and performance appraisal after clarifying its initial concerns:

> "Yes, the workers' council needed more clarification. If you do this, what do you want to do with this, what is your aim? And then we explained it to them. Then the workers' council said it's okay. [. . .] (Case C: I1, 1).

In summary, the case data in the managerial adapting style do not present a uniform picture of employees being included in the adapting processes, especially in decision-making processes in NPOs. In particular, the patterns of the variety of HR and the degree of involvement of the workers' council provide in-depth insight into how the employees' needs, goals, and motivations played little role in shaping the individual adapting processes. Once the HR practice was imitated from the state association, the employees were only minimally involved as members of the workers' council. Instead, only the high commitment of middle managers fostered the decision-making processes in the managerial adapting style. These patterns help to understand why the unique attributes of HR influenced adapting. This pattern regarding the importance of the commitment of middle managers provides further insight into the managerial adapting style, revealing the ways in which the managers at both the top and middle levels dominate and steer the adapting processes. These findings reflect the emphasis in this style on managerial level influences rather than lower level employees in shaping the adapting processes.

Lacking the Managerial Capability to Consider Organizational Structure and Deploying the Managerial Capability of Resource Allocation

Finally, in the managerial adapting style, which is characterized by managers dominating the few adapting activities, the managers did not even consider organizational structure when implementing the HR practice, thereby hindering adapting. Case C provides an illustrative example of the *absence of the managerial capability to consider organizational structure*. The manager was unable to consider the centralized, traditional hierarchical structure and transfer the necessary resources, which had a negative effect on the implementation of the HR practice. This finding provides a better understanding of the managerial adapting style in which the managers fail to engage in resource reconfiguration. The following statement by the executive director depicts the restricting effect of not having considered the organizational structure:

> "[We had problems during the implementation] in terms of time. We have a really tight administrative structure. I also wanted to be at every feedback discussion, to be there at the last talk. It wasn't possible for us in terms of time." (Case C: I1, 1).

Rather than responding to this constraint stemming from the absence of this managerial capability, the executive director merely stated that the organization had failed to properly implement the HR practice (Case C: I1, 1). As is characteristic of the managerial adapting style, the executive director continued to dominate the adapting processes.

Finally, even in the managerial adapting style in which the managers rarely or failed to engage in resource reconfiguration activities, deploying the *managerial capability of resource allocation* still influenced adapting.

Although the goal setting and performance appraisal practice has no impact on financial resources because of the organization's collective wage scale, implementing the HR practice aided the manager in determining whether more resources are necessary for the employees to achieve their goals. As the executive director commented, he is enabled in estimating these resources in restructuring processes:

> "Has the goal been met and if not, why was it not met? Was the goal unrealistic or were the resources not available in order to reach that goal? And we look a lot more closely now." (Case C: I1, 1).

Thus, the data show that even the low level of resource reconfiguration activities in the managerial adapting style was encouraged by the deployment of this managerial capability in that it enabled determining the necessary resources for achieving employees' goals. Yet lacking the capability to consider organizational structure during the introduction of the HR practice made it difficult to properly transfer resources, leading to the overall failure in implementing the HR practice. These findings shed further light on why managers fail to engage in resource reconfiguration in the managerial adapting style. The managerial adapter did not respond to these constraints because the manager dominated the adapting processes and failed to reflect on his own role in the alteration of HRM. Nonetheless, the findings reveal that managerial capabilities emerge as central influences on adapting in this style in which the managers engaged in few adapting activities.

Discussion of the Managerial Adapting Style

Although managers must interpret new events and developments (Teece, 2007), in the managerial adapting style, adapting activities are rarely encouraged at all. The multiple stakeholders' demands did not influence adapting in this style, which is predominantly characterized by managers steering the direction of search, dominating decision-making processes, and rarely or failing to engage in resource reconfiguration. As the executive directors rely on their past managerial decisions and experience with the HR practice, the unique attributes of HR also have little influence on adapting processes. Once the HR practice was imitated from the state association, the employees' representatives were only symbolically involved in the development and implementation of the HR practice. Instead, the adapting processes were only encouraged by the managers' experience of the HR practice being aligned with the mission, middle managers' willingness to change, and the managerial capability to determine necessary resources. Yet even these path dimensions provide further insight into how managers dominate the adapting processes (Jurkiewicz & Massey, 1998).

First, ensuring a fit between the espoused mission and the introduction of the HR practice indicates more precisely how managers play a dominant role in this adapting style in terms of their managerial experience of the HR

Table 5.10   Influence of Path Dimensions on Adapting Styles

	FOSTER ADAPTING	HINDER ADAPTING	NO INFLUENCE ON ADAPTING	CONSEQUENCES ON LEARNING
VALUES-DRIVEN STRATEGIC ORIENTATION	Managerial adapting style Local adapting style Decentralized adapting style	Local adapting style		Local adapting: *none*: additional learning activities did not occur
MULTIPLE STAKEHOLDERS' DEMANDS	Local adapting style Decentralized adapting style	Local adapting style Decentralized adapting style	Managerial adapting style	Local adapting: *none*: allow the conflicts with the external stakeholders to continue
				Decentralized adapting: *encourages* further learning activities (experience accumulation and knowledge articulation)
UNIQUE ATTRIBUTES OF HR	Managerial adapting style Local adapting style Decentralized adapting style	Local adapting style Decentralized adapting style		Local adapting: *none*: inevitability of the hindering effects
				Decentralized adapting: *none*: resigned acceptance
MANAGERIAL CAPABILITIES	Managerial adapting style Local adapting style Decentralized adapting style	Managerial adapting style Local adapting style Decentralized adapting style		Managerial adapting: *none*: managers dominated the adapting processes themselves
				Local adapting: *none*: managers succumbed to path dependencies of past change processes
				Decentralized adapting: *none*: failed to acknowledge the changes needed at the level of the middle managers

practice. This finding also adds on to the studies suggesting that NPOs must honor their value-expressive character in the way that they operate (Jeavons, 1992), especially with managers leading by example. Furthermore, the unique attributes of HR encouraged decision-making processes through the commitment of the middle managers, reflecting again the emphasis in this style on managerial level rather than lower level employee influences. This finding provides additional insight into the role of managers by revealing how managers at both the top and middle levels dominate and steer the adapting processes.

Moreover, failing to consider the organizational structure hindered the implementation of the HR practice especially in terms of resource reconfiguration, and not responding to this constraint points to the failure of the managers to reflect on their own dominating role in the alteration of HRM. This confirms research indicating that managers often do not see what is changing or do not respond in a timely fashion (Helfat et al., 2007). These findings provide even further insight into how the dominance of managers negatively affects adapting in the managerial adapting style. Rather than incorporating the past experience of their employees and external stakeholders, the managers relied solely on their own capabilities and knowledge bases. This blindsided the managers, e.g., from perceiving the need to add or transfer any managerial resources for the implementation of the HR practice. Through their narrow beliefs, managers constrained adapting in this style and thus did not act in ways that contribute to the creation, extension, or modification of the resource base (Helfat et al., 2007). This is in line with the dynamic capabilities literature, which points out that managers can become trapped by their assumptions, information filters, and problem-solving strategies (Teece, 2007).

PATH AS A SOURCE OF VARIATION IN THE ADAPTING STYLES

Analyzing the influence of the path dimensions on adapting suggests that adapting is subject to the influence of path and that the values-driven strategic orientations, multiple stakeholders' demands, unique attributes of HR, and managerial capabilities influenced the three adapting styles differently. The rich case data expose the different effects of these path dimensions across the adapting styles, thus providing in-depth insight into how and why the adapting styles varied. Table 5.10 depicts the path dimensions that influenced the adapting styles and their direction of influence on adapting, as well as their further consequences on learning.

Values-Driven Strategic Orientation

In contrast to its influence on learning, the path dimension of the values-driven strategic orientation exerts an influence across all of the adapting styles. Yet the data from the local and managerial adapting styles only partially confirmed the studies, which emphasize that NPOs should not compromise on their values and should instead maintain routines and practices that are in accordance with their mission for adapting to change (Alexander et al., 1999; Salipante & Golden-Biddle, 1995). On the one hand, incorporating the organizational values espoused in the mission in the alteration of HRM is further confirmed (Alatrista & Arrowsmith, 2004), as this enabled adapting processes in the managerial adapting style. Yet, in the local adapting style, emphasizing structural issues at the expense of the mission was also seen to foster adapting processes. Similarly, the emphasis on performance-related management rather than the mission enabled decision making about the alteration of HRM in the decentralized adapting style. Adding on to the discussion in the nonprofit literature on change in the mission being one of accommodation, proactive change, reorientation, or even mission displacement (Minkoff & Powell, 2006), this study provides evidence that accommodating for performance and structural issues in relation to the mission is not always detrimental to adapting in NPOs, especially if these changes remain in line with past structural changes. However, these results are tempered because the lack of a fit with the values-driven strategic orientation has an idiosyncratic influence in the local adapting style.

Unique Attributes of HR

Second, the analysis regarding the unique attributes of HR shows that idiosyncratic patterns emerged in the different styles, especially with respect to how this path dimension shaped the adapting processes. The adapting styles were influenced, e.g., by the variety and acceptance of HR, which are constitutive of path in that they capture the experience, skills, and resources of the employees (Mahoney, 1995). The finding that middle managers' commitment fostered decision-making processes in the realm of HRM expands on the nonprofit literature on employee commitment to the organization's cause (Armstrong, 1992) and one's profession (Newman & Wallender, 1978), revealing how NPOs can make decisions that ease the implementation of HR practices with the support of their employees, even in the managerial adapting style. Furthermore, the degree of involvement of the workers' council plays a crucial role in influencing adaptation in the decentralized and local adapting styles. The findings indicate that sufficiently involving the workers' council fostered decision making through providing input and gaining their support early on in the change process. Yet the analysis unearths the interesting finding that involving the workers' council is much like a double-edged sword, as their involvement delayed decision-making processes when they did not participate in sharing the burden of the work. Furthermore, the findings on involving employees and the workers' council in the alteration of HRM in the decentralized and local adapting styles support research, which suggests that greater employee participation functions as a barrier to change and results in lengthier decision-making processes while simultaneously enhancing the acceptance of the HR practice (Armstrong, 1992; Cunningham, 2001; Jackson et al., 2005; Kellock Hay et al., 2001). Overall, the findings on the influence of this path dimension on adapting yield further evidence of the role of employees as a barrier to change (Kellock Hay et al., 2001), with the employees' different preferences and perspectives, dissatisfaction, resistance to change, and the involvement of the workers' council hindering adapting processes during the alteration of HRM. Yet the costs of failing to involve the employees blocked adapting and were perceived as far greater than those associated with including the employees. This study demonstrates that enabling the employees to put their own values into practice (Alatrista & Arrowsmith, 2004), add in their heterogeneous perspectives, and use their specific knowledge and expertise was a necessary tradeoff in order to increase the employees' acceptance of the HR practice and ensure transparency during the development and implementation of the HR practice. Finally, employees were not always broadly included in decision-making processes as seen in the local and managerial adapting styles, thereby reflecting the varied results on employee involvement prevalent in the nonprofit literature (Cunningham, 2001; Jackson et al., 2005; McMullen & Brisbois, 2003; Sheehan, 1998).

Managerial Capabilities

Third, the managerial capabilities also influenced adapting in all three of the styles, confirming the importance of managers in change processes especially through managerial decision making (Adner & Helfat, 2003; Helfat et al., 2007). The local and managerial adapters drew only partially on their employees or not at all when identifying opportunities for the alteration of HRM, with the HR managers or executive directors solely developing the HR practices and determining the direction of search. These findings support the importance of executive directors in initiating change (Durst & Newell, 2001). The managerial capabilities to consider organizational structure and allocate resources are in line with research that suggests the importance of organizational structure and internal resources and operations during change (Dibella, 1992; Parsons & Broadbridge, 2004; van der Pijl & Sminia, 2004). Just as previous nonprofit research shows the need to consider organizational structure in the implementation of HRM (Alatrista & Arrowsmith, 2004; Cunningham, 2001; Palmer, 2003), the present study yields supporting evidence that the managerial capability to consider the organizational structure aids managers in making quick decisions about the future direction of the organization in the local adapting style. The absence of managerial capabilities also illuminates how managers can play a role in failing to adapt in the decentralized and managerial adapting styles. For example, failing to consider an organization's centralized, traditional hierarchical structure was detrimental for altering HRM, leading to difficulties in terms of conflicting goals and communicating changes in goals within the organization and a failure to engage in resource reconfiguration. In particular, because the managers did not always consider the organizational structure, this had negative effects on linking information about changes in organizational goals and communicating these changes throughout the organization. Thus, the managerial failure to consider organizational structure and its effects on knowledge management also proved to be a barrier to learning in this study. Building on the research which maintains that executives are crucial for gaining resources (Jurkiewicz & Massey, 1998), adapting was encouraged by the managers strategically allocating resources in the adapting styles. In particular, strategic visionary thinking and managerial scope in allocating financial and human resources enhance decision-making and restructuring processes.

Multiple Stakeholders' Demands

Fourth, the multiple stakeholders' demands emerged as an idiosyncratic influence of path, influencing adapting only in the local and decentralized adapting styles. They did not influence the managerial adapting style because the board and funders were not involved in developing or implementing HRM. The hindering influence of external stakeholders' demands, conflicting interests, and low levels of external input on search and decision making adds on to the discussion of varying stakeholder expectations and problems of gaining acceptance across diverse constituencies as obstacles to introducing new HR practices (Cunningham, 1999; Palmer, 2003). Furthermore, the findings suggest that external stakeholders can also foster adapting through providing input and scope to the employees to develop the HR practice and delegating tasks. Expanding on studies about the need for the constant effort to maintain an effective fit among the organization, managers, and the board (Bailey & Grochau, 1993), the role of trust emerged from the data, pointing further to the importance of a fit between managers and the board as their trusting relationship fostered decision making. Thus, the local adapting style also reveals the active role of the board in decision making in NPOs (Durst & Newell, 2001; Harlan & Saidel, 1994) and adds to this literature by providing evidence of the board's involvement in the context of the alteration of HRM.

Influence of Path on Adapting Styles

Yielding insight into how the influence of the path dimensions differed across the adapting styles, it is first noteworthy that all of the path dimensions had both a fostering and hindering influence on the adapting processes. Regarding the values-driven strategic orientation, mixed results emerged showing that even subsuming the mission and organizational values to structural or performance management issues aided the processes through which the HR practices were developed and implemented. Yet, in the local adapting style, the lack of a fit with the values-driven strategic orientation also hindered adapting by leading to disharmony in the organization and its member organizations. Although the local adapters recognize the importance of responding to prioritizing structural issues over values by engaging in further learning activities, they relied instead on their current knowledge base rather than involving the employees in additional knowledge articulation processes. This finding suggests that the local adapters are aware that mobilizing learning processes can support adapting but remain trapped in their accumulated knowledge base rather than mobilizing learning in a timely fashion. Thus, the values-driven strategic orientation both fosters and hinders adapting.

Furthermore, it is unusual that the deployment of a managerial capability hinders adapting. Yet the analysis demonstrates that the managerial capabilities not only support adapting but also hinder it through detracting from the organizational goals. The three adapting styles did not respond to the constraints stemming from managerial capabilities by drawing on additional learning activities. Instead, the managers failed to reflect on their own roles in the alteration of HRM as they dominated these processes, succumbed to path dependencies of structural changes within the prior alteration of HRM, and failed to acknowledge the changes needed at the level of middle managers. Iterating with the literature points to the lack of a capability to change their managerial capabilities, which can be understood as a lack of a dynamic managerial capability (Adner & Helfat, 2003).

As in the data on path and learning, the unique attributes of HR and the multiple stakeholders' demands have a fostering as well as a hindering influence on adapting. In the local and decentralized adapting styles, however, the constraints stemming from the unique attributes of HR were tolerated rather than the organizations engaging in further learning activities. The analysis reveals that the hindering influence of the employees was merely accepted, with the managerial responses ranging from resigned acceptance in the decentralized adapting style to the inevitability of the hindering effects in the local adapting style. The constraints that were placed on the adapting processes by employees were viewed as a necessary tradeoff in order to increase the employees' acceptance of the HR practice and ensure transparency. This is in line with the literature that suggests that employee participation in change management affects employees' acceptance of change (Campbell, 2008; Filipovitch, 2006; Kong, 2007). In summary, the findings imply that the unique attributes of HR foster and hinder adapting.

Finally, the data reveal that the decentralized adapters responded to the constraints from the multiple stakeholders' demands by engaging in further learning activities. Cycling back to the data shows that as the direction of adapting changed given the influence of this path dimension, managers responded by mobilizing learning processes to support adapting. Whereas in the local adapting style, the conflicts with the external stakeholders were merely tolerated and allowed to continue, the managers in the decentralized adapters responded by mobilizing additional experience accumulation and knowledge articulation processes to enable the external search activities that had been prohibited by the low levels of input of the organization's subsidiary. This differentiated approach appears to have to do with the nature of the input and demands of the individual external stakeholders. In the local adapting style, managers felt they had no choice because these struggles stemmed from past grievances, and they had to succumb to the threat-like input of the representatives of member organizations. In the decentralized adapting style, the managers appeared to be spurred on by the insufficient external stakeholder input to engage in these learning processes. This example shows precisely how external stakeholders can foster learning in NPOs (Fyles, 2003). The findings show that the multiple stakeholders' demands both foster and hinder adapting and foster further learning. In summary, the findings reveal that, given the constraints from the path dimension of multiple stakeholders' demands, learning processes are drawn on and activated by the managers to support adapting processes. If the managers perceive they have scope in the matter, they employ these further learning processes once the direction of adapting changes when being hindered by path. Stemming from this analysis of path, learning processes also emerge as activities that reinforce the adapting processes through which NPOs develop and implement their HR practices.

Overall, several implications on the relationship between path and adapting have emerged from the analysis of the adapting styles. From the discussion, it has become evident that narrow managerial beliefs, path-dependent adapting relying on past experience, and path-breaking adapting involving the lower levels of the organization account for the differences in the adapting styles and thus explain why path and adapting are related. The perspectives of path have provided a deeper understanding of the specific differences among the individual path dimensions, their influence on the adapting styles, and the relationship between path and the adapting styles. Although the individual path dimensions had a more prevalent influence on the adapting styles than the learning styles, the analysis still shows in detail how and why the concept of path can explain the variation across the adapting styles.

6 Discussion, Conclusions, and Implications for the Alteration of HRM in NPOs

Guided by the concept of methodological fit (Edmondson & McManus, 2007), this study was designed to make a contribution to the nonprofit literature and the dynamic capabilities approach by extending this theory to the novel setting of the nonprofit sector. Both the conclusions drawn from this exploratory case study and the series of implications for the alteration of HRM in NPOs that are developed in this chapter provide initial, key insights into a topic that has thus far lacked empirical attention in the nonprofit literature. First, the main findings related to the research questions will be examined. Thereafter, the contribution to the nonprofit literature and theory will be discussed in relation to the extant studies reviewed in Chapters 2 and 3. Positioning these insights within the wider debate on convergence in HRM across the sectors, implications are drawn that guide managers in balancing the distinguishing nonprofit characteristics with investing in learning and adapting when altering HRM in NPOs. Finally, the book closes with a brief discussion of the study's limitations and directions for future research.

DISCUSSION OF MAIN FINDINGS RELATED TO THE RESEARCH QUESTIONS

Despite the increasing relevancy of HRM in NPOs with regard to improving efficiency and coping with uncertain environments (Conway & Monks, 2008; McMullen & Brisbois, 2003), the review of the nonprofit literature on HRM has demonstrated a broad research gap on the alteration of HRM. Although the current studies provide some insight on what is causing HRM to be altered in NPOs and the implications thereof, there is still scant research on the actual processes involved in altering HRM. In addition, research is lacking on the influences, i.e., the specific nonprofit characteristics, which shape the introduction of new or modified HR practices. Drawing on the theoretical background of the dynamic capabilities approach as it emphasizes the role of path and the underlying organizational processes through which organizations alter their resource base to adapt to their environments (Helfat et al., 2007; Teece, 2007; Teece et al., 1997), this study sought to bridge this gap by examining how and why NPOs develop and implement new or modified HR practices through learning and adapting processes. This study also explored how and why path influences these learning and adapting processes.

Using within- and cross-case analysis in a multiple exploratory case study, learning and adapting styles were identified, which are characterized by the varying degree to which they encourage learning and adapting during the development and implementation of HR practices. Having demonstrated how the styles of learning and adapting differ in terms of their aggregated patterns, the concept of path was subsequently drawn on to provide a better understanding of why these differences among the learning and adapting styles emerge. In the following sections, the main findings with regard to these learning styles, adapting styles, and the relationships between path and the learning and adapting styles will be discussed, in particular in terms of how these findings contribute to the dynamic capabilities and nonprofit literature.

Findings Related to the Learning Styles

An *integrative learning style* was identified in which NPOs develop and implement their HR practices by encouraging all three of the learning processes. The findings reveal that higher investments in learning are discovered to stem from the co-presence of all three learning mechanisms. Extending the theoretical literature which claims that the investment in learning reaches the highest point with codification (Zollo & Winter, 2002), the integrative learners show the necessity of combining experience accumulation and knowledge articulation with knowledge codification for a higher investment in learning when altering HRM. Integrative learners encourage a high degree of learning by achieving a balance between exploration through acquisitive learning and exploitation of the existing knowledge within the organization (March, 1991). The findings add on to the literature on learning to show that as in experiential learning (Keil, 2004), acquisitive learning also entails adapting the knowledge to the organization-specific context through maintaining learning practices that are in line with the nonprofit organization's values, mission, and goals. Integrative learners place an emphasis on aligning learning practices with the organization's values-driven strategic orientation, whether in vicarious learning from nonprofits' experiences, hiring external support versed in the specifics of NPOs, or adapting the imitated materials to nonprofit values. Furthermore, the compatibility of pre-existing knowledge, previous experience, or externally acquired knowledge about the HR practice facilitates both utilizing and integrating knowledge, providing support for the assumption in the literature that complementary internal knowledge enhances the assimilation of external knowledge (Zahra & George,

2002). Again, this complementarity concerns sector-specific knowledge that is in alignment with the organization's values and mission. From these findings, it can be concluded that a high investment in learning during the alteration of HRM (*integrative learning style*) depends on a co-presence of all three key learning mechanisms and is especially supported by being *aligned with the nonprofit organization's values, mission, and goals*, as seen in the *compatibility* between internal and externally gained knowledge about the HR practice.

The second style of learning that was identified, the *experiential learning style*, reveals that the HR practice can be developed and implemented by acquiring knowledge about the HR practice through direct experience, thereby confirming the literature on the lack of complementarity between the knowledge base and the external sources (Zahra & George, 2002). This learning style is unique in that it is the only style that provides evidence for first-hand self-learning about developing the HR practice in the NPOs. Iterating with the theoretical literature, Zollo and Winter (2002) view the evolution of knowledge as beginning in the generation of ideas of how to address old problems or new challenges, followed by evaluating these ideas for their potential in the organization. Both of the experiential learners initiated the alteration of HRM stemming from their internal and external challenges through their learning routines of engaging in discussions with the employees, which led to the creation of organization-specific knowledge about the HR practice. Corroborating the literature that codification supports experiential learning and is necessary as the implications of experience are likely to be lost in organizations (Keil, 2004; Levitt & March, 1988), experiential learners require detailed documentation of the HR practice to enhance transparency and serve as a justification for the need for the HR practice. Thus, it can be concluded that self-learning during the alteration of HRM (*experiential learning*) results in creating organization-specific knowledge about the HR practice that is supported by *learning routines with the employees* and *detailed codification* for the transfer and evaluation of the newly generated ideas throughout the organization.

Furthermore, the *exploratory learning style* was identified, which engages in the acquisition of second-hand experience and pursuit of new alternatives for developing and implementing the HR practice mainly from outside of the organization. Exploring new alternatives, however, can reduce the speed with which skills related to existing knowledge are improved. Moreover, the search for new ideas has more diffuse effects than the further development and refinement of existing ideas (March, 1991). As exploratory learning occurs at the expense of developing the limited pre-existing knowledge about the HR practice, these learners are prone to a vicious cycle in which the organization's lack of complementary internal knowledge prompts them to engage in further external acquisitive learning activities without adjusting and improving on their existing learning routines (Zollo & Winter, 2002). Imitative learning (Levitt & March, 1988) and exploring these new alternatives of HR practices is facilitated by the perception that sector-specific barriers do not exist as the HR instruments are deemed universally applicable. Given the emphasis on buying HR practices externally, exploratory learners make little use of codification during the alteration of HRM, furthering the risk that the existing skills with developing and implementing HR practices are not refined and extended from HR practice to HR practice. In conclusion, learning through the acquisition of second-hand experience during the alteration of HRM (*exploratory learning*) depends on the *pursuit of new alternatives* especially through imitating HR practices, which *neglects developing the organization's knowledge of and skills in* altering HRM.

Finally, a fourth style of learning was identified, the *administrative learning style*, which displays weaknesses in the ways in which NPOs gain, share, and document knowledge during the alteration of HRM. Representing the lowest degree of learning in all of the learning styles, the administrative learning style provides support that the level of investment in learning is related to the time, efforts, and resources expended in codification processes (Zollo & Winter, 2002). As administrative learners predominantly copy best practices in HRM, this necessitates the pursuit of only few and simple codification activities and results in neglecting to codify the method of introducing the HR practice. Despite the prevalence of imitative learning (Levitt & March, 1988), the analysis suggests that the pursuit of acquisitive learning is beset by barriers that stem from a lack of knowledge and experience about the HR practice in the nonprofit sector, leading to less acquisitive learning in this style. Furthermore, lacking routines of information distribution and employee participation throughout the organization, the employees are merely informed but not involved in developing or implementing the HR practices. With this limited investment in employee learning, the administrative learners fail to draw on their potential skills and experiences in altering HRM, thereby perpetuating the situation that Huber (1991) refers to as organizations often not knowing what they know. Not only highlighting the lack of routines as a hindrance to learning (Collinson & Wilson, 2006), administrative learners are also unable or unwilling to learn by failing to adapt the HR practice being copied to the organization's values and needs. Thus, it can be concluded that a low investment in employee learning during the alteration of HRM (*administrative learning*) depends on *copying best practices* in HRM and is beset by weaknesses of *limited routines of employee participation, knowledge distribution and adaptation* to the organization's values, as well as *nonprofit sector barriers* to gaining knowledge about the HR practice.

These findings on the learning styles contribute to the nonprofit literature in several ways. First, they add on to the nonprofit literature on the *conditions that can enhance organizational learning* in NPOs. Supplementing the research on flexible structures, norms, and rules as enabling learning and accessing organizational knowledge in NPOs (Meyer & Mühlbacher,

2001), the findings on the learning styles highlight the relevance of nonprofit sector-specific or organization-specific knowledge sources that entail compatibility between external and internal knowledge and support accessing and integrating external knowledge. This finding also coincides with the case study by Fyles (2003), which maintains that the practices which facilitate learning in NPOs include access to information from a vast range of external and internal sources. Although there is evidence in the exploratory and administrative learning styles that the knowledge gained from the for-profit sector is viewed as universally applicable to all sectors, maintaining practices that are in line with the nonprofit organization's needs and goals characterizes accessing knowledge about the HR practice in the integrative and experiential learning styles. Confirming the importance of engaging in knowledge-sharing activities outside of the organization (Strichman et al., 2008), this study also demonstrates the integrative, experiential, and administrative learning styles' participation in interorganizational and intraorganizational networks that take nonprofit differences into account.

Second, the findings about the learning styles add on to research on the *barriers to learning in NPOs*, ranging from weak communication mechanisms to poor documenting and disseminating habits, and information overload, which prevent the integration and interpretation of information (Fyles, 2003). Although some of these studies suggest that NPOs are documenting their experiences more and replacing informal knowledge exchange with formal mechanisms (Strichman et al., 2008), others highlight that in making implicit knowledge explicit, NPOs face challenges that are exacerbated by the tendency to personalize and the informal structures (Bruckner, 2001). The present study provides additional empirical support by showing that learning was hindered in the various learning styles when failing to use formal networks to share knowledge beyond the organization. This is in line with research on hindrances to knowledge flows and challenges in evaluating, formalizing, and storing tacit knowledge, with knowledge being widespread, fragmented, and rarely formalized as knowledge is shared through informal contacts rather than codifying it and sharing it within a network (Lettieri et al., 2004). Additionally, across the learning styles, barriers to knowledge assimilation were of a cultural, sectoral, and organization-specific nature. For example, the experiential learners provide evidence of facing constraints in the integration of externally acquired knowledge due to cultural and sectoral differences, as well as fundamental differences in the implementation of HR practices. The findings suggest that in addition to sectoral differences, a lack of complementary knowledge about altering HRM is a barrier to learning processes in NPOs.

Finally, the present study departs from the research that claims NPOs are plagued by poor documentation habits to show that knowledge is being formalized in all of the learning styles (Fyles, 2003). The findings point out that while engaging in the infrequent task of altering HRM, the level of engaging in codification activities and the degree of detail is varied to fit the needs of the learning style. In contrast to the integrative and experiential learners that confirm the research on codification being important for learning from experience (Keil, 2004; Levitt & March, 1988; Zollo & Winter, 2002), exploratory learners focus mainly on buying HR practices and administrative learners imitate best practices in HRM, necessitating the pursuit of only a few and simple codification activities. Thus, the data show that different levels and detail of codification are appropriate for different learning styles that emphasize developing their HR practice themselves or acquiring the HR practice externally. In summary, the findings suggest that managers may benefit from varying their codification efforts according to their learning style when altering HRM.

As a result, this discussion of the learning styles adds on to the existing nonprofit research by unearthing further facilitators of and barriers to the learning processes through which NPOs develop and implement their HR practices. The findings on the integrative, experiential, exploratory, and administrative approaches to learning reveal differences in the underlying mechanisms of the development and implementation of HR practices in NPOs. The different investments in learning during the alteration of HRM stem from engaging in a mixture of all three learning processes with an emphasis on alignment with the organization's values and mission, generating organization-specific knowledge through learning routines with the employees, externally pursuing new alternatives of HR practices through imitation, and copying best practices given limited routines as well as nonprofit sector barriers to knowledge acquisition. In summary, these learning styles shed light on the different ways in which the NPOs develop and implement their HR practices.

Findings Related to the Adapting Styles

In identifying the *decentralized adapting style*, the analysis unearths that developing and implementing the HR practice through a decentralized approach of incorporating the lower level organizational members and various external stakeholders aided these organizations in their adapting processes. Teece (2007) has highlighted the role of decentralization in helping sustain the ability to adapt to change because it reduces the organizational layers that create structural rigidities and constrain responsiveness. This study reveals that a decentralized approach to adapting aided in identifying opportunities, problems, and areas for altering HRM by drawing on the organizational members who were often the source of information regarding the need for initiating change in HRM. The study shows that decentralization also helps in identifying opportunities for the alteration of HRM by accessing existing external connections through the employees' interorganizational and intraorganizational ties. Furthermore, a decentralized approach to adapting during the alteration of HRM fostered reaching a consensus about the HR practice by engaging both employees and stakeholders. Consensus seeking poses a particular challenge in NPOs given their associative nature, which mandates a large consensus of agreed values in the face of unclear, vague goals and multiple stakeholders (Barragato, 2002; Simsa, 2003; Stone et al., 1999). Autonomy in decision making in the decentralized adapters especially helped to minimize resistance to the HR practice and coordination difficulties during the implementation of the HR practice. Finally, a decentralized approach also aided in accomplishing the implementation of the HR practice by ensuring employee responsiveness through directly involving the employees in resource reconfiguration. From these findings, it can be concluded that a decentralized approach to adapting during the alteration of HRM (*decentralized adapting style*) depends on *incorporating the lower level organizational members and accessing various external stakeholders* in the development and implementation of HR practices. Decentralization contributes to *problem recognition and consensus making* during the development of HR practices, as well as the *minimization of resistance, reduction of coordination barriers, and heightened employee responsiveness* during the implementation of HR practices.

The *local adapting style* developed and implemented HR practices by encouraging adapting that remained close to past change processes. The study demonstrates that the local adapters have no incentive for conducting broader search processes beyond the nonprofit sector and instead rely on the same external consultants in altering HRM, confirming that organizations' locus of search depends on their past experience and remains in close proximity to the accumulated knowledge base (Cohen & Levinthal, 1990; Nelson & Winter, 1982; Zahra & George, 2002). Local adapters neglect the employees' external connections and close relationships to sources of knowledge regarding the HR practice, which could open up the potential to examine the organization's periphery and escape deeply ingrained assumptions (Teece, 2007). Finally, the success of search activities that remain in proximity of the local adapter's current experience constrains the search horizon during the development of the HR practice. As a result, there is no perceived need to devote scarce resources of attention to broad-based distant search when altering HRM in the local adapting style (Teece, 2007). Moreover, local adapters engage in self-reinforcing decision-making behavior about their HR practices by relying on past experience and previous problem-solving strategies (Finkelstein & Haleblian, 2002; Leonard-Barton, 1992; March et al., 1991), although this may not meet the demands of the current alteration of HRM. In line with this emphasis on past processes, the local approach to adapting also points to the rigidity and path dependency of restructuring when implementing HR practices, especially as the reconfiguration activities result in making changes in the organizational structure that remain in line with past change experiences. Again, managers frame their new problems with the lens of their past experiences, which can lead to inefficient solutions in the face of new alternatives in the changing environment (Sydow et al., 2009). In conclusion, a local approach to adapting during the alteration of HRM (*local adapting style*) depends on relying on *past experience and outdated knowledge bases*. This contributes to *constraints in the perception of new opportunities* for the development of HR practices and perpetuates *self-reinforcing decision behavior* and *adopting past solutions* in the implementation of HR practices.

Finally, the *managerial adapting style* was the third adapting style identified in the analysis. Although a number of researchers have pointed to the importance of managers in change (Adner & Helfat, 2003; Helfat et al., 2007; Teece, 2007), not all functions should rely on their cognitive traits because managers often fail to respond to change in a timely fashion (Helfat et al., 2007). Consistent with this perspective, the managerial adapting style points to weaknesses as the search for opportunities for altering HRM is dominated solely by the executive directors who can become easily trapped by their information filters (Teece, 2007). The analysis shows that identifying the opportunity to alter HRM without considering the employees leaves the managerial adapting styles vulnerable to relying solely on intraorganizational ties and subject to a perceived lack of sector-specific information when developing their HR practices. Furthermore, the study reveals that the managerial-level decision making about the introduction of the HR practice is not consultative because the input of employees and stakeholders is not gained in these decision-making processes. In this respect, the literature highlights that managers can run the risk of bias associated with hierarchical decision-making processes and the inability to see what is changing (Helfat et al., 2007; Teece, 2007). Finally, the managerial adapting style is associated with shortcomings in implementing the HR practices throughout the entire organization given the managerial failure to perceive the need to add or transfer supportive resources. This finding is in line with research on the constraints of managerial cognitive representations (Helfat et al., 2007; Tripsas & Gavetti, 2000) and provides empirical evidence for how these managerial misjudgments about the scope of the implementation of HR practices can play a significant role in the failure to adapt. Rather than reflecting on their own roles and adapting their mental models to the changing demands of implementation, narrow managerial beliefs constrained the NPOs from responding to resource gaps in the implementation of HR practices. In conclusion, a managerial approach to adapting during the alteration of HRM (*managerial adapting style*) depends on *managerial beliefs and judgments*, which, if not adjusted to the changing demands of the alteration of HRM, can contribute to the *failure to garner input from employees and stakeholders* during the development of the HR practice and the *failure to allocate resources* for the implementation of the HR practice.

Contributing to the nonprofit literature on adapting, the present study also conveys *mixed findings on how the adapting styles identify the need for change*. Although nonprofit studies suggest that the executive director and the board are the main catalysts for undertaking change efforts (Durst & Newell, 2001), others indicate that changes are driven mainly by internal initiatives from staff and are only relayed back to the board (Filipovitch, 2006; Kong, 2007). This study is also characterized by opportunities for altering HRM being recognized and initiated by the managers in all of the adapting styles, yet the alteration of HRM especially in the decentralized adapting style is also triggered through introspective searching that draws on the internal resources of the employees and different stakeholders who dominate the direction of search, including the board. This latter finding supports existing empirical research that boards attempt to direct nonprofits and shape management decisions (Durst & Newell, 2001) and goes beyond this literature to show how initiating the alteration of HRM in the decentralized adapters was also aided by external stakeholders who gave the organization and its employees scope to manage this change as they saw fit. Furthermore, the literature emphasizes nonprofit leaders participating in internal and external networks to develop relationships (King, 2004), as well as maintaining interorganizational ties and being active in networks to bring in new resources and opportunities (Alexander, 2000). The findings demonstrate too that across all three adapting styles, the NPOs identified the need for altering HRM by drawing on their external ties. Not only were the external linkages to the university, external stakeholders, as well as interorganizational and intraorganizational ties used to initiate the introduction of the HR practice, but these connections were also used to transfer resources during the implementation of the HR practice. Thus, this study provides additional evidence for the importance of networks in recognizing opportunities and acquiring resources.

In line with previous literature, this study also displays *mixed findings on the degree of including employees in decision making in NPOs.* Employees were not always broadly included in decision-making processes about the introduction of HR practices, thereby reflecting the varied findings on employee involvement that are prevalent in the nonprofit literature (Cunningham, 2001; Jackson et al., 2005; McMullen & Brisbois, 2003; Sheehan, 1998). The present study provides partial support for the consultative and discursive nature of decision making in NPOs as the decentralized adapters exercise autonomy in decision making at the lower levels of the organization and include various external stakeholders in decision making. Additional empirical support is provided for the effects of involving multiple participants in decision making on enhancing the acceptance of the HR practice and on the pace of developing and implementing HR practices (Armstrong, 1992; Kellock Hay et al., 2001). While including multiple participants is perceived to increase acceptance of the HR practice, at the same time, this study shows more precisely that delays in decision-making processes in the decentralized and local adapting styles arise out of involving the employees and external stakeholders due to their conflicting views. Thus, this study adds on to the literature by showing how the overly discursive nature of decision making in NPOs (von Eckardstein, 2002) can eradicate the quick decision making that arises from the considerable autonomy of organizational units (Teece, 2007). Furthermore, shedding light on how top managers influence change in NPOs beyond their intuitive strategic decision-making styles that are supported by accumulated tacit organizational knowledge bases (Ritchie et al., 2007), managers not only rely on their own knowledge and capabilities but do well to garner the expertise of employees and external stakeholders in making decisions during the alteration of HRM.

Finally, building on the nonprofit research on *resource acquisition* which maintains that executives play a crucial role in gaining resources (Jurkiewicz & Massey, 1998), this study indicates that employees also facilitated resource transfer through their expertise and their acceptance of change as manifested in their trusting relationships with the managers. Thus, the study shows that HR practices are implemented in the NPOs with managers *and* employees engaging in resource reconfiguration activities. The findings also reveal how managers are pivotal for resource allocation (Helfat et al., 2007; King, 2004), in that the managerial failure to perceive the need for resources is associated with an unsuccessful implementation of the HR practice. Furthermore, adding on to studies which suggest that NPOs deal with their demands for professionalization through coping strategies that include reducing staff and increasing workloads (Alexander et al., 1999), the findings show how the decentralized and local adapters also cope by integrating and modifying HR practices, strategically aligning the organizational structure with goals, and deploying employees to new areas within the organization.

As a result, this discussion of the adapting styles extends the nonprofit literature by revealing how the adapting processes through which HR practices are developed and implemented are fostered and hindered. Overall, the decentralized, local, and managerial approaches to adapting provide a better understanding of the different ways in which the NPOs develop and implement their HR practices. Specifically, these NPOs differ in their underlying mechanisms of altering HRM in terms of incorporating lower levels of employees and stakeholders, continually emphasizing past experience when altering HRM and possessing shortcomings in developing and implementing HR practices due to narrow managerial beliefs and judgments.

Findings on the Relationships between Path and the Learning and Adapting Styles

Although other theoretical perspectives may be useful in explaining the differences across the learning and adapting styles, following the conceptual framework guiding this study, the theoretical concept of path was drawn on. Findings have been provided that shed light on the relationships between path and the learning and adapting styles. It can be concluded from these findings that the concept of path yields in-depth insight into why the styles of learning and adapting vary considerably across the NPOs in the development and implementation of HR practices. The analysis has demonstrated that path has an idiosyncratic influence on the learning and adapting styles, and the variations in the influence of path are associated with differences in the styles that entail various consequences for the alteration of HRM. With regard to learning, the examination of path leads to the development of the following four tentative propositions about the relationship between path and the learning styles.

- First, when NPOs consider their values-driven strategic orientation, multiple external stakeholders' demands, unique attributes of HR, as well as their managerial capabilities in the alteration of HRM, they are more likely to make a high investment in learning that combines all three learning processes (*integrative learning*). In terms of the consequences for the alteration of HRM, the differences incurred from following the mission as well as involving the employees and the external stakeholders prohibit the direct transfer of HR practices from the for-profit or public sectors.

- In contrast, when NPOs solely include their managerial capabilities during the development and implementation of HR practices, they are less likely to invest in learning and focus instead on copying best practices (*administrative learning*). These managers invest little in involving the knowledge and experience of employees or external stakeholders in developing the HR practices and focus instead on imitating best practices. Regarding the implications for the alteration of HRM, when failing to invest in learning beyond managers' routines and past experience, NPOs are not prohibited from directly copying HR practices from the for-profit sector.

- Furthermore, when NPOs consider the unique attributes of HR in terms of the breadth of HR, acceptance of HR, and the concerns of the workers' council, they are more likely to engage in self-learning (*experiential learning*). In terms of the alteration of HRM, the differing proclivities of the employees and their organization-specific knowledge restrict NPOs from imitating best practices, resulting in internally developing their HR practices.

- Yet when NPOs draw less on the experience of their employees as seen in incorporating only the concerns of the workers' council, they are more likely to explore new alternatives of HR practices externally (*exploratory learning*). This entails consequences for HRM as the NPOs are able to buy the HR practice without adapting it to the needs of the organization and its employees. Instead, exploring these new alternatives of HR practices is facilitated by the perception that organization- and sector-specific barriers do not exist as the HR instruments are deemed universally applicable.

These tentative propositions capture the newly identified relationships between path and learning that reveal the importance of values and the experience of managers, employees, and external stakeholders for the way learning occurs during the alteration of HRM in NPOs. These findings can be understood in relation to the literature on path-dependent learning, which points to organizations leveraging their prior experience onto new projects (Pisano, 2000). Conceptual and empirical work on the path dependency of learning maintains that although constraints can arise from organizations' previous experiences (Levitt & March, 1988), previous knowledge also enables future processes (Nelson & Winter, 1982; Teece et al., 1997). As learning takes place from the introduction of one HR practice to the next HR practice, it is path-dependent. The previous knowledge becomes available for future change processes (Pisano, 2000). The findings reflect that the previous knowledge and experience embedded in the path dimensions account for differences across the learning styles.

Cycling back and forth between the findings and this theoretical background, the high encouragement of a combination of learning processes in the integrative learners is facilitated by incorporating the previous experience of their managers, external stakeholders, and their employees with introducing past HR practices. More specifically, the integrative learners were able to draw on this previous knowledge and experience and leverage it to the current development and implementation of the HR practice (Pisano, 2000). In addition, the integrative learners remain in line with their experience of orienting the mission of the organization with the development and implementation of the HR practice. As a result, the integrative learners can deepen their knowledge base given the variety of experience they draw on and highly encourage a mixture of all three individual learning processes (Zollo & Winter, 2002). In contrast, the administrative learners, who had limited pre-existing knowledge about the HR practice and are only influenced by incorporating the experience of their managers in learning processes, rarely encourage learning processes. They are not able to develop a deeper knowledge base because they did not draw on the variety of experience within and beyond the organization. Whereas the exploratory learners minimally incorporated the employees' experience through the workers' council, the experiential learners went beyond to include their employees' experience in terms of the breadth of HR, acceptance of HR, and the workers' council. These learning styles thus differed in the degree to which they drew on employees' experience, as seen in the greater emphasis on self-learning and internally developing the HR practice in the experiential learning style, as opposed to a focus on engaging in several acquisitive learning activities and externally acquiring the HR practice in the exploratory learning style.

In summary, these findings are interpreted to maintain that differences in incorporating managerial, stakeholder, and employees' knowledge and experience, as well as experience gained from following the mission, account for differences in the learning styles across the organizations. Thus, previous knowledge and experience serves as a crucial factor in understanding the relationship between path and the learning styles. This complements studies on the path dependency of learning, which reveal that organizations develop capabilities through learning that depends on pre-existing know-how and previous knowledge from past projects (Camuffo & Volpato, 1996; Helfat, 1997; Marsh & Stock, 2006).

Yet as Pisano (2000) points out, when it comes to learning, the link between learning and experience remains poorly understood because it is not entirely straightforward. Some experiences allow organizations to determine the underlying cause–effect relationships, which then become applicable for future processes (Teece et al., 1997). Although possessing previous experience may provide opportunities for learning, whether learning occurs from experience can depend on specific organizational actions and management decisions (Pisano, 2000). In a similar vein, a conclusion from this case study is that external stakeholder expertise, experience derived from following the mission, and employees' knowledge and experience play a crucial role in learning. Whether learning that entails a high investment in and integrates all three learning processes takes place depends critically on managerial actions and decisions to incorporate this experience. If managers incorporate the experience from the mission, employees, and external stakeholders, the more likely it is that a high investment in learning during the alteration of HRM will occur. In contrast, if managers neglect to take actions that enable them to draw on and learn from a variety of employee and stakeholder experience, a mere imitation of best practices in HRM can arise, and learning is likely to be only rarely encouraged. The alteration of HRM occurs without a synergistic relationship to the organizational mission and values. If self-learning is the aim of the organization, managers should pay attention to broadly incorporating the experience of their employees beyond the minimal legal requirement of consulting the workers' council, which leads to learning that predominantly emphasizes acquiring HR practices. This study specifically sheds light on the poorly understood link between learning and experience (Pisano, 2000), showing that different styles of learning are associated with incorporating different kinds of previous experience. These findings both confirm and add on to the conceptualization of path in the literature, which has been understood as constituted by the organization's values, routines, past managerial decisions, and experience (Mahoney, 1995), to show the importance of values and experience of employees as well as that of external stakeholders for the way learning processes evolve in organizations. Learning occurs to differing degrees during the alteration of HRM depending on managerial action and attention being devoted to the various kinds of experience within and outside of the organization.

Given the importance of both the values-driven strategic orientation and unique attributes of HR for learning in the integrative, experiential, and exploratory learning styles, these findings bear implications when organizations need to invest in these styles of learning during the alteration of

HRM because they cannot merely copy HR practices directly from the for-profit sector as in the administrative style. Instead, the organizational values and proclivities of employees differ across NPOs and need to be taken into consideration. In addition, incorporating the knowledge and experience of the external stakeholders also appears to account for differences in learning, thereby prohibiting the direct transfer of HR practices that fail to take the heterogeneity of external stakeholders' demands and past experiences into account when investing in integrative learning. In summary, the theoretical concept of path helps to understand these differences across the learning styles given that the path dependency of learning entails that previous experience influences future learning processes (Pisano, 2000).

In terms of adapting, the study also shows that differences in the influence of path are associated with differences in adapting styles, which entail various consequences for the alteration of HRM. From the analysis of path, the following three tentative propositions can be developed about the relationship between path and the adapting styles:

- When NPOs are able to break from the past alteration of HRM with regard to their strategic orientation by engaging in adapting processes that widely involve their external stakeholders and employees, they are more likely to highly encourage adapting during the alteration of HRM (*decentralized adapting*). Although the consultative, consensus-oriented adapting with internal and external stakeholders entails longer adapting processes that draw out the development of the HR practice, decentralization aids the alteration of HRM through decision-making scope and broad discretion. These findings have added on to the theoretical literature on decentralization (Teece, 2007) by showing that a decentralized approach to the alteration of HRM supports escaping path dependencies. NPOs are aided in recognizing opportunities to alter HRM and in reaching a consensus by including these employees' and external stakeholders' experiences. Furthermore, employees are responsive through their sufficient involvement, and coordination difficulties are minimized. As a consequence for the alteration of HRM, the development and implementation of HR practices are enabled.

- In contrast, when NPOs remain trapped in path-dependent adapting processes that occur close to their past decisions, structures, and practices of altering HRM, they are more likely to engage in adapting to a moderate degree (*local adapting*). These findings reflect that path dependency stems from being dependent on past inefficient practices, as the local adapters relied heavily on their past negative experience and knowledge of their prior change processes even when the current situation differed substantively. The local adapting style is constrained in its adapting processes as the current knowledge base is protected at the expense of change. This entails consequences for the alteration of HRM in that it poses barriers to developing and implementing HR practices, especially when adopting past solutions in the implementation of HR practices.

- Finally, when NPOs fail to incorporate the experience of their employees and external stakeholders and are solely dominated in their adapting processes by their managerial capabilities, they are less likely to engage in adapting (*managerial adapting*). This fits with the characteristics of the managerial adapting style, which entails a sole reliance on managers' past decisions, experience, capabilities, and knowledge bases, with neither external stakeholder nor employee input being taken into account. These findings point to the literature on managers becoming trapped by their assumptions (Teece, 2007). As managers constrain adapting through their narrow beliefs and failure to perceive resource gaps, the implications for the alteration of HRM can entail a failure to implement the HR practice consistently.

These tentative propositions reflect the newly identified relationships between path and adapting that shed light on how stakeholder involvement, relying on past experience, and managerial beliefs account for differences in adapting during the alteration of HRM in NPOs. The interpretation of the findings shows that these mechanisms behind path-breaking adapting, path-dependent adapting, and the absence thereof account for the differences in the way the various styles adapt during the alteration of HRM.

According to the theoretical literature, path-breaking change occurs through interventions that require reflection on the drivers of path dependency (Sydow et al., 2009). External interventions enable organizational members to grasp the inconsistency between espoused theories and behavior. Encouraging dialogue to address these hidden defenses and embrace errors is also claimed to function as a learning trigger (Bradshaw, 2002). In the decentralized adapter, external interventions were undertaken, which enabled critical reflection of the organization's processes by engaging the lower levels of the organization in a discourse about performance issues. These findings provide initial empirical evidence that a decentralized approach to altering HRM may aid in breaking up regimes of path dependency. Thus far, the role of decentralization has been emphasized in the literature in terms of aiding organizations in their ability to reconfigure their resources (Teece, 2007; Teece et al., 1997). While this study corroborates that it facilitates resource reconfiguration, it also expands on the literature to show how decentralization is associated with path-breaking behavior. These organizations were able to break free from the logic of path dependency in their strategic orientation as the interventions encourage a decentralized, organization-wide dialogue that addresses the hidden assumptions and defenses, thereby irritating the system of routines and rules that had dominated within the organization. Thus, this study shows that escaping the organizational path entails unearthing the ineffective dynamics of the organization (Sydow et al., 2009), and this can be facilitated by stakeholder involvement at the lower levels of the organization. This finding confirms the study's initial assumption that when the experience, skills, and resources of the employees are included in the alteration of HRM, managers have the potential to bring about path-breaking change in NPOs, shedding new light on the role of decentralization in adapting.

In contrast, in the local adapting style, the findings confirm that path dependency stems from being dependent on previous experience. In the local adapters, previous knowledge was transferred from the alteration of one HR practice to the next HR practice. By reverting to previous solutions, such as structures and change practices that were unsuccessful, the findings in the local adapting style confirm that path dependency is often associated with inefficiency because organizations become locked in to one path regardless of new alternatives or changed internal or external conditions (Sydow et al., 2009). Thus far, the concept of path dependency has proven useful within the public sector literature for understanding how previous events and decisions may affect the organization's development into a particular path (Gains et al., 2005; Kay, 2005). Yet path dependency has only recently gained attention in the nonprofit literature, with organizational commitment to founding values, past experience of leaders, and entrenched routines being identified as path-dependent factors that constrain adaptation (Ramanath, 2009). The present study confirms that the experience of managers was a path-dependent factor as seen in the managers' reliance on their experience in terms of engaging in local search, repeating past change routines, not responding to past grievances, and reverting to their old organizational structure from the previous alteration of HRM. The theoretical literature on path dependency points to several mechanisms of self-reinforcement that can help to explain why the adapting processes in the local adapting style are sticky or persistent (Arthur, 1994; Mahoney, 2000; Pierson, 2000a). This can provide further insight into the dynamics of path dependency, moving the analysis from describing the influence of path to come to explanations for why path influenced the style in this manner (Pierson, 2000c). The analysis has confirmed that self-reinforcing mechanisms including learning effects and benefits from power reproduce the past patterns in the local adapters (Arthur, 1994; Mahoney, 2000). Coinciding with the literature on learning effects (Pierson, 2000c), the knowledge gained and skills accumulated from the use of the structure in the past aids in reproducing the path of the prior structure. Power also played a crucial role in encouraging managers in the local adapting style to not respond to external stakeholders' past grievances and conflicts and continue movement down a specific path (Mahoney, 2000). As a result of these self-reinforcing dynamics, search, decision-making, and restructuring processes remained in line with past changes in the organization. Local adapters engaged in highly path-dependent adapting processes because they rely heavily on the experience and knowledge gained from previously altering HRM.

The managerial adapting style forms an exception in that there is no evidence of path-breaking or path-dependent behavior with regard to the adapting processes. Instead, the rare participation in adapting processes is dominated by managers' experience of the HR practice being aligned with the mission, middle managers' willingness to change, and the managerial capability to determine necessary resources. By relying solely on their own capabilities and knowledge bases, managers failed to reflect on their own role in the alteration of HRM and were blindsided from perceiving the resource gaps in the implementation of the HR practice. Thus, instead of incorporating the variety of experience embedded in the path dimensions, the mechanism driving the adapting processes in the managerial adapting style appears to be the managerial beliefs. These narrow managerial beliefs and judgments play a role in the failure to engage in adapting processes (Tripsas & Gavetti, 2000). These findings add on to the literature by demonstrating how adapting can be damaged when relying on the cognitive traits of only a few individuals (Teece, 2007) and are in line with research on managers often not seeing what is changing or failing to respond in a timely fashion (Helfat et al., 2007). Rather than incorporating the knowledge of their employees and external stakeholders, the narrow managerial beliefs prevent managers from responding to shortcomings in the implementation of the HR practice. The managers constrained adapting through their beliefs and thus did not act in ways that contribute to the alteration of HRM.

Therefore, the mechanisms of stakeholder involvement, relying on past experience and managerial beliefs behind path-breaking adapting, path-dependent adapting and the absence thereof have been identified as critical to understanding the relationships between path and the adapting styles during the alteration of HRM. This study confirms the conceptualization of path in the literature (Mahoney, 1995) by revealing that when adapting processes depend heavily on the manager's past experience in altering HRM, they evolve in a cumulative way. Initial empirical evidence is provided of path-breaking behavior that instigated a shift from values in the organization's strategic orientation, which suggests that organizations are not entirely trapped by their past, although the new path still remains a product of the earlier structure of existing activities, resources, and actors (Hakansson & Lundgren, 1997; Teece, 2007). Thus, the findings imply that if managers incorporate employees and external stakeholders in organization-wide processes, the more likely it is that a decentralized approach to adapting that can break from past alteration of HRM will occur. In contrast, if managers rely heavily on past experience through prioritizing organizational structure over values and adhere to past decisions, structures, and practices, the more likely local adapting will occur that remains path-dependent and close to the past alteration of HRM. Furthermore, if managers fail to incorporate the experience of employees and external stakeholders and their narrow beliefs and judgments solely dominate the adapting processes, the more likely a managerial adapting style will occur in which the managers fail to respond to shortcomings in the alteration of HRM and adapting is rarely encouraged. These differences in path account for the variation in encouraging adapting across the styles.

Thus, a central contribution of the book entails identifying these foundations of the concept of path, which are the relevant management concepts for exploring learning and change in NPOs. These findings aid in making sense of the mix of stability and change that characterizes the alteration of HRM in NPOs. It can be concluded that path functions as an appropriate concept to gain insight into the influence of the distinguishing nonprofit characteristics on the alteration of HRM. Viewing the learning and adapting styles together when weighing the influence of these individual distinguishing nonprofit characteristics entails the following main conclusions about the alteration of HRM in NPOs.

First, although values play a dominant role in influencing learning across several of the styles, contrary to assumptions in the literature, altering HRM is not predominantly mission-driven. Granted, maintaining learning practices that are in line with the nonprofit organization's values, needs, and goals and complementary sector-specific knowledge provides insight into why best practices are not suitable for these NPOs. Yet rather than being primarily mission-driven, the NPOs retain a focus on their managerial capabilities in learning and adapting. Although it is not surprising that managerial capabilities feature as a dominant influence, they only remain a starting point for the alteration of HRM. This study also reveals the deficits of solely relying on these capabilities, especially as the managerial beliefs constrained the implementation of the HR practice. In addition, the findings demonstrate that employees emerge as a critical stakeholder in the alteration of HRM. This suggests the importance of investing in the unique strengths and expertise of the HR pool and highlights the need for further research on the double-edged role of employees in the alteration of HRM. Finally, in contrast to the literature, the varying expectations of multiple external stakeholders were not a dominant influence on the alteration of HRM, yet this study also unearths the role of board in the context of altering HRM. Future research needs to devote attention to the relationship between the board and managers and the issues stemming from the dual management structure of NPOs for HRM. On the whole, these conclusions highlight the interactions with both the internal and external environments of NPOs during the alteration of HRM. Although learning and adapting can be precipitated by changes in the external environment, this study clearly points to the importance of the organization's internal environment as well when examining the dominating influences on how these organizations learn and adapt.

CONTRIBUTION TO THE NONPROFIT LITERATURE

The distinguishing nonprofit characteristics both facilitated and hindered the development and implementation of HR practices, suggesting that factors distinctive to NPOs matter and even pose challenges when altering HRM. These findings confirm and contradict the current nonprofit research and shed light on new phenomena that have not yet been addressed in the literature. In the following section, the contribution of these empirical findings to the nonprofit literature will be discussed, and several broader implications for the alteration of HRM in NPOs will be drawn.

Organizational Values in Learning in NPOs

Surprisingly, the analysis reveals that the salient role of organizational values, while not a barrier to change, is more relevant to learning than adapting in NPOs. The findings only partially confirm the studies which emphasize that NPOs should not compromise on their values and instead maintain routines and practices that are in accordance with their mission for adapting to change (Alexander et al., 1999; Frumkin & Andre-Clark, 2000; Salipante & Golden-Biddle, 1995). Rather, this study provides evidence that accommodating for performance and structural issues in relation to the mission is not always detrimental to adapting in NPOs (Minkoff & Powell, 2006). Yet more so than with regard to adapting, the findings expand on the current nonprofit research to show the centrality of organizational values for learning. These values foster learning in NPOs as the need to maintain a fit with the mission, culture, and nonprofit goals encouraged the organizations to engage in knowledge articulation and codification. Moreover, it affected the organization's decisions about what type of knowledge to gain and where to gain this knowledge from. Knowledge that reflects nonprofit values and goals is crucial to learning because differences between the sectors often limited knowledge sharing and the ability to access new information. These findings extend the argument that traditionality may aid NPOs (Salipante & Golden-Biddle, 1995) by specifying how considering the historically embedded values of the mission encourages learning.

Board as an HR Change Initiator and Its Trusting Relationship with Managers

Although the empirical findings confirm previous research which suggests that multiple external stakeholders complicate the management of change (Kellock Hay et al., 2001; Ospina et al., 2002; Stone et al., 1999), this study also shows that the board enhanced the development and implementation of HR practices in NPOs. On the one hand, the analysis provides evidence of an active role of the board, initiating the introduction of the HR practice and actively making changes during adapting processes. This active involvement of the board confirms the role of the board as a change initiator (Harlan & Saidel, 1994), yet this study goes beyond previous research to show that the board can even function as an HR change initiator. On the other hand, rather than being highly involved in HR decision making in

NPOs (Durst & Newell, 2001; McMullen & Brisbois, 2003), the analysis overwhelmingly suggests that the board gave managers and employees the decision-making scope to develop and implement their HR practices. In this respect, maintaining a trusting relationship between the board and the managers is a finding that has not been significantly addressed in studies on the relationship between internal and external stakeholders. Although research has discussed the roles of the board (Harlan & Saidel, 1994), it has focused less on the interaction between the board and executives or employees and the involvement of the board in developing and implementing HRM (Akingbola, 2006a; McMullen & Brisbois, 2003). Thus, this finding underscores the importance of board-related leadership for managers (Herman & Heimovics, 1990a, 1990b) in the area of HRM, corroborating that the relationship between boards and executive directors is characterized by a climate of trust rather than conflict in NPOs (Miller, 2002).

Employees as Necessary Barriers to Change

The cross-case analysis overwhelmingly demonstrates that the inclusion of employees in learning and adapting processes hindered the development and implementation of HR practices. Involving employees in the alteration of HRM was found to prevent learning and delay the adapting processes, supporting research which suggests that greater employee participation functions as a barrier to change and results in lengthier decision-making processes (Armstrong, 1992; Kellock Hay et al., 2001). The findings bolster the nonprofit studies which claim that employee participation in change management affects employees' acceptance of change and that their limited willingness to change may hinder the management of change (Campbell, 2008; Filipovitch, 2006). Furthermore, the employees' conflicting views and differing preferences during the development and implementation of the HR practice yield additional empirical evidence that the employees in nonprofits have different goals, priorities, and values that diverge from those of the organization (Fenwick, 2005; Minkoff & Powell, 2006). These findings are in line with prior studies that identify loyalties of staff and internal resistance to change as possible constraints on introducing HRM (Alatrista & Arrowsmith, 2004; Cunningham, 1999).

Although employee involvement was a barrier to adapting, the phenomenon emerges that their involvement was necessary because the costs of failing to involve the employees were perceived as far greater than those associated with including the employees. This study demonstrates that not only enabling the employees to put their own values into practice (Alatrista & Arrowsmith, 2004), but also adding in their diverse perspectives and using their specific knowledge and expertise during the development and implementation of the HR practice was a necessary tradeoff in order to increase the employees' acceptance of the HR practice and ensure transparency throughout the process. Furthermore, the case data provide evidence of the negative effects of failing to involve the workers' council on time and to a sufficient degree. Based on the analysis, the study highlights that employees are necessary barriers to change that must be included in developing and implementing HR practices in NPOs.

Managerial Scope, Strategic Visionary Thinking, and Beliefs

The managerial capabilities to integrate past change experience, employ learning routines, consider organizational structure, and allocate resources that emerged from the data confirm and expand on the nonprofit literature. These findings are in line with research that suggests the necessity of considering organizational structure, internal resources and operations, and the manager's accumulated knowledge base during change in NPOs (Parsons & Broadbridge, 2004; van der Pijl & Sminia, 2004). Extending previous research which indicates that a lack of resources features as a barrier to introducing HRM (Cunningham, 1999; Kellock Hay et al., 2001), this study shows that managerial scope in allocating financial and human resources and strategic visionary thinking that anticipates change enables the alteration of HRM. Thus, managers can influence change, especially through sensing changes in the environment or within the organization and reconfiguring organizational resources (Teece, 2007).

However, the absence of managerial capabilities illuminates how managers can play a role in failing to adapt. For example, failing to consider an organization's structure was detrimental for altering HRM given conflicting goals. This finding supplements previous research which reveals that organizational structure can function as a barrier to the adoption of new HR practices, especially as the organizational structures lack a common perspective on goals and priorities (Alatrista & Arrowsmith, 2004; Cunningham, 2001; Palmer, 2003). Yet NPOs may have an overall advantage in this respect given their flatter, more democratic structures, which allow for the better coordination of organizational change (Tassie et al., 1996). Moreover, the finding that the managers did not respond to hindrances points to the failure of managers to adapt their mental models to changes in the demands associated with altering HRM. Their managerial beliefs constrained them from perceiving new opportunities to alter HRM and addressing resource gaps in the implementation of the HR practice. Overall, these findings suggest the importance of managerial cognition in terms of strategic visionary thinking and beliefs for understanding the development and implementation of HR practices in NPOs.

Implications for the Alteration of HRM in NPOs

Against the background of isomorphic behavior within and between the sectors (Bies, 2010; Leiter, 2008; Ramanath, 2009; Verbruggen et al., 2011) and the narrow debate on adopting best practices from the for-profit sector

(Brooks, 2002; Helmig et al., 2004; Speckbacher, 2003), this study clearly implies that the influence of the distinguishing nonprofit characteristics prevents managers from directly transferring HR practices from the for-profit or public sector. The exploratory empirical research demonstrates in several cases how specific factors distinctive to NPOs shape the way they alter their HRM, leading to the conclusion that these characteristics render the introduction of HR practices different from a direct imitation of HR practices from the other sectors. Granted, broader management trends result in HRM becoming more similar across the sectors, and several elements identified in this study indicate the alteration of HRM is merging aspects that are common to the other sectors. For example, evidence is provided of an emphasis on performance management in professionalizing HRM that reflects a convergence among the sectors, confirming previous studies in the literature that cite changing employment relations and working conditions in NPOs (Cunningham, 2008a, 2010b; Hurrell et al., 2011; Kellock Hay et al., 2001). This development could also be seen in the introduction of pay for performance schemes and practices that entail performance appraisal across the cases. Furthermore, several case examples demonstrate HR practices being imitated or bought externally from the for-profit sector. The findings reveal that NPOs orient themselves strongly toward for-profit experiences with HR practices when engaging in learning and adapting.

However, rather than isomorphic pressures in HRM toward best practices arising from the demands of maintaining public sector funding and power relations between government agencies and employers (Cunningham, 2008b, 2010b; Palmer, 2003; Parry et al., 2005), the case study reveals that NPOs are responding to pressures in their internal organizational environments as well, such as employee dissatisfaction or challenges in recruitment or coordination. Granted, several of the cases were introducing HR practices to proactively deal with budgetary constraints stemming from state cutbacks, yet the explored NPOs were not shifting their HRM toward a specific public sector approach. In particular, the reasons for altering HRM suggest, in contrast to the literature (Akingbola, 2006a), that NPOs are matching changes in their strategic direction with change in their HRM. Thus, some of the cases provide examples of a proactive approach to altering HRM in order to address future challenges and funding restrictions. Surprisingly, despite these budgetary constraints, the NPOs still had the capability to strategically allocate the necessary human and financial resources in designing and implementing HRM. In contrast to the literature, the HR function was not constrained and under-resourced (Cunningham, 2010b); instead, the managers were given access to the necessary resources for the alteration of HRM. Finally, going beyond viewing changes in HRM with regard to the relations to the state (Cunningham, 2008b), this exploratory study highlights the influence of a variety of external stakeholders beyond the state, for example, boards, advisory committees, subsidiaries, and member organizations, shedding light on the ways in which HR managers face pressure and seek to reconcile external demands when adopting HR practices.

On the one hand, positioning these findings within the wider debate on isomorphic behavior in the sectors does corroborate a shift toward a strategic, performance-related emphasis in HRM that is reflective of the tendency in for-profit and public sectors. On the other hand, the exploratory multiple case study reveals that HRM is being altered in NPOs in distinctive ways that are not adequately explained by the aforementioned convergence across the sectors. Instead, the distinguishing features of NPOs shape the development and implementation of their HR practices and can lead to several challenges that render the alteration of HRM different from the private and public sectors. As the alteration of HRM is influenced by the organization's specific path, adopting for-profit management models directly to NPOs ignores the values and experience of employees and the heterogeneity of multiple external stakeholders. The findings confirm that NPOs have values-based reasons for selecting their HR practices that fit with the organization's culture and management philosophy (Eaton, 2000). Thus, the risks of professionalizing HR practices do not lie merely in a lack of resources, capabilities, and expertise in HRM (Kellock Hay et al., 2001), but in imitating best practices or buying HR practices externally without adapting them to the specific needs of the organization and its employees or without a synergy to the organization's values. As such, this study provides empirical evidence for the obstacles to the introduction of HRM entailing distinguishing nonprofit characteristics such as the existing values, expectations of the diverse constituencies, loyalties of staff and inherent resistance to change, as well as the participative culture and organizational structures that lack a common perspective on goals in NPOs (Cunningham, 1999; Palmer, 2003). Thus, the implications drawn from the analysis of the influence of values, external stakeholders, and nonprofit employees challenge the direct adoption of HR practices that are developed in the for-profit sector and derived from for-profit strategies.

For example, although there is evidence that NPOs benefit from aligning the development and implementation of their HR practices with the values-driven strategic orientation in learning, the study shows that the decision making by and influence of managers and external stakeholders on the alteration of HRM can contribute to a disconnect between HRM and the values-driven strategic orientation. This is likely to entail the danger of installing HR practices that deviate from the strategic direction of the mission and may lead, for example, to recruiting employees that are not oriented toward the strategy, thus posing a threat to the organization's mission (Akingbola, 2006a). Managers must be aware that altering HRM can bear implications for the organization in terms of deviating from the mission. Finally, regarding the challenges that NPOs face in altering HRM, the analysis shows that this entails managing several, contradictory bottom lines in NPOs (Anheier, 2005). Instead of relying solely on their capabilities, managers must balance the varying stakeholder and employee expectations and attend to the dual management structure with boards. In summary, by drawing on their distinctive values and heterogeneous stakeholders' experiences and investing in the unique strengths of their employees in addition to the capacities of managers, NPOs can invest in learning and adapting that aids them in accomplishing the alteration of HRM.

CONTRIBUTION TO THEORY

By examining the learning and adapting styles and the influence of path on these styles in the new context of nonprofits, this study aimed to make a contribution to theory. Extending the dynamic capabilities approach to the nonprofit setting creates the opportunity to make a theoretical contribution, e.g., by unearthing anomalies or breakdowns in the data (Alvesson & Kärreman, 2007). These outliers and surprises can help to build better explanations and extend theory (Miles & Huberman, 1994). Theory extension entails empirically grounding the concepts of path and processes in a new context other than in which the concept was first developed or intended to be used (Colquitt & Zapata-Phelan, 2007; Snow, 2004). The nonprofit setting has proven especially fruitful in unpacking the influence of path on the learning and adapting styles and shedding new light on the relationships among path, learning, and adapting that affect the current understanding of the relationships in the dynamic capabilities approach, thereby addressing the how element of theory (Whetten, 1989). Discussing these empirical findings in light of the existing theory provides the opportunity to broaden the initially introduced concepts and achieve analytical generalization (Eisenhardt, 1989; Yin, 2009). The following section discusses how this study contributes to a better understanding of the relationship between path and processes in the dynamic capabilities approach.

First, grounding path in the novel context of the nonprofit setting has revealed that the theoretical concept of path accounts for the differences across the learning and adapting styles. Path enables insight into the ways in which the learning and adapting styles were constrained or enabled in the development and implementation of HR practices, yielding initial evidence of both path-dependent and path-breaking behavior. While the conceptualization of path as being constituted by values and experience is confirmed in the literature (Mahoney, 1995), exploring path in the nonprofit sector also reveals more specifically that not only the experience of managers or employees, but also the experience of external stakeholders and experience gained from following the mission explains the differences in the way the learning processes across the learning styles evolve. In this manner, this study further contributes to understanding the link between learning and experience (Pisano, 2000). The role of experience is also corroborated in the path dependency of adapting processes, with these processes evolving cumulatively due to drawing heavily on managerial experience. Thus, a central contribution of this study is shedding light on the sustained persistence of learning and adapting processes in which experience is the main path-dependent factor that reproduces a certain solution (Sydow et al., 2009). In terms of further understanding the differences across the adapting styles, this study also makes a contribution to the literature on path-breaking behavior. Confirmatory evidence is provided of escaping path-dependent regimes by integrating an exogenous perspective (Bradshaw, 2002; Sydow et al., 2009), yet this study also expands on the literature by revealing that a decentralized approach aids in unearthing hidden assumptions and defenses through critical reflection together with the lower levels of the organization. Given the discursive internal decision-making processes in NPOs in which they tend to consider the needs of their members (von Eckardstein, 2002), organizations in the nonprofit sector may have an inherent advantage for engaging in path-breaking adapting through this decentralized approach.

Second, analyzing the learning and adapting styles in the nonprofit sector contributes to the literature on dynamic capabilities in several ways. Having identified and discussed the four learning styles through which NPOs alter their HRM, findings emerge that expand on and further refine the literature on learning. These findings in the integrative learning style depart from the research on the role of learning mechanisms in the dynamic capabilities approach (Zollo & Winter, 2002), as higher investments in learning are observed in this study to stem from the co-presence of all three learning mechanisms, rather than solely codification processes. Furthermore, the analysis of the four learning styles shows that when altering HRM, acquisitive learning that involves gaining and internalizing knowledge from outside of the organization dominates over experiential learning. Less evidence is provided for first-hand experiential learning (Pisano, 1994; Zahra et al., 1999), as the analysis shows that second-hand learning is crucial in all of the learning styles for building up new knowledge when taking up a new activity, such as when organizations alter their HRM (Keil, 2004; Mahoney, 1995; March et al., 1991). In addition, while codification is confirmed to support experiential learning during the alteration of HRM (Keil, 2004; Levitt & March, 1988), the findings extend the literature by showing that the level and detail of codification can be varied to fit the learning style in order to aid future employees who face similar tasks (Zollo & Winter, 2002). Moreover, expanding on the literature on the complementarity between the knowledge base of the firm and external sources (Zahra & George, 2002), a lack of complementary internal knowledge is shown to trigger further external acquisitive learning activities, as seen in the exploratory learning style. Finally, this study yields additional empirical evidence of learning processes supporting each other (Kale & Singh, 1999; Marsh & Stock, 2006; Verona & Ravasi, 2003), as knowledge codification encourages knowledge articulation by ensuring knowledge transfer throughout the organization.

Furthermore, by identifying and investigating into the adapting styles through which NPOs develop and implement their HR practices, the aforementioned findings call for extending the research within the dynamic capabilities approach to include the initial insights on the difficulties of overcoming path dependencies in reconfiguration. In contrast to the literature on reconfiguration (Teece, 2007), path dependencies in the local adapting style are maintained rather than escaped in restructuring given the reliance on past experience (Pisano, 2000). The findings add on to the literature on decentralization (Teece, 2007) by showing that a decentralized approach aids in adapting and especially in engaging in path-breaking behavior. Moreover, this study shows that when researching into restructuring processes, managerial beliefs are pivotal for understanding how managers can be detrimental to adapting. In particular, it supplements the research on managerial cognitive representations inhibiting the organization from adapting to change (Tripsas & Gavetti, 2000) to show how narrow managerial beliefs constrain restructuring processes as managers fail to respond to resource gaps.

In addition, exploring the influence of path on processes in the nonprofit setting sheds further light on the relationship between learning and adapting in the dynamic capabilities approach. After analyzing the learning and adapting styles, it was noted that learning and adapting appear related, but it remained unclear how and why they are linked to each other. Indeed, the connections between learning and adapting are still poorly understood, with most of the literature explicating the relationship between organizational processes and dynamic capabilities (Maritan & Peteraf, 2007). Teece (2007) advances the discussion on the linkages between learning and adapting by stating that sensing requires learning as the microfoundations of the capability to recognize opportunities depend on the learning capacities of the individual or the organization. He also maintains that learning, knowledge-sharing, and knowledge-integrating procedures are important for the realignment of assets yet does not delve into the relationship between these knowledge management processes and reconfiguring resources. This study adds on to this discussion as restructuring processes are aided by knowledge sharing beyond the organization in that this learning activity enables the further transfer of resources during the implementation of HR practices. This provides additional empirical support for learning as an *enabling process* that facilitates the reconfiguration of existing resources (Easterby-Smith & Prieto, 2008; Pavlou & El Sawy, 2005). Organizational processes are not only conceptually linked, such as experience accumulation and search processes (Pandza & Thorpe, 2009), as this study also provides empirical evidence that links knowledge articulation or codification with supporting decision-making processes. Maritan and Peteraf (2007) propose that there may be individual supporting processes underlying dynamic capabilities that are not only consistent elements but have reinforcing complementarities as well. This study yields evidence that decision-making and restructuring processes are supported by the additional learning processes of experience accumulation and knowledge articulation. Further research is necessary to examine the reinforcing complementarities these learning processes may feature with the adapting processes.

Finally, the tentative propositions developed in this study capture the newly identified relationships and provide a basis for further research on the approaches to learning and adapting during the alteration of HRM. In this respect, the findings emerging from analyzing the relationships among path and the learning and adapting styles can help to better understand how learning and adapting are linked. Both the analysis of the learning styles and the adapting styles has shown that the constraining influence of path results in the mobilization of learning processes. Just as latent routines or a pool of resources can be mobilized by managers in adaptable organizations (Collinson & Wilson, 2006), the phenomenon was identified that once the direction of learning or adapting shifts given the hindering influence of path, the managers respond by activating learning processes. Learning processes thus emerge as activities that managers draw on to reinforce adapting. By participating in further experience accumulation and knowledge articulation activities with employees, the workers' council or external stakeholders, the managers sought to move the development and implementation of the HR practice forward. A key function of managers appears to be drawing on these complementary individual learning processes when organizations are hindered in learning or adapting, thereby providing additional empirical support for the critical role of managers in adapting to change (Adner & Helfat, 2003; Helfat et al., 2007). These findings help to make sense of the relationship between path and learning that goes beyond the explanation that processes of learning are enabled by being close to the accumulated knowledge base and past processes (Nelson & Winter, 1982; Teece et al., 1997). Thus, one of this study's contributions lies in further clarifying the role of path and processes in the dynamic capabilities literature. Although a first step has been taken toward understanding the processes of and influences on the alteration of HRM, additional research is needed to validate these linkages among path, learning, and adapting. The learning and adapting styles and their identified relationships to path provide a framework that may guide further research.

Thus far, this discussion has demonstrated that the dynamic capabilities approach was appropriate for analyzing this study's research questions. This study shows that this theoretical approach is also applicable to organizations with goals that do not include profit maximization and thus extends beyond the conditions of wealth creation it was initially designed to explain. The findings on the relationship between path and processes that emerge from exploring the dynamic capabilities approach in this novel empirical domain testify to its relevancy for the nonprofit context as well, thereby broadening the theory's range. By merging insights gained inductively from the nonprofit sector with the extant dynamic capabilities approach, the exploratory multiple case study sheds light on the established constructs and suggests new connections among path and processes that render further empirical research necessary. Thus, the dynamic capabilities framework provides insight into how and why the learning and adapting styles emerge and differ. It accounts for idiosyncrasies in the way NPOs respond to changes in their environment and internal conditions. In summary, this theoretical approach has proven fruitful for understanding the alteration of HRM in NPOs by providing the underlying logic for the observed relationships between the distinguishing nonprofit characteristics and the learning and adapting styles through which NPOs develop and implement their HR practices.

LIMITATIONS AND DIRECTIONS FOR FUTURE RESEARCH

Although this study has taken an important first step toward understanding the learning and adapting processes through which NPOs alter their HRM, much empirical work remains to be done. The implications of this study are, of course, subject to limitations in both method and scope. First, regarding the method, key informants who were directly involved in planning, decision making, and implementing the HR practices were selected for conducting interviews, which in most cases included either the executive directors or HR managers. Although intensive direct observation in Case A allowed for gathering the experiences of line managers in addition to the HR managers, additional research could benefit from gaining first-hand data from the employees regarding their perspectives of the development and implementation of HR practices in NPOs. Second, this study was limited to solely exploring the processes through which NPOs alter their HR practices. Further studies could explore the link between these implemented HR practices and outcomes, such as their impact on the nonprofit's ability to meet performance goals or their responsiveness to change. Such quantitative-oriented empirical research would afford nonprofit practitioners with insights into how these new or modified HR practices may better equip their organizations in fulfilling their mission and facing internal and external changes.

Furthermore, the analysis focused solely on the development and implementation of HR practices. As a result, the findings may be limited to the nature of altering HRM. Additional empirical research is called for to examine the findings in other change contexts, e.g., regarding the development and implementation of organizational strategies or innovations. The learning and adapting processes explored in this study might take on different configurations according to the contexts in which they take place. Moreover, exploring the dynamic capabilities approach in NPOs has shown that it is relevant for the nonprofit sector as well, thereby broadening the range of this theoretical approach beyond the for-profit and public sectors. Yet additional empirical research in the nonprofit sector is needed to validate the newly identified connections among path, learning, and adapting. Although the analysis is based on the specific experiences of eight NPOs, these new relationships provide a framework that may guide further research. As the empirical findings in this study emerged as common patterns stemming from NPOs across a range of diverse fields, these findings may apply to other NPOs in similar fields. Initial common insights have been gained into the complex relationship between path and processes, yet empirical research is still needed to investigate the differentiated implications of the role of path to examine the extent to which similar change behavior is elicited. Furthermore, this book has highlighted that NPOs in Germany are facing similar environmental constraints and pressures as NPOs in the U.S. or the U.K., e.g., rising demand for services given demographic changes, funding cutbacks, increasing competition from the other sectors, and a stronger emphasis on performance and efficient management. Additional research is necessary to examine the extent to which the lessons learned from these cases can provide insight into organizational change and HRM in NPOs beyond Germany. Finally, the findings exhibit the value of case study research for examining organizational change, as the learning and adapting processes are dependent on the individual path the organization has taken. This study underscores the need for more fine-grained qualitative research into processes and the influence of path to inform the dynamic capabilities literature. Ultimately, this may require merging existing theory with the insights developed inductively using qualitative data from new settings, such as the nonprofit sector.

Appendix

Table A.1 Learning Dimensions

	EXPERIENCE ACCUMULATION PROCESSES
Dimension	The extent to which the NPO engages in external acquisitive learning activities.
Dimension	Whether the NPO has internal knowledge about the HR practice.
++	*High extent of engaging in external acquisitive learning activities; The NPO has internal knowledge about the HR practice.*
- -	*The NPO does not engage in external acquisitive learning activities; The NPO does not have internal knowledge about the HR practice.*
	KNOWLEDGE ARTICULATION PROCESSES
Dimension	The extent to which the NPO shares knowledge within and beyond the organization.
Dimension	Whether the NPO utilizes pre-existing knowledge and integrates the externally acquired knowledge.
++	*High extent of knowledge sharing within and beyond the organization; The NPO utilizes pre-existing knowledge and integrates the externally acquired knowledge.*
- -	*Knowledge is not shared within and beyond the organization; The NPO does not utilize pre-existing knowledge and integrate the externally acquired knowledge.*
	KNOWLEDGE CODIFICATION PROCESSES
Dimension	The extent to which the NPO engages in codification activities using written or electronic tools.
Dimension	Whether the NPO codifies the content, method, and rationale behind the HR practice.
++	*High extent of engaging in codification activities using written or electronic tools; The NPO codifies the content, method, and rationale behind the HR practice.*
- -	*The NPO does not engage in codification activities using written or electronic tools; The NPO does not codify the content, method, and rationale behind the HR practice.*

5-Point Scale of Participation

  - -   No   - Low   0 Medium   + Fair   ++ High

Table A.2   Adapting Dimensions

SEARCH PROCESSES	
Dimension	The extent to which the NPO explores within the organization and beyond the organization in the development and implementation of the HR practice.
Dimension	Whether the NPO engages in local and distant search.
++	*High extent of exploring within the organization and beyond the organization in the development and implementation of the HR practice; The NPO engages in local and distant search.*
- -	*The NPO does not explore within the organization and beyond the organization in the development and implementation of the HR practice; The NPO does not engage in local and distant search.*

DECISION-MAKING PROCESSES	
Dimension	The extent to which the NPO internally and externally integrates resources and activities to make decisions about the development and implementation of the HR practice.
Dimension	Whether the NPO engages in lower and higher level decision making.
++	*High extent of internally and externally integrating resources and activities to make decisions about the development and implementation of the HR practice; The NPO engages in lower and higher level decision making.*
- -	*The NPO does not internally and externally integrate resources and activities to make decisions about the development and implementation of the HR practice; The NPO does not engage in lower and higher level decision making.*

RESTRUCTURING PROCESSES	
Dimension	The extent to which the NPO adds, transfers, deletes, or recombines resources for the development and implementation of the HR practice.
Dimension	Whether the NPO engages in generating new resource combinations to better match the environment.
++	*High extent of adding, transferring, deleting, or recombining resources for the development and implementation of the HR practice; The NPO engages in generating new resource combinations to better match the environment.*
- -	*The NPO does not add, transfer, delete, or recombine resources for the development and implementation of the HR practice; The NPO does not engage in generating new resource combinations to better match the environment.*

5-Point Scale of Participation

- - No   - Low   0 Medium   + Fair   ++ High

Table A.3 Interview Question Guideline

Interview Questions

1. New and Modified HR Practices

1.1. How would you describe your current HRM system? What are the HR practices in your organization?

1.2. What HR practices are being/have been introduced or changed recently?

1.3. Please describe this HR practice.

1.4. Why did you introduce/change this HR practice?

1.5. What are the expected benefits of introducing/changing the HR practice?

2. Path

Values-driven strategic orientations:

2.1. What is the mission and what are the values of your organization?

Unique attributes of HR:

2.2. How would you describe and estimate the needs and motivations of the employees?

Demands of multiple stakeholders:

2.3. Who are your stakeholders and what are their main interests regarding the HR practice?

Financial resources:

2.4. How is your organization financed?

Organizational structure:

2.5. How would you describe the structure of your organization?

3. Adapting: Search

3.1. How did you introduce/change the HR practice?

3.2. Was a plan to introduce/change the HR practice formulated and, if so, how? What are the goals and content of this plan?

3.3. To what extent were the stakeholders involved in the planning phase?

3.4. What resources aided during the planning phase?

3.5. What problems did you face during the planning phase? How did you try to resolve these problems?

4. Learning: Experience Accumulation

4.1. How did you obtain information about the HR practice?

4.2. From which source(s) was your information about the introduction/change of the HR practice gathered?

4.3. What were the (expected) benefits of gaining information?

4.4. What problems did you face in gathering information about the introduction/change of the HR practice? How did you try to resolve these problems?

Path and Learning: Existing Knowledge

4.5. What previous experiences did you or others in the organization have with the HR practice?

4.6. Have previous experiences with and information about altering HRM played a role in the introduction/change of the practice and if so, how?

Continued

Table A.3   Continued

4.7. Have prior experiences with and information about altering HRM influenced the way new information was gathered about altering HRM and, if so, how?

4.8. Was the new information gathered combined with these prior experiences and information about altering HRM and, if so, how?

5. Learning: Knowledge Articulation

5.1. How was the new information shared?

5.2. With whom was the new information shared in the organization?

5.3. To what extent were the stakeholders involved in the process of information sharing?

5.4. What were the (expected) benefits of information sharing?

5.5. What problems did you face in sharing information about the introduction/change of the HR practice? How did you try to resolve these problems?

6. Adapting: Decision Making

6.1. How were decisions made regarding the introduction/change of the HR practice?

6.2. Who was involved in making the decision to introduce/change the HR practice? Who was involved in making decisions about how to introduce/change the HR practice?

6.3. Was the expertise of the employees included and, if so, how?

6.4. What role did the stakeholders play in decision making?

6.5. How quickly was the decision made to introduce/change the HR practice?

6.6. What resources aided in the decision-making phase?

6.7. What problems did you face during the decision-making phase? How did you try to resolve these problems?

7. Adapting: Restructuring

7.1. Has the new/changed HR practice been implemented and, if so, how?

7.2. What resources aided in the implementation phase?

7.3. Were existing resources reconfigured to aid in implementing the new/changed HR practice and, if so, how?

7.4. Was the new/changed HR practice implemented through a pilot phase and, if so, how? What have your past experiences been with using a pilot phase?

7.5. What problems did you face during the implementation phase? How did you try to resolve these problems?

8. Learning: Knowledge Codification

8.1. Have the actions taken during the introduction/change of the HR practice been documented and, if so, how?

8.2. With which activities and tools have the actions taken during the introduction/change of the HR practice been documented?

8.3. How will you proceed with the documentation of the introduction/change of the HR practice?

8.4. What were the (expected) benefits of documenting the introduction/change of the HR practice? What did you learn through documenting the process?

8.5. What problems did you face in documenting information about the introduction/change of the HR practice? How did you try to resolve these problems?

9. Path, Learning, and Adapting: Values-Driven Strategic Orientations

9.1. Have these values been considered during the introduction/change of the HR practice and, if so, how? Have these values shaped the introduction/change of the HR practice and, if so, how?

9.2. Have these values been shaped by the introduction/change of the HR practice and, if so, how?

10. Path, Learning, and Adapting: Unique Attributes of HR

10.1. Have the employees' needs and motivations been considered in the introduction/change of the HR practice and, if so, how? Have these needs and motivations shaped the introduction/change of the HR practice and, if so, how?

Continued

Table A.3 Continued

10.2. Have these needs and motivations been shaped by the introduction/change of the HR practice and, if so, how?
11. Path, Learning, and Adapting: Multiple Stakeholders' Demands
11.1. Have the demands of the stakeholders been considered in the introduction/change of the HR practice and, if so, how? Have these demands shaped the introduction/change of the HR practice and, if so, how?
11.2. Have the demands of the stakeholders been shaped by the introduction/change of the HR practice and, if so, how?
12. Path, Learning, and Adapting: Financial Resources
12.1. Have the financial resources been considered in the introduction/change of the HR practice and, if so, how? Have the financial resources shaped the introduction/change of the HR practice and, if so, how?
12.2. What are the financial consequences of introducing/changing the HR practice?
13. Path, Learning, and Adapting: Organizational Structure
13.1. Has the organizational structure been considered in the introduction/change of the HR practice and, if so, how? Has the organizational structure shaped the introduction/change of the HR practice and, if so, how?
13.2. Has the organizational structure been shaped by the introduction/change of the HR practice and, if so, how?
14. Path, Learning, and Adapting: Existing HR Practices
14.1. Have the existing HR practices shaped the introduction/change of the HR practice and, if so, how?
14.2. What are the (expected) consequences of the implementation for the existing HR practices?
15. Path, Learning, and Adapting: Existing Routines
15.1. What are your previous experiences with introducing/changing HR practices or overall change management?
15.2. How has the current process differed from these previous experiences with introducing/changing HR practices or overall change management?
15.3. Have prior ways of introducing/changing HR practices or overall change management influenced the introduction/change of the HR practice and, if so, how?
16. Adapting
16.1. How does/will the new or modified HR practice influence the ability of the organization to address change?
16.2. What went well during the process of introducing/changing the HR practice?
16.3. What problems did you encounter during the process of introducing/changing the HR practice and how were they resolved?
17. Concluding Questions
17.1. Is there anything else you would like to share that was not addressed thus far?
17.2. What did you expect from this interview?

Table A.4   Public and Internal Document Material

CASE		TYPES OF DOCUMENTS
Case A: Social services state association	Public	Annual reports, brochures, mission statement, organization's magazine, press releases, strategy report, website information
	Internal	Case study, contracts, discussion paper, documents regarding organizational goals and HR practices, draft and final HR practice-related questionnaires, draft and final workers' council agreements, external presentations, HR practice-related checklists, internal PowerPoint presentations, memos, organization chart, project assignment, project timetable, sample performance appraisal systems
Case B: Museum	Public	Mission statement, organizational and interorganizational brochures, publications, website information, workshop proceedings
	Internal	Annual work planning report, bylaws, documents regarding HR practices, organization chart
Case C: Social services local chapter	Public	Website information
	Internal	HR practice-related questionnaire, mission statement, organization chart, organizational handbook on quality management
Case D: Environmental organization	Public	Documents regarding HR practices, organization chart, website information
	Internal	Bylaws, discussion paper, internal reports, internal power point presentations, memos
Case E: Sports organization	Public	Mission statement, organization chart, press release regarding the OD process, website information
	Internal	Board resolutions, bylaws, guidelines and regulations, contract with external consultants, draft papers, documents regarding the formulation of organizational goals and the OD process, documents regarding HR practices, letters, results of working groups, timetable
Case F: Teaching hospital	Public	Mission statement, organization chart, website information
	Internal	Draft papers, external presentations, HR practice-related questionnaire and brochure, internal PowerPoint presentations, internal and third-party reports, magazine articles, memos, statistics, workers' council agreements
Case G: Foundation	Public	Annual reports, bylaws, mission statement, reports, organization chart, organization magazine, website information
	Internal	External presentations, documents regarding HR practices and organizational goals, HR practice-related questionnaire, brochure, documents, internal PowerPoint presentations
Case H: Religious organization	Public	Mission statement, organization chart, website information
	Internal	Documents regarding HR practices, internal memos, internal proposals, letters, strategy, evaluation reports

Bibliography

Adner, R., & Helfat, C. E. (2003). Corporate Effects and Dynamic Managerial Capabilities. *Strategic Management Journal, 24*, 1011–1025.

Akingbola, K. (2004). Staffing, Retention and Government Funding: A Case Study. *Nonprofit Management & Leadership, 14*(4), 453–465.

Akingbola, K. (2006a). Strategy and HRM in Nonprofit Organizations: Evidence from Canada. *International Journal of Human Resource Management, 17*(10), 1707–1725.

Akingbola, K. (2006b). Strategic Choices and Changes in Non-Profit Organizations. *Strategic Change, 15*(6), 265–281.

Alatrista, J., & Arrowsmith, J. (2004). Managing Employee Commitment in the Not-For-Profit Sector. *Personnel Review, 33*(5), 536–548.

Alexander, J. (2000). Adaptive Strategies of Nonprofit Human Service Organizations in an Era of Devolution and New Public Management. *Nonprofit Management & Leadership, 10*(3), 287–303.

Alexander, J., Nank, R., & Stivers, C. (1999). Implications of Welfare Reform: Do Nonprofit Survival Strategies Threaten Civil Society? *Nonprofit and Voluntary Sector Quarterly, 28*(4), 452–475.

Almond, S., & Kendall, J. (2000a). *Paid Employment in the Self-Defined Voluntary Sector in the Late 1990s: An Initial Description of Patterns and Trends* (Civil Society Working Paper, No. 7). Retrieved from http://eprints.lse.ac.uk/29038

Almond, S., & Kendall, J. (2000b). Taking the Employees' Perspective Seriously: An Initial United Kingdom Cross-Sectoral Comparison. *Nonprofit and Voluntary Sector Quarterly, 29*(2), 205–231.

Alvesson, M., & Kärreman, D. (2007). Constructing Mystery: Empirical Matters in Theory Development. *Academy of Management Review, 32*(4), 1265–1281.

Ambrosini, V., & Bowman, C. (2009). What Are Dynamic Capabilities and Are They Useful Constructs in Strategic Management? *International Journal of Management Reviews, 11*(1), 29–49.

Amit, R., & Schoemaker, P. J. H. (1993). Strategic Assets and Organizational Rent. *Strategic Management Journal, 14*(1), 33–46.

Anheier, H. K. (1992). An Elaborate Network: Profiling the Third Sector in Germany. In B. Gidron, R. M. Kramer, & L. M. Salamon (Eds.), *Government and the Third Sector: Emerging Relationships in Welfare States* (pp. 31–56). San Francisco: Jossey-Bass.

Anheier, H. K. (2005). *Nonprofit Organizations: Theory, Management, Policy.* London: Routledge.

Anheier, H. K., & Seibel, W. (1993). *Defining the Nonprofit Sector: Germany* (Working Papers of the Johns Hopkins Comparative Nonprofit Sector Project, No. 6). Retrieved from http://ccss.jhu.edu/index.php?section=content&view=16&sub=34&tri=49

Anheier, H. K., & Seibel, W. (2001). *The Nonprofit Sector in Germany: Between State, Economy and Society*. Manchester: Manchester University Press.

Armstrong, M. (1992, December). A Charitable Approach to Personnel. *Personnel Management*, pp. 28–32.

Arthur, J. B., & Boyles, T. (2007). Validating the Human Resource System Structure: A Level-Based Strategic HRM Approach. *Human Resource Management Review, 17*(1), 77–92.

Arthur, W. B. (1994). *Increasing Returns and Path Dependence in the Economy*. Ann Arbor: University of Michigan Press.

Backman, E. V., Grossman, A., & Rangan, V. K. (2000). Introduction. *Nonprofit and Voluntary Sector Quarterly, 29*(1), 2–8.

Bailey, D., & Grochau K. E. (1993). Aligning Leadership Needs to the Organizational Stage of Development: Applying Management Theory to Nonprofit Organizations. *Administration in Social Work, 17*(1), 23–45.

Ban, C., Drahnak-Faller, A., & Towers, M. (2003). Human Resource Challenges in Human Service and Community Development Organizations. *Review of Public Personnel Administration, 23*(2), 133–153.

Barley, S. R. (2006). When I Write My Masterpiece: Thoughts on What Makes a Paper Interesting. *Academy of Management Journal, 49*(1), 16–20.

Barman, E. A. (2002). Asserting Difference: The Strategic Response of Nonprofit Organizations to Competition. *Social Forces, 80*(4), 1191–1222.

Barney, J. B. (1991). Firm Resources and Sustained Competitive Advantage. *Journal of Management, 17*(1), 99–120.

Barney, J. B. (1992). Integrating Organizational Behaviour and Strategy Formulation Research: A Resource-Based Analysis. In P. Shrivastava, A. Huff, & J. Dutton (Eds.), *Advances in Strategic Management* (8th ed., pp. 39–61). Greenwich, CT: JAI Press.

Barney, J. B. (2001a). Is the Resource-Based "View" a Useful Perspective for Strategic Management Research? Yes. *Academy of Management Review, 26*(1), 41–56.

Barney, J. B. (2001b). Resource-Based Theories of Competitive Advantage: A Ten-Year Retrospective on the Resource-Based View. *Journal of Management, 27*(6), 643–650.

Barr, P. S. (2004). Current and Potential Importance of Qualitative Methods in Strategy Research. In D. Ketchen & D. Bergh (Eds.), *Research Methodology in Strategy and Management* (Vol. 1, pp. 165–188). Oxford: Elsevier.

Barragato, C. A. (2002). Linking for-Profit and Nonprofit Executive Compensation: Salary Composition and Incentive Structures in the U.S. Hospital Industry. *Voluntas, 13*(3), 301–311.

Bartunek, J. M., Rynes, S. L., & Ireland, R. D. (2006). What Makes Management Research Interesting, and Why Does It Matter? *Academy of Management Journal, 49*(1), 9–15.

Basinger, N. W., & Peterson, J. R. (2008). Where You Stand Depends on Where You Sit: Participation and Reactions to Change. *Nonprofit Management & Leadership, 19*(2), 243–257.

Beattie, R. S. (2006). Line Managers and Workplace Learning: Learning from the Voluntary Sector. *Human Resource Development International, 9*(1), 99–119.

Beattie, R. S., Hamlin, R., & Ellinger, A. (2005). *Facilitating Learning: Are Public Sector Managers Any Different?* Paper presented at the Ninth International Research Symposium on Public Management, Milan, Italy.

Beck, M. (2002). Fachtagung: Personal gewinnen und halten. *Sozialwirtschaft Aktuell, 10*, 10–12.

Becker, B., & Gerhart, B. (1996). The Impact of Human Resource Management on Organizational Performance: Progress and Prospects. *Academy of Management Journal, 39*(4), 779–801.

Ben-Ner, A., Ren, T., & Paulson, D. F. (2011). A Sectoral Comparison of Wage Levels and Wage Inequality in Human Services Industries. *Nonprofit and Voluntary Sector Quarterly, 40*(4), 608–633.

Benz, M. (2005). Not for the Profit, but for the Satisfaction? Evidence on Worker Well-Being in Non-Profit Firms. *KYKLOS, 58*(2), 155–176.

Berg, B. L. (2007). *Qualitative Research Methods for the Social Sciences* (6th ed.). Boston: Pearson/Allyn & Bacon.

Bies, A. L. (2010). Evolution of Nonprofit Self-Regulation in Europe. *Nonprofit and Voluntary Sector Quarterly, 39*(6), 1057–1086.

Bingham, C. B., Eisenhardt, K. M., & Furr, N. R. (2007). What Makes a Process a Capability? Heuristics, Strategy and Effective Capture of Opportunities. *Strategic Entrepreneurship Journal, 1*(1), 27–47.

Bode, I. (2003). Flexible Response in Changing Environments: The German Third Sector Model in Transition. *Nonprofit and Voluntary Sector Quarterly, 32*(2), 190–210.

Borzaga, C., & Depedri, S. (2005). Interpersonal Relations and Job Satisfaction: Some Empirical Results in Social and Community Care Services. In B. Gui & R. Sugden (Eds.), *Economics and Social Interaction. Accounting for Interpersonal Relations* (pp. 125–149). Cambridge: Cambridge University Press.

Borzaga, C., & Tortia, E. (2006). Worker Motivations, Job Satisfaction, and Loyalty in Public and Nonprofit Social Services. *Nonprofit and Voluntary Sector Quarterly, 35*(2), 225–248.

Boselie, P. (2009). A Balanced Approach to Understanding the Shaping of Human Resource Management in Organisations. *Management Revue, 20*(1), 90–108.

Boselie, P., Dietz, G., & Boon, C. (2005). Commonalities and Contradictions in HRM and Performance Research. *Human Resource Management Journal, 15*(3), 67–94.

Bowman, C., & Ambrosini, V. (2003). How the Resource-Based and the Dynamic Capability Views of the Firm Inform Corporate-Level Strategy. *British Journal of Management, 14*(4), 289–303.

Bradshaw, P. (2002). Reframing Board-Staff Relations: Exploring the Governance Function Using a Storytelling Metaphor. *Nonprofit Management & Leadership, 12*(4), 471–484.

Brandl, J., & Güttel, W. H. (2007). Organizational Antecedents of Pay-for-Performance Systems in Nonprofit Organizations. *Voluntas, 18*(2), 176–199.

Brandl, J., Güttel, W. H., Konlechner, S., Beisheim, M., von Eckardstein, D., & Elsik, W. (2006). Entwicklungsdynamik von Vergütungssystemen in Nonprofit-Organisationen. *Zeitschrift für Personalforschung, 20*(4), 356–374.

Brooks, A. C. (2002). Can Nonprofit Management Help Answer Public Management's "Big Questions?" *Public Administration Review, 62*(3), 259–266.

Brown, W. A., & Iverson, J. O. (2004). Exploring Strategy and Board Structure in Nonprofit Organizations. *Nonprofit and Voluntary Sector Quarterly, 33*(3), 377–400.

Brown, W. A., & Yoshioka, C. F. (2003). Mission Attachment and Satisfaction as Factors in Employee Retention. *Nonprofit Management & Leadership, 33*(1), 5–18.

Bruckner, W. (2001). Mit Wissen entscheiden—Wissensmanagement in NPOs. In R. Simsa (Ed.), *Management der Nonprofit Organisation* (pp. 132–142). Stuttgart: Schäffer Poeschel.

Buckmaster, N. (1999). Associations between Outcome Measurement, Accountability, and Learning for Non-Profit Organisations. *The International Journal of Public Sector Management, 12*(2), 186–197.

Bundesarbeitsgemeinschaft der Freien Wohlfahrtspflege e.V. (2009). *Einrichtungen und Dienste der Freien Wohlfahrtspflege Gesamtstatistik 2008.* Berlin: Bundesarbeitsgemeinschaft der Freien Wohlfahrtspflege.

Burgelman, R. A. (1994). Fading Memories: A Process Theory of Strategic Business Exit in Dynamic Environments. *Administrative Science Quarterly, 39*(1), 24–56.

Burt, E., & Taylor, J. A. (2000). Information and Communication Technologies. Reshaping Voluntary Organizations? *Nonprofit Management & Leadership, 11*(2), 131–143.

Campbell, D. A. (2008). Getting to Yes . . . or No: Nonprofit Decision Making and Interorganizational Restructuring. *Nonprofit Management & Leadership, 19*(2), 221–241.

Campbell, D. T. (1975). "Degrees of Freedom" and the Case Study. *Comparative Political Studies, 8*(2), 178–193.

Camuffo, A., & Volpato, G. (1996). Dynamic Capabilities and Manufacturing Automation: Organizational Learning in the Italian Automobile Industry. *Industrial and Corporate Change, 5*(3), 813–838.

Carlile, P., & Christensen, C. M. (2004). *The Cycles of Theory Building in Management Research* (Working paper, No. 05–057). Retrieved from http://www.hbs.edu/research/pdf/05–057.pdf

Chetkovich, C., & Frumkin, P. (2003). Balancing Margin and Mission: Nonprofit Competition in Charitable Versus Fee-Based Programs. *Administration & Society, 35*(5), 564–596.

Cillo, P., & Verona, G. (2008). Search Styles in Style Searching: Exploring Innovation Strategies in Fashion Firms. *Long Range Planning, 41*(6), 650–671.

Cohen, M. D., Burkhart, R., Dosi, G., Egidi, M., Marengo, L., Warglien, M., & Winter, S. (1996). Routines and Other Recurring Action Patterns of Organizations: Contemporary Research Issues. *Industrial and Corporate Change, 5*(3), 653–698.

Cohen, W. M., & Levinthal, D. A. (1990). Absorptive Capacity: A New Perspective on Learning and Innovation. *Administrative Science Quarterly, 35*(1), 128–152.

Collinson, S., & Wilson, D. C. (2006). Inertia in Japanese organizations: Knowledge Management Routines and Failure to Innovate. *Organization Studies, 27*(9), 1359–1387.

Collis, D. J. (1994). How Valuable Are Organizational Capabilities? *Strategic Management Journal, 15*(Special Issue: Competitive Organizational Behavior), 143–152.

Colquitt, J. A., & Zapata-Phelan, C. P. (2007). Trends in Theory Building and Theory Testing: A Five-Decade Study of the Academy of Management Journal. *Academy of Management Journal, 50*(6), 1281–1303.

Conway, E., & Monks, K. (2008). HR Practices and Commitment to Change: An Employee-Level Analysis. *Human Resource Management Journal, 18*(1), 72–89.

Corley, K. G., & Gioia, D. A. (2004). Identity Ambiguity and Change in the Wake of a Corporate Spin-Off. *Administrative Science Quarterly, 49*(2), 173–208.

Creswell, J. W. (2009). *Research Design: Qualitative, Quantitative, and Mixed Methods Approaches* (3rd ed.). Thousand Oaks, CA: Sage.

Cunningham, I. (1999, April–June). Human Resource Management in the Voluntary Sector: Challenges and Opportunities. *Public Money and Management,* pp. 19–25.

Cunningham, I. (2001). Sweet Charity! Managing Employee Commitment in the UK Voluntary Sector. *Employee Relations, 23*(3), 226–239.

Cunningham, I. (2005). *Struggling to Care: Employee Attitudes to Work at the Sharp End of Service Provision in the Voluntary Sector.* Paper presented to the Annual Labour Process Conference at the University of Strathclyde, Glasgow, Scotland.

Cunningham, I. (2008a). *Employment Relations in the Voluntary Sector: Struggling to Care.* New York: Routledge.

Cunningham, I. (2008b). A Race to the Bottom? Exploring Variations in Employment Conditions in the Voluntary Sector. *Public Administration, 86*(4), 1033–1053.

Cunningham, I. (2010a). Drawing from a Bottomless Well? Exploring the Resilience of Value-Based Psychological Contracts in Voluntary Organizations. *The International Journal of Human Resource Management, 21*(5), 699–719.

Cunningham, I. (2010b). The HR Function in Purchaser-Provider Relationships: Insights from the UK Voluntary Sector. *Human Resource Management, 20*(2), 189–205.

Cunningham, I., & James, P. (2011). *Voluntary Organizations and Public Service Delivery.* New York: Routledge.

Dathe, D., Hohendanner, C., & Priller, E. (2009). Wenig Licht, viel Schatten—der Dritte Sektor als arbeitsmarktpolitisches Experimentierfeld. In J. Allmendinger (Ed.), *WZBrief Arbeit 3 (Oktober).* Berlin: Wissenschaftszentrum Berlin für Sozialforschung.

Dathe, D., & Kistler, E. (2005). Arbeit(en) im Dritten Sektor. In S. Kotlenga, B. Nägele, N. Pagels, & B. Ross (Eds.), *Arbeit(en) im dritten Sektor. Europäische Perspektiven* (pp. 54–65). Mössingen-Talheim: Talheimer.

De Cooman, R., de Gieter, S., Pepermans, R., & Jegers, M. (2011). A Cross-Sector Comparison of Motivation-Related Concepts in for-Profit and Not-for-Profit Service Organizations. *Nonprofit and Voluntary Sector Quarterly, 40*(2), 296–317.

De Prins, P., & Henderickx, E. (2007). HRM Effectiveness in Older People's and Nursing Homes: The Search for Best (Quality) Practices. *Nonprofit and Voluntary Sector Quarterly, 36*(4), 549–571.

Deci, E. L., & Ryan, R. M. (1980). The Empirical Exploration of Intrinsic Motivational Processes. In L. Berkowitz (Ed.), *Advances in Experimental Social Psychology* (pp. 39–80). New York: Academic Press.

Deckop, J. R., & Cirka, C. C. (2000). The Risk and Reward of a Double-Edged Sword: Effects of a Merit Pay Program on Intrinsic Motivation. *Nonprofit and Voluntary Sector Quarterly, 29*(3), 400–418.

Denis, J., Lamothe, L., & Langley, A. (2001). The Dynamics of Collective Leadership and Strategic Change in Pluralistic Organizations. *Academy of Management Journal, 44*(4), 809–837.

Denzin, N. K. (2001). *Interpretive Interactionism* (2nd ed.). Newbury Park, CA: Sage.

DiBella, A. J. (1992). Planned Change in an Organized Anarchy: Support for a Postmodernist Perspective. *Journal of Organizational Change Management, 5*(3), 55–65.

DiMaggio, P. J., & Powell, W. W. (1983). The Iron Cage Revisited: Institutional Isomorphism and Collective Rationality in Organizational Fields. *American Sociological Review, 48*(2), 147–160.

Dolan, D. A. (2002). Training Needs of Administrators in the Nonprofit Sector. *Nonprofit Management & Leadership, 12*(3), 277–292.

Dooley, L. M. (2002). Case Study Research and Theory Building. *Advances in Developing Human Resources, 4*(3), 335–354.

Dosi, G., & Teece, D. (1998). Organizational Competencies and the Boundaries of the Firm. In R. Arena & C. Longhi (Eds.), *Markets and Organizations* (pp. 281–302). New York: Springer.

Durst, S. L., & Newell, C. (2001). The Who, Why and How of Reinvention in Nonprofit Organizations. *Nonprofit Management & Leadership, 11*(4), 443–458.

Easterby-Smith, M., Lyles, M. A., & Peteraf, M. A. (2009). Dynamic Capabilities: Current Debates and Future Directions. *British Journal of Management, 20*(1), 1–8.

Easterby-Smith, M., & Prieto, I. M. (2008). Dynamic Capabilities and Knowledge Management: An Integrative Role for Learning? *British Journal of Management, 19*(3), 235–249.

Easterby-Smith, M., Thorpe, R., Jackson, P. R., & Lowe, A. (2008). *Management Research* (3rd ed.). Los Angeles: Sage.

Easterby-Smith, M., Thorpe, R., & Lowe, A. (2000). *Management Research: An Introduction* (13th ed.). London: Sage.

Ebrahim, A. (2002). Information Struggles: The Role of Information in the Reproduction of NGO-Funder Relationships. *Nonprofit and Voluntary Sector Quarterly, 31*(1), 84–114.

Ebrahim, A. (2005). Accountability Myopia: Losing Sight of Organizational Learning. *Nonprofit and Voluntary Sector Quarterly, 34*(1), 56–87.

Eckardstein, D. von (2002). Personalmanagement in NPOs. In C. Badelt (Ed.), *Handbuch der Nonprofit Organisationen* (3rd ed., pp. 309–336). Stuttgart: Schaeffler-Poeschel.

Eckardstein, D. von, & Simsa, R. (2004). Introduction. In A. Zimmer & E. Priller (Eds.), *Future of Civil Society. Making Central European Nonprofit-Organizations Work* (pp. 245–251). Wiesbaden: VS Verlag für Sozialwissenschaften.

Edmondson, A. C., & McManus, S. E. (2007). Methodological Fit in Management Field Research. *Academy of Management Review, 32*(4), 1155–1179.

Eisenhardt, K. M. (1989). Building Theories from Case Study Research. *Academy of Management Review, 14*(4), 532–550.

Eisenhardt, K. M. (1991). Better Stories and Better Constructs: The Case for Rigor and Comparative Logic. *Academy of Management Review, 16*(3), 620–627.

Eisenhardt, K. M., & Graebner, M. E. (2007). Theory Building from Cases: Opportunities and Challenges. *Academy of Management Journal, 50*(1), 25–32.

Eisenhardt, K. M., & Martin, J. A. (2000). Dynamic Capabilities: What Are They? *Strategic Management Journal, 21*(10–11), 1105–1121.

Elsbach, K. D. (2005). Weird Ideas from Qualitative Research. In K. D. Elsbach (Ed.), *Qualitative Organizational Research* (pp. 1–13). Greenwich, CT: Information Age Publishing.

Emanuele, R., & Higgins, S. (2000). Corporate Culture in the Nonprofit Sector: A Comparison of Fringe Benefits with the For-Profit Sector. *Journal of Business Ethics, 24*(1), 87–93.

Feldman, D. C. (2004). What Are We Talking About When We Talk About Theory? *Journal of Management, 30*(5), 565–567.

Fenton, N. E., & Inglis, S. (2007). A Critical Perspective on Organizational Values. *Nonprofit Management & Leadership, 17*(3), 335–348.

Fenwick, M. (2005). Extending Strategic International Human Resource Management Research and Pedagogy to the Non-Profit Multinational. *International Journal of Human Resource Management, 16*(4), 497–512.

Filipovitch, A. J. (2006). Organizational Transformation of a Community-Based Clinic. *Nonprofit Management & Leadership, 17*(1), 103–116.

Finkelstein, S., & Haleblian, J. (2002). Understanding Acquisition Performance: The Role of Transfer Effects. *Organization Science, 13*(1), 36–47.

Flick, U. (2007a). *Managing Quality in Qualitative Research.* London: Sage.

Flick, U. (2007b). *Designing Qualitative Research.* London: Sage.

Fontana, A., & Frey, J. H. (2005). The Interview—From Neutral Stance to Political Involvement. In N. K. Denzin & Y. S. Lincoln (Eds.), *The Sage Handbook of Qualitative Research* (3rd ed., pp. 695–727). Thousand Oaks, CA: Sage.

Forrant, R., & Flynn, E. (1999). Skills, Shop-Floor Participation and the Transformation of Brimfield Precision: Lessons for the Revitalization of the Metal-Working Sector. *Industrial and Corporate Change, 8*(1), 167–188.

Frankel, R. M. (1999). Standards of Qualitative Research. In B. F. Crabtree & W. Miller (Eds.), *Doing Qualitative Research* (pp. 333–346). Thousand Oaks, CA: Sage.

Freeman, R. E. (1984). *Strategic Management: A Stakeholder Approach.* Boston: Pitman.

Frey, B. S., & Jegen, R. (2001). Motivation Crowding Theory. *Journal of Economic Surveys, 15*(5), 589–611.

Frumkin, P., & Andre-Clark, A. (2000). When Missions, Markets, and Politics Collide: Values and Strategy in the Nonprofit Human Services. *Nonprofit and Voluntary Sector Quarterly, 29*(1), 141–163.

Frumkin, P., & Kim, M. T. (2001). Strategic Positioning and the Financing of Nonprofit Organizations: Is Efficiency Rewarded in the Contributions Marketplace? *Public Administration Review, 61*(3), 266–275.

Fyles, R. (2003). *How Does Oxfam Canada Learn?* Montreal, Canada: McGill University Press.

Gains, F., John, P. C., & Stoker, G. (2005). Path Dependency and the Reform of English Local Government. *Public Administration, 83*(1), 25–45.

Galaskiewicz, J., & Bielefeld, W. (1998). *Nonprofit Organizations in an Age of Uncertainty: A Study of Organizational Change.* New York: Aldine de Gruyter.

Galunic, D. C., & Eisenhardt, K. M. (1996). The Evolution of Intracorporate Domains: Divisional Charter Losses in High-Technology, Multidivisional Corporations. *Organization Science, 7*(3), 225–282.

Gavetti, G., & Levinthal, D. (2000). Looking Forward and Looking Backward: Cognitive and Experimental Search. *Administrative Science Quarterly, 45*(1), 113–137.

Geertz, C. (1973). *The Interpretation of Culture.* New York: Basic Books.

George, G. (2005). Learning to Be Capable: Patenting and Licensing at the Wisconsin Alumni Research Foundation 1925–2002. *Industrial and Corporate Change, 14*(1), 119–152.

Gephart, R. P. (2004). From the Editors—Qualitative Research and the Academy of Management Journal. *Academy of Management Journal, 47*(4), 454–462.

Gibbert, C. G., Ruigrok, W., & Wicki, B. (2008). What Passes as a Rigorous Case Study? *Strategic Management Journal, 29*(13), 1465–1474.

Gibbs, G. R. (2007). *Analyzing Qualitative Data.* Los Angeles: Sage.

Gilbert, C. G., & Christensen, C. M. (2005). Anomaly-Seeking Research: Thirty Years of Development in Resource Allocation Theory. In J. l. Bower & C. G. Gilbert (Eds.), *From Resource Allocation to Strategy* (pp. 71–89). New York: Oxford University Press.

Glaser, B. G. (1978). *Theoretical Sensitivity.* Mill Valley, CA: Sociology Press.

Glick, W. H., Huber, G. P., Miller, C. C., Doty, D. H., & Sutcliffe, K. M. (1990). Studying Changes in Organizational Design and Effectiveness: Retrospective Event Histories and Periodic Assessments. *Organization Science, 1*(3), 293–312.

Gobo, G. (2004). Sampling, Representativeness and Generalizability. In C. Seale, G. Gobo, J. F. Gubrium, & D. Silverman (Eds.), *Qualitative Research Practice* (pp. 405–426). Thousand Oaks, CA: Sage.

Golden, B. R. (1992). The Past Is the Past—or Is It? The Use of Retrospective Accounts as Indicators of Past Strategy. *Academy of Management Journal, 35*(4), 848–860.

Golden-Biddle, K., & Rao, H. (1997). Breaches in the Boardroom: Organizational Identity and Conflicts of Commitment in a Nonprofit Organization. *Organization Science, 8*(6), 593–611.

Grant, R. M. (1991). The Resource-Based Theory of Competitive Advantage: Implications for Strategy Formulation. *California Management Review, 33*(3), 114–135.

Grant, R. M. (1996). Toward a Knowledge-Based Theory of the Firm. *Strategic Management Journal, 17*(Special issue: Knowledge and the Firm), 109–122.

Guba, E. G., & Lincoln, Y. S. (1989). *Fourth Generation Evaluation*. Newbury Park, CA: Sage.

Guest, D. E. (1997). Human Resource Management and Performance: A Review and Research Agenda. *The International Journal of Human Resource Management*, 8(3), 263–276.

Hailey, J., & James, R. (2002). Learning Leaders: The Key to Learning Organisations. *Development in Practice*, 12(3), 398–408.

Hakansson, H., & Lundgren, A. (1997). Paths in Time and Space—Path Dependence in Industrial Networks. In L. Magnusson & J. Ottosson (Eds.), *Evolutionary Economics and Path Dependence* (pp. 119–137). Cheltenham, UK: Elgar.

Haley-Lock, A., & Kruzich, J. (2008). Serving Workers in the Human Services: The Roles of Organizational Ownership, Chain Affiliation, and Professional Leadership in Frontline Job Benefits. *Nonprofit and Voluntary Sector Quarterly*, 37(3), 443–467.

Hall, P. D. (1990). Conflicting Managerial Cultures in Nonprofit Organizations. *Nonprofit Management & Leadership*, 2, 153–165.

Handy, F., & Katz, E. (1998). The Wage Differential between Nonprofit Institutions and Corporations: Getting More by Paying Less? *Journal of Comparative Economics*, 26(2), 246–261.

Hansmann, H. (1980). The Role of Nonprofit Enterprise. *Yale Law Journal*, 89(3), 835–901.

Harlan, S. L., & Saidel, J. R. (1994). Board Members' Influence on the Government-Nonprofit Relationship. *Nonprofit Management & Leadership*, 5(2), 173–196.

Hatten, M. L. (1982). Strategic Management in Not-for-Profit Organizations. *Strategic Management Journal*, 3(2), 89–104.

Heimovics, R. D., Herman, R. D., & Coughlin, C. L. J. (1993). Executive Leadership and Resource Dependence in Nonprofit Organizations: A Frame Analysis. *Public Administration Review*, 53(5), 419–427.

Helfat, C. E. (1994). Evolutionary Trajectories in Petroleum Firm R&D. *Management Science*, 40(12), 1720–1747.

Helfat, C. E. (1997). Know-How and Asset Complementarity and Dynamic Capability Accumulation: The Case of R&D. *Strategic Management Journal*, 18(5), 339–360.

Helfat, C. E. (2000). Guest Editor's Introduction to the Special Issue: The Evolution of Firm Capabilities. *Strategic Management Journal*, 21(10/11), 955–959.

Helfat, C. E. (2007). Stylized Facts, Empirical Research and Theory Development in Management. *Strategic Organization*, 5(2), 185–192.

Helfat, C. E., Finkelstein, S., Mitchell, W., Peteraf, M. A., Singh, H., Teece, D. J., & Winter, S. (Eds.) (2007). *Dynamic Capabilities: Understanding Strategic Change in Organizations*. Malden, MA: Blackwell.

Helmig, B., Jegers, M., & Lapsley, I. (2004). Challenges in Managing Nonprofit Organizations: A Research Overview. *Voluntas*, 15(2), 101–116.

Henderson, R., & Cockburn, I. (1994). Measuring Competence? Exploring Firm Effects in Pharmaceutical Research. *Strategic Management Journal*, 15(Special Issue: Competitive Organizational Behavior), 63–84.

Herman, R. D., & Heimovics, R. D. (1990a). The Effective Nonprofit Executive: Leader of the Board. *Nonprofit Management & Leadership*, 1(2), 167–180.

Herman, R. D., & Heimovics, R. D. (1990b). An Investigation of Leadership Skill Difference in Chief Executives of Nonprofit Organizations. *American Review of Public Administration*, 20(2), 107–124.

Herman, R. D., & Heimovics, R. D. (1994). Executive Leadership. In R. D. Herman (Ed.), *The Jossey-Bass Handbook of Nonprofit Leadership and Management* (pp. 137–153). San Francisco: Jossey-Bass.

Hodgkin, C. (1993). Policy and Paper Clips: Rejecting the Lure of the Corporate Model. *Nonprofit Management & Leadership*, 3(4), 415–429.

Hoffmann, E. A. (2006). The Ironic Value of Loyalty: Dispute Resolution Strategies in Worker Cooperatives and Conventional Organizations. *Nonprofit Management and Leadership*, 17(2), 163–177.

Huber, G. P. (1991). Organizational Learning: The Contributing Processes and the Literatures. *Organization Science*, 2(1), 88–115.

Huber, G. P., & Power, D. J. (1985). Retrospective Reports of Strategic-Level Managers: Guidelines for Increasing Their Accuracy. *Strategic Management Journal*, 6(2), 171–180.

Hudson, M. (1999). *Managing without Profit: The Art of Managing Third-Sector Organizations* (2nd ed.). London: Penguin Books.

Hurrell, S. A., Warhurst, C., & Nickson, D. (2011). Giving Miss Marple a Makeover: Graduate Recruitment, Systems Failure, and the Scottish Voluntary Sector. *Nonprofit and Voluntary Sector Quarterly*, 40(2), 336–355.

Iansiti, M., & Clark, K. B. (1994). Integration and Dynamic Capability: Evidence from Product Development in Automobiles and Mainframe Computers. *Industrial and Corporate Change*, 3(3), 557–605.

Irons, J. S., & Bass, G. (2004). *Recent Trends in Nonprofit Employment and Earnings: 1990–2004*. Washington, D.C.: OMB Watch.

Jackson, T., Festing, M., & Okech, J. (2005). *Managing People in International NGOs: International HRM Policies and Practices of British and German Development NGOs*. Paper presented at the 8th Conference on International Human Resource Management, Cairns, Australia.

Jarzabkowski, P. (2008). Shaping Strategy as a Structuration Process. *Academy of Management Journal*, 51(4), 621–650.

Jeavons, T. H. (1992). When Management Is the Message: Relating Values to Management Practice in Nonprofit Organizations. *Nonprofit Management & Leadership*, 2(4), 403–417.

Jick, T. D. (1979). Mixing Qualitative and Quantitative Methods: Triangulation in Action. *Administrative Science Quarterly*, 24(4), 602–611.

Jurkiewicz, C. L., & Massey, Jr., T. K. (1998). The Influence of Ethical Reasoning on Leader Effectiveness: An Empirical Study of Nonprofit Executives. *Nonprofit Management & Leadership*, 9(2), 173–186.

Kale, P., & Singh, H. (1999). *Alliance Capability & Success: A Knowledge-Based Approach*. Philadelphia: The Wharton School, University of Pennsylvania.

Kanter, R. M., & Summers, D. V. (1987). Doing Well while Doing Good: Dilemmas of Performance Measurement in Nonprofit Organizations and the Need for a Multiple-Constituency Approach. In W. W. Powell (Ed.), *The Nonprofit Sector: A Research Handbook* (pp. 154–166). New Haven, CT: Yale University Press.

Karim, S., & Mitchell, W. (2000). Path-Dependent and Path-Breaking Change: Reconfiguring Business Resources Following Acquisitions in the U.S. Medical Sector, 1978–1995. *Strategic Management Journal*, 21(11), 1061–1081.

Kay, A. (2005). A Critique of the Use of Path Dependency in Policy Studies. *Public Administration*, 83(3), 553–571.

Keil, T. (2004). Building External Corporate Venturing Capability. *Journal of Management Studies*, 41(5), 799–825.

Kellock Hay, G., Beattie, R. S., Livingstone, R., & Munro, P. (2001). Change, HRM and the Voluntary Sector. *Employee Relations*, 23(3), 240–255.

Kendall, J., & Knapp, M. (2000). Measuring the Performance of Voluntary Organizations. *Public Management Review*, 2(1), 105–132.

Kim, S. E. (2005). Balancing Competing Accountability Requirements: Challenges in Performance Improvement of the Nonprofit Human Services Agency. *Public Performance and Management Review*, 29(2), 145–163.

Kim, S. E., & Lee, J. W. (2007). Is Mission Attachment an Effective Management Tool for Employee Retention? An Empirical Analysis of a Nonprofit Human Services Agency. *Review of Public Personnel Administration*, 27(3), 227–248.

King, G., Keohane, R. O., & Verba, S. (1994). *Designing Social Inquiry: Scientific Inference in Qualitative Research.* Princeton: Princeton University Press.

King, N. K. (2004). Social Capital and Nonprofit Leaders. *Nonprofit Management & Leadership, 14*(4), 471–486.

Koch, J. (2008). Strategic Paths and Media Management—A Path Dependency Analysis of the German Newspaper Branch of High Quality Journalism. *Schmalenbach Business Review, 60,* 50–73.

Kogut, B., & Zander, U. (1992). Knowledge of the Firm, Combinative Capabilities, and the Replication of Technology. *Organization Science, 3*(3), 383–397.

Kong, E. (2007). The Strategic Importance of Intellectual Capital in the Non-Profit Sector. *Journal of Intellectual Capital, 8*(4), 721–731.

Kor, Y. Y., & Mahoney, J. T. (2005). How Dynamics, Management, and Governance of Resource Deployments Influence Firm-Level Performance. *Strategic Management Journal, 26*(5), 489–496.

Kramer, R. (1990). *Voluntary Organizations in the Welfare State: On the Threshold of the '90s* (Working Paper, No. 8). London: London School of Economics, Centre for Voluntary Organisation.

Kvale, S. (2007). *Doing Interviews.* London: Sage.

Langley, A. (1999). Strategies for Theorizing from Process Data. *Academy of Management Review, 24*(4), 691–710.

Langley, A., Denis, J. L., & Lamothe, L. (2003). Process Research in Healthcare: Towards Three-Dimensional Learning. *Policy & Politics, 31*(2), 195–206.

LeCompte, M. D., & Goetz, J. P. (1982). Problems of Reliability and Validity in Ethnographic Research. *Review of Educational Research, 52*(1), 31–60.

Lee, T. W. (1999). *Using Qualitative Methods in Organizational Research.* Thousand Oaks, CA: Sage.

Lee, T. W., Mitchell, T. R., Wise, L., & Fireman, S. (1996). An Unfolding Model of Voluntary Employee Turnover. *Academy of Management Journal, 39*(1), 5–36.

Leete, L. (2000). Wage Equity and Employee Motivation in Nonprofit and for-Profit Organizations. *Journal of Economic Behavior and Organization, 43*(4), 423–446.

Leete, L. (2001). Whither the Nonprofit Wage Differential? Estimates from the 1990 Census. *Journal of Labor Economics, 19*(1), 136–170.

Leete, L. (2006). Work in the Nonprofit Sector. In W. W. Powell & R. Steinberg (Eds.), *The Nonprofit Sector: A Research Handbook* (2nd ed., pp. 159–179). New Haven, CT: Yale University Press.

Leiter, J. (2008). Nonprofit Isomorphism: An Australia–United States Comparison. *Voluntas, 19*(1), 67–91.

Leonard-Barton, D. (1990). A Dual Methodology for Case Studies: Synergistic Use of a Longitudinal Single Site with Replicated Multiple Sites. *Organization Science, 1*(3), 248–266.

Leonard-Barton, D. (1992). Core Capabilities and Core Rigidities: A Paradox in Managing New Product Development. *Strategic Management Journal, 13*(Special Issue), 111–125.

Lepak, D. P., Marrone, J. M., & Takeuchi, R. (2004). The Relativity of HR Systems: Conceptualizing the Impact of Desired Employee Contributions and HR Philosophy. *International Journal of Technology Management, 27*(6/7), 639–655.

Lettieri, E., Borga, F., & Savoldelli, A. (2004). Knowledge Management in Non-Profit Organizations. *Journal of Knowledge Management, 8*(6), 16–30.

Letts, C., Ryan, W. P. A., & Grossman, A. (1999). *High Performance in Nonprofit Organizations.* New York: John Wiley and Sons.

Levinthal, D., & March, J. G. (1993). The Myopia of Learning. *Strategic Management Journal, 14*(Special Issue: Organizations, Decision Making and Strategy), 95–112.

Levitt, B., & March, J. G. (1988). Organizational Learning. *Annual Review of Sociology, 14,* 319–340.

Lewis, D. (2007). *The Management of Non-Governmental Development Organizations* (2nd ed.). New York: Routledge.

Light, P. C. (2002). The Content of Their Character: The State of the Nonprofit Workforce. *The Nonprofit Quarterly, 9*(3), 6–16.

Lindenberg, M. (2001). Are We at the Cutting Edge or the Blunt Edge? Improving NGO Organizational Performance with Private and Public Sector Strategic Management Frameworks. *Nonprofit Management & Leadership, 11*(3), 247–270.

Luo, Y. (2000). Dynamic Capabilities in International Expansion. *Journal of World Business, 35*(4), 355–378.

Lynn, D. B. (2003). Symposium: Human Resource Management in Nonprofit Organizations. *Review of Public Personnel Administration, 23*(2), 91–96.

MacVicar, A., Foley, M., Graham, M., Ogden, S., & Scott, B. (2000). Flexible Working Practices in the Public, Not-for-Profit, and Commercial Leisure Sectors in Scotland. *Public Management Review, 2*(2), 263–271.

Mahoney, J. T. (1995). The Management of Resources and the Resource of Management. *Journal of Business Research, 33*(2), 91–101.

Mahoney, J. T. (2000). Path Dependence in Historical Sociology. *Theory and Society, 29*(4), 507–548.

March, J. G. (1991). Exploration and Exploitation in Organizational Learning. *Organization Science, 2*(1, Special Issue: Organizational Learning: Papers in Honor of (and by) James G. March), 71–87.

March, J. G., Sproull, L. S., & Tamuz, M. (1991). Learning from Samples of One or Fewer. *Organization Science, 2*(1), 1–13.

Maritan, C. A. (2001). Capital Investment as Investing in Organizational Capabilities: An Empirically Grounded Process Model. *Academy of Management Journal, 44*(3), 513–532.

Maritan, C. A., & Peteraf, M. A. (2007). Dynamic Capabilities and Organizational Processes. In C. E. Helfat, S. Finkelstein, W. Mitchell, M. A. Peteraf, H. Singh, D. J. Teece, & S. Winter (Eds.), *Dynamic Capabilities: Understanding Strategic Change in Organizations* (pp. 30–45). Malden, MA: Blackwell.

Marsh, S. J., & Stock, G. N. (2006). Creating Dynamic Capability: The Role of Intertemporal Integration, Knowledge Retention, and Interpretation. *Journal of Product Innovation Management. 23*(5), 422–436.

Marshall, C., & Rossman, G. B. (2006). *Designing Qualitative Research* (4th ed.). Thousand Oaks, CA: Sage.

Maxwell, S. E., & Delaney, H. D. (2004). *Designing Experiments and Analyzing Data: A Model Comparison Data* (2nd ed.). Mahwah, NJ: Lawrence Erlbaum Associates.

McMullen, K., & Brisbois, R. (2003). *Coping with Change: Human Resource Management in Canada's Non-Profit Sector* (CPRN Research Series on Human Resources in the Non-Profit Sector, No. 4). Ottawa, Ontario: Canadian Policy Research Networks.

McMullen, K., & Schellenberg, G. (2003a). *Job Quality in Non-Profit Organizations* (CPRN Research Series on Human Resources in the Non-Profit Sector, No. 2). Ottawa, Ontario: Canadian Policy Research Networks.

McMullen, K., & Schellenberg, G. (2003b). *Skills and Training in the Non-Profit Sector* (CPRN Research Series on Human Resources in the Non-Profit Sector, No. 3) Ottawa, Ontario: Canadian Policy Research Networks.

Merlot, E. S., Fenwick, M., & de Cieri, H. (2006). Applying a Strategic International Human Resource Management Framework to International Non-

Governmental Organisations. *International Journal of Human Resources Development and Management*, 6(2/3), 313–327.

Meyer, M., & Mühlbacher, J. (2001). Organisationales Lernen in NPOs. In R. Simsa (Ed.), *Management der Nonprofit Organisation* (pp. 107–129). Stuttgart: Schäffer Poeschel.

Miles, M. B. (1979). Qualitative Data as an Attractive Nuisance: The Problem of Analysis. *Administrative Science Quarterly*, 24(4), 590–601.

Miles, M. B., & Huberman, A. M. (1994). *Qualitative Data Analysis: An Expanded Sourcebook* (2nd ed.). Thousand Oaks, CA: Sage.

Miller, J. (2002). The Board as a Monitor of Organizational Activity. *Nonprofit Management & Leadership*, 12(4), 429–450.

Minkoff, D. C., & Powell, W. W. (2006). Nonprofit Mission: Constancy, Responsiveness, or Deflection? In W. W. Powell & R. Steinberg (Eds.), *The Nonprofit Sector: A Research Handbook* (2nd ed., pp. 591–611). New Haven, CT: Yale University Press.

Mirvis, P. (1992). The Quality of Employment in the Nonprofit Sector: An Update on Employee Attitudes in Nonprofits versus Business and Government. *Nonprofit Management & Leadership*, 3(1), 23–41.

Montealegre, R. (2002). A Process Model of Capability Development: Lessons from the Electronic Commerce Strategy at Bolsa de Valores de Guayaquil. *Organization Science*, 13(5), 514–531.

Moore, M. H. (2000). Managing for Value: Organizational Strategy in For-Profit, Nonprofit, and Governmental Organizations. *Nonprofit and Voluntary Sector Quarterly*, 29(1), 183–204.

Moore, M. H. (2003). *The Public Value Scorecard: A Rejoinder and an Alternative to "Strategic Performance Measurement and Management in Non-Profit Organizations" by Robert Kaplan* (Hauser Center for Nonprofit Organizations Working Paper Series, No. 18). Retrieved from http://www.hks.harvard.edu/hauser/publications/working_papers/ workingpaperlist.htm

Nelson, R. R., & Winter, S. G. (1982). *An Evolutionary Theory of Economic Change* (4th ed.). Cambridge, MA: Belknap Press of Harvard University Press.

Netting, F. E., O'Connor, M. K., Thomas, M. L., & Yancey, G. (2005). Mixing and Phasing of Roles Among Volunteers, Staff, and Participants in Faith-Based Programs. *Nonprofit and Voluntary Sector Quarterly*, 34(2), 179–205.

Newey, L. R., & Zahra, S. A. (2009). The Evolving Firm: How Dynamic and Operating Capabilities Interact to Enable Entrepreneurship. *British Journal of Management*, 20(1), 81–100.

Newman, W. H., & Wallender, H. W. (1978). Managing Not-for-Profit Enterprises. *Academy of Management Review*, 3(1), 24–31.

Nickson, D., Warhurst, C., Dutton, E., & Hurrell, S. (2008). A Job to Believe in: Recruitment in the Scottish Voluntary Sector. *Human Resource Management Journal*, 18(1), 20–35.

Nygren, D. J., Ukeritis, M. D., McClelland, D. C., & Hickman, J. L. (1994). Outstanding Leadership in Nonprofit Organizations: Leadership Competencies in Roman Catholic Religious Orders. *Nonprofit Management & Leadership*, 38(4), 375–391.

Osborne, S. P. (1996). What Is "Voluntary" about the Voluntary and Non-Profit Sector? In S. P. Osborne (Ed.), *Managing in the Voluntary Sector. A Handbook for Managers in Charitable and Non-Profit Organizations* (pp. 5–17). London: International Thomson Business Press.

Ospina, S., Diaz, W., & O'Sullivan, J. F. (2002). Negotiated Accountability: Managerial Lessons from Identity-Based Nonprofit Organizations. *Nonprofit and Voluntary Sector Quarterly*, 31(1), 5–31.

Paauwe, J. (2009). HRM and Performance: Achievements, Methodological Issues and Prospects. *Journal of Management Studies*, 46(1), 129–142.

Pablo, A. L., Reay, T., Dewald, J. R., & Casebeer, A. L. (2007). Identifying, Enabling and Managing Dynamic Capabilities in the Public Sector. *Journal of Management Studies, 44*(5), 687–708.

Palmer, G. (2003). *Employee Relations in the Voluntary Sector.* Paper presented to British Universities Industrial Relations Association Annual Conference, Leeds, UK.

Pandza, K., & Thorpe, R. (2009). Creative Search and Strategic Sense-Making: Missing Dimensions in the Concept of Dynamic Capabilities. *British Journal of Management, 20*, 118–131.

Parry, E., Kelliher, C., Mills, T., & Tyson, S. (2005). Comparing HRM in the Voluntary and Public Sectors. *Personnel Review, 34*(5), 588–602.

Parsons, E., & Broadbridge, A. (2004). Managing Change in Nonprofit Organizations: Insights from the UK Charity Retail Sector. *Voluntas, 15*(3), 227–242.

Patton, M. Q. (2002). *Qualitative Research and Evaluation Methods.* Thousand Oaks, CA: Sage.

Pavlou, P. A., & El Sawy, O. A. (2005). *Understanding the "Black Box" of Dynamic Capabilities* (Working Paper). Los Angeles, CA: Anderson Graduate School of Management, University of California Press.

Pavlou, P. A., & El Sawy, O. A. (2006a). From IT Leveraging Competence to Competitive Advantage in Turbulent Environments: The Case of New Product Development. *Information Systems Research, 17*(3), 198–227.

Pavlou, P. A., & El Sawy, O. A. E. (2006b). *Decomposing and Leveraging Dynamic Capabilities* (Working Paper). Los Angeles, CA: Anderson Graduate School of Management, University of California Press.

Penrose, E. T. (1959). *The Theory of the Growth of the Firm.* Oxford: Oxford University Press.

Perry, J. L., Mesch, D. J., & Paarlberg, L. (2006). Motivating Employees in a New Governance Era: The Performance Paradigm Revisited. *Public Administration Review, 66*(4), 505–514.

Pettigrew, A. M. (1990). Longitudinal Field Research on Change: Theory and Practice. *Organization Science, 1*(3), 267–292.

Piekkari, R., Welch, C., & Paavilainen, E. (2009). The Case Study as Disciplinary Convention: Evidence from International Business Journals. *Organizational Research Methods, 12*(3), 567–589.

Pierson, P. (2000a). Increasing Returns, Path Dependence, and the Study of Politics. *American Political Science Review, 94*(2), 251–267.

Pierson, P. (2000b). The Limits of Design: Explaining Institutional Origins and Change. *Governance, 13*(4), 475–499.

Pierson, P. (2000c). Not Just What, but When: Timing and Sequence in Political Processes. *Studies in American Political Development, 14*(1), 72–92.

Pisano, G. P. (1994). Knowledge, Integration, and the Locus of Learning: An Empirical Analysis of Process Development. *Strategic Management Journal, 15*(*Special Issue*), 85–100.

Pisano, G. P. (2000). In Search of Dynamic Capabilities: The Origins of R&D Competence in Biopharmaceuticals. In G. Dosi, R. R. Nelson, & S. G. Winter (Eds.), *The Nature and Dynamics of Organizational Capabilities* (pp. 129–154). Oxford: Oxford University Press.

Pitt-Catsouphes, M., Swanberg, J. E., Bond, J. T., & Galinsky, E. (2004). Work-Life Policies and Programs: Comparing the Responsiveness of Nonprofit and For-Profit Organizations. *Nonprofit Management & Leadership, 14*(3), 291–312.

Poole, M. S., van de Ven, A. H., Dooley, K., & Holmes, M. E. (2000). *Organizational Change and Innovation Processes.* New York: Oxford University Press.

Pratt, M. G. (2008). Fitting Oval Pegs into Round Holes: Tensions in Evaluating and Publishing Qualitative Research in Top-Tier North American Journals. *Organizational Research Methods, 11*(3), 481–509.

Preston, A. (1989). The Nonprofit Worker in a For-Profit World. *Journal of Labor Economics, 7*(4), 438–463.

Preyra, C., & Pink, G. (2001). Balancing Incentives in the Compensation Contracts of Nonprofit Hospital CEOs. *Journal of Health Economics, 20*(4), 509–525.

Provan, K. G. (1991). Receipt of Information and Influence over Decisions in Hospitals by the Board, Chief Executive Officer and Medical Staff. *Journal of Management Studies, 28*(3), 281–298.

Punch, K. F. (2005). *Introduction to Social Research: Quantitative and Qualitative Approaches* (2nd ed.). Thousand Oaks, CA: Sage.

Pynes, J. E. (1997). *Human Resources Management for Public and Nonprofit Organizations*. San Francisco, CA: Jossey-Bass Publishers.

Ragin, C. C. (2004). Combining Qualitative and Quantitative Research. In C. C. Ragin, J. Nagel, & P. White (Eds.), *Workshop on Scientific Foundations of Qualitative Research* (pp. 109–115). Arlington, VA: National Science Foundation.

Ramanath, R. (2009). Limits to Institutional Isomorphism: Examining Internal Processes in NGO–Government Interactions. *Nonprofit and Voluntary Sector Quarterly, 38*(1), 51–76.

Rapley, T. (2004). Interview. In C. Seale, G. Gobo, J. F. Gubrium, & D. Silverman (Eds.), *Qualitative Research Practice* (pp. 15–33). Thousand Oaks, CA: Sage.

Rawls, J., Ullrich, R., & Nelson, O. (1975). A Comparison of Managers Entering or Reentering the Profit and Nonprofit Sectors. *Academy of Management Journal, 18*(3), 616–623.

Richards, L. (2005). *Handling Qualitative Data: A Practical Guide*. London: Sage.

Ridder, H.-G., Bruns, H.-J., & Neumann, S. (2004). Nonprofit-Organisationen im Spannungsfeld von normativer und ökonomischer Rationalität—Der Beitrag des Human Resource Management zum Veränderungsmanagement. *Zeitschrift für öffentliche und gemeinwirtschaftliche Unternehmen, 27*(1), 31–55.

Ridder, H.-G., & Hoon, C. (2009). Qualitative Methods in Research on Human Resource Management. *Zeitschrift für Personalforschung, 23*(2), 93–106.

Ridder, H.-G., Hoon, C., & McCandless, A. (2009). The Theoretical Contribution of Case Study Research to the Field of Strategy and Management. In D. J. Ketchen & D. D. Bergh (Eds.), *Research Methodology in Strategy and Management* (pp. 137–178). San Diego, CA: Elsevier.

Ridder, H.-G., & McCandless, A. (2010). Influences on the Architecture of Human Resource Management in Nonprofit Organizations: An Analytical Framework. *Nonprofit and Voluntary Sector Quarterly, 39*(1), 124–141.

Rindova, V. P., & Kotha, S. (2001). Continuous "Morphing": Competing through Dynamic Capabilities, Form, and Function. *Academy of Management Journal, 44*(6), 1263–1280.

Ritchie, W. J., Kolodinsky, R. W., & Eastwood, K. (2007). Does Executive Intuition Matter? An Empirical Analysis of Its Relationship with Nonprofit Organization Financial Performance. *Nonprofit and Voluntary Sector Quarterly, 36*(1), 140–155.

Rodwell, J. J., & Teo, S. T. T. (2004). Strategic HRM in For-profit and Non-Profit Organizations. *Public Management Review, 6*(3), 312–331.

Rogers, E. W., & Wright, P. M. (1998). Measuring Organizational Performance in Strategic Human Resource Management: Problems, Prospects, and Performance Information Markets. *Human Resource Management Review, 8*(3), 311–331.

Rondeau, K. V., & Wagar, T. H. (2001). Impact of Human Resource Management Practices on Nursing Home Preferences. *Human Services Management Research, 14*(3), 192–202.

Roomkin, M., & Weisbrod, B. (1999). Managerial Compensation and Incentives in For-Profit and Nonprofit Hospitals. *Journal of Law, Economics, and Organizations, 15*(3), 750–781.

Roper, L., & Pettit, J. (2002). Development and the Learning Organisation: An Introduction. *Development in Practice, 12*(3/4), 258–271.

Rosenbloom, R. S. (2000). Leadership, Capabilities, and Technological Change: The Transformation of NCR in the Electronic Era. *Strategic Management Journal, 21*(10/11), 1083–1103.

Ruhm, C. J., & Borkoski, C. (2003). Compensation in the Nonprofit Sector. *Journal of Human Resources, 38*(4), 992–1021.

Rumelt, R. P. (1984). Towards a Strategic Theory of the Firm. In R. B. Lamb (Ed.), *Competitive Strategic Management* (pp. 556–570). New York: Prentice-Hall.

Rumelt, R. P. (1994). Invited Forward to Strategic Thinking. In G. Hamel & A. Hene (Eds.), *Competence Based Competition*. Sussex: John Wiley & Sons.

Ryan, W. P. (1999, January–February). The New Landscape for Nonprofits. *Harvard Business Review*, pp. 127–136.

Salamon, L. M. (2002a). The Resilient Sector: The State of Nonprofit America. In L. M. Salamon (Ed.), *The State of Nonprofit America* (pp. 3–61). Washington, DC: Brookings Institution Press.

Salamon, L. M. (2002b, Winter). What Nonprofit Wage Deficit? *The Nonprofit Quarterly*, pp. 61–62.

Salamon, L. M., & Anheier, H. K. (1992). In Search of the Nonprofit Sector: I. The Question of Definitions. *Voluntas, 3*(2), 125–151.

Salamon, L. M., & Anheier, H. K. (1996). *The International Classification of Nonprofit Organizations: ICNPO-Revision* (Working Papers of the Johns Hopkins Comparative Nonprofit Sector Project). Retrieved from http://ccss.jhu.edu/index.php? section=content&view=16&sub=34&tri=49

Salamon, L. M., & Anheier, H. K. (1998). The Social Origins of Civil Society: Explaining the Nonprofit Sector Cross-Nationally. *Voluntas, 9*(3), 213–248.

Salamon, L. M., Anheier, H. K., List, R., Toepler, S., & Sokolowski, S. W. (Eds.). (1999). *Global Civil Society: Dimensions of the Nonprofit Sector*. Baltimore, MD: Johns Hopkins Center for Civil Society Studies.

Salamon, L. M., & Dewees, S. (2002). In Search of the Nonprofit Sector: Improving the State of the Art. *American Behavioral Scientist, 45*(11), 1716–1740.

Salamon, L. M., Sokolowski, S. W., & List, R. (2004). Global Civil Society: An Overview. In L. M. Salamon & S. W. Sokolowski (Eds.), *Global Civil Society. Dimensions of the Nonprofit Sector* (2nd ed., pp. 3–60). Bloomfield: Kumarian Press.

Salipante, P. F., & Golden-Biddle, K. (1995). Managing Traditionality and Strategic Change in Nonprofit Organizations. *Nonprofit Management & Leadership, 6*(1), 3–20.

Salvato, C. (2003). The Role of Micro-Strategies in the Engineering of Firm Evolution. *Journal of Management Studies, 40*(1), 83–108.

Schepers, C., DeGieter, S., Pepermans, R., Du Bois, C., Caers, R., & Jegers, M. (2005). How Are Employees of the Nonprofit Sector Motivated? A Research Need. *Nonprofit Management & Leadership, 16*(2), 191–208.

Schmid, H. (1992). Strategic and Structural Change in Human Service Organizations: The Role of the Environment. *Administration in Social Work, 16*(3/4), 167–186.

Schneider, U. (2008). Dimensionen der Wertschöpfung durch Non-Profit-Organisationen. In J. König, C. Oerthel, & H. J. Puch (Eds.), *In Soziales investieren. Mehr Werte schaffen* (pp. 117–138). München: Allitera-Verlag.

Seale, C. (1998). Qualitative Interviewing. In C. Seale (Ed.), *Researching Society and Culture*. London: Sage.

Seale, C. (1999). *The Quality of Qualitative Research*. London: Sage.

Seibel, W. (1990). Government/Third-Sector Relationship in a Comparative Perspective: The Case of France and West-Germany. *Voluntas, 1*(1), 42–60.

Seidel, J., & Kelle, U. (1995). Different Functions of Coding in the Analysis of Textual Data. In U. Kelle (Ed.), *Computer-Aided Qualitative Date Analysis* (pp. 53–61). London: Sage.

Shah, S. K., & Corley, K. G. (2006). Building Better Theory by Bridging the Quantitative-Qualitative Divide. *Journal of Management Studies, 43*(8), 1821–1835.

Sheehan, J. (1998). *NGOs and Participatory Management Styles: A Case Study of CONCERN Worldwide, Mozambique* (International Working Paper Series, No. 2). London: London School of Economics, Centre for Voluntary Organisation. Retrieved from http://eprints.lse.ac.uk/29090/

Siggelkow, N. (2007). Persuasion with Case Studies. *Academy of Management Journal, 50*(1), 20–24.

Silverman, D. (2006). *Interpreting Qualitative Data* (3rd ed.). London: Sage.

Simon, H. A. (1997). *Models of Bounded Rationality* (Vol. 3). Cambridge, MA: MIT Press.

Simsa, R. (2002). NPOs im Lichte gesellschaftlicher Spannungsfelder: Aktuelle Herausforderungen an das strategische Management. In R. Schauer, R. Purtschert, & D. Witt (Eds.), *Nonprofit-Organisationen und gesellschaftliche Entwicklung: Spannungsfeld zwischen Mission und Ökonomie* (pp. 39–61). Linz: Trauner.

Simsa, R. (2003). Fighting Heroes, Repair-Workers or Collaborators? Strategies of NPOs and Their Consequences. *Financial Accountability & Management, 19*(3), 225–241.

Simsa, R. (2004). *Necessary Sisyphus Work: Work-Satisfaction, Work-Pressure and Motivation of Employees in Social Service Organizations.* Paper presented at the ISTR Sixth International Conference "Contesting Citizenship and Civil Society in a Divided World", Toronto, Canada.

Singh, H., & Zollo, M. (1998). *The Impact of Knowledge Codification, Experience Trajectories and Integration Strategies on the Performance of Corporate Acquisitions* (Working Paper, No. 98-24). Philadelphia, PA: University of Pennsylvania, The Wharton School.

Snow, C. C., & Thomas, J. B. (1994). Field Research Methods in Strategic Management: Contributions to Theory Building and Testing. *Journal of Management Studies, 31*(4), 457–480.

Snow, D. (2004). Thoughts on Alternative Pathways to Theoretical Development: Theory Generation, Extension and Refinement. In C. C. Ragin, J. Nagel, & P. White (Eds.), *Workshop on Scientific Foundations of Qualitative Research* (pp. 133–136). Arlington, VA: National Science Foundation.

Speckbacher, G. (2003). The Economics of Performance Management in Nonprofit Organizations. *Nonprofit Management & Leadership, 13*(3), 267–281.

Stake, R. E. (2005). Qualitative Case Studies. In N. K. Denzin & Y. S. Lincoln (Eds.), *The Sage Handbook of Qualitative Research* (3rd ed., pp. 443–465). Thousand Oaks, CA: Sage.

Statistisches Bundesamt Deutschland. (2008). *Statistisches Jahrbuch für die Bundesrepublik Deutschland (Statistical Yearbook for Germany 2008).* Wiesbaden: Statistisches Bundesamt Deutschland.

Stone, M., Bigelow, B., & Crittenden, W. (1999). Research on Strategic Management in Nonprofit Organizations: Synthesis, Analysis, and Future Directions. *Administration & Society, 31*(3), 378–423.

Stone, M., & Brush, C. (1996). Planning in Ambiguous Contexts: The Dilemma of Meeting Needs for Commitment and Demands for Legitimacy. *Strategic Management Journal, 17*(8), 633–652.

Strichman, N., Bickel, W. E., & Marshood, F. (2008). Adaptive Capacity in Israeli Social Change Nonprofits. *Nonprofit and Voluntary Sector Quarterly, 37*(2), 224–248.

Sutton, R. I. (1997). The Virtues of Closet Qualitative Research. *Organization Science, 8*(1), 97–106.

Sutton, R. I., & Staw, B. M. (1995). What Theory Is Not. *Administrative Science Quarterly, 40*(3), 371–384.

Sydow, J., Schreyögg, G., & Koch, J. (2009). Organizational Path Dependence: Opening the Black Box. *Academy of Management Review, 34*(4), 689–709.

Szulanski, G. (1996). Exploring Internal Stickiness: Impediments to the Transfer of Best Practice Within the Firm. *Strategic Management Journal, 17*(Special Issue: Knowledge and the Firm), 27–43.

Tassie, B., Zohar, A., & Murray, V. (1996). The Management of Change. In S. P. Osborne (Ed.), *Managing in the Voluntary Sector. A Handbook for Managers in Charitable and Non-Profit Organizations* (pp. 137–153). London: International Thomson Business Press.

Teece, D. J. (2007). Explicating Dynamic Capabilities: The Nature and Micro-foundations of (Sustainable) Enterprise Performance. *Strategic Management Journal, 28*(13), 1319–1350.

Teece, D. J., & Pisano, G. (1994). The Dynamic Capabilities of Firms: An Introduction. *Industrial and Corporate Change, 3*(3), 537–556.

Teece, D. J., Pisano, G., & Shuen, A. (1997). Dynamic Capabilities and Strategic Management. *Strategic Management Journal, 18*(7), 509–533.

Theuvsen, L. (2004). Doing Better While Doing Good: Motivational Aspects of Pay-for-Performance Effectiveness in Nonprofit Organizations. *Voluntas, 15*(2), 117–136.

Tonkiss, F., & Passey, A. (1999). Trust, Confidence and Voluntary Organisations: Between Values and Institutions. *Sociology, 33*(2), 257–274.

Tripsas, M., & Gavetti, G. (2000). Capabilities, Cognition, and Inertia: Evidence from Digital Imaging. *Strategic Management Journal, 21*(10/11), 1147–1161.

Trochim, W. M. K. (2001). *Research Methods Knowledge Base.* Cincinnati, OH: Atomic Dog Publishing.

Truss, C., & Gratton, L. (1994). Strategic Human Resource Management: A Conceptual Approach. *International Journal of Human Resources Management, 5*(3), 663–720.

van de Ven, A. H. (1992). Suggestions for Studying Strategy Process: A Research Note. *Strategic Management Journal, 13*(Special Issue: Strategy Process: Managing Corporate Self-Renewal), 169–191.

van de Ven, A. H. (2007). *Engaged Scholarship: A Guide for Organizational and Social Research.* Oxford: Oxford University Press.

van de Ven, A. H., & Huber, G. P. (1990). Longitudinal Field Research Methods for Studying Processes of Organizational Change. *Organization Science, 1*(3), 133–143.

van de Ven, A. H., Polley, D. E., Garud, R., & Venkataraman, S. (1999). *The Innovation Journey.* New York: Oxford University Press.

van der Pijl, K., & Sminia, H. (2004). Strategic Management of Public Interest Organizations. *Voluntas, 15*(2), 137–155.

van Maanen, J. (1979). Reclaiming Qualitative Methods for Organizational Research: A Preface. *Administrative Science Quarterly, 24*(4), 520–526.

van Maanen, J., Sorensen, J. B., & Mitchell, T. R. (2007). The Interplay Between Theory and Method. *Academy of Management Review, 32*(4), 1145–1154.

VanWynsberghe, R., & Khan, S. (2007). Redefining Case Study. *International Journal of Qualitative Methods, 6*(2), 80–94.

Vaughan, D. (1992). Theory Elaboration: The Heuristics of Case Analysis. In C. C. Ragin & H. S. Becker (Eds.), *What Is a Case? Exploring the Foundations of Social Inquiry* (pp. 173–202). Cambridge: Cambridge University Press.

Verbruggen, S., Christiaens, J., & Milis, K. (2011). Can Resource Dependence and Coercive Isomorphism Explain Nonprofit Organizations' Compliance with Reporting Standards? *Nonprofit and Voluntary Sector Quarterly, 40*(1), 5–32.

Verona, G., & Ravasi, D. (2003). Unbundling Dynamic Capabilities: An Exploratory Study of Continuous Product Innovation. *Industrial and Corporate
Change*, 12(3), 577–606.

Vigoda, E., & Cohen, A. (2003). Work Congruence and Excellence in Human
Resource Management. *Review of Public Personnel Administration*, 23(3),
192–216.

Walton, J. (1992). Making the Theoretical Case. In C. C. Ragin & H. S. Becker
(Eds.), *What Is a Case? Exploring the Foundations of Social Inquiry* (pp. 121–
137). Cambridge: Cambridge University Press.

Wang, C. L., & Ahmed, P. K. (2007). Dynamic Capabilities: A Review and Research
Agenda. *International Journal of Management Reviews*, 9(1), 31–51.

Watson, M. R., & Abzug, R. (2005). Finding the Ones You Want, Keeping the
Ones You Find: Recruitment and Retention in Nonprofit Organizations. In R.
D. Herman (Ed.), *The Jossey-Bass Handbook of Nonprofit Leadership and
Management* (2nd ed., pp. 623–659). San Francisco, CA: Jossey-Bass.

Weick, K. E. (1995). *Sensemaking in Organizations*. Thousand Oaks, CA: Sage.

Weick, K. E. (2005). The Experience of Theorizing: Sensemaking as Topic and
Resource. In K. G. Smith & M. A. Hitt (Eds.), *Great Minds in Management:
The Process of Theory Development* (pp. 394–413). New York: Oxford Uni-
versity Press.

Weisbrod, B. A. (1998). Guest Editor's Introduction: The Nonprofit Mission and
Its Financing. *Journal of Policy Analysis and Management*, 17(2), 165–174.

Wernerfelt, B. (1984). A Resource-Based View of the Firm. *Strategic Management
Journal*, 5(2), 171–180.

Whetten, D. A. (1989). What Constitutes a Theoretical Contribution? *Academy of
Management Review*, 14(4), 490–495.

Whittemore, R., Chase, S. K., & Mandle, C. L. (2001). Validity in Qualitative
Research. *Qualitative Health Research*, 11(4), 522–537.

Winter, S. G. (2000). The Satisficing Principle in Capability Learning. *Strategic
Management Journal*, 21(10/11), 981–996.

Winter, S. G. (2003). Understanding Dynamic Capabilities. *Strategic Management
Journal*, 24(10), 991–995.

Wittmer, D. (1991). Serving the People or Serving for Pay: Reward Preferences
among Government, Hybrid Sector, and Business Managers. *Public Productivity and Management Review*, 14(4), 369–383.

Wright, P. M., & Boswell, W. R. (2002). Desegregating HRM: A Review and Synthesis of Micro and Macro Human Resource Management Research. *Journal of
Management*, 28(3), 247–276.

Wright, P. M., Gardner, T. M., Moynihan, L. M., & Allen, M. R. (2005). The
Relationship between HR Practices and Firm Performance: Examining Causal
Order. *Personnel Psychology*, 58(2), 409–446.

Yin, R. K. (2009). *Case Study Research: Design and Methods* (4th ed.). Thousand
Oaks, CA: Sage.

Zahra, S. A., & George, G. (2002). Absorptive Capacity: A Review, Reconceptual-
ization, and Extension. *Academy of Management Review*, 27(2), 185–203.

Zahra, S. A., Nielsen, A. P., & Bogner, W. C. (1999, Spring). Corporate Entrepreneurship, Knowledge, and Competence Development. *Entrepreneurship:
Theory and Practice*, 23, 169–189.

Zahra, S. A., Sapienza, H. J., & Davidsson, P. (2006). Entrepreneurship and
Dynamic Capabilities: A Review Model and Research Agenda. *Journal of Management Studies*, 43(4), 917–955.

Zimmer, A., Gärtner, J., Priller, E., Rawert, P., Sachße, C., Walz, R., & Graf Stra-
chwitz, R. (2004). The Legacy of Subsidiarity: The Nonprofit Sector in Germany. In A. Zimmer & E. Priller (Eds.), *Future of Civil Society. Making Central*

European Nonprofit-Organizations Work (pp. 681–711). Wiesbaden: VS Verlag für Sozialwissenschaften.

Zimmer, A., & Priller, E. (2001). Der Dritte Sektor in Deutschland: Wachstum und Wandel. *Gegenwartskunde*, *50*(1), 121–147.

Zimmer, A., Priller, E., & Hallmann, T. (2001). Zur Entwicklung des Nonprofit-Sektors und den Auswirkungen auf das Personalmanagement seiner Organisationen. *Zeitschrift für Personalforschung*, *15*(3), 207–225.

Zimmermann, J. A. M., & Stevens, B. W. (2006). The Use of Performance Measurement in South Carolina Nonprofits. *Nonprofit Management & Leadership*, *16*(3), 315–327.

Zollo, M., & Winter, S. G. (2002). Deliberate Learning and the Evolution of Dynamic Capabilities. *Organization Science*, *13*(3), 339–351.

Index

managerial capabilities, 17–18, 48–49, 177, 178, 184–186, 192–194, 197–199, 201–205, 207–208, 216–219, 227–231, 234–237, 239–241, 253, 257, 259–260, 263

managerial skills, 17–18, 41, 48, 153, 205. *See also* managerial capabilities

market: developments, 3, 30, 34–35, 64; marketization of NPOs, 13, 66; orientation, 1, 4, 5, 44

marketing, 4, 91, 94, 196

member organizations, 68–69, 93, 96–97, 110, 145, 147, 150, 172, 189, 210–211, 219–220, 222–223, 240–241, 264

metaphors, 82, 118, 127, 128, 178, 198

methodological fit, 56–58, 60, 61, 85, 87

methodological rigor, 83–86

methodology, 56–62; *See also* case studies; method

mission, 5, 13, 23, 68–69; as a distinguishing feature of NPOs, 6, 13–14; as a factor influencing employee recruitment, motivation and retention, 16–17, 19–20, 23, 26; as an influence on learning and adapting, 13, 25, 47–48, 50, 176, 180, 186, 199, 203, 207–208, 210–211, 220–221, 229, 231–232, 235, 237, 238, 240, 244–245, 248, 253–255, 259, 260, 261, 266; drift in, 238, 265;

motivation. *See* employee motivation, intrinsic motivation

multiple case studies, 10, 56, 58–62, 71, 73, 83, 85, 87–88, 175, 265, 270

multiple stakeholders, 5, 6, 14–15, 17, 18, 25, 27, 47–48, 51, 176–178, 180–182, 189–190, 195–196, 200–201, 204, 206, 208, 211–213, 218, 222–224, 229, 230, 232, 235, 236, 240, 241, 253–260, 261–262, 265, 266. *See also* external stakeholders; internal stakeholders

museum, 68, 74, 91–92, 126, 130–133, 164, 199–203

N

neo-institutionalism, 6

networks, 4, 15, 18, 38, 50, 52, 110–111, 120–121, 129, 143–144, 150, 158, 193, 247, 251

non-participant observation,73, 75–76, 78, 79, 86, 270

non-profit-distributing criterion/non-profit distribution constraint, 2, 63

nongovernmental organizations, 1

nonprofit organizations: specific characteristics of, 2–7, 12–18, 23–24, 25, 26, 27, 47–48, 63–64, 176–178, 203–207, 237–240, 253–260, 261–266; types, 1, 63 structural-operational definition of, 1, 63. *See also* employees; external environment; funding; internal environment; human resource management; management; mission; multiple stakeholders

nonprofit wage differential, 20–21, 23

O

operational capabilities, 29–32, 34, 35–36, 37–42, 163, 175, 255

organizational capabilities. *See* operational capabilities

organizational change, 13, 15, 27, 32, 48, 49, 171, 176, 263, 271; acceptance of, 17, 18, 24, 25, 26, 48, 177, 184, 190–194, 196, 201, 205, 206, 213, 215–216, 224, 226, 232, 233, 236, 238, 240, 241, 251, 252, 253, 254, 262

organizational development, 69, 96, 228

organizational goals, 5, 13, 20, 53, 67–69, 90, 113, 269; fit with, 17, 21, 106–108, 118, 127, 128, 150, 152, 159, 176, 186, 195, 198, 199, 203, 207, 208, 209, 217, 227, 228, 229, 241, 244, 245, 247, 252, 260, 261; multiple, 6, 12, 13, 14, 24, 25, 47, 48, 176, 177, 225, 239, 249, 263, 265. *See also* values-driven strategic orientation

organizational hierarchy, 53, 68–69, 89, 81, 94, 96, 98, 148, 150, 220, 234, 239, 217

organizational processes. *See* processes (organizational)